In the Shadow of *Dred Scott*

IN THE SHADOW OF DRED SCOTT

St. Louis Freedom Suits and the Legal Culture
of Slavery in Antebellum America

KELLY M. KENNINGTON

The University of Georgia Press
ATHENS

© 2017 by the University of Georgia Press
Athens, Georgia 30602
www.ugapress.org

Most University of Georgia Press titles are available from popular e-book vendors.

Printed digitally

Library of Congress Cataloging-in-Publication Data

Names: Kennington, Kelly M. (Kelly Marie), author.
Title: In the shadow of Dred Scott : St. Louis freedom suits and the legal culture of slavery
   in antebellum America / Kelly M. Kennington.
Description: Athens : University of Georgia Press, [2017] | Series: Early American Places |
   Includes bibliographical references and index.
Identifiers: LCCN 2016028172 | ISBN 9780820345512 (cloth : alk. paper) | 9780820345529
   (pbk. : alk. paper) | 9780820350851 (ebook)
Subjects: LCSH: Slaves—Legal status, laws, etc.—Missouri—Saint Louis. | Region—
   History—19th century—Cases.
Classification: LCC KF482 .K46 2017 | DDC 342.77808/7—dc23 LC record available at
   https://lccn.loc.gov/2016028172

For Mike and Diane

Contents

Acknowledgments   xi

Note on Sources   xvii

Introduction: The Legal Culture of Slavery   1

1   Setting the Scene   17

2   Bringing Suit   41

3   Crafting Strategy   67

4   A World in Motion   93

5   Double Character   116

6   Defending Suits   142

7   Political Repercussions   167

Conclusion: After the Verdict   191

Appendix   197

Notes   215

Bibliography   261

Index   281

Acknowledgments

In the five years since my daughter Olivia arrived, I have frequently repeated the phrase "it takes a village to raise a child" with newfound appreciation. The saying also comes to mind as I think about the long process it took to "birth" this book. Completing a book definitely takes a village. While the book's flaws remain my own, there are many people and institutions who were critical to helping me bring this project to fruition. I am deeply grateful for my "village."

My research has benefited from the generous support of several research and writing fellowships. Thank you to Duke University for the Anne Firor Scott and Summer Research fellowships; the Julian Price Endowment for the travel and research support; and the Anne T. and Robert M. Bass family for the Instructorship that supported my last year of research in graduate school. The William Nelson Cromwell Foundation and the American Society for Legal History, the William E. Foley Research Fellowship from the Missouri State Archives, and a Summer Grant from Auburn University's College of Liberal Arts helped fund the travel for the final stages of the book.

I am so thankful for the support of the members of my writing groups during my years at Duke: Gordon Mantler, Sebastian Lukasik, Steve Inrig, Felicity Turner, Orion Teal, and Eric Weber, who shared wine, food, and writing advice. Two dear friends deserve separate mention: Heidi Giusto has read and commented on countless drafts of my work over the years and is one of my best sources of support and advice; Julia Gaffield's boot camp was vital to my early research and writing, and her last-minute text references helped answer a couple of late questions. Thanks also to Anne-Marie Angelo, Fahad Bishara, Elizabeth Brake, Jenny Crowley, Seth Dowland, Karlyn Forner, Mitch Fraas, Katharine French-Fuller, Reena Goldthree, Alisa Harrison, Paul Johstono, Max Krochmal, Pam Lach, Noeleen McIlvenna, Erin Parish, Bryan Pitts, Paul Quigley, Jacob Remes, Phil Rubio, Liz Shesko, David Silkenat, Silvermoon, Michael Weisel, Paige Welch, and Kristin Wintersteen for being such excellent colleagues and friends.

Laura Edwards has pushed me to excel at all stages of my work on this project. Her gentle, insightful, and thorough comments on the early research, the numerous drafts, and the final book manuscript were invaluable, and she continues to be the type of mentor and scholar I most admire and aspire to be. Thank you also to Ed Balleisen, Peter Wood, and Adriane Lentz-Smith for your careful reading of my work, your thoughtful advice on the early stages of the project, and your support for my research. I want to give special thanks to Margaret Humphreys for her generous support over the years. In addition, the early stages of my work benefited from generous conversations with Daina Ramey Berry, Sally Deutsch, Lil Fenn, John French, Barry Gaspar, David Gilmartin, John Hart, Reeve Huston, Jonathan Ocko, Tom Robisheaux, Alex Roland, John Thompson, and the members of the Triangle Legal History Seminar.

Howard Erlanger and the Institute for Legal Studies at the University of Wisconsin Law School deserve special recognition for welcoming me and providing research and institutional support during my year as the Law and Society Postdoctoral Fellow. Madison is a magical place, and Howie and others made my time there productive and memorable. My year began with the exceptional advice and community provided by Barbara Welke and the members of the 2009 Hurst Summer Institute for Legal History. For reading my dissertation and helping me rethink my ideas and move forward to write this book, I am especially grateful to Howie, Steve Kantrowitz, Mitra Sharafi, and Karl Shoemaker. While at UW, I also benefited from conversations and feedback on my writing from Christy Clark-Pujara, Mary Claypool, Ariela Gross, Dirk Hartog, Martha Jones, Adam Malka, Lauren McCarthy, Dylan Penningroth, Ryan Quintana, Mitra Sharafi, Karl Shoemaker, and Jim Sweet. Thanks also to Lauren McCarthy for her research assistance and friendship.

Auburn is a vibrant community of scholars whom I am so fortunate to call my colleagues and friends. Rupa Mishra and I began our teaching careers together, and I am deeply grateful for her friendship, support, and advice over the years. In the final stages of writing and revisions, the close network of the "cul-de-sac" has provided welcome laughs and distractions, answered questions and given suggestions, and been there to encourage me through the process. Thanks also to Ken Noe, Ralph Kingston, Kathryn Braund, Jenny Brooks, Chris Ferguson, Ruth Crocker, Carolyn Day, Sunny Stalter-Pace, the members of the Nineteenth Century Studies group, and all of my colleagues in the history department for your helpful advice on pieces of the project. Emily Friedman, Chase Bringardner, Becky Brunson, Eden McLean, and Danilea Werner have each provided support and guidance when I needed it the most, and I appreciate their friendship.

One of the things I have most enjoyed about becoming a historian is traveling for research and to professional events where I get to meet new colleagues and make friends who share my interests. In doing so, I have accumulated many professional debts over the years that I am happy to be able to briefly acknowledge here. I only hope I do not forget anyone. For reading portions of the work at its various stages, I thank Melissa Blair, Diane Mutti Burke, Kristen Epps, Eden McLean, Michael Schoeppner, Christine Sears, Rachel Shelden, and Karen Tani. Rabia Belt and Martha Jones read and commented on the entire manuscript, and it is much improved as a result of their suggestions. For enriching the project through their comments and suggestions at conferences, I am grateful to Rob Baker, Robert Cottrol, Jim Gigantino, Mark Graber, Ariela Gross, Sally Hadden, Bernard Herman, Tony Kaye, Ted Maris-Wolf, Stephen Middleton, Christopher Morris, Jesse Nasta, Susan O'Donovan, Gautham Rao, Josh Rothman, Daniel Sharfstein, Leslie Schwalm, Rebecca Scott, Anne Twitty, Lea VanderVelde, Kirt von Daacke, and Eva Sheppard Wolf. I thank Randy Sparks and the late Judy Schafer for their mentorship and support from my earliest research stages. I also want to thank Lauren Araiza, Adam Arenson, Ari Bryen, Catherine Conner, Deborah Doroshow, Samantha Gervase, Hilary Green, Jonathan Hancock, Luke Harlow, Melissa Hayes, Rana Hogarth, Jennifer Holland, Julia Irwin, David Konig, Susanna Lee, Todd Olzewski, Steve Prince, Sharon Romeo, and Lauren McIvor Thompson for sharing their insights on the research and writing process, providing a laugh or an understanding ear, and cheering me on as I worked on this project. My online support system, especially my Summer Writing Group and the members of the #Graftonline, helped me push through the last round of revisions on the book.

The University of Georgia Press has been a joy to work with; I appreciate your patience with a new author. Thank you to Walter Biggins and

Beth Snead for answering my many questions and supporting this project. Thanks also to the three anonymous reviewers for the press; this work is a much stronger book because of the detailed, insightful comments offered by each of the readers. I also want to thank the *Journal of Southern History* and its editorial staff for granting permission for me to include material from my article "Geography, Mobility, and the Law" (53, no. 3 [2014]: 575–604) in the book.

Several archivists provided me with assistance, and so I enthusiastically thank the staff of the Missouri History Museum, the Missouri State Archives–St. Louis, and the Western Historical Manuscripts Collection. Personal relationships can make quite a difference in the course of a research project, and I am fortunate to know the people I met through my archival journeys. In particular, I want to thank Molly Kodner and Dennis Northcott at the Missouri History Museum; Patricia Barge (here's our book, Pat!), Sharon Kenny, Nik Henle, Bill Glankler, and Eben Lehman at the Missouri State Archives–St. Louis branch; Dennis Snead, Valerie J. Munzlinger, and the Marion County Clerk's office; Ruth Ann Hager at the St. Louis County Library; and Elizabeth Dunn at the Daniel Rubenstein Library. Kristin E. S. Zapalac deserves special thanks for her kindness and her willingness to share some of her unending knowledge about Missouri's freedom suits. Finally, I want to thank Bob Moore of the National Parks Service, who generously shared with me his extensive freedom suit expertise and research, as well as personal notes and photographs. Mel Conley of the Civil Court Records archive and Bob Moore deserve the gratitude of all scholars who study the St. Louis freedom suits for identifying these valuable resources and working to separate, organize, and preserve them for future researchers.

My family has been a constant source of support through the research and writing of this project. My mom, Leslie Kennington, has read the entire book and offered feedback as well as given countless hours of encouragement and confidence when I needed it most. My dad and stepmom, Rohn and Terrie Kennington, have given generously from the "Rohn Kennington Scholarship," and I am so grateful for their assistance and their faith in me. Thanks also to Hillary Mount, Courtney Saddler, Celeste Kennington, Caleb Kennington, and Gene and Sharon Brandewie. I want to thank Rebecca Gordon and Ellen Overmyer Lloyd for their friendship and their patience while listening to me talk about this project; you ladies are my family, too.

Over the past several years, Kim Welch has become not only my writing buddy, my accountability partner, and my sounding board for new ideas, she has become one of my dearest friends. She read numerous drafts of the book, talked me through challenging passages, and pushed me to keep going whenever I was discouraged. Thank you, Kim, for all that you do.

Kevin Brandewie has lived with this project from its inception, and yet he is still willing to help me think through difficult sections of material, provide comfort and comic relief when I need it, and support me at every step of the way. I am so fortunate to get to share this journey with him. Our two beautiful children, Olivia and Alex, arrived as I worked on this book (Alex just two weeks after my initial submission), and their bright smiles and infectious personalities make coming home from work each day a pleasure.

Finally, I cannot say enough good things about Mike and Diane Everman. Mike is the archivist at the Missouri State Archives–St. Louis, and Diane is the archivist for Enterprise and for the Jewish Community Archives (among her many projects). From my first foray into the St. Louis archives, Mike and Diane helped me immerse myself in the beautiful city, driving me through neighborhood enclaves, introducing me to the world-class museums, and dining with me at the best restaurants. They invited me to stay with them on my many return research trips and then provided countless nights of fun conversations, fabulous food, and Cardinals' games. Their passion for the city's history—especially its less well-known residents like the enslaved plaintiffs chronicled in this book—is infectious. This book is lovingly dedicated to them for their many kindnesses to me and others.

In the pages that follow, the case files of more than three hundred enslaved individuals who sued for freedom in St. Louis (in 287 cases, several of which involved multiple enslaved plaintiffs) will serve as the basis for a broader discussion of the legal culture of slavery and the processes of negotiation that occurred in and around freedom suits. The St. Louis freedom suits are located in the Missouri State Archives' St. Louis branch, as part of the St. Louis Circuit Court Historical Records Project, and are nearly all available online through the Historical Records Project website. A handful of newly discovered freedom suits from the General Court for the Territory of Louisiana (which included St. Louis and the territory that became Missouri) came to the author's attention in the final stages of this project. More freedom suits undoubtedly exist in this collection of early territorial court records and will be an exciting avenue for future research into early St. Louis. Additional local St. Louis court cases—debt cases, disputes over slave sales, and other types of legal action—and legal records relating to the freedom suits and local legal culture, such as circuit court record books, execution books, and manumission records, help to flesh out the use of the legal system by enslaved individuals and their enslavers.

The St. Louis freedom suits contain varying levels of complexity that sometimes defy simple categorizing. Certain case files are rich and complete, and others contain only a petition and a few related documents. The outcomes of the cases are not always known or entirely clear. For example, some cases have no verdict in the case file. Circuit Court record books and other supporting documents can sometimes indicate the likely outcome of the case, but even when a verdict is known, the enslaved person's status is not always fully identifiable. For that reason, defining cases as "successful" or not is fraught with the possibility of oversimplification. This book does include some rough numbers and several charts in the appendix, which classify cases by whether or not the plaintiff was freed by the case or if their status could not be determined by the case's outcome.

Although not systematically comparative in method, this study surveys more than eight hundred state supreme court freedom suits to provide a broader context for St. Louis's cases and to begin to make some connections between the St. Louis example and other jurisdictions. The impressive collection of appellate records involving people of African descent collected by Helen Tunnicliff Catterall (*Judicial Cases Concerning American Slavery and the Negro*, 5 vols. [Washington, DC: Carnegie Institution of Washington, 1926]) yielded a list of cases involving disputes over personal status. Because freedom suits happened throughout the United States, using appellate records is one way to get a sense of how these additional locations compared to the local legal culture of St. Louis and to suggest avenues for further local research of freedom suits elsewhere.

Although freedom suit case files and related legal records form the heart of this project, occasionally personal manuscript collections (mostly of lawyers, slaveholding defendants, and other prominent members of the St. Louis community), newspapers, and additional types of records help complete the picture of St. Louis's freedom suits. Letters are an important part of capturing—to the best possible extent—the web of negotiations and concerns swirling around outside the courtroom action in freedom suits. Much of the relevant correspondence involved prominent St. Louis attorneys and judges whose letters have survived in archival collections. Though letters are imperfect in recovering the full panoply of conversations that took place beyond the courtroom, they indicate the many related exchanges that happened between slaveholding defendants, attorneys, and other participants that made up a crucial part of the legal culture of slavery.

The numerous misspellings in all quotes are original. For purposes of clarity, the term "*sic*" after each misspelled word is avoided.

IN THE SHADOW OF *DRED SCOTT*

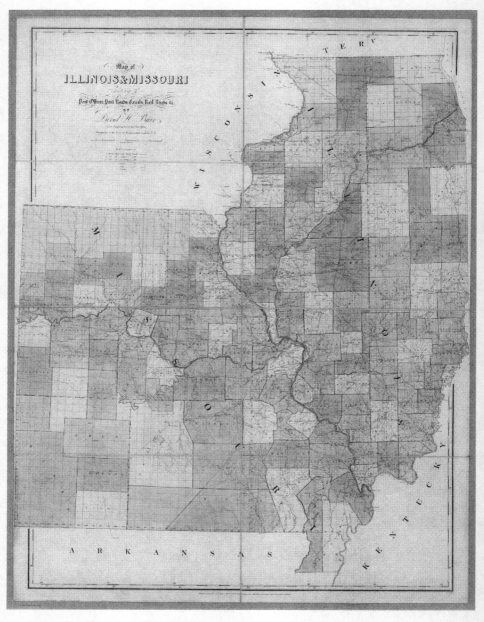

FIGURE 1. David H. Burr, "Map of Illinois & Missouri," in *The American Atlas* (Washington, DC, 1839). Courtesy of the David Rumsey Map Collection, www.davidrumsey.com.

Introduction: The Legal Culture of Slavery

When Alsey, a thirty-eight-year-old enslaved woman, sued for freedom in the St. Louis Circuit Court in March 1841, she initiated a series of legal processes that continued for more than a decade. According to her petition, sometime in the late 1810s, Robert Cross granted permission for his son-in-law to take fourteen-year-old Alsey from Kentucky to Illinois to live and work for his family as a slave. Several witnesses testified to her residence in Illinois, where the state's 1818 constitution prohibited slavery (with one exception that did not fit Alsey's circumstances), though the witnesses disagreed over a few key issues.[1] Cross's son-in-law confirmed Alsey's version of events—that he took her to Illinois with Cross's permission, and five years later, he sold her to pay off a debt.[2] The buyer then transferred Alsey to William Campbell, who took her back to Kentucky. Defense witnesses countered this narrative by suggesting that Cross's son-in-law took Alsey without Cross's permission, held her in Illinois against his wishes, and sold her without any legal claim to ownership. According to one witness, Alsey's alleged owner, Robert Cross, accompanied the witness to search for her but only after she had lived in Illinois for five years. The pair traveled first to the Illinois residence of Cross's son-in-law (who took Alsey from Cross) and then to William Campbell's Kentucky home, where Campbell refused to give Alsey to Cross and "compelled us [Cross and the witness] at the point of arms to desist."[3] Facing the threat of deadly force, Cross retreated; he later regained possession of Alsey after successfully suing Campbell in Kentucky. Alsey most likely learned of her right to freedom based on her residence in the free territory of Illinois,

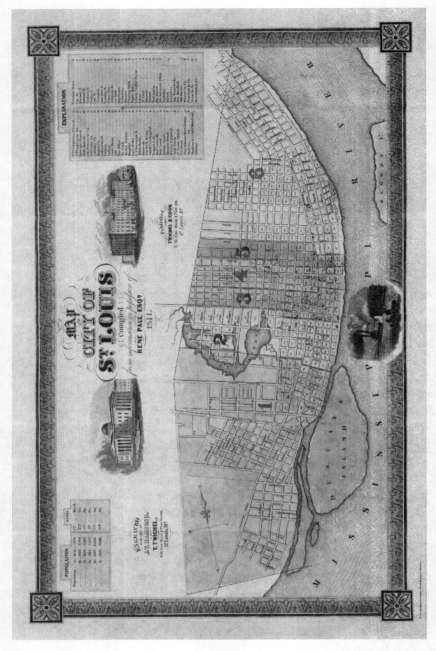

Figure 2. Rene Paul, "Map of the City of St. Louis compiled from information in the possession of Rene Paul Esqr." Published by Twichel and Cook N.W. Cor. Main and Pine Sts. St. Louis, Mo. Engraved at the Office of J. T. Hammond, by T. Twichel. N.W. Cor. Main and Pine Streets. St. Louis, Mo., 1844. Courtesy of the David Rumsey Map Collection, www. davidrumsey.com.

or she first had the opportunity to sue for freedom, years later, when Cross brought her to St. Louis and sold her to a prominent St. Louis attorney and Circuit Court judge, Robert Wash. Wash eventually sold Alsey and her son to William Randolph, who became the defendant in her freedom suit.[4]

The process of freedom suits, and their outcomes, often relied on interpersonal relationships and local influences. For example, one witness elaborated on his personal problems with Judge Robert Wash—who bought Alsey in St. Louis and sold her to the defendant, Randolph. The witness remained bitter about losing his own human property in numerous freedom suits. He blamed Judge Wash, testifying that he was "sorry to know such a man" whose decisions against him "were neither legal nor constitutional." The witness even offered to give $100 to help Alsey win her freedom, hoping to force Wash to lose his investment in Alsey, because he "very much dislikes the man."[5] Personal conflict seeped into the decision-making process of freedom suits, connecting the web of people who each brought their unique set of motivations to these cases: in this instance, even a slaveholder and defendant in a handful of St. Louis freedom suits willingly offered to help an enslaved plaintiff prosecute her case.

Freedom suits spawned additional litigation and struggles—in and out of court—when enslavers tried to avoid losing financial resources after an enslaved plaintiff won his or her freedom, as Alsey did with the jury's verdict in 1843 and again in the 1844 appeal.[6] Shortly after the initial verdict for Alsey's freedom, the defendant, William S. Randolph, sued Robert Wash for selling Alsey and her son as slaves. Wash failed to appear in the Circuit Court, which resulted in a judgment for Randolph by default.[7] Wash appealed twice to the Missouri Supreme Court after the Circuit Court refused to reinstate his case.[8] Freedom suits held substantial financial repercussions for defendants who lost valuable human property. Each freed slave left a trail of slave traders desperate to pass the buck and avoid the loss. As Wash learned, some enslavers managed to dodge their responsibility by pursuing additional legal recourse against earlier buyers and sellers of the legally free plaintiff.

After Robert Wash lost his multiple appeals, he tried to pass his financial losses on to the person who sold Alsey to him: her initial owner, Robert Cross.[9] The effects of freedom suits like Alsey's rippled out beyond the initial lawsuits, resulting in additional legal battles, heated conversations, and occasionally, documentation. Private correspondence allows a glimpse into these conflicts, though undoubtedly many of the fights and accusations that followed when an enslaved person won freedom remain unrecorded. Writing to J. T. Barbour in Illinois (possibly a friend or legal agent), Wash explained that his "claim is founded . . . on a Bill of sale from Robt. F. Cross for two of the children (Burrie + Louisa) + . . . on the record of a Judgment rendered against me [Wash] after

Alsy obtained her freedom, which liberated also her son Moses."[10] In a second letter, Wash pleaded with Barbour to recover at least a portion of his losses from Cross, but Barbour informed Wash that he lacked a "private letter of his [Cross's], that would make him liable."[11] Wash needed more direct evidence of Cross's culpability if he hoped to avoid getting stuck with the bill for Alsey and her son. Wash's lack of documentation doomed his efforts, but the lawsuits he defended and the letters he wrote reveal the chain of additional legal and extralegal efforts that freedom suits generated.

Alsey's petition, her legal strategies, and her experiences mirrored those of hundreds of enslaved men and women who used the legal system to seek free status as plaintiffs in St. Louis's freedom suits (defined as any case in which the ultimate outcome decided the future personal status of a person held in slavery). Alsey presented the most often used argument for freedom made in the antebellum years—that her residence in free territory effected her release from slavery. Her case stretched into multiple legal actions across a number of years, a common result of these complicated battles. The rich surviving records in Alsey's case detail the relationships, additional litigation, and maneuverings outside the formal legal system and across multiple states that characterized local contests over the meaning of slavery and freedom. When Alsey, Dred and Harriet Scott, and hundreds of other enslaved men and women approached the St. Louis courts to sue for freedom, they became active contributors to the legal culture of slavery. By sharing their experiences and crafting their arguments, these individuals, with the assistance of their attorneys, participated in the larger struggle over the meanings of slavery and freedom in the antebellum legal arena.

The term "legal culture" refers to the constellation of attitudes and experiences concerning law in a particular time and place—separate from formal legal institutions like statutes and court proceedings, though these institutions certainly influenced how antebellum Americans understood law and legal authority. Focusing on the process of freedom suits reveals how legal authority operated in the lives of ordinary people, which involved a combination of their experiences of local court dealings along with more informal conversations, negotiations, and debates. Legal culture is primarily concerned with how communities discuss and think about law and how their views on law shape everyday lives and practices.[12] Encompassed within legal culture is legal consciousness: individuals' view of law, their experience of the law, and the considerations they make when approaching the legal system for assistance.[13] Legal culture includes communal attitudes and practices, whereas legal consciousness focuses on individuals' motivations and concerns and their conceptions about the role of law in their lives.

Legal culture emerged through the day-to-day workings of local communities—in the example of freedom suits, legal culture includes not only the cases themselves but also the many practices occurring before, during, and after the lawsuits. In antebellum St. Louis, legal disputes over slavery and freedom took place largely, but not exclusively, in freedom suit courtrooms. Freedom suits were hubs around which interconnected legal actions, conversations, and negotiations developed. These webs of personal interests, violence, power, and deception influenced the course of each person's battle over slavery. Enslaved men, women, and children were central players in these processes of determining personal status.

In antebellum St. Louis, the legal culture of slavery emerged from the multitude of voices and processes that struggled over the meaning of slavery and freedom. Alsey's case illustrates the legal culture of slavery through the multiple (and sometimes competing) conversations it generated about the law of slavery; Judge Wash's suit against the man who bought Alsey from him in St. Louis, Wash's letters to Illinois concerning Alsey's freedom suit and the financial losses it generated, and the attitude of Alsey's witness toward Judge Wash (because of earlier freedom suit decisions) all underscore the wide range of perspectives and reactions Alsey's lawsuit invoked. By contrast, Alsey's individual legal consciousness refers to the manner in which she learned about the law and her right to sue for freedom, the considerations she made before bringing suit, and how her experience in her case affected her understanding of law.

A host of voices contributed to the developing legal culture of slavery in antebellum America, and enslaved men and women were not merely victims or passive subjects of this development—they were active participants in the conversation.[14] The legal culture of slavery, for the purposes of this book, is specifically the areas of law and legal practice related to enslaved individuals. Enslaved men, women, and children encountered the law in their daily lives through legal regulations and restrictions on their behavior, property clauses that might result in transfers of direct control over their labor, and the occasional lawsuit initiated by them. Enslaved individuals knew about limits placed on their mobility when they requested a pass or encountered a slave patrol. Enslaved captives also recognized law's role when an enslaver died, forcing his or her slaves to move to a relative's house or possibly face the auction block. Given the dire consequences, it should come as little surprise that enslaved people realized that knowledge of the law was paramount for their survival in the system of American slavery and that they sometimes managed to make the legal system work to their advantage.

In the Shadow of Dred Scott contributes to a vibrant literature on enslaved and other subordinated peoples' use of law.[15] Ariela Gross's *Double Character* has served as a partial model for this study because it uses a single locale

(Natchez, Mississippi) to discover the many ways enslaved people contributed to the legal process. Gross also brings in appellate opinions to contextualize the issues she explores in Natchez, arguing that enslaved individuals influenced the legal process in unexpected and indirect—but also effective—ways. Gross's important book paved the way for additional scholars to look at enslaved individuals' interactions with law in a variety of different contexts. This project builds on Gross's work not only by focusing on suits for freedom but also by finding more direct, conscious engagement by African Americans and their attorneys in the legal culture of slavery.[16]

This book uses the process of freedom suits and the legal culture of slavery to reveal how daily interactions, personal relationships, and arguments presented in court shaped the legal debate over slavery and freedom. Building on examples like the work of Gross, Laura Edwards, and Martha Jones, *In the Shadow of* Dred Scott views the relationship between formal legal institutions and more informal legal processes as fluid and contested.[17] Local and appellate case law were central to the process of entrenching slavery in nineteenth-century America; but courts were not the only places making law, nor were they the exclusive purview of wealthy white men.[18] Including suits for freedom in discussions of legal process and legal culture means broadening the cast of players to include enslaved and free African Americans, attorneys working with these individuals, and the interests and arguments of local communities.[19]

Despite this attention to the legal experiences of a variety of subordinated groups, and although the *Dred Scott* case has been the subject of voluminous scholarly attention, few studies discuss the thousands of individuals who sued for freedom in the years prior to Dred Scott's case.[20] This book treats Dred and Harriet Scott's freedom suits as merely the most famous examples of a phenomenon that was more common than many scholars have generally recognized.[21] Freedom suits constituted a significant element of the legal culture of slavery in antebellum America. Although their frequency should not be overstated, the number of local suits in St. Louis, combined with the hundreds of appellate cases from throughout the United States, suggest a broader awareness of legal access and a deeper engagement of enslaved individuals with local and appellate courts than is typically discussed in the scholarly literature.

Incorporating ideas and questions gleaned from the field of legal studies, including legal anthropology, legal sociology, and legal history, this study uses freedom suits to explore the construction of the legal categories of slavery and freedom and the ways in which these categories remained variable throughout the antebellum years.[22] Legal scholarship has largely focused on the contributions of legal professionals—judges, lawyers, and legislators—when discussing the creation of law and legal culture.[23] Following the anthropologist Laura Nader's arguments for a more plaintiff-centered approach to decision making, this book takes seriously the efforts and risks taken by enslaved plaintiffs when approaching the court, sharing their stories, and challenging the control of enslavers.[24] When enslaved individuals chose to bring a suit for freedom, they challenged the dominion of enslavers by wielding the law's authority to frustrate enslavers' designs and assert legal personhood. Although largely following existing lines of reasoning, enslaved plaintiffs and their attorneys also pushed the boundaries of these scripts. Enslaved plaintiffs approached the law with certain expectations, beginning a process they could not always control. The outcome of each case—with the plaintiff winning freedom or, conversely, remaining in slavery—matters less than the overall effect of forcing enslavers to defend their position and answer to the rule of the law. By arguing over a central political issue of the era, the many participants in freedom suits contributed to conversations over the boundaries of slave and free status in the antebellum years. These boundaries shifted and remained unsettled, demonstrating how these conversations transferred an element of power to the plaintiffs as they fought over meaning in the arena of law.

Three main themes within contests over slavery and freedom are particularly apparent in the St. Louis cases: mobility, geography, and negotiations.[25] A central concern of nineteenth-century Americans, mobility formed the basis for many St. Louis freedom suits. When enslavers traveled with enslaved individuals to free territory, these enslaved persons used the doctrine of free soil to argue for freedom in court. Closely related is the significance of geography to enslaved individuals' ability to sue. In St. Louis, the city's proximity to free states and its location on the Mississippi River provided opportunities for its enslaved population to sue for freedom, but the city's geography also created the danger of removal from the city or even sale to the Deep South. Enslaved plaintiffs leveraged the possibilities, made available by their mobility and the city's geography, to negotiate for certain advantages—though these efforts were not always successful. Negotiations surrounding freedom suits involved lawyers making deals, defendants seeking loopholes, and countless arrangements that took place within the courtroom and outside it. Together, the multiple interests surrounding freedom suits contributed to the legal culture of slavery and linked it with the major political currents of the era.

No other American city highlights enslaved litigants' role in antebellum debates over slavery like St. Louis. The city was the heart of the

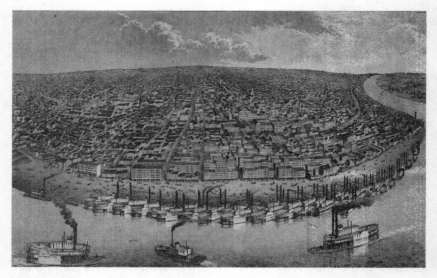

FIGURE 3. "A view of the city of St. Louis from the Mississippi River, ca. 1859." "Our City (St. Louis, Mo.)," lithograph by A. Janicke and Co., St. Louis, as accessed through the Library of Congress (http://www.loc.gov/pictures/item/94513619/).

American West, and its location on the Mississippi River cemented its role as a connector of peoples from north, south, east, and west, as well as the various groups of immigrants who moved into the American interior searching for land and opportunity. Although St. Louis's population mirrored much of the broader United States, the city's location on the border of slave and free states also created an increasing ambiguity surrounding personal status, as well as a fluidity—in terms of population and social conditions—that characterized the Border South. Law is often challenged and developed on its borders, where multiple legal orders collide and people from a variety of backgrounds interact with one another.[26] The city's position on the border of the slave state of Missouri and the free state of Illinois created space for negotiations over personal status and expanded the available routes to freedom for the enslaved residents of the region.[27]

Clashes over slavery happened throughout the United States in the first half of the nineteenth century; in many places, the courts proved to be crucial battlegrounds for these contests, making decisions that had real consequences for the men and women involved in each case. Delving into a single local setting like St. Louis reveals the multitude of actors who argued over slavery and freedom in local communities and how these contests extended beyond lawsuits for freedom. Both local and appellate courts issued decisions that shaped conversations over slavery and freedom and formed legal doctrines used by judges and attorneys in St. Louis. Legal doctrine was a central influence on the legal culture of slavery, as communities learned about, discussed, and argued over judicial opinions from St. Louis and elsewhere. Local decisions in St. Louis form the heart of this investigation into these debates, but St. Louis's courts did not operate in a vacuum. Judges and attorneys in St. Louis sought to understand a broader legal landscape that included appellate courts in Missouri as well as other jurisdictions. Studying the legal culture of slavery is necessarily a local enterprise—much of the hard work of legal and extralegal wrangling, conversations, and personal interactions took place within local communities like St. Louis—though the local scene was never divorced from state, regional, and national dialogue surrounding slavery. The legal culture of slavery connected multiple jurisdictions and also helped distinguish each particular geographic area of focus.

Because the existing historiography does not yet allow for broader comparisons of local freedom suit courts throughout the United States, this study surveys more than eight hundred appellate opinions in freedom suits to place St. Louis's cases in a broader context. Legal doctrine from appellate courts provides a frame of reference for the local study of St. Louis's freedom suits, allows for certain issues to be discussed in greater detail than the St. Louis records permit, and starts the process of trying to understand broader patterns and trends in freedom suits—a process that additional studies of local records will help to complete, as new caches of local freedom suits become available.

The book's structure generally follows the trajectory of a freedom suit, starting with the establishment of the legal framework for suits for freedom in Missouri and concluding with the results and political ramifications of the cases. Because the story centers on suits for freedom as an element of the developing legal culture of slavery, the overarching arc emphasizes the process of this type of lawsuit, with chapters covering particular stages and perspectives that made up these contests. Tracing the practices of freedom suits in this way highlights how various people experienced these cases. Each group—enslaved plaintiffs, slaveholding defendants, legal professionals, and the broader community—worked to influence the outcomes and control the process of making meaning through the law.

A brief sketch of the outcomes of St. Louis's freedom suits offers a sense of some of the available data generated by the cases, though the complex nature of local legal outcomes and the fact that many of the final results are unknown do not allow for many broader conclusions based solely on the numbers of cases.[28] Of the 287 suits for freedom in St. Louis from 1810 to 1860, 110 suits (38 percent) concluded with the enslaved plaintiff receiving free status, 84 cases (30 percent) failed to win freedom, and in 93 freedom suits (32 percent), the plaintiff's status could not be definitively determined by the available historical records.[29] Of these 93 undetermined suits, 49 cases ended when the enslaved plaintiffs voluntarily allowed his or her case to be dismissed or agreed not to further prosecute the case.[30] St. Louis plaintiffs sued for freedom based on three major categories of arguments: freedom after residence on free soil (209 cases, resulting in freedom in 79 cases, or 38 percent); freedom from the time of birth, which often meant birth to a free mother (116 cases, resulting in freedom in 57 cases, or 49 percent); and freedom based on prior manumission or an agreement for manumission (62 cases, resulting in freedom in 24 cases, or 39 percent).[31] Women slightly outnumbered men in St. Louis freedom suits, and many St. Louis plaintiffs sued in groups of family members or with other people claimed as slaves by the same enslaver.[32] Although these numbers present more questions than they can answer, they suggest that enslaved plaintiffs managed to definitively win freedom in more than a third of their suits in St. Louis, a somewhat surprising number when one considers that all judges, attorneys, jurors, and most witnesses were white men and that early American legislatures often designed the law of slavery to protect enslavers and to uphold white supremacy above the interests of people of African descent. The number of St. Louis cases resulting in freedom is remarkably similar to the numbers in Keila Grinberg's work on freedom suits in Brazil. Grinberg's results concluded that out of a total of 400 cases, 158 cases (39.5 percent) resulted in freedom, 28 cases (7 percent) ended with conditional freedom, 165 cases (41.25 percent) left the plaintiff in slavery, and 49 cases (12.25 percent) had unknown outcomes.[33]

The corpus of St. Louis freedom suits includes two major periods of change—the early 1820s and the mid- to late 1840s—which are discussed in chapters 1 and 7 of this book. The early years of the freedom suits, from 1810 to the mid-1820s, witnessed greater informality and new precedent-setting cases that established the patterns of litigation for the next couple of decades. The low number of cases that occurred in the early years, from 1810 to 1825 (33 cases, or 11 percent), can be partially explained by the small population of St. Louis at the time, which had only 10,049 residents at the time of the first available census data in 1820.[34] The vast majority of the freedom suits occurred from 1825 to 1845 (217 cases, or 76 percent), with the number of cases falling off sharply after 1845. The second major shift in the freedom suit litigation in St. Louis happened after 1845, when changes to the freedom suit statute, followed in 1852 by the Missouri Supreme Court decision in Dred Scott's case, resulted in far fewer cases (37 cases, or 13 percent) in the later antebellum years (1846–60). Because most of the suits occurred in between these two periods of change with little variation in terms of patterns of arguments and outcomes, and in order to emphasize the importance of process and perspective to the legal culture of slavery in freedom suits, the book is organized thematically.

In the Shadow of Dred Scott begins by providing the background to Missouri's legal system, antebellum slave laws, and the statutes and forms that allowed enslaved men and women to sue for freedom. Chapter 1, "Setting the Scene," briefly examines the legal heritage of St. Louis and the Missouri region, beginning with the earliest French settlement of the area. French, and later Spanish, legal traditions influenced the development of Missouri's legal apparatus through statutes and through the participation of the largely French population of St. Louis, which continued to be a major factor in the city's politics into the 1830s. The chapter examines the codification of slave law and legal practice in the region, including Missouri's early statutes, and compares Missouri's slave laws to those of other slave states. The precise legal form differed slightly in various jurisdictions, but freedom suit statutes reveal a notable degree of continuity across time and place. The chapter also explains the process by which an enslaved individual sued for freedom, including the various steps taken from the beginning to the end of a case. Following a suit through its various stages reveals how the format of legal actions left a great deal of room for maneuvering—both within and outside the courtroom, although the conclusion of a legal suit often was not the end of the person's struggles to win and maintain legal freedom.

Chapter 2, "Bringing Suit," takes the perspective of the enslaved litigants to consider the process by which these individuals determined to sue for freedom. Enslaved men and women had a couple of additional options for becoming free, including the possibility of running away, which was a common occurrence in St. Louis, and manumission, which became increasingly difficult for enslaved individuals in the later antebellum decades. The chapter considers how enslaved individuals learned about freedom suits, through their attorneys but especially through the existing networks of communication among slaves and free people of color.[35] Once enslaved individuals heard of the opportunity for suing for freedom, they considered the risks involved when suing their owners. Freedom suits held dangerous consequences for some enslaved plaintiffs, who might suffer mental and physical abuse as a result of their cases or be sold away from the court's jurisdiction as a way to prevent the court from declaring them free. For these reasons, enslaved men and women mulled over their options and weighed the risks before beginning their suits, a process that indicates a high degree of legal consciousness among the enslaved population of St. Louis.

The character of St. Louis's legal community and its involvement in freedom suits is traced in chapter 3, "Crafting Strategy." Enslaved plaintiffs directed the course of their lawsuits by approaching the court or an attorney and sharing their life circumstances in the hope of proving illegal enslavement. Despite their vital role in this process, enslaved individuals relied on attorneys at every stage of the legal action—making the efforts of attorneys a critical part of the struggles over slavery and freedom taking place in and around these cases. Freedom suit statutes codified the existing process for prosecuting this type of legal action, but, like statutes relating to other types of litigation, they said nothing about how the suits could be argued or decided. A brief survey of the arguments used and the forms they took in various jurisdictions reveals the creativity of enslaved plaintiffs and their attorneys when prosecuting freedom suits. When appellate court decisions restricted the use of particular arguments for freedom, local litigants and their attorneys crafted ways around these limits, creating new strategies for winning freedom. The ways in which each argument for freedom developed suggest a culture of negotiation, not only between alleged slaves and their supposed owners but also between litigants and the judges and juries deciding their cases.

Chapter 4, "A World in Motion," highlights the themes of geography and movement in freedom suits, especially the location of St. Louis on the border of the free state of Illinois, as well as the significance of mobility to freedom suits and to interstate comity.[36] The primary argument made by enslaved plaintiffs in St. Louis's freedom suits, including *Dred Scott*, was that the enslaved individual had lived or traveled in free territory. This argument enjoyed reasonable success for much of the antebellum period because of the English precedent in *Somerset v. Stewart* (1772) and because of the doctrine of interstate comity, which required each state to respect other states' laws.[37] Following these legal doctrines meant that Missouri courts ended up freeing a number of enslaved individuals—like Alsey in the opening example—who had traveled or lived in Illinois, a phenomenon that is also reflected in freedom suits from other regions of the country. The antebellum era witnessed an increase in mobility for many Americans, both because of improvements in transportation and also because of people's desire to move west for land and new opportunities outside the eastern seaboard settlements. Freedom suits in other jurisdictions also relied on mobility to create arguments for freedom: some included issues of comity, whereas others dealt with regionally specific statutes that allowed for freedom suits when enslavers violated established rules limiting their mobility with their enslaved property. Mobility therefore influenced the trajectory of freedom suits in St. Louis and elsewhere.

Chapter 5, "Double Character," employs as its starting point the central argument made in Ariela Gross's book of the same title, that enslaved individuals had a "double character" in law as both persons and property.[38] Whereas Gross examines property cases in which enslaved individuals managed to interject their personhood, and the work of other legal historians of slavery tends to differentiate between areas where the law considered slaves as property (such as disputes over sales), and areas where the law considered slaves to be persons (such as the criminal law), freedom suits are one area of law that simultaneously highlights both legal aspects of enslaved individuals. Prosecuting a freedom suit meant granting legal personhood and therefore recognizing the undeniable humanity of the enslaved plaintiff, but these cases also often revolved around strict property disputes, such as slave sales or manumissions by will or deed. This chapter looks at how the central tension of slaves as both people and property played out in the courtroom, where community relations and a person's reputation could influence the court's determinations. The chapter also delves into the negotiations over freedom that took place between enslaved persons and enslavers, including arrangements for an enslaved individual to purchase freedom, and how the law responded to disputes that arose when enslavers violated these agreements.

In chapter 6, "Defending Suits," the focus shifts to the enslavers who became defendants in freedom suits. Freedom suit defendants were often leading members of their communities who used their spheres of power and influence to try to thwart the efforts of enslaved plaintiffs and their attorneys. Like enslaved plaintiffs, defendants understood the law's restrictions on them, and yet many enslavers openly flaunted their disregard for legal measures—at least until they found themselves facing a freedom suit. Defendants employed a variety of strategies for success in freedom suits, engaging in legal wrangling both in and out of the courtroom to avoid losing their valuable human property. Lawyers also played an important role in this story, working alongside enslavers and aiding their efforts to avoid prosecution. Much of the scholarship on slave law has emphasized the perspective of white enslavers—in this book, their voices are merely one of many significant actors shaping debates over personal status.

The example of St. Louis is placed in a larger political context in chapter 7, "Political Repercussions," which examines the repercussions of the cases in the years prior to the U.S. Supreme Court's *Dred Scott* decision in 1857. The chapter argues that freedom suits did not occur in isolation: these cases both influenced and were influenced by national and local politics, bringing major changes in terms of process and results in the last decade and a half of freedom suit case law. Dred Scott's case is perhaps the best example of this relationship, but other freedom suits also carried political implications because successful freedom suits increased the number of free people of color in local populations and could result in property losses for the community's leading citizens. The 1840s and 1850s were an era of increasing tensions over the slavery issue in both local and national politics, and this changing atmosphere contributed to a general push for tighter legal restrictions on enslaved and free people of color.[39] At the same time, St. Louis's politics began to diverge from the rest of the state; as the city's population became increasingly diverse and included large numbers of immigrants, St. Louis began to shift its political loyalties. By the late 1850s, the city voted Republican, signifying a break with the political tradition of its French elites and delivering a blow to the goals of the city's enslavers. In the midst of these political currents, St. Louis's freedom suits also underwent a number of changes. For example, an 1845 statute required enslaved plaintiffs to provide financial security to guarantee the costs of their freedom suits. This new requirement made suing for freedom much more difficult for Missouri slaves, who often lacked access to financial resources. As a result, the number of freedom suits plummeted in the late 1840s and 1850s, and the outcomes also shifted to reflect the changing political climate of the city. In the last fifteen years of freedom suits in St. Louis, the Circuit Court failed to find a single case in favor of the slaveholding defendant. In this way, political currents happening in and around the local legal arena brought tremendous consequences for enslaved individuals.

In the Shadow of Dred Scott traces the story of St. Louis's freedom suits, providing context and background to Dred Scott's infamous case, but the book also explores the larger themes of local legal culture and the relationship between subordinated peoples and the law. White enslavers dominated the antebellum legal system in St. Louis and throughout the slaveholding states, but that did not mean that the legal system ignored the concerns of the poor whites, women, immigrants, enslaved men and women, and free people of color who made up the vast majority of the American population. Examining a local example of one subordinated group's encounters with the law and placing it into conversation with similar themes, arguments, and circumstances that arose in appellate cases from throughout the slaveholding states sheds light on the ways in which the legal system responded to the demands of a variety of different actors. The legal culture of slavery encompassed a broad range of experiences by enslaved individuals and their communities. Freedom suits constituted a small but valuable segment of this culture. This book is an effort to understand the process of these cases and how the multiple concerns that clashed in and around lawsuits for freedom contributed to debates over the meaning of slavery and freedom in antebellum America.

1 /   Setting the Scene

When Arch and Jack sued Barnabas Harris for freedom in 1818, both men searched for the best strategy to obtain freedom in the St. Louis courts.[1] Harris claimed that the men belonged to Eusebius Hubbard of Kentucky after an 1811 indenture transferred property (including the two enslaved men) to Hubbard from his wife. The document decreed that Arch and Jack serve Hubbard until his death and then become the property of his heirs.[2] Such an arrangement—passing human property between spouses or family members in what the legal community referred to as a life estate, which granted temporary control to the beneficiary—was not unusual, though it raised complicated questions about ownership rights and control over human property.[3]

Jack claimed freedom based on an 1817 manumission ordering that Jack be freed after Hubbard's death. The manumission deed declared that Jack was to "be fully Emancipated and completely discharged from the claim or claims to any servitude, bondage or authority whatsoever."[4] Arch's manumission arrangement included an additional requirement that he serve Hubbard's daughter for fifteen years before receiving his freedom.[5] When Hubbard died shortly after issuing the deeds, Jack and Arch passed into the possession of his heirs, who, as later evidence makes clear, were well aware of the manumission agreements. Recognizing that they now held illegitimate title to free men, the heirs quickly sold the alleged slaves to Barnabas Harris for an unnamed price in order to avoid prosecution.[6] After the sale, the two enslaved men sued Harris for freedom, inaugurating a series of legal processes that centered on their freedom suits but were not confined to the courtroom.

The term "freedom suit" can refer to a variety of types of legal contests, though statutes often specified the particular type of legal action required to determine the issue of personal status in each state. In the pages that follow, the term refers to any lawsuit in which one of the primary issues the court had to decide was the personal status (as legally free or enslaved) of one or more alleged slaves. Often initiated by a person or persons held in slavery or by someone else on their behalf, freedom suits also originated from disputes over wills, habeas corpus petitions, and other types of legal actions. The form and process of these cases depended on the type of legal action pursued, which varied according to each particular state's statutes and existing practices.[7]

Process and strategy were integral elements influencing how enslaved individuals learned about law, thought about law, and transmitted their ideas about law. For this reason, understanding how a freedom suit operated in practice is essential for getting at the relationship between enslaved individuals and the legal system. Various points in the legal procedure of a freedom suit offered enslaved plaintiffs opportunities for interacting with attorneys and other legal professionals, deepening their awareness of legal culture, and inching toward freedom. The process of suing for freedom could—and often did—take years to complete: years full of affidavits, summonses, testimony, and continuances, leaving plaintiffs in a type of legal limbo. Some enslaved plaintiffs spent the bulk of this time working for temporary hirers, others remained with their alleged owners, and a few individuals spent the majority of the time that passed during their cases in the St. Louis jail. During the years spent waiting for a decision in a freedom suit, enslaved plaintiffs, although certainly terrified of the potentially negative outcome of their cases, eagerly participated in the process and contributed to the conversations that took place within each lawsuit.

The location, statutes, and process of freedom suits set the parameters for discussions over slavery and freedom taking place in local communities across the country. In St. Louis, the area's legal heritage and its early relationship to slavery affected later conflicts in the antebellum decades. By the early nineteenth century, the St. Louis community was only beginning to debate the existence of slavery in the legal arena. The maneuverings of the city's enslaved population forced these questions into the public sphere—jump-starting local conversations about slavery, even as communities, legislatures, and courts throughout the United States wrestled over similar issues.

Early St. Louis

When Arch and Jack began searching for a remedy for their illegal enslavement in the late 1810s, the town of St. Louis was less than seventy years old and had witnessed several shifts in imperial control. Beginning with the town's initial eighteenth-century European settlement, St. Louis embraced a diverse population; its legal culture grew out of this tradition of French and Spanish heritage, as well as the city's commitment to racial slavery and the near-constant tensions with Native Americans in the surrounding area.

Slow European settlement in an area that was already home to multiple groups of Native Americans contributed to Missouri's multiculturalism. In the early eighteenth century, Missouri and Osage Indians inhabited the lands around the banks of the Mississippi and Missouri Rivers, near present-day St. Louis. Europeans made a few failed attempts at settlement in the early decades of the century before establishing the first permanent outpost in 1750, when France claimed the entire region as part of French Louisiana. In 1764, in an attempt to recover financial losses following the Seven Years' War (1754–63), the French adventurer Pierre Laclède and his stepson, Auguste Chouteau, traveled north along the Mississippi River from New Orleans and founded the settlement of St. Louis near the confluence of the Mississippi and Missouri Rivers.[8] Soon after, new groups of permanent settlers began arriving, and the young village seemed to "spring into existence."[9] French colonists dominated this initial influx, moving west across the Mississippi River after word arrived from Europe that France had surrendered all of its territory east of the river to the British. By late 1764, when news of the French cession of Louisiana to Spain reached St. Louis, the area had around forty or fifty families living there.[10]

St. Louis's shifting imperial loyalties brought a mixed population of settlers; among the early arrivals was the family of Arch and Jack's enslaver, Eusebius Hubbard. The remote inland territory's failure to produce riches made it something of a colonial hot potato, bouncing from France to Spain, back to France, and finally to the new United States, all in the space of only forty years. After years of conflicts and failed settlement attempts, the Spanish relinquished Missouri to the French, who then quickly sold it to the United States in the Louisiana Purchase of 1803. Shortly after the United States assumed control of the territory, Eusebius Hubbard married and received three hundred acres of land in St. Louis, and eleven enslaved persons, as part of his marriage arrangement.[11]

Throughout the territorial period, Native Americans along with French, a few Spanish, and Anglo-American settlers intermingled to construct Missouri's unique social landscape, which also included a substantial population of enslaved and free people of African descent.

St. Louis's European settlers committed the town to forced labor from its inception. The earliest known St. Louis inventory of goods and property, from March 1766, showed "two negroes," apparently brought from the Illinois Territory by a French official.[12] In a reference from 1768, a trader agreed to "take a negro in place of the said sum of eight hundred livres in peltries" as payment for one of his debts.[13] Additionally, the first book registering births, marriages, and deaths in the Catholic parish of St. Louis contains an entry dated October 4, 1770, when the sexton of the church "interred the body of Gregory, a free negro man."[14] Although a lack of solid population data makes it impossible to pinpoint the number of enslaved and free people of color living in the settlement in its earliest decades, a later newspaper reference suggests that the Catholic Church baptized and buried hundreds of enslaved and free people of color, in addition to the predominantly French inhabitants of the village.[15]

Enslavers in St. Louis quickly seized on the strategy of trying to divide loyalty in order to better control their human property. For example, on May 15, 1787, Marie-Thérèse Chouteau received $600 in silver for the value of her enslaved man, who died trying to help recapture two escaped Indian slaves. One nineteenth-century historian described the incident, writing, "This affair was one of absorbing interest to the inhabitants of our little community, furnishing the gossips of the day a fruitful topic to engage their attention. . . . Not so much from the death of the negro itself, *for that was a circumstance of minor importance at that day,* as from the high social position that all concerned [in] it occupied in the community."[16] The enslaved man's death came as a result of trying to help capture runaway Indian slaves, an indicator of the divisive plan attempted by enslavers in these early years. Marie-Thérèse Chouteau was the mother of Auguste Chouteau and the mistress of Pierre Laclède, the two men who together founded the village of St. Louis. A wealthy and powerful woman, her social standing no doubt influenced the award she received to compensate her for the loss of her human property.[17]

The indenture transferring Arch and Jack from Eusebius Hubbard's wife to Hubbard and then to his heirs took place in late 1811, just before the outbreak of imperial conflict in the War of 1812. The end of the fighting brought significant change to St. Louis and the region that later became the state of Missouri: with the war over and the British presence in the Northwest Territory eliminated, more settlers from further east and south entered the area. After 1815, the population of the area now called the Missouri Territory (with roughly the same boundaries as the state of Missouri) increased exponentially, driving explosive growth in its largest town, St. Louis. From 1815 to 1818, the population of St. Louis doubled to more than three thousand residents.[18] Many of these new settlers brought enslaved captives with them from eastern seaboard states like Virginia and the Carolinas, helping, along with the founding French residents, to build a solid foundation of powerful slaveholding families in the region.

Arch and Jack brought their freedom suits just before the slavery question catapulted Missouri into national debates over the future of the institution in the American West. The Compromise of 1820, also known as the Missouri Compromise, resulted from the question of whether Missouri would allow enslaved and free people of color to migrate to the region. Northerners, many of whose states had already abolished or were in the process of abolishing slavery, feared that allowing Missouri to enter as a slave state would upset the balance of power in the U.S. Senate. Southerners wanted to guarantee the ability of enslavers to bring their human property into new territories, therefore preserving their own power in Congress and protecting the institution they viewed as crucial to the region's survival. With enslavers forcing groups of enslaved laborers to migrate to the region, white Missourians erupted in protest over the suggestion that they would not be admitted as a slave state.[19] The eventual Compromise admitted Missouri as a slave state and Maine as a free state, which preserved the balance of power in the Senate. Even more important for future debates over slavery, the Compromise created a line at the 36°30' parallel to denote that new states admitted to the United States north of this line would not have slavery and those territories south of the line would allow slavery. Although the Missouri Compromise left both sides with battle scars in the form of added distrust and increased tension, it did manage to keep slavery in the background of national politics for more than two decades.[20] In 1821, when Missouri joined the Union as a state permitting slavery, Missouri's 20,000 enslaved residents represented roughly 15 percent of the population; St. Louis alone had over 10,000 total residents, and its 1,800 enslaved people constituted 18 percent of the city's population.[21] At the same time, the number of free people of color in the territory decreased to only 347, possibly because of tight legal restrictions placed on all people of African descent, enslaved and free.[22]

Enormous population growth in the space of only a few years created a tense environment in St. Louis and the surrounding area, which is reflected in the city's attempts to maintain control of its African-descended population. One particularly sensational St. Louis example of this tension was the legal case of *United States v. Elijah* (1818), involving an enslaved man who faced charges of conspiracy to commit murder for plotting to kill his enslaver's wife. Elijah's case received widespread attention and eventually resulted in a guilty verdict and his execution.[23] Fears of slave uprising further unsettled the social relations in the area. As a result, state and local officials passed a variety of ordinances designed to control enslaved and free people of African descent.[24] These new legal restrictions built on a long tradition of slave law under the French and Spanish.

Creating a Law of Slavery

By the 1810s, Arch and Jack attempted to navigate a legal system built on a foundation of varying imperial codes that emphasized informal negotiations. In the eighteenth century, St. Louis and surrounding settlements west of the Mississippi operated under successive French and Spanish civil law codes before shifting in the early nineteenth century to a legal code that more closely resembled the English common law tradition.[25] After the Spanish officially assumed control of St. Louis from the French in May 1770, Spanish officials called commandants administrated justice and settled local disputes in St. Louis, often without formal judicial proceedings. Commandants preferred arbitration or informal settlement to court proceedings, and the right of trial by jury did not exist in the Spanish legal system.[26]

When France transferred control of the Missouri region to the United States in 1803, a combination of Spanish civil law, the legal traditions of the predominantly French population, and English common law brought in by the new, American government and Anglo-American settlers all worked to create a hodgepodge of rules and precedents for the new American courts—and individuals looking for legal remedies—to digest. For the most part, existing laws and practices remained in place unless directly altered by the new governmental authorities. Justices of the peace administered law on the local level, and litigants could appeal their decisions to the Court of Quarter Sessions of the Peace (the precursor to the Circuit Court).[27] The tremendous growth of the colony in the 1810s, with many new Anglo-American settlers moving in, brought changes to the court system in St. Louis. Congress created the Territory of Missouri in June 1812 and affirmed existing legal practices not specifically changed by the territorial legislature. In 1813, the courts operating in St. Louis combined to form the Court of Common Pleas, which exercised civil, criminal, and probate jurisdiction for St. Louis County until the creation of the Circuit Court on February 15, 1815. At the inception of the St. Louis Circuit Court—where Arch, Jack, and most other illegally enslaved plaintiffs brought suit for freedom—it provided civil, criminal, chancery, and probate authority in St. Louis.[28]

When plaintiffs like Arch and Jack built their arguments for freedom, they drew on the combination of French, Spanish, and English legal traditions that constituted Missouri's system of slave law. By the mid-eighteenth century, slave laws and conditions in North America varied considerably from place to place. Even so, slavery had become a strict, race-based system of exploitation and social domination, regardless of the European power in control. St. Louis was no exception. French law governed the earliest enslaved persons in St. Louis. In 1724, the French established the *Code Noir*, or Black Code, for Louisiana, which also constituted the first law of slavery in Missouri. Based on the Roman system of slavery, the *Code Noir* provided for a minimum standard of care for enslaved persons, and it allowed them to marry with the permission of their enslavers.[29] When the Spanish took control of the Louisiana Territory and eventually modified the *Code Noir* after 1764, they allowed enslaved men and women to own property, restricted Native American slavery, and instituted the practice of allowing enslaved individuals to purchase freedom (with or without their enslavers' consent), or *coartación*.[30] Spanish residents could keep their existing Indian slaves, as long as they registered them with local authorities, but Spanish codes forbade the further importation and the buying and selling of enslaved Native Americans. These policies opened the door to a number of later freedom suits based on Native American ancestry, including the first freedom suit in the new U.S. Territory of Missouri. Although the Spanish instituted elaborate slave codes, the predominantly French population kept them from being fully enforced by Spanish authorities.[31]

When the United States government arrived in Missouri, it kept the existing laws in place unless altered by the territorial legislature—which later Americanized the legal code, reflecting the national trend toward greater restrictions on people of African descent. Although the influence of the *Code Noir* and Spanish slave law continued through the powerful French families residing in the territory and their experience with

Spanish legal practices, the legislature passed a new set of laws regulating slavery in Missouri on October 1, 1804, that resembled the slave codes of older U.S. states, especially Virginia and Kentucky. These laws prohibited enslaved individuals from unlawfully assembling, traveling without a pass, or carrying firearms or other weapons.[32] The new legislation defined all persons held in slavery as "personal estate" (movable property) and defined a "mulattoe" as anyone with at least one-fourth "negro blood." It also prohibited any "negro or mulattoe," including enslaved and free persons, from being "a witness [in court] except in pleas of the United States against negroes or mulattoes, or in civil pleas where negroes alone shall be parties."[33] The law committed escaped slaves to jail, claiming that "many times slaves runaway and lie hid and lurking in swamps, woods and other obscure places, killing hogs and committing other injuries to the inhabitants of this district."[34] These restrictions on the mobility of enslaved individuals were typical of state codes elsewhere and reflected a growing sense of unease among the nation's enslavers as the spread of slavery continued to the South and West—and began to contract in the North. Enslaved individuals' use of migration to shape arguments for freedom substantiated legislators' concerns with slave mobility in this early legislation.

Arch's and Jack's freedom suits directly engaged the new territorial statutes' limits on overseers and holders of slaves—including restrictions on their ability to control, sell, or manumit enslaved men and women. The laws prohibited enslavers from allowing an enslaved person to "go at large, or hire him or herself out." If a slaveholder permitted an enslaved individual to hire his or her own time, any person could apprehend the slave and commit him or her to jail. After giving notice in the newspaper, the sheriff or officer of the court could sell the person to the highest bidder.[35] The new statutes further prohibited whites and free blacks from stealing enslaved persons or knowingly "selling any free person for a slave," with the latter infraction subjecting violators to execution, though there are no known cases of this criminal restriction having been enforced. The law did permit enslavers to manumit their slaves by deed, as Eusebius Hubbard did for Arch and Jack, or by will, but only if the court deemed the person "of sound mind and body" and the bondsman or bondswoman was under forty-five years of age and older than eighteen for females and twenty-one for males.[36] If the enslaver chose to manumit a slave by will, his or her estate had to be free of debt, or the enslaved person could be sold to cover any deficiency.

Manumissions were one of the primary ways enslaved individuals like Arch and Jack became free, but when enslavers violated manumission

agreements or otherwise ignored the law to enslave freed persons, statutes set up the remedy of suing for freedom. This option for freedom
existed in North American colonies before the American Revolution,
though the overall number of pre-Revolution freedom suits remains
unclear and in need of further exploration.[37] By the early nineteenth-
century, freedom suits certainly existed in considerable numbers, and
earlier precedents influenced the form and content of these cases. In
many instances, slaveholding states continued to use their colonial statutes for freedom suits with only slight alterations, and new territories
and states borrowed heavily from their predecessors when establishing
their own avenues for suing for freedom.

Anatomy of a Freedom Suit

Missouri's freedom statute, which Arch and Jack eventually used to
sue for freedom, was a product of heavy legal borrowing and codified
existing legal practices from throughout the United States. Although
the extent to which the statute came directly from another state's laws
is unclear, freedom statutes from across the United States shared many
common features—as did much of America's slave law.[38] Europeans
arriving in the Americas and colonizing the Atlantic coast drew on the
legal heritage of the Caribbean sugar islands to develop their understand-
ings of slavery.[39] Likewise, migrants moving west in the generations of
the late eighteenth and early nineteenth centuries brought with them the
legal training, case law, and statute books of the eastern seaboard states.
Virginia, in particular, contributed to the legal heritage of Kentucky and
other western enclaves.[40] Legal borrowing not only eased the transition
of immigrants to their new residences; in addition, the ability to draw on
earlier precedents was an integral part of the common law that provided
further authority to early settlers' statutes and court decisions.

Legislators recognized the importance of statutes for shaping debates
over slavery in court, though the example of freedom suit litigation
makes clear how plaintiffs and defendants could stretch their interpretation of the statutes or craft arguments to get around statutory provisions. Legislators sought to rein in potentially revolutionary tendencies
in the legal system, but they also recognized the need for a remedy in
cases of illegal enslavement. Freedom suits provide one example of how
attorneys, judges, and litigants contributed to local cultures that sometimes allowed for freedom in the midst of seemingly rigid slaveholding
societies. For enslavers, whose paranoia over rebellion and direct violent

confrontation over slavery in the antebellum era is well documented in the historical literature, the existence of a large corpus of freedom suits would also have been frightening.[41] Not every colony, territory, and state saw high numbers of freedom suits in their jurisdictions, but the existence of explicit statutory provisions for freedom suits in nearly every slaveholding jurisdiction—and case law even in those rare jurisdictions that lacked freedom suit statutes—no doubt raised enslavers' concerns.

Legislators occasionally indicated how certain community considerations drove the creation and the design of particular elements of freedom suit statutes in their states. For example, Delaware's 1760 colonial statute explained legislators' worries about the illegal enslavement of the children born to white women and "Negro or mulatto fathers and their descendants" who, lawmakers feared, could be sold outside of the colony.[42] A more surprising justification was in Georgia's 1851 statute, which indicated that its passage was necessary to prevent free people of color from being taken and "illegally held in a state of slavery, by wicked white men" in that state.[43] Georgia's law is unusual because it suggested a desire to protect free people of color in a Deep South state and it passed in the 1850s, when most southern states moved to tighten restrictions on free people of African descent and prevent additions to this incendiary population in their communities.

Explicit rationales for freedom suit legislation were rare, and rarer still were explanations that indicated a desire to protect free persons of color held illegally as slaves; more common explanations showed concern for enslavers' property rights and a determination to shield them from the interference of antislavery agitators. For example, Virginia's 1795 freedom suit statute specified that "great and alarming mischiefs" happening in other states necessitated the new statutory guidelines to prevent "heavy expenses in tedious and unfounded law suits" from impinging on the right to control human property. By providing a specific mode of redress in cases of illegal enslavement, Virginia's lawmakers hoped to thwart the practices of antislavery activists and, especially, societies formed for that purpose. Virginia's statute also included specific punishments to discourage outsiders from assisting enslaved people suing for their freedom. If the court found an individual "aiding and abetting" an unsuccessful freedom suit, that person owed a $100 penalty to the alleged owner, who could sue any person who refused to pay these damages.[44] Although Missouri never legislated punishment for community members who helped enslaved plaintiffs, community involvement—and especially the perceived involvement of abolitionists—did exist in a few examples. Before Jack sued for freedom in St. Louis in the fall of 1818, his enslaver, Barnabas Harris, sued a third party, Joseph McClurg, two separate times for stealing Jack from Harris. In both cases, McClurg insisted that he had not stolen Jack because Jack was a free man, but that did not protect McClurg from also facing a criminal charge for slave stealing.[45] The potential meddling of community members like McClurg was a central concern in the St. Louis freedom suits as well as in other southern states. In 1822, Mississippi's lawmakers imposed a $100 penalty on individuals helping enslaved people bring unsuccessful freedom suits.[46] South Carolina held the enslaved plaintiff's guardian liable for the costs of bringing any suit deemed "groundless" by the court.[47] These types of repercussions added an additional financial stake—beyond the value of the alleged slave—to the outcome of freedom suits, perhaps limiting the number of white community members willing to assist the illegally enslaved. The existence of legal prescriptions against antislavery activism suggests that the involvement of these activists in freedom suits was a common problem, even if only a few examples of this issue appear in the specific context of St. Louis's cases. These laws could also point to the growing paranoia among enslavers that abolitionists threatened their rights and therefore endangered the system of slavery itself.[48]

Missouri's freedom statute codified existing legal practice and created a space for conversations among enslaved plaintiffs, their attorneys, and the many other actors involved in these contests over personal status. Missouri's original 1807 territorial statute, and the 1824 state law, stated, "It shall be lawful for any person held in slavery to petition the general court . . . praying that such person may be permitted to sue as a poor person, and stating the grounds on which the claim to freedom is founded." If courts found these grounds sufficient, they "may direct an action of assault and battery, and false imprisonment, to be instituted in the name of the person claiming freedom against the person who claims the petitioner as a slave, to be conducted as suits of the like nature between other persons."[49] Most Missouri freedom suits were trespass cases, including assault-and-battery or false-imprisonment claims, but some enslaved individuals also used habeas corpus actions to gain release from slavery or to get access to the court to file an action for freedom. Sometimes a single case combined several of these actions. Enslaved men and women used these legal forms, as dictated by the statute, in order to raise the issue of illegal enslavement and challenge their personal status. Because Missouri's freedom suit statute ordered enslaved plaintiffs to sue for assault and battery or false imprisonment, the issue of the individual's freedom became a preliminary issue that had to be decided to determine whether the defendant committed the tort, or civil wrong. In other words, if the court decided that the plaintiff was legally enslaved, the defendant would not be guilty of assaulting or falsely imprisoning the plaintiff (because existing practice allowed enslavers to assault and imprison their human property with no penalty), but if the plaintiff was a free person, the defendant could not legally assault or imprison the plaintiff. Missouri's enslaved persons established illegal enslavement using a variety of legal strategies, though their strategies followed the specific legal formats dictated by the statute.

Statutes outside Missouri did not always specify the type of legal action available to persons who considered themselves illegally detained in slavery, but when statutes did prescribe a case type, they tended to be similar to Missouri's statutory requirements.[50] As in Missouri, several state statutes required the form of trespass to bring a freedom suit. In the early nineteenth century, trespass included not only property crimes but also crimes on a person's body, such as assault and battery and false imprisonment. Arkansas adopted an identical freedom suit statute to Missouri's in 1807 and kept nearly the same format when it codified the state statute in 1837, most likely because both Missouri and Arkansas were territories (and, eventually, states) formed out of the Louisiana Territory.[51] Similar freedom statutes in Georgia and South Carolina specified that freedom suits should be brought as trespass in ravishment-of-ward cases and added the requirement that illegally enslaved plaintiffs (designated as wards) have a guardian—Georgia eventually mandated a free white guardian—to approach the court and give an oath testifying to the illegal enslavement.[52] Florida's 1824 statute allowed enslaved individuals to bring an action of trespass.[53] In Delaware, a 1760 statute expanded its provisions to allow the enslaved to raise the issue of freedom in any other action at law, though it included a reference to trespass for false-imprisonment cases.[54]

Assault and battery, false imprisonment, and the more general category of trespass were popular forms of legal action even in jurisdictions whose statute did not require these formats. A slight majority of statutes—eight of fourteen—did not set out a specific type of case for enslaved plaintiffs seeking freedom.[55] In most of these jurisdictions, the existing court opinions refer to the cases as "petitions for freedom," "suits for freedom," or "suits to try freedom." An 1833 Alabama case simply listed the action as a "petition according to the statute."[56] The issue of an enslaved person's status as free or enslaved also came up in challenges to the alleged owner's last will and testament, and these will disputes could take on several forms—though actions relating to wills often looked similar to claims for other types of property. When enslaved persons fled their enslavement, their alleged owner could bring an "action to recover slaves," forcing the escaped persons to defend their freedom. Legislators perhaps felt no need to lay out the precise legal format for freedom suits because the cases could fit within existing property and personal claims, which allowed the courts to recognize a broad range of complaints that might allow for considerations of personal status.

States did try to limit freedom suits, with legislators imposing additional restrictions and levying threats on plaintiffs who sought freedom in the courts. The most extreme of these risks was the possible imposition of physical violence that both South Carolina and Georgia included in their freedom suit statutes—both states mandated corporal punishment "not to exceed life or limb"—in the case of an unsuccessful freedom suit.[57] Enslaved plaintiffs made a number of considerations prior to instituting their suits; in these two states, the men and women considering a freedom suit had to assess not only the risk of physical violence at the hands of angry enslavers but also the possibility of violence at the hands of the state.[58] Missouri, Florida, Georgia, and Arkansas all specified that the burden of proof in suits for freedom was on the plaintiff, though Missouri's and Arkansas's statutes expressed courts' willingness to accept more than the usual forms of written proof in the cases of enslaved plaintiffs, thus recognizing the difficulties for enslaved individuals trying to secure written documentation or direct white testimony of their free status.[59]

In order for illegally enslaved individuals like Arch and Jack to present their claims for freedom to the broader community, they needed to know where to go to initiate their cases. In nearly every state, the venue for initial jurisdiction in freedom suit complaints was the Circuit Court or the County Court, though some statutes mentioned Courts of Common Pleas, Superior Courts of law or equity, or even simply the magistrate of the county where the enslaved person—or his or her alleged owner—lived.[60] For example, illegally enslaved residents of Baltimore needed to bring their cases to the Criminal Court, but other Maryland residents needed to approach the Circuit Court of their county of residence.[61] It is unclear how knowledge of the correct venue and steps for suing reached illegally enslaved persons, though many enslaved individuals undoubtedly heard about the process through local communication networks. Legal information spread in slave communities, especially in urban areas, through the grapevine telegraph, as well as through the popularity and broader community awareness of freedom suits.[62]

The question of how enslaved individuals actually brought their petitions is difficult to answer because the historical record contains few clues or explanations for how persons held in slavery could learn about and initiate a lawsuit, even when the statute allowed them to bring this type of legal case. From the scant evidence available in the local setting of St. Louis, enslaved persons most likely began their lawsuits in one of two ways. First, some enslaved plaintiffs directly approached an attorney, perhaps stopping him in the street or visiting the office of his legal practice. In another possible scenario, the potential plaintiff went straight to the courthouse, where the judge appointed one or more attorneys to assist in drawing up a petition. Courthouses were a central feature of antebellum towns and cities, drawing diverse crowds to the spectacle of court day and providing one of the primary venues for entertainment and community gossip.[63] As such, these crucial meeting places were well known among the enslaved population, who might accompany enslavers to court sessions or pass by while performing their required labor. In each of these two scenarios, once enslaved individuals connected with a lawyer, they then shared their life stories with the attorney in the hopes of being able to sue for freedom.

Arch and Jack each pursued different legal remedies in the St. Louis Circuit Court. In May 1818, Arch filed a habeas corpus petition against Harris, ordering him to justify the legal basis for his claim to ownership. True to the ad hoc nature of St. Louis's early court system, the initial summons ordered Harris to bring Arch before Judge Nathaniel Beverly Tucker "*at his house* in the County of St. Louis & Township of St. Ferdinand."[64] Harris attempted to defend his claim to Arch as his slave by showing the judge the bill of sale from Hubbard's heirs. The judge responded by denying his authority to decide this question and suggesting a different remedy for Arch, writing about the case, "[It] presents a question which I am incompetent to try."[65] Judge Tucker claimed he could not issue a final decision because the suit involved "a controversy in which a right to personal liberty is alleged on the one hand, and a claim to property on the other," so Arch needed to file a trespass claim. The judge instructed Arch, "The legislature . . . passed a law providing the remedy of persons claimed as slaves. . . . I can do nothing therefore in this case, but leave the applicant in the possession of Barnabas Harris, to pursue the Remedy which the Law has pointed out."[66] Recognizing that Arch's case required a jury, Judge Tucker suggested that Arch sue directly for freedom using the 1807 freedom suit statute by making a complaint of trespass rather than a habeas corpus claim to win freedom. In response to the judge's suggestion, Arch instituted a freedom suit claiming that Eusebius Hubbard executed "an instrument in writing" and "emancipated [him] after the death of . . . the said Eusebius."[67] When Arch's initial attempt at navigating the legal realm failed, Judge Tucker suggested that Arch avail himself of the statutory procedure.

Jack began his legal struggle for freedom with the second strategy employed by Arch, filing suit in October 1818 for trespass and false imprisonment (as specified by the Missouri territorial statute) with Joshua Barton as his attorney. Most people of African descent in antebellum America were illiterate, forcing their reliance on attorneys to record their initial arguments for freedom in a petition to the court.[68] In Missouri, the law mandated that attorneys' fees be part of the costs associated with the suit.[69] A number of states provided an attorney, usually by asking the court to appoint one for enslaved plaintiffs, although it is not always apparent whether the enslaved plaintiff approached the attorney prior to coming to court or whether the court involved the attorney after hearing the initial complaint of the plaintiff. Five jurisdictions— Missouri, Arkansas, Virginia, the District of Columbia, and Maryland— included the assignment of attorneys in their statutes, and two of these jurisdictions—Virginia and the District of Columbia—added the restriction that attorneys working for enslaved plaintiffs should do so "without fee or reward" for their services.[70] Lawyers working for enslaved plaintiffs without payment may seem odd, though the practice of providing attorneys for enslaved defendants in criminal cases was well established.[71] In Maryland, attorneys in losing freedom suits actually paid the costs of the case, perhaps encouraging the appointed attorneys to prosecute these cases to the best of their ability. The example of St. Louis's attorneys indicates that attorneys sometimes failed to prosecute freedom suits, leading judges to dismiss these cases before enslaved plaintiffs could receive additional help.

Plaintiffs' attorneys like Barton crafted petitions explaining the circumstances or preliminary arguments for freedom, filed their petitions with the court, and awaited the court's response. The judge responded by either approving or denying each petition as sufficient to prove a right to freedom and officially assigning the attorney or attorneys to work for the plaintiff. Missouri's statute allowed enslaved plaintiffs to sue *au pauperis*, or as "poor persons," meaning they lacked the necessary funds to bring a suit. If the judge approved the request to sue *au pauperis*, the fees of the suit would be covered by the state if the plaintiff lost his or her suit or by the defendant in a successful action for freedom. This method of suit (at the state's expense) ended with an 1845 Missouri law requiring plaintiffs to provide security, or financial resources, to cover the costs of their suits.[72]

The expense of bringing a legal case could be a barrier to suing but was largely absent from freedom suits through much of the antebellum period. The bonds of security provided by enslavers could be used to cover the expenses of freedom suits when defendants failed to prove their claim to an enslaved individual. In other forms of civil litigation, courts usually assigned costs of the suit to the losing party, though the limited resources of enslaved plaintiffs in freedom suits raised questions about who should cover the costs in these cases. Though it might be tempting to read into legislators' and judges' assignment of costs a particular concern for protecting illegally enslaved individuals or even encouraging freedom suits, the existing common law provision for suing *au pauperis* was a long-standing practice that many freedom suit jurisdictions used when determining who should pay for these cases. Some states' statutes specified that illegally enslaved individuals could sue as poor persons, whereas other states allowed this request in practice even if the statute did not specifically mention it.[73] The District of Columbia directed that losing parties pay the costs, either through their existing resources or through their labor, and in other instances, bonds of security (mentioned earlier) could also be required of enslaved plaintiffs or their guardians in order to begin to prosecute their freedom suits.[74]

Once an attorney filed a petition on the enslaved plaintiff's behalf, each case followed a similar legal process. First, the attorney produced a declaration complaining that the defendant had assaulted and falsely imprisoned the enslaved plaintiff, which he maintained was illegal because the plaintiff was a free person, not a slave. The declaration sometimes included graphic detail of the violence involved in the alleged assault. For example, in an 1821 freedom suit, the declaration complained that the defendant "beat, wounded and ill-treated the said Tempe [plaintiff] whereof the said Tempe was in great danger of losing her life."[75] In another example, the declaration detailed that the defendant assaulted the plaintiff, beating and striking her with a whip and with his fists several times all over her body, on "the head face, chest, back, shoulders; arms legs and abvers other parts of the body."[76] While it is certainly possible that attorneys sometimes exaggerated this violence to demonstrate an assault had occurred or that attorneys could be relying on the type of formal language necessary to any assault-and-battery charge, the level of detail in a number of petitions suggests that the violent descriptions sometimes recounted actual events. The declaration explained the tort and allowed the plaintiff's status (as slave or free) to become the main issue for the court to decide. For example, a free person could claim assault and battery or false imprisonment, but the law of slavery allowed enslaved individuals to be assaulted and imprisoned with no penalty. The court had to first rule on whether the alleged victim was free in order to determine if he or she could be a victim of the tort.

Once a judge approved the plaintiff's petition, he then issued several orders of protection—instructing the sheriff to summon the defendant to court, to allow the enslaved plaintiff to see his or her attorney, and to prevent the defendant from removing the plaintiff from the court's jurisdiction—because of the many threats defendants made to their alleged slaves who sued for freedom. In some instances, the judge required the defendant to put up a bond guaranteeing the safety of the plaintiff and that the defendant would not remove the alleged slave from the court's jurisdiction. Even with orders of protection in place, slaveholding defendants often removed or attempted to remove plaintiffs from the court's jurisdiction. In one particularly striking case, an enslaved plaintiff wrote a letter to her attorney from outside St. Louis, where the defendant had removed her to prevent her freedom suit. She wrote, "Sir i wish to inform that Mr. felps is trying his best to keep me a slave; he has got me out of the county where i cannot do nothing for my self and he says that he will keep me out of your reach if possible."[77] Judges' orders might fail when an enslaver ignored the court's instructions and removed the enslaved person from the court's jurisdiction to avoid losing the freedom suit, but judges did recognize the real dangers in bringing a freedom suit.

Nearly every antebellum freedom statute recognized the risk involved in bringing suit for freedom and offered some measure of protection during the pending suit.[78] As in Missouri, six additional statutes required a bond of security from the enslaver to guarantee that the enslaved plaintiff would have reasonable access to his or her attorney and would not be subject to any "severity" as a result of the freedom suit. Five states mandated similar bonds of security and indicated that, if an alleged owner failed to provide this financial show of good faith, the sheriff should hire the enslaved plaintiff out to a temporary owner (who must provide the same bond of security).[79] In Tennessee, two enslaved women brought a separate chancery suit (or a suit in equity, to provide a specific remedy not raised in the civil case) during their pending freedom suit because they feared being sold outside the court's jurisdiction. The Tennessee Supreme Court ruled that the enslaved plaintiffs could also draw on the "more ample" powers of chancery to protect them from sale.[80] Kentucky legislators added an extra protection by making it a misdemeanor—punishable by a fine of not less than $500 and not greater than $2,000—to remove an enslaved plaintiff from the state of Kentucky during his or her freedom suit.[81]

Along with these initial orders, judges required the sheriff to summon the defendant to court to answer the charge. The summonses often appear in the case file, along with notes indicating whether the sheriff served them on the defendant. The summons in Jack's case does not indicate if the sheriff served Harris, though sometimes a notation on the summons stated that the defendant "refused to hear" the summons, and in one case, the defendant "refused to hear it read in consequence of his being hard of hearing."[82] Freedom suit case files might also include summonses for witnesses, with notes reporting whether the sheriff was able to serve the person. The summonses in a case file also demonstrate that sometimes defendants in freedom suits did not live in St. Louis, or a defendant may have fled the area when hearing of the impending lawsuit.

After filing the initial charges and petitions, both parties entered pleas. In most of the St. Louis records, the defendant followed the summons by entering a plea of not guilty, claiming that the law allowed the defendant to assault or imprison the plaintiff because the defendant held the plaintiff as a slave. In Jack's case, the case file contains the plea of Harris's administrator, Frederick Hyatt (who became the defendant after Harris died), who declared that Jack "was the property of Barnabas Harris + a slave for life."[83] Plaintiffs could then respond to the defendant's plea in a replication. In one St. Louis woman's freedom suit, her replication appeared immediately after her alleged owner pleaded not guilty, by stating that the woman should not be barred from bringing suit because she "was + still is a free person + not the slave of the said defendant."[84] The legal jockeying of pleas and replications to the plea were part of the negotiations taking place during a freedom suit, though the statements involved in these documents tended to be formulaic—written according to basic legal convention.

From the plea and replication forward, the evidence available in the case files is increasingly scattered and frustratingly incomplete. The limited nature of nineteenth-century court records meant that they lacked materials that became a standard part of the record in twentieth-century trials. Freedom suit case files lack transcripts of the trial proceedings, witness testimony in open court, and the oral arguments presented by attorneys. In the days before court reporters kept a transcript of a case, it is difficult to piece together what might have happened in court during each freedom suit. Though testimony in open court was not collected for the case file, freedom suit case files often included depositions recorded outside St. Louis and sent to the St. Louis Circuit Court to be read in evidence at the trial. Much of the richest documentation of the lives of enslaved plaintiffs and their interactions with the law is found in this material. Depositions varied in length and detail, and they suffer from limitations similar to other examples of oral testimony or interviews.[85] Despite these problems, depositions from witnesses provide glimpses into the evidence of freedom suits, revealing the intricacies of debating slavery and freedom in the broader communities from which these disputes originated.

Arch's case file does not contain depositions or details about his evidence; Jack's case file is more complete and indicates how freedom suit litigants offered evidence to support their causes. Jack presented what appears to be a strong case; not only did he manage to produce a copy of the manumission deed that Hubbard executed for him, but he procured white testimony to authenticate it.[86] This evidence bolstered Jack's argument for freedom based on the manumission. Barnabas Harris answered Jack's arguments and called witnesses to challenge the validity of the manumission. Harris's attorney ordered depositions taken in Kentucky to confirm that the sale of Arch and Jack to Harris was legitimate.[87] When the defense notified Jack's attorney of the time and place for the depositions, he allowed Jack to be present, an unusual instruction absent from later cases that suggests the informality of the procedural rules in the early years of these cases. The depositions presented testimony that in 1802, Eusebius Hubbard sold Arch and Jack to his son and son-in-law, George Hubbard and John Proctor, for $1,000. This sale would nullify the deed of manumission because Eusebius Hubbard did not hold a legal title to the enslaved men at the time he attempted to manumit them. The witness also claimed that when he recently spoke with Jack, Jack admitted to being a part of this transaction, therefore alleging that Jack recognized that he legally belonged to George Hubbard and John Proctor before they sold him to Harris. If the court believed this testimony, it would mean that Jack's own statements might have undermined his claim to freedom.[88]

Communities became involved in freedom suits in a variety of ways, by presenting evidence in depositions, by appearing as witnesses in court, or through the service of white male community members on freedom suit juries. Not all freedom suits were jury trials, but in Missouri and at least seven additional jurisdictions, juries are mentioned as either required or allowed.[89] Washington, D.C.'s statute permitted either party in the freedom suit to request a jury, and it even specified the number of preemptory challenges given to each side when selecting the jury.[90] Other states, such as Delaware, granted the judge the ability to issue summary judgment in a freedom suit without opening the case to a jury's discretion.[91] Although there is no clear pattern for which statutes allowed juries, required juries, or failed to mention juries, the involvement of white jurors clearly affected the outcome of freedom suits. Virginia and Mississippi specified that no members of antislavery organizations could serve as jurors in freedom suits, though presumably, enslavers' attorneys would challenge any antislavery activists and prevent their participation, even when the legislation did not specifically prohibit their service.[92] Community members also sometimes acted as guardians—a role required in certain states—and in other instances, enslaved plaintiffs directly approached the courts. The participation by community members no doubt contributed to disseminating information about these cases beyond the courtroom.[93]

Judicial instructions to the jury can be significant elements for analyzing the arguments presented in freedom suits, as well as the negotiations taking place in the courtroom; though they do not exist in every case file, jury instructions appear with enough frequency to allow for some cautious generalizations. After attorneys for each party presented their case, the attorneys requested that the judge give particular instructions to the jury, which could include points of law, as well as whether the jury could consider specific pieces of the arguments presented at trial. The judge then chose which elements to include in his charge to the jury. This discretionary power gave judges influence over how the juries decided because it allowed them to dictate what elements of the case the jury could consider in its deliberations.[94] For example, in one St. Louis woman's case, the judge refused to give the jury the instruction that if "the plaintiff is not one quarter of African descent," she should be free.[95] Although the judge refused to give this instruction, the jury in the plaintiff's case set her free, possibly because of her argument that she was an indentured servant and was, in the words of one of her witnesses, "a bright mulatto, nearly white."[96] In almost every St. Louis freedom suit, a jury decided the outcome of the case and whether damages should be awarded. Jury instructions, then, signaled a judge's influence over the jury's decision, but they also point out the times when juries ignored the legal prescriptions and found verdicts that suggest a stronger role for the beliefs of the wider communities from which these cases arose.

The judge's role in determining Jack's case discloses the discretionary power of judges in these types of actions or, at least, Jack's perception of that influence. In an August 23, 1819, motion listing reasons for the court to grant a new trial, Jack's attorney argued that "the Court misdirected the Jury in this, to wit: that if they believed the sale in Kentucky was intended as a fraud upon all the world, That still it was good."[97] A second motion complained "that the Court rejected the Evidence that was offered by the Plff [plaintiff] that E. Hubbard had during his life often declared that it was his intention at his death to set the said Plff free and that he had promised to the said Plff to do so."[98] In other words, the judge took no interest in the accuracy of the testimony about the sale; even a fraudulent sale would not help Jack's case. Instead, the judge directed the jury to ignore the question of the sale's legitimacy. The judge also prevented the jury from considering evidence that Hubbard had wanted to free Jack. Based on these instructions, which limited the jury's options, the verdict signed by the jury's foreman concluded that "the jury do find in favor of the Defendant."[99]

A final element of freedom suit cases that has survived in some of the case files is the jury verdict. The jury foreman usually recorded the jury's decision on a small scrap of paper, which may be why this piece has been lost from some of the records. Circuit Court Record Books (records that detailed the proceedings of court each day) helped fill in the gaps and determine the outcome of the majority of the St. Louis freedom suits. The verdict would almost certainly have been the most significant piece of the case file for freedom suit litigants, though for historians, the verdicts often come with a frustrating lack of context or explanation.[100] The verdicts sometimes aligned quite closely with the evidence presented and the judge's instructions, though the majority of verdicts require a bit more interpretation to attempt to explain why certain freedom suits enjoyed success while others failed to result in freedom for the alleged slave. For example, why did two almost-identical juries (with ten of twelve jurors in common) on the same day find a verdict for the plaintiff in one woman's case but find for the defendant in another freedom suit?[101] The answers to this question call for a more in-depth analysis that includes not only a consideration of the evidence in each case but also the judge's instructions to the jurors. In both of these cases, the jury seems to have followed the judge's instructions. In the case found for the defendant, though, the appellate court reversed and remanded the case, finding against the judge's instructions.

The question of whether an enslaved plaintiff should receive damages for the time he or she spent illegally enslaved spoke to the plaintiffs' legal standing, as well as the power of the state over alleged owners of enslaved persons. Like Missouri, statutes in at least five other jurisdictions—South Carolina, Arkansas, Kentucky, Virginia, and Georgia—allowed enslaved plaintiffs to receive compensatory damages; Delaware also specified that damages could accrue if anyone restrained a plaintiff after the court declared the individual to be free.[102] Georgia's 1861 statute specified that enslavers could be charged damages unless the jury believed that the defendant was "bona fide" in his or her mistake; in other words, if the jury felt that the alleged owner had a reason to believe the plaintiff was his or her slave, the plaintiff could not receive damages.[103] Missouri eliminated the possibility of damages in the mid-1830s, and Arkansas followed suit in 1837, suggesting that the courts believed that free status should be enough restitution for enslaved plaintiffs held illegally as slaves.[104]

The verdict and declaration of damages rarely marked the end of these contests over personal status. Following each decision, the losing side could (and often did) ask the judge to overturn the verdict or request a new trial, as Jack's attorney did in 1819. For example, in a typical motion for a new trial, one defendant's attorney complained to the judge that the verdict was "against evidence" and "against law" and that the court "erred in giving the instructions prayed for by the plaintiff to the jury," among other complaints.[105] When the judge refused to grant the losing side a new trial, the attorney then asked for an appeal to the Missouri Supreme Court. The Supreme Court heard appeals in roughly 10 percent of St. Louis freedom suits, though these appellate decisions wielded considerable influence over the subsequent cases brought in the Circuit Court. While the percentage of appeals in the St. Louis example cannot be assumed to accurately reflect the number of appeals elsewhere, if they are even slightly indicative of the frequency of appeals in other jurisdictions, the 807 appellate freedom suit decisions examined for this study suggest that freedom suits occurred more regularly than historians have previously noted.[106] Appellate decisions tried to offer closure on a particular matter of law or evidence, but in Missouri, the Supreme Court's judgment often remanded the case for a new trial, sometimes instructing the trial judge to follow the directions of the Supreme Court.

Arch and Jack struggled to determine what types of legal actions to bring to court, and at the same time, St. Louis judges and juries also squabbled over how to determine the outcome of each case. Conflicting testimony forced judge and jury to decide whom to believe and how much weight to give to that testimony, a problem that came up in freedom suits throughout the antebellum years. Enslaved plaintiffs and their allies employed a variety of legal strategies to win freedom in court, but defendants also drew on a multitude of countertactics to defend these actions. In the early years of freedom suits, courts' interpretations were not always predictable, which allowed for complex maneuvering to try to influence the outcome of the suits.

Equally important to these battles over personal status were the actions of white enslavers in the St. Louis community, who knew about the possibility of freedom suits and tried to find ways around becoming defendants in these types of cases. Looking beyond the case files reveals that Harris expected Arch and Jack to sue for freedom and did not intend to pay for the men until the courts resolved the freedom suits. In a letter to his brother in Kentucky, Harris wrote, "Mr. Ballew [most likely Ballus] and Procter . . . should decline receiving pay for the negroes I purchased of them until the suits is decided which I expect they intend. I wish they may and rather intend they shall unless it would disoblige them verry much."[107] A second letter, from Thomas Ballus to Harris, explained that Ballus and Proctor had sent Harris their "bill of sale with a full Receipt theirof we wish you to make use of them as your council and wisdom may direct."[108] The letter also references an earlier letter from Harris, suggesting that Ballus and Proctor procure their own counsel because they could be named as defendants in the freedom suits. Ballus's response to this suggestion is instructive: "sir we have consulted our minds on the subject & we do not feel disposed so to act. *we let you have those boys at a reduced price in consiquence of some trouble that we thougt their might arise,* we never expected any on the grounds it has arose, and we perceive none yet, we trust sir to your wisdom and candure in the whole proceedings."[109] Ballus and the others knew of the enslaved men's claims to freedom—fully expecting the men to sue, they offered them for sale at a lower price to avoid prosecution and leave Harris to deal with the lawsuits on his own. But Ballus also quickly backed off this admission, claiming that he and Proctor "never expected" trouble "on the grounds it has arose." Enslavers like Ballus and Proctor conspired to secure their safety from prosecution and conviction at the expense of enslaved people whom they realized could be legally free.

Suits for freedom in local jurisdictions throughout the slaveholding states likely followed a similar process to that outlined here in Missouri, though as the cases of Arch and Jack suggest, there were a number of actions and responses that occurred around each suit for freedom. While the details of the case files outlined here should not be interpreted to dictate the exact contents of the case files in other jurisdictions, the statutes often mandated similar rules and forms for bringing suit for freedom. For this reason, this description of the trajectory of a typical freedom suit—and the examples of Arch's and Jack's cases—should be taken as a rough guide for how each case would have proceeded. The form and content of freedom suits suggest the multiplicity of concerns that clashed in these contests, as well as the pivotal roles played by attorneys, judges, defendants, and the broader community members who served as witnesses, guardians, and jurors.

The legal structure discussed in this chapter became the starting point for a series of negotiations surrounding freedom suit litigation that forced enslaved plaintiffs and their attorneys to adjust their strategies in response to the arguments of judges, juries, and defendants. Multiple interests collided in these contests over personal status, but the process began with enslaved plaintiffs. The following chapters take into consideration these various perspectives; even so, the key actors in these legal dramas were the enslaved men, women, and children who chose to take the momentous step and approach a lawyer to sue for freedom. Enslaved men and women living throughout the United States knew about the possibility of achieving freedom through the courts, and they understood the risks associated with challenging an enslaver's property rights. Each of these plaintiffs carefully considered their options before bringing suit. Although individuals held in slavery had limited opportunities for freedom and a severely restricted ability to negotiate—they were certainly not treated as equal players in these struggles—there were examples of enslaved people entering agreements with enslavers for self purchase or manumission, as well as taking the dangerous step of fleeing their bondage. Initiating a freedom suit took enormous courage because these cases came with a host of risks. As enslaved individuals were well aware, these life-changing lawsuits could bring free status or continued slavery, independence or physical violence, legal protection or the auction block.

As young Lucy Delaney waited for the judge to announce her fate, she trembled in her seat. She later described the scene as "a bright, sunny day, a day which the happy and carefree would drink in with a keen sense of enjoyment." But, she said, "my heart was full of bitterness." Lucy recognized the gravity of her situation—within minutes, the judge would announce the jury's decision and declare her legally free or permanently enslaved. "I could not tell one person from another," Lucy wrote. "Friends and foes were as one, and vainly did I try to distinguish them. I felt dazed, as if I were no longer myself."[1] Lucy sat bewildered as the trial resumed and her lawyer asked the court to release her.[2] The judge agreed to release her after reading the jury's verdict, granting Lucy her freedom. In response, the defense attorney leaped from his seat to protest and demand that Lucy be returned to jail until he could begin further proceedings, but Lucy's attorney successfully defended her right to liberty. Writing years later, Lucy expressed some sense of the overwhelming joy she felt at the time. "Oh! The overflowing thankfulness of my grateful heart at that moment, who could picture it? None but the good God above us! I could have kissed the feet of my deliverers, but I was too full to express my thanks."[3] Lucy's triumph followed nearly seventeen months of suffering in jail awaiting trial, years of contemplating a way to escape her enslaver, and a lifetime of abuse in slavery.

Lucy Delaney's story, recounted in her 1892 memoir, *From the Darkness Cometh the Light; or, Struggles for Freedom*, illustrates the process of freedom suits from the viewpoint of an enslaved plaintiff.[4] Lucy argued for freedom based on her mother's successful freedom suit, but she did not sue immediately after her mother's case; the numerous considerations that preceded Lucy's decision to bring suit reflect her knowledge of the legal process—its risks and its rewards. Though published decades after she appeared in court, Lucy's narrative details the legal consciousness of the enslaved men and women who made calculated decisions to rely on formal legal institutions, to participate in a broad array of informal legal processes, or to find alternative avenues to freedom.

St. Louis's freedom suits are merely the most visible manifestations of the elaborate debates over slavery that took place in the city and throughout the antebellum South. As such, the lawsuits contain only part of the larger story of conversations, considerations, and battles over personal status that happened outside the courtroom. Prior to enslaved plaintiffs beginning their cases, they examined their available options for freedom, including both legal and extralegal means of escaping their enslavement. Suing for freedom brought enormous risks that could mean violent reprisal or painful separation from friends, family, and home. Although the exact deliberations that plaintiffs made before, during, and after their cases remain largely hidden, Lucy's experience highlights some of the considerations involved in taking the fateful step to sue for free status.

When enslaved men, women, and children like Lucy faced these fearful possibilities and brought suit, they expected that the courts would take their grievances seriously. Because powerful whites dominated legislatures and judicial appointments, one might anticipate that the system would capitulate to them in arguments between enslavers and their human property. Courts had the authority to issue decisions in controversies over personal status, granting judges and juries great power over both enslaved plaintiffs and wealthy whites who sought to control enslaved individuals. The law of slavery denied enslaved persons many of their basic human freedoms, and it aided enslavers in controlling and abusing their enslaved property. Still, this same law could also act to protect the circumscribed position of persons of color, including recognition of illegal enslavement in freedom suits. The law regulated enslaved individuals and their enslavers, acting as a check on the absolute power of slave ownership, which contributed to enslaved individuals' understanding of the role of law and their willingness to sue for legal freedom.[5] Lucy's freedom suit ended with the court releasing her from the bonds of slavery, though as Lucy realized during her long battle for freedom, the outcome was far from a foregone conclusion. Lucy's narrative makes several brief references to her encounters with the law of slavery in the years prior to her 1844 freedom suit.[6] Lucy's familiarity with the law's power and its limits speaks to the ubiquity of legal information in the slave community and the complex processes that took place beyond the confines of freedom suit courtrooms.

Communication

Uncovering the ways in which legal knowledge traveled among the enslaved and free black populations, even those who lived in rapidly expanding urban areas, is a tricky process.[7] Given that most people of African descent were illiterate, there is little available written material to substantiate the ways in which legal information spread among this subordinated group within southern society. There were a number of possible sources for enslaved plaintiffs to learn about law—and specifically, about the option of suing for freedom—but the most likely explanation is that enslaved and free persons of color heard about these possibilities through the varied and extensive oral communication networks that existed among nonwhite residents of the community, especially in a thriving river town like St. Louis.[8] Enslaved and free people of African descent in the city lived and worked in close proximity to one another and could share information about the laws allowing these types of cases, practical advice about bringing a lawsuit, and anecdotal reports about the success of prior claims.[9]

Lucy's narrative suggests that slaves learned about the existence of freedom suits from other enslaved and free people of African descent and that in St. Louis, the option of suing for freedom was well known in the city's enslaved community. Especially in urban locations, enslaved people came into frequent contact with other enslaved and free people of color who lived and worked near one another. Through these connections, they shared experiences and information that might include discussions of laws and legal pathways to freedom.[10] Delaney described the decision of her mother, Polly Wash, to sue for her freedom in language implying that the possibility of suing was common knowledge among the enslaved and free black populations of St. Louis. According to Lucy's narrative, Wash first attempted to run away to freedom, but when slave catchers found her in Chicago, her fear for Lucy's safety led her to return to slavery in St. Louis. Delaney's memoir recalls that after her mother returned from her abortive escape, she "decided to sue for her freedom, and for that purpose employed a good lawyer."[11] This language implies that Wash knew of her ability to sue for freedom but chose not to do so until after she failed to secure her freedom by fleeing to a free state. She began her legal suit after exhausting other options. Delaney's selection of words is notable: when Wash returned, she simply "decided" to sue for freedom and "employed a good lawyer." In describing the decision to sue without referencing how Wash knew about her ability to do so, Delaney made it sound like this was an obvious, available course of action.

The language in Lucy Delaney's memoir also indicates that her mother was familiar enough with the St. Louis legal community to know how to contact and employ a person she considered to be a "good lawyer." The memoir does not mention how Wash learned about her attorney or his reputation, though a closer examination of his record in freedom suits suggests that although Wash was able to find an attorney who helped her win her case and her freedom, the attorney had a less-than-ideal track record in prosecuting freedom suits. The freedom suit case files reveal that Wash's attorney, Harris L. Sproat, worked in at least two other freedom suits prior to accepting her case.[12] Not only did Sproat's clients fail to win freedom in both instances, but in a freedom suit brought by Sproat's first enslaved client, the woman complained of having to initiate a second freedom suit five years after the first because Sproat neglected her initial case. In that case, Sproat's client argued that it was his failure to appear in court—despite her having paid him fifty dollars in fees—that caused the court to discontinue her suit.[13] So although Wash was able to locate and hire an attorney, her lawyer may not have deserved Lucy's later description of him as a "good lawyer." Legal knowledge in the enslaved community, though widespread, was far from perfect or complete.

Whether driven by money or principle, some attorneys contributed to the spread of legal information among the enslaved population when they encouraged enslaved persons to sue for freedom. In a study of manumission and freedom suits in New Orleans, the historian Judith Kelleher Schafer has suggested that in several of the numerous freedom suits brought in the 1840s and 1850s in that city, one particular attorney sought out and encouraged suits for freedom.[14] In St. Louis, the instances of a single attorney prosecuting multiple suits for freedom usually involved family members or closely related cases, making it logical that the same attorney would prosecute the suits. In at least a couple of examples, the community began to associate certain attorneys with working for clients of African descent. Anxious enslavers sometimes complained that these antebellum ambulance chasers would stir up discontent and disobedience among the enslaved population by encouraging frivolous suits for freedom.[15] An 1880 narrative describing Dred Scott's case commented that two attorneys, "Burd and Risk, who were called the 'nigger lawyers,'" approached him and "urged Scott to sue for his freedom, telling him he was entitled to do so."[16] The attorneys referenced in this account developed a reputation for working for enslaved clients in freedom suits because of their work prosecuting a combined total of fifty-five freedom suits in St. Louis.[17]

Although attorneys sometimes encouraged freedom suits, community knowledge of a lawyer's legal reputation came from multiple sources, including the experiences of men and women of African descent. White elites in St. Louis and throughout the slaveholding states feared the existence of enslaved and free black communication links because they believed these channels could foster slave revolts, aid escaped slaves, or even offer a form of legal counsel.[18] Enslavers' anxiety over their enslaved men and women intermingling with one another is evident in the legislation that slave-state legislatures passed to restrict black people's movement, their ability to gather in groups, and their access to education. These laws existed throughout the slaveholding states, expressing the widespread fear of enslaved people's ability to disseminate information.[19] For example, the earliest digest of Missouri state laws (1824) implemented the pass system, requiring enslaved persons traveling beyond their enslavers' homes or plantations to carry a pass granting them permission to leave. Missouri law also prohibited enslaved persons from meeting in groups without permission from their enslavers. An 1804 statute against slave gatherings started with the preamble, "To prevent the inconvenience, arising from the meeting of slaves." The "inconvenience" that white legislators recognized was that these meetings were often spaces for the enslaved gatherers to share information. The next statute in the same digest prescribed punishment for "any white person, free negro or mulatto . . . found in company with slaves at any unlawful meeting."[20] Free people of color and whites, as well as enslaved men and women, could spread dangerous information or encourage unruliness through these clandestine gatherings. The very existence of such laws suggests how difficult it was to prevent enslaved people from developing contacts and relationships beyond the control of their enslavers.

Freedom suit case files also offer clues to how plaintiffs learned about the law. Several freedom suit petitions state that the plaintiff was "informed" and "believe[d]" he or she was entitled to freedom. One example stated that the plaintiff was "advised and believe[d]" he was entitled to his freedom.[21] This language is formulaic, but it was not part of all of the cases—suggesting it could have had a more particular meaning when the petitioner chose to use it. Although the cases do not specify who "advised" these plaintiffs about their right to sue, the language indicates that information traveled along a grapevine that must have included both enslaved and free blacks, as well as opportunistic or sympathetic white community members.

Cities and towns fostered communication between enslaved and free people of African descent. Enslaved individuals in cities interacted daily with other enslaved people, free blacks, and whites far more easily than on isolated rural plantations—though highly effective communication systems existed beyond the cities as well.[22] Such contact worried enslavers who recognized that close and crowded quarters allowed for the physical gap between enslaved individuals and their enslavers to be "filled" with people they viewed as subversive, such as free people of African descent and poor whites. Relatively large populations of free people of color made enslavers especially uneasy because free blacks shared physical characteristics with enslaved individuals, but their status suggested the possibility of freedom.[23] Some free people of African descent secured their freedom by successfully using the courts to sue for their status, and these individuals must have made enslavers particularly nervous.

Enslavers recognized that living in a river community like St. Louis provided a means of accessing information and possibly learning tricks and legal strategies to be used in freedom suits and other types of litigation. An 1841 St. Louis newspaper editorial highlighted the concern of enslavers that time spent on the river allowed enslaved individuals to make connections and learn of the possibilities for escape through their interactions with other enslaved and free people of color or even abolitionists. The editor complained of the social relationships formed on the river: "This communication renders the slaves restless and induces them to run away, and furnishes them a means of escape."[24] Enslaved individuals' access to boats and, perhaps more importantly, their exchanges with enslaved and free boat workers or travelers frightened enslavers who realized that while steamboat commerce brought goods and financial resources to St. Louis, it might also provide dangerous sources of information and, in addition, legal knowledge.

A number of observers, both within and outside St. Louis, commented on how the ability to mix and mingle on city streets, docks, and markets meant that information channels constantly evolved, grew, and adapted to changing circumstances among urban enslaved populations. Discussions of the power and influence of the slave community as a source of information occurred in a number of venues. The northern observer Frederick Law Olmsted noted of enslaved people in cities that "slaves can never be brought together in denser communities, but their intelligence [i.e., knowledge] will be increased to a degree dangerous to those who enjoy the benefit of their labor."[25] The spread of information by word of mouth was a powerful force that outsiders to the slave system recognized and that enslavers feared. Enslavers believed—or at least, they argued when defending the peculiar institution—that living in slavery was beneficial for people of African descent, who, in these slaveholders' eyes, were not capable of caring for themselves or working hard to provide for their families. Because of their belief in the moral superiority of whiteness and the positive nature of slavery for people of African descent, some white elites felt sure that their enslaved property would not sue for freedom without encouragement. One of the few mentions of freedom suits in any St. Louis newspaper focused on the role of oral communication in contributing to the spread of legal knowledge. The condescending tone of the article in the *Missouri Argus* also referenced the fear of enterprising attorneys who could offer "legal advice" to the enslaved: "Tom wants his freedom, and sallies in quest of legal advice; he states his case, and right or wrong, is flattered to proceed. Pleased with his prospects, he brags to Dick, who after a little scratching and bumping of his reminiscences, takes a notion that he has a right to freedom too. . . . Fired with untried hope, Dick flies to Ned. . . . Ned catches flame and communicates it to Big Bill—Big Bill to little Jim, and little Jim to everything that wears wool."[26] Although the author of the *Argus* article took issue with the attorneys who "flattered" enslaved men and women to proceed with their cases, whether "right or wrong," the author also complained of the spread of this legal information among the enslaved community. The article significantly indicated that it was Tom who initially "sallie[d] in quest of legal advice." Tom's actions suggest widespread knowledge of freedom suits—and perhaps other opportunities for interacting with the legal system—among the city's enslaved community.

Options

Although enslaved people like Lucy and her mother came to court to acquire legally recognized freedom, suing was not their only option for becoming free. Manumission required the consent of an enslaver and was thus a rare path to freedom, but enslavers did free their human property using a variety of types of arrangements that included selling freedom to the enslaved individual (or to a friend or relative of the enslaved person), rewarding meritorious behavior, or freeing elderly slaves to avoid having to care for them, to name only a few examples. Manumission was not common, but it was a separate legal path to freedom that almost one thousand enslaved persons in St. Louis managed to secure between 1828 and 1865.[27] Escaping slavery and fleeing to freedom was another option for enslaved individuals, especially those who lived along the border to free states, and thus, attempting a permanent escape from slavery was a popular option for enslaved individuals living in border states like Missouri.[28] For the vast majority of enslaved individuals, possibilities for asserting freedom were temporary and came by attempting to control certain aspects of their lives, such as by stealing time for themselves, taking food or other goods from their owners, or maneuvering so they could be purchased by or hired out to the enslaver of their choice.[29] Despite the higher frequency of these temporary forms of respite, some individuals did attempt a more permanent escape from their enslavement.

Lucy Delaney's memoir richly documents two stories of fleeing slavery—those of her sister, Nancy, and her mother, Polly Wash—that suggest some of the considerations enslaved women (and men) took into account when planning to abscond.[30] Lucy recalled how her mother, who grew up in a free state, urged her daughters to escape whenever possible. When Lucy's sister, Nancy, accompanied her new enslavers on their honeymoon in Philadelphia, she used the opportunity of their celebration to sneak onto a boat and flee to Canada. Writing in Nancy's voice, Delaney explains, "as the boat stole away into the misty twilight and among crushing fields of ice, though the air was chill and gloomy, I felt the warmth of freedom as I neared the Canada shore."[31] After Nancy's escape, Lucy's mother plotted constantly to take Lucy and join Nancy: "Mother was always planning and getting ready to go, and while the fire was burning brightly, it but needed a little more provocation to add to the flames."[32] That provocation came in the form of an argument between Polly Wash and her mistress, who then sold Wash on the auction block. To avoid the sale and separation from Lucy, Wash fled the area and made it as far as Chicago, where slave catchers found her and returned her to St. Louis. Polly Wash brought her 1839 freedom suit only after she had failed in her attempted escape to Canada.[33]

Lucy's sister and her mother chose the most well-known option for freedom (and the one that has received much of the modern scholarly and popular attention): the possibility of escaping slavery and fleeing to freedom in a free state or in a new community. In St. Louis, the proximity of the city to Illinois, along with the anonymity provided in the urban environment, made it a popular destination for runaway slaves and the slave catchers who hunted them.[34] St. Louis's enslaved population knew that the free state of Illinois was just across the Mississippi River, so a number of the city's enslaved residents found ways to cross the river to freedom. Although it is impossible to determine the exact number of runaway slaves in the antebellum era, undoubtedly many people reached free soil and never appeared in the historical record. The precarious nature of freedom in the North led others to invoke the law to confirm their right to freedom. Escaped slaves faced extreme danger, and they could never establish themselves in their communities in the way that legal freedom allowed. For this reason, some individuals decided to use the courts to establish freedom, after considering (and sometimes attempting) an escape from slavery. Enslaved individuals turned to the courts to provide them with *legal* freedom, which allowed them to establish themselves as free persons in their communities with less risk of capture or reenslavement.

Runaway slaves like Lucy's mother found themselves thrust into the legal process, forcing them to rely on the courts. Despite the precarious position of African Americans accused of escaping slavery, they also made a variety of demands on the legal system—including initiating legal actions and lodging complaints against jailers and supposed owners. Suspected runaway slaves appeared in court to argue against their imprisonment, which forced them to provide evidence of their freedom and sometimes to bring a separate suit for freedom. Anyone suspecting that a person was a runaway slave could ask the sheriff or a justice of the peace to jail the person until the alleged owner could claim his or her human property.[35] While sheriffs held suspected runaways in jail, they advertised their confinement in St. Louis newspapers to summon enslavers to collect their enslaved "property."[36] After a specified amount of time, alleged fugitives could be sold at auction if their supposed owners did not retrieve them.

In response to this imprisonment, a number of suspected runaways brought suits for freedom or habeas corpus petitions to establish their right to legal freedom and to gain their release from jail. One St. Louis man brought a habeas corpus claim to protest his imprisonment as a runaway slave, arguing "that he is free born and entitled to his freedom," so he asked "that he be discharged."[37] By making freedom the issue before the court, he sought legal recognition to confirm his free status and protect him from a fraudulent sale as a slave. Because these petitions could appear in front of justices of the peace in addition to the Circuit Court, estimates of the total number of people in this position are impossible to determine.[38] In a July 1835 freedom suit, one enslaved woman petitioned the court to release her because the sheriff "did imprison the said Mary Ann in the Common Gaol [jail] of said County & kept & detain[ed] her in prison there as a runaway slave for the space of ten days."[39] By instituting suit for freedom against the sheriff, this woman began a series of legal processes to establish her free status.

For Lucy Delaney and others, fleeing the control of their alleged owners was a necessary precursor to initiating a suit for freedom. These individuals needed to run in order to be able to approach the court. In addition, a number of runaways whose stories entered the courts ran *to* St. Louis *from* the Northwest, usually from Illinois, which may seem odd because slavery was illegal in Illinois and legal in Missouri. But freedom in Illinois was precarious, with many persons of color serving lifelong indentures or being held as slaves despite the existence of laws against slavery.[40] For this reason, at least some people viewed St. Louis as a destination where they could obtain freedom, either through the courts or through the anonymity provided by an urban setting. Running away was a difficult and extralegal method for freeing oneself; filing a freedom suit, while also risky, had the possibility of bestowing permanent free status on successful plaintiffs.

The fact that some individuals managed to escape long enough to file suit meant that they were well aware of the legal right of suing for freedom and merely needed to make it to court to exercise that right. For these enslaved plaintiffs, their mobility and flight was a central part of their strategy for winning freedom. For example, an enslaver filed a petition in the St. Louis Circuit Court stating that "Joe and Ralph black persons . . . are runaway slaves and now lurking about the county of St. Louis and that he verily believes that the said Negroes are now hid in the said county and at the house of Gustavus H. Bird."[41] For this reason, the enslaver asked a justice of the peace to arrest the two men. The sheriff responded by explaining, "Joe & Ralph surrendered themselves to me and are now in Jail—They claim to be free men—have sued for their freedom and have been ordered to be hired out untill the termenation of the suit."[42] Ralph and Joe, along with others, needed to get away from their enslaver's immediate control in order to be able to sue for freedom. Once they instituted their cases, they agreed to wait in jail and answer the charge of running away.

Running away to sue for freedom was not only about escaping alleged owners' control long enough to make it to court; for some plaintiffs, fleeing their homes was part of a strategy to obtain the best possible outcome for their suits. If an alleged owner held a position of wealth or power in a community, as many of the St. Louis defendants did, escaping to a neighboring jurisdiction or requesting a change of venue in court could help an enslaved person win freedom. A brief look at similar cases outside St. Louis indicates that this practice also occurred on the eastern seaboard, where enslaved plaintiffs hoped that they might receive a better outcome outside the local sphere of influence exercised by their alleged owners—though existing laws and judicial interpretations sometimes thwarted their efforts. For example, Virginia's statutes forbid this type of legal forum shopping.[43] When a group of siblings sued and won their freedom in one Virginia county, the Virginia Supreme Court reversed the case after learning that the family did not actually live in that county. Citing the statute's requirement that freedom suit plaintiffs must sue "where the complainant shall reside, and not elsewhere," the appellate opinion explained that "it could never have been in the contemplation of the legislature, that, in controversies about jurisdiction . . . the will or choice of the [enslaved] complainant could . . . [have] any influence in solving questions as to his residence."[44] The Virginia Supreme Court interpreted the statutes as prohibiting enslaved plaintiffs in freedom suits from traveling to a new location in an attempt to obtain a favorable outcome in their case. These cases suggest that the legal knowledge of enslaved individuals included valuable information about how various courts might receive their freedom suits.

Maryland's law—adopted by the District of Columbia—allowed courts greater leeway. For example, the District of Columbia allowed an enslaved family whose owner lived in Maryland to sue within their district: "The plea [of the slaveholding defendant] does not deny that they were then residing here, but only that they were not residing here under the direction of their master; which is a negative pregnant with this affirmative, that they were residing here. If the petitioners were, at the time of filing their petition, residing here, and holden in slavery by the defendant, we think this court had jurisdiction; and it is certain that this court has exercised jurisdiction in many such cases."[45] The District of Columbia judge indicated a willingness to permit an enslaved person to flee his county of residence and sue in its courts, stating, "If he were taken up as a runaway, and confined in the county jail, by authority of his master, he would be residing there under the direction of his master, and might there petition for his freedom."[46] Like Lucy and other St. Louis plaintiffs who ran away to bring their suits, examples from courts in Virginia and D.C. also recognized how slipping away from enslavers' control facilitated freedom suits.

Lucy fled her enslavement and hid in her mother's protection when she learned of her impending sale away from St. Louis on a steamboat.[47] For Lucy and other enslaved plaintiffs, mobility was a key factor in the story of their freedom suits—escaping the control of enslavers could be a tactic for freedom in itself or a means to approaching the court to sue. Although running away was one of the primary choices open to the enslaved when considering routes to freedom, bringing a legal suit offered a somewhat more stable—though potentially treacherous—position by enlisting the courts to declare and protect their free status. Freedom suits often dragged on for years, leaving plaintiffs in a legal limbo and subjecting them to all kinds of horrors in the process.

Risk of Removal and Sale

Lucy Delaney sued for freedom after her enslaver, David Mitchell, arranged to send her on a steamboat down the Mississippi River. Fearing her impending sale and separation, Lucy raced to her mother's home in the city, where she cowered in the darkness until her mother returned from her day's labor. As Lucy described these terrifying moments, "my imagination had almost converted the little cottage into a boat, and I was steaming down South, away from my mother, as fast as I could go."[48] Mitchell was "furious" when he learned about Lucy's escape. He took his anger out by beating his coachman, hoping to elicit information about Lucy's whereabouts. When this violence failed to locate Lucy, he hired "negro catchers" to find her and bring her back for departure on the steamboat *Alexander Scott*. Upon learning that Lucy's mother had sued him for Lucy's freedom, Mitchell—like numerous other freedom suit defendants—was irate.[49]

Although the evidence suggests that only a handful of defendants in the St. Louis freedom suits actually managed to sell enslaved plaintiffs away from the city—usually to areas further down the Mississippi River—the possibility of sale must have loomed large in the minds of the city's enslaved population. Lawmakers and judges acknowledged this danger and created legal protections for enslaved plaintiffs in freedom suits to limit the type of violent reaction from enslavers that many individuals experienced. Missouri's freedom suit statute specified that plaintiffs "shall not be taken nor removed out of the jurisdiction of the courts, nor be subjected to any severity" because of their suit.[50] When a judge granted a person permission to sue for freedom, his orders included this prohibition. These fears were well grounded. Enslavers perpetrated these types of abuses despite courts' efforts to prevent them.

Numerous plaintiffs filed motions asking a judge to prevent the defendant(s) from removing them from the court's jurisdiction, placing their hope in the courts to provide protection. One enslaved plaintiff's petition stated that because his alleged owner threatened to sell him away from St. Louis, he was "afraid" and had "good reasons to fear."[51] An enslaved mother of three small children explained the trepidation involved in filing a suit when she told the judge that "she knows of no person to whom . . . she thinks she could safely confide her intention of instituting a suit for her freedom, without incurring the hazard of being deprived of the opportunity . . . by being sent out of the jurisdiction of this court."[52] Freedom suit plaintiffs feared the ability and determination of enslavers to avoid prosecution and to try to preserve their investments in their human property.

The threat of sale to areas "down the river," usually to the Mississippi Valley region around Natchez or New Orleans, was a real possibility that enslavers in Upper South states like Missouri used as a way to threaten their human property and prevent prosecution in freedom suits. One St. Louis attorney filed a motion stating that his client's supposed owner had "recently sent or caused said Pelagie [his client] to be conveyed to Ste. Genevieve, and there to be shiped on board of some boat for New Orleans—and beyond the jurisdiction of this court . . . with a view of having her sold as a slave beyond the reach of justice."[53] Motions about removing plaintiffs from the court's jurisdiction often made reference to the "reach of justice" or the "ends of justice," as if leaving St. Louis also meant moving beyond the realm of judicial protection—suggesting that plaintiffs believed the courts of St. Louis provided certain advantages in freedom suits or that other jurisdictions could be less willing to recognize freedom. These types of statements appealed to the court to elevate the legal protection of enslaved captives over the preservation of slavery and the interests of enslavers.

Enslaved plaintiffs like Lucy Delaney sometimes reached out to third parties for assistance. When Delaney made it to her mother's home, she relied on a white neighbor woman—who, as she recalled, "sympathized" with her—to help pick her mother's lock, allowing Lucy to hide until her mother's return.[54] In another example from the St. Louis freedom suits, an enslaved woman detailed how the defendants tried to prevent her case by taking her aboard a steamboat. The complaint she filed explained,

"The Captain of the boat learning that your petitioner was entitled to her freedom refused to take your petitioner on board of his boat."[55] Although her petition does not say so explicitly, it is likely that she was the person who informed the captain of her free status, asking that he protect her and perhaps even reminding him of the potential consequences if he refused to do so. Although prosecution for these crimes was relatively rare, the threat of prosecution was enough to compel boat captains to exercise caution when transporting people of African descent.[56]

One example in particular reveals the desperate pleas for help that enslaved plaintiffs made and the anguish they experienced when the people they turned to for help failed to protect them from removal. In a remarkable letter written by the enslaved plaintiff Dorinda to a prominent St. Louis attorney, she pleaded for his assistance after her first attorney died and her second attorney neglected to take depositions for her case.[57] Although she likely received assistance in writing her letter because most people of African descent could not write, Dorinda's ability to contact a prominent attorney while held in captivity is unusual.[58] Dorinda's letter recalled the strategy that her owner, Avington Phelps, employed to prevent her suit, as well as her understanding of Phelps's intentions. Her desperation that the court act to protect her from Phelps's attempts to prevent her suit comes through in her language.[59] She wrote,

> Sir i wish to inform that Mr. felps is trying his best to keep me a slave; he has got me out of the county where i cannot do nothing for my self and he says that he will keep me out of your reach if possible. therefore i hope you will do the more for me. for i believe that he will not apear to court from what i can see and does not intend to fetch me unless he is made to do so. and you know that he was ordered by the court not to fetch me out of the county where the court sets. And he told the court that he was going to take me to Lualin [ill.] Browns about 9 miles from St. Louis and when he got me there he forced me on to Clarksvill where he has kep me ever sense and said i shold not go back to St. Louis untill spring.[60]

The fact that Dorinda knew to send her letter to a renowned St. Louis attorney after both of her original attorneys had failed her suggests the extent of her knowledge of St. Louis's legal community and her interactions with the law. She turned to this lawyer for protection when her enslaver ignored the orders of the court and tried to sell her away from St. Louis, forcing her to attempt new strategies for securing her freedom. Although the Circuit Court records do not indicate the outcome of

Dorinda's suit, her letter contained a notation on the back that it reached the recipient after the court dismissed her case for lack of prosecution—because no attorney appeared to argue her case. In other words, the letter arrived too late for the attorney to help her efforts in St. Louis, though her extensive legal knowledge may have led her to continue searching for help elsewhere.

Violence

Like the possibility of sale, physical violence was an ever-present threat made by enslavers, especially for plaintiffs in suits for freedom. Lucy Delaney described her response when her alleged owner, Mrs. Mitchell, attempted to whip her: "I rebelled against such government and would not permit her to strike me; she used shovel, tongs and broomstick in vain, as I disarmed her as fast as she picked up each weapon."[61] For Lucy, the threat of violence preceded her suit for freedom, though her recollections of the Mitchells' violent tempers suggest that they would not respond peacefully to her legal claim. Enslaved plaintiffs endured the ire of those whom they sued; their cases outraged enslavers, who seethed at the audacity of their "property" dragging them to court to demand release from slavery. Enslavers did recognize the courts' authority to emancipate slaves, even if they did not always respect or obey the courts' decisions. Because of the Missouri statute's requirement that freedom suits be brought as assault cases, nearly every St. Louis freedom suit describes an incident of violence. Although some of these accounts could be exaggerated or even fabricated to meet the demands of the particular legal form of assault and battery or false imprisonment, the level of detail involved in many of these descriptions suggests that at least some of the physical violence happened as described. The prevalence of abuse in response to freedom suits makes sense when one considers the crucial role that violence played in keeping enslaved people subjected to the rule of enslavers.[62]

As Lucy's story of Mrs. Mitchell's attack makes clear, when an enslaved man or woman disobeyed his or her alleged owner's orders or questioned the owner's authority, the response was often immediate and physical. Few offenses angered enslavers more than a slave suing them for freedom. Not only did freedom suits mean that the defendant was in danger of losing control of his or her valuable property, but these cases also invested people of African descent with the backing of the law—a direct challenge to the absolute authority of enslavers. Freedom suits limited the power of slaveholders in a society based on the enslavers' fantasy that the will of the enslaved person could be completely subjected to the will of the master.[63]

In a society where violence was ubiquitous—especially for the enslaved—physical brutality often became even more pronounced once a plaintiff filed his or her case.[64] When one enslaved plaintiff sued for freedom a second time, she reported that "she has been treated with great cruelty severity and oppression" since her previous suit. Therefore, she "verily believes that the same severe and oppressive treatment will be exercised toward her on account of this application."[65] For this plaintiff, emphasizing the violent reaction to her initial petition was one way of signaling to the court her awareness of the risks involved in a second attempt for freedom and asking for protection from this threat.

Evidence of violence or mistreatment existed in the majority of these cases in order to demonstrate that the defendant assaulted the plaintiff because this was the legal form for Missouri freedom suits, but it does not follow that plaintiffs and their attorneys invented or embellished all descriptions of this type of violence to fit the guidelines set down in the statute.[66] Regardless of whether each attack happened as described by the plaintiff, the frequency and level of detail in these accounts had to be believable in order to enjoy success in court. For this reason, complaints of violence suggest patterns of abuse based in reality.[67] For example, one enslaved plaintiff not only complained in her petition that the defendant assaulted her to the point where she "was in great danger of losing her life."[68] A later petition in this woman's case described even more mistreatment: she complained that since the beginning of her case, her alleged owner had "frequently abused and beaten her (and particularly on yesterday) for no other cause that she knows of but her present application for freedom." In addition to the physical punishment, the defendant had "refused to supply her with clothing necessary for comfort and decency, alleging as a reason that *he expected soon to lose her.*" Defendants had little incentive to properly clothe and care for enslaved plaintiffs in freedom suits, as investing money into a person who may soon be released from the enslaver's control seemed to be an unnecessary expenditure. The defendant also forced the woman to work harder because of her suit, and "her duties as a servant are rendered much more hard than that of the other servants in the family, and . . . she is seldom spoken to by Mr. Price [the defendant] accept with ill humor and abusive language."[69] For this woman and other enslaved plaintiffs, the cruelty they experienced exceeded the usual day-to-day violence of slavery.

Enslavers throughout the South strategically used violence to keep enslaved plaintiffs (and potential plaintiffs) from prosecuting suits for freedom. An example from Louisiana echoes the type of violence described in St. Louis's case files. In this instance, a group of kidnappers used physical intimidation to try to prevent their enslaved victim from suing for freedom. The kidnappers hoped that their years of violent control over an enslaved victim would persuade the court to uphold their alleged property rights to the woman. The judge's explanation of the nature of enslavement is instructive: "The relation of master and slave while it subsists in fact, implies power on one side and subjection on the other."[70] Even after recognizing the inherent element of control involved in master-slave relations, the court refused to allow a group of kidnappers to deny freedom to an enslaved plaintiff simply because they had managed to keep her in slavery for fifteen years. The opinion continued, "It is, besides, proved in this case, that violence was employed by the defendants to keep the plaintiff quiet in her apparent condition."[71] Violence was a widely accepted, *legal* element of the slave system. Using physical brutality to force a free person into slavery was illegal, and the court stepped in to regulate the illicit violence of enslavers.[72]

The majority of defendants in St. Louis's freedom suits did not deny the accusations of violence leveled against them. Instead, defendants maintained their right to discipline their property with force, if necessary. One defendant claimed in his explanation to the court that he used "no more force and violence *than was absolutely necessary* to ensure the obedience and service of his said servant."[73] In order to justify his abuse, another defendant blamed the behavior of his alleged slave. As he explained, the plaintiff "neglected her duty" as his slave and "behaved and conducted herself in a disorderly, saucy, contumacious and improper mannour toward the said defendant." When she "resisted and refused to obey the lawful commands" of the defendant, he "did modestly chasten and correct . . . the said plaintiff . . . and in so doing did *necessarily and unavoidably* a little beat, bruise, and ill treat the said plaintiff."[74] Other defendants commonly used similar language when explaining their use of force to the court, asserting their rights as owners of human property to punish enslaved persons when they failed to obey.

Slave law sanctioned the use of physical force, though in freedom suits, the central question of each case was whether the abuse alleged was legal (because the person was legally enslaved) or whether their free status meant the assault became an actionable tort. The form of freedom suits in Missouri and elsewhere required an assertion of violence: the defendant's guilt rested on the court's determination of the plaintiff's status as slave or free. Although legal restrictions existed to prevent abuse as a result of a suit for freedom, the examples detailed here indicate the limitations of that protection. Enslaved plaintiffs recognized that the daily violence that pervaded the system of slavery would only increase when they initiated legal cases for freedom against their violent oppressors. This realization was an important element in deciding whether to file a case.

Jail

Lucy Delaney's narrative warned of an additional consideration for enslaved men and women when weighing the option of suing for freedom—the likelihood that their enslavers or the court would order them to be confined to the St. Louis jail during their suits. Because these cases could sometimes last several years, enslaved plaintiffs feared the prospect of spending years in jail as a consequence of their freedom suits.[75] Lucy complained of her imprisonment for "seventeen long and dreary months" in the St. Louis jail, writing, "My only crime was seeking for that freedom which was my birthright!"[76] Lucy's mother, Polly Wash, even filed complaints with the court about her sufferings in the cold, damp jail cell.[77] Plaintiffs in most freedom suits spent at least part of the time during their cases in the local jail, a factor that likely entered their minds when considering whether to sue.

Imprisonment in an antebellum jail was rarely intended as a punishment for the individuals detained there. In Missouri, one key difference between American law and Spanish colonial law was that after the United States took possession of the territory, incarceration was not a sentence for any crime committed by an enslaved person.[78] The exception was persons confined on suspicion of being runaway slaves, some of whom would have eventually become freedom suit plaintiffs or filed habeas corpus actions to demand their release from jail before trying their right to freedom.[79]

Rather than trying to punish enslaved plaintiffs, the courts—and sometimes alleged owners—placed these litigants in jail for "safekeeping," to protect them from enslavers who might harm them or sell them or to allow their supposed owners to shirk the responsibility of feeding and clothing them.[80] When one enslaved plaintiff brought his freedom suit, the court asked the jailer why he kept the plaintiff in prison. The jailer explained that he held the alleged slave "for safe keeping & for no other cause" and that he took the plaintiff into custody after two men threatening him were "arrested by virtue of a warrant for kidnapping."[81] In many cases, the court ordered the sheriff to take possession of the plaintiff and hold the person in jail for the duration of the suit. In these instances, the court exerted its authority over enslavers by protecting plaintiffs while they sued for freedom.

Although courts often proposed the jail as a shelter from the violence of slaveholding defendants in freedom suits, jails could also be sites where abuses and mistreatment of enslaved plaintiffs occurred. Consider the case of a mulatto man who sued for freedom in 1842. After ten years of continuances in his case, an August 1852 motion brought before a justice of the peace stated that the alleged slave "was locked up in a cell of the jail of the County of St. Louis & whipped violently on account of his claim for freedom." The man was also "restrained of the reasonable liberty of attending his counsel & the Court."[82] Perhaps it was the long duration of his case or the amount of time and suffering he endured in jail, but eventually the keepers of the jail told the court that having "observed his conduct" daily, they believed the individual was "at times of unsound mind and insane" and perhaps was "insane the whole time of his incarceration."[83] There is no mention that the plaintiff's imprisonment led to his "strange conduct," but ten years in jail—and enduring violent whippings while imprisoned there—could not have helped his mental state.

The St. Louis jail, like most county jails in the antebellum period, was not a pleasant place. Cramped quarters and poor sanitary conditions added to the misery that enslaved plaintiffs felt during their suits. The St. Louis Grand Jury regularly filed reports of the city's jail, detailing complaints about the facility's security as well as its cleanliness and size; multiple reports suggested the need for repairs.[84] A February 1834 report found the condition of the jail at that time "greatly jeopardized" the health and safekeeping of the prisoners. By the time the city had begun the repairs (in February 1835), the grand jury suggested the efforts were too little too late, calling them a "waste of public money" because "no repairs . . . can be made to . . . make it secure." Despite recommending a new building in a report filed July 22, 1835, and finding the building to be "deficient in size and strength" in a November 1837 report, the same statement contained the questionable reassurance that "the prisoners therein make no complaint."[85] An 1865 inspection found that the cells in the St. Louis jail measured only eight feet square with ten-foot ceilings, and they usually held from three to six prisoners.[86] The inspectors described the scene in the St. Louis county jail as follows: "How pestilential must be the moral atmosphere of these crowded cells, where employment is impossible" and "where the professional burglar and thief and the young transgressor, or perchance the wholly innocent boy, are shut up together, with nothing to do."[87] Long-term confinement in these conditions must have been a dismal experience, but it was something many enslaved plaintiffs were willing to risk.

In Lucy Delaney's case, the defendant, Mitchell, sent Lucy to jail both to avoid caring for her and also to prevent her from absconding. Defendants like Mitchell also placed enslaved plaintiffs in jail to avoid paying a bond ensuring the plaintiff's safety and care during the suit. Enslavers did not want to use their resources clothing and feeding men and women who might soon be freed from their service; for this reason, some enslaved plaintiffs ended up spending much of their suits in jail, shifting the responsibility for their care and maintenance from their alleged owners to the county where they sued. Counties paid for enslaved plaintiffs' food and other needs during their cases, although county officials usually hired out enslaved men and women to help defray these costs. Responsibility for upkeep of the jail and its prisoners fell to the sheriff, who delegated daily management to a jailer, including the task of locating hirers for freedom suit plaintiffs to help offset the expense of their cases.[88]

Mitchell was not the only freedom suit defendant trying to avoid the cost of caring for alleged slaves who might soon be freed; the issue of cost came up in numerous other state appellate examples. Although freedom statutes did not mandate that enslaved plaintiffs stay in jail during these cases, it was a common practice for alleged slaves to be imprisoned for their protection or for the convenience of their alleged owners. For example, in one early nineteenth-century case, the Supreme Court of Virginia charged the defendant with the costs of the enslaved plaintiff's time spent in jail.[89] In contrast, Alabama's freedom statute required enslaved plaintiffs to provide a bond of security for their costs (which most plaintiffs would have done through a third party). In a case brought by a jailer for costs incurred keeping a plaintiff in jail during his freedom suit, the Alabama Supreme Court found that the person who provided the bond of security did not have to pay for the costs of jailing the plaintiff during the freedom suit.[90] Arguments over the responsibility of paying for plaintiffs' care during freedom suits contributed to cost-cutting measures, with potentially devastating effects for the individuals left to languish in jail.

Receipts from freedom suit case files offer additional details of the treatment of prisoners housed in the St. Louis jail. The available figures suggest that St. Louis's enslaved litigants received a lower standard of care than prisoners elsewhere, and—given the segregation of jails and the racial attitudes of the antebellum era—sheriffs and jailers most likely spent less money on prisoners of African descent than on white prisoners. One study found that as early as 1796, Tennessee sheriffs received 25 cents a day to care for prisoners. By the 1850s, Alabama sheriffs received 50 cents daily to care for their prisoners.[91] In Missouri, an 1835 statute lists a sheriff's fee of 37.5 cents per day for "furnishing a prisoner with board."[92] In other words, the sheriff received a total of 37.5 cents per day per prisoner, which included not only the sheriff's pay but also the jailer's pay and the prisoner's board. After one enslaved plaintiff brought his case in 1844, he spent more than three and a half years in the St. Louis jail. The abstract of court costs in his case included the jailer's request for only 30 cents per day for the man's care during this long stretch.[93] As late as 1860, the St. Louis jailer caring for another freedom suit plaintiff received only $27 for ninety days, or 30 cents per day.[94] A report on prisons and jails made after the Civil War found that jailers in St. Louis received 80 cents per day per prisoner—a sum that included the jailers' salaries—but the report suggested that it only cost around 15–20 cents per day to feed prisoners in the ways the reporters observed. The report did not distinguish by race, and by the late 1860s, it had no need to distinguish by condition of servitude; the circumstances for enslaved plaintiffs were likely worse than those found in this later report.[95]

Responsibility for the daily care of jailed plaintiffs lay with the sheriffs and jailers, who did not want to be held responsible for "damage" to enslaved property. One concerned St. Louis sheriff submitted an affidavit to the court about the conditions of a particular enslaved mother, Elsa Hicks, and her infant son, who lived in the jail during Hicks's 1847 freedom suit. Having housed Hicks and her son for over a year, the sheriff found himself unable to fulfill the court's order to hire her out. His affidavit stated, "I have tried diligently to hire said woman out," but "I think there is very little probability that I shall be able to dispose of the said woman & child" because of the high bond asked for her hire and because of her deteriorating health. He explained that "since said woman & child have been confined in jail the health of both of them appears to have become impaired the woman has reduced in flesh & looks badly."[96] When it seemed as though Hicks's case would continue past the fall term in 1848, the sheriff warned the court that "if she shall remain in jail til said suit is determined the consequence will probably [be] very serious to her health & to that of her child & *may be fatal to one or both of them*."[97] Sheriffs provided for jailed plaintiffs out of their own funds until the conclusion of the case, when the losing party had to pay the costs of the suit. If a plaintiff remained in jail for a particularly long period of time, the sheriff could incur considerable expense if the losing party refused or was unable to pay. Because no bond of security was given in Hicks's case, the sheriff complained, "if her suit shall be dismissed I know of no responsible party who will be liable to pay for the expense of keeping her in jail." For this reason, he asked, "If I am required to perform further duties & incur further expenses with said negro that the court will require some security to be given for any costs & expenses & trouble so required."[98] For Elsa Hicks and her ailing child, the time they spent in jail clearly threatened tragic consequences for their health and well-being.

Hiring

The sheriff's complaint in Elsa Hicks's case mentions a related risk that enslaved plaintiffs faced during their freedom suits: sheriffs usually hired out enslaved plaintiffs held in the jail to the highest bidder to help cover the cost of the suit or to avoid responsibility for caring for the alleged slave. Hiring helped offset the costs of freedom suits and the care and upkeep of plaintiffs kept in jail during these cases, which gave jailers and sheriffs considerable motivation to try to strike a deal and hire out an enslaved person. The resulting negotiations were akin to the wheeling and dealing that took place over the sale of an enslaved person, and sometimes sheriffs faced difficulty hiring people out if the bond the court required was too high—as was the case with Elsa Hicks and her child.[99] In these instances, the failure of the sheriff to hire out a plaintiff forced that person to remain in jail for long stretches of time. In one case, the court asked for $1,000 bond for the plaintiff's hire, so his attorney filed a motion and successfully persuaded the court to reduce this amount.[100] One month later, the attorney again asked that bond be reduced, stating that "the same is excessive in view of the value of the property, which is not worth more than four hundred dollars." The plaintiff in this instance argued that his own sale value was lower, most likely because he wanted to get out of jail. The motion also states that "the Plaintiff is confined in a dungeon without having committed any offense, and has simply presented his petition for his freedom."[101] Imprisonment clearly felt like punishment to this individual and the numerous other men and women confined in jail for extended periods of time.

In slaveholding states throughout the antebellum South, slave hiring occurred with the greatest frequency in cities, where the dearth of large-scale plantation agriculture encouraged enslavers to find new employment for their human property.[102] In St. Louis, the most frequent posts for hiring out enslaved women included various forms of domestic service, while men were most readily hired along the bustling waterfront for tasks linked to the levy and the riverboats tied up there. But the incessant demand for labor in the growing urban area meant that enslaved workers could be assigned to a wide range of tasks, including some of the least pleasant and most dangerous jobs available in the city. When the sheriff hired out an enslaved plaintiff, the court required that he also collect a bond from the hirer to guarantee the hired person's safety. The lack of long-term investment in the enslaved people hired gave hirers less incentive to care for these men and women; for this reason, bonds of security were intended to keep the hirer from mistreating plaintiffs or removing them from the court's jurisdiction. Bonds of security may have helped to incentivize the care of the hired person, but for enslaved plaintiffs in freedom suits—claiming to be free and therefore able to work and earn wages for themselves—the process of being bargained for in the streets or on the courthouse steps must have felt like an especially egregious insult, not to mention the fear that came from the unknown hirer, who may abuse the hired worker or subject him or her to brutal or unfamiliar types of labor.

Although Lucy Delaney remained in jail during her freedom suit, the jailer did hire out Lucy's mother, Polly Wash, when she sued for freedom five years earlier. At the conclusion of her case, Wash successfully sued for and received the wages she earned during her freedom suit, despite the fact that the courts usually hesitated to award back wages to freed plaintiffs.[103] Some plaintiffs appeared to prefer being hired out to living in jail, even if hiring out also had its dangers. Enslaved individuals throughout the South were more likely to be hired out at some point in their lives than to be sold.[104] But unlike other slave-hiring situations, the purpose of hiring in freedom suits was to cover the costs of caring for the enslaved person and of bringing a legal case. Enslaved plaintiffs earned funds that contributed to the costs of their legal cases by working for their hirers during their freedom suits.

Reasons to Sue

The substantial perils associated with suing for freedom raise questions about why an enslaved individual would brave these uncertainties to file suit. At least some potential litigants must have weighed the many risks involved and decided not to sue. Freedom was clearly important to men and women held in slavery, but it was not their only consideration. The fact that thousands of men and women across the South chose to face these dangers and sue speaks to their perseverance, to their willingness to trust the legal system and demand its assistance, and to their tremendous desire for legal freedom.[105] Free people of color faced numerous restrictions on their free status, and laws passed throughout the United States limited their ability to travel freely, to own certain types of property, and to fully participate in the political process.[106] Despite these limitations, the ability to be legally free and control one's own wages, have access to one's family, and make decisions about one's own welfare all contributed to the longing for freedom evident in nearly all of the writings, interviews, and testimony of enslaved or recently freed people of African descent.[107] When Lucy Delaney wrote of the difficulties she faced after she received freedom, including the premature deaths of her children, she wrote, "One consolation was always mine! Our children were born free and died free!"[108] For Delaney as for many other freedpeople, even the sorrows and restrictions on freedom for people of African descent were preferable to a life lived in slavery.

Exigent circumstances sometimes led enslaved individuals to brave the risks and file a suit for freedom: fear of being sold or violent mistreatment could be both cause and effect of freedom suits. Though many enslaved plaintiffs suffered abuses and threats as a result of their suits, other enslaved individuals sued to combat similar sufferings. For example, just as the threat of being sold away from the court's jurisdiction affected numerous enslaved plaintiffs, the fear of being sold further south could be the initial impetus for bringing a freedom suit. When enslaved men or women learned of an enslaver's intention to sell them, they could choose to institute suit to prevent the sale by asking the court for protection. For Lucy Delaney, it was only after she had a serious argument with Mrs. Mitchell and realized that her greatest fear—being sold away from St. Louis—was a real possibility that she made the decision to sue. After the argument, Delaney wrote, "I was not surprised to be ordered by Mr. Mitchell to pack up my clothes and get ready to go down the river, for I was to be sold that morning, and leave, on the steamboat

Alex. Scott, at 3 o'clock in the afternoon."[109] Some freedom suit plaintiffs, then, decided to sue only when threatened with the worst abuses of the system of slavery.

St. Louis freedom suit plaintiffs decided to bring their cases for a variety of reasons, but one powerful motivator was that in St. Louis, as elsewhere, the court sometimes sided with alleged slaves over enslavers. In St. Louis's cases, more than a third of the suits resulted in free status for the enslaved plaintiff.[110] These cases demonstrate enslavers' obligation to abide by judicial decisions, though the existence of multiple suits brought by the same enslaved plaintiff suggests that defendants did not always follow the court's instructions. In freedom suits, legislators and courts provided illegally enslaved men and women a venue to grant or restore their legal freedom. It is for this reason and because of the limited options available to enslaved plaintiffs for legally recognized freedom that they relied on the same legal authority that was designed to protect the interests of white enslavers to set them free. These men and women brought their grievances before the law because they believed that there was a chance the courts would acknowledge the injustice of their treatment and grant them legal freedom, and they also hoped that enslavers would recognize and obey the court's ruling.

People of African descent possessed a variety of sources of legal information, and although most of them did not sue for freedom, knowledge of the law—and, most likely, of the option of bringing suit—was widespread. Given the dangers and risks involved, enslaved plaintiffs did not make the decision to start a legal case lightly. Rather, plaintiffs would have weighed their risks and possible rewards carefully, perhaps exploring other possibilities before initiating their cases. Some individuals, like Lucy Delaney's mother, chose to sue only after pursuing other alternatives like attempting to escape. Other people sued after the arrangements for legal freedom that they made with owners failed to come to fruition; when enslavers reneged on their promises, enslaved negotiators turned to the courts to try to enforce these extralegal agreements. Still other enslaved plaintiffs—including Lucy Delaney—sued when they found themselves in immediate danger: after threats of sale, to combat physical abuse they suffered, or whenever they feared that either of these possible hazards might become a reality.[111] Taking a closer look at the spread of legal information, the options for freedom, the risks of bringing suit, and the high number of cases despite these dangers reveals the determination of enslaved plaintiffs in freedom suits and also indicates the existence of countless community conversations about slavery that included the voices of people of African descent. Enslaved plaintiffs' personal stories formed the basis for their claims to freedom, though the limits of their position within antebellum society meant that they could not combat their enslavers alone.

3 / Crafting Strategy

Litchfield, Connecticut, native Rufus Pettibone arrived in St. Louis with his family in May 1818, completing a cross-country journey from New York to search for work as a lawyer in the bustling river town. Pettibone brought with him three years of reading law in prominent attorneys' offices and just under ten years of experience as a practicing lawyer. Pettibone formed a partnership with another Litchfield, Connecticut, native—"one of the most experienced lawyers then at the St. Louis bar"— and worked for less than three years before receiving an appointment as judge of the Second Judicial Circuit in the newly admitted state of Missouri in 1821. Two years later, at age thirty-nine, he became a justice on the Missouri Supreme Court, a position he held from 1823 until his death in 1825. Shortly before he died at age forty-one, the legislature appointed Pettibone and another prominent legal scholar to revise and publish the state's first collection of revised statutes.[1] In less than ten years, Pettibone ascended the political ladder of Missouri and participated in several pivotal moments for the new state's legal community.

Like many lawyers working in St. Louis in the 1810s and 1820s, Pettibone enmeshed himself in the numerous contemporary debates surrounding slavery in St. Louis, including courtroom disputes over personal status. One sketch of his life recalled that, during the debates over slavery in Missouri in 1820, Pettibone ran as a candidate for the minority of Missouri residents who opposed the further extension of slavery in the proposed state.[2] He worked for both plaintiffs and defendants in freedom suits, became a defendant in a series of freedom suits relating to one enslaved family, and presided over freedom suit courtrooms as a judge. Whatever his particular beliefs on slavery, Pettibone embodies the complex web of personal interests and professional responsibilities that swirled around suits for freedom.

As Pettibone's example makes clear, each individual participant in these contests over slavery brought his or her own expectations and interests into court, and those interests could change based on the person's position within each case. Exploring the strategies that lawyers crafted with their enslaved clients—and, specifically, the arguments presented in freedom suits—highlights the creativity and the legal maneuvering that took place in and around the antebellum courtroom. Much of this legal wrangling was a result of the attorneys assigned to work in freedom suits, but lawyers relied on enslaved litigants to share their stories, find key witnesses, and bring in support from the broader community.

Freedom suits indicate how a variety of legal actors contrived to secure or prevent free status for enslaved individuals. Although plaintiffs came to the table from a drastically unequal bargaining position, enslaved clients and their attorneys participated in give-and-take interactions with their enslavers that were a common part of life in slaveholding societies.[3] The ability to navigate within the prescribed legal form provided a space for debating issues of slavery and freedom through the courts. Some of these negotiations took place by exploring various legal avenues, such as by bringing a habeas corpus petition or finding a more favorable venue to bring suit for freedom. But enslaved individuals and their attorneys also negotiated when they crafted strategies for freedom suits, adjusted arguments on the basis of appellate decisions, or worked to find the right mix of arguments and evidence to establish freedom in the courts.

Creativity in crafting legal strategies is evident in the arguments plaintiffs and their attorneys presented to the courts when trying to establish freedom. For example, while the majority of St. Louis's freedom suits argued for freedom based on time spent on free soil (usually in Illinois), the ways in which plaintiffs' attorneys made this claim shifted in response to previous court decisions, both in St. Louis and in the Missouri Supreme Court. When the Missouri Supreme Court began to make the distinction between an enslaver merely passing through Illinois with his or her human property and the enslaver establishing residence in a free state, the attorneys for enslaved plaintiffs looked for witness testimony to prove the alleged owner and the enslaved plaintiff moved and became residents of Illinois for the required length of time. Freedom suits, and the related litigation that developed around these cases, paint a rich picture of the types of arrangements enslavers made with their human property to allow for the possibility of freeing them, including what happened when enslavers failed to honor their promises and agreements.

Lawyers

Attorneys like Rufus Pettibone played a critical role in helping enslaved plaintiffs in freedom suits bring their cases to court and present their arguments. A brief sketch of the lawyers in nineteenth-century Missouri and their reasons for involvement in freedom suits—including financial gain, experience, ideological motives, or a sense of duty—highlights their importance to prosecuting and defending these cases. Because so many lawyers worked for both sides in freedom suits, ideological motives were not always the main reason lawyers agreed to work for enslaved plaintiffs, though in at least a couple of examples, sympathetic beliefs may have played a role. There was no contradiction between supporting slavery (either by slave ownership or by other legal relationships with enslavers) and prosecuting freedom suits for enslaved plaintiffs.[4] Many attorneys in St. Louis—as elsewhere—owned human property and worked regularly for the interests of the powerful enslavers of their community. These same individuals got involved in freedom suits for a complicated assortment of reasons. The background of the attorneys in St. Louis contributed to the type of legal culture that emerged around suits for freedom through the number of lawyers involved, the experience they brought to the cases, and their relationships with the broader community.

The legal profession developed early in the nineteenth century in Missouri. Rufus Pettibone and other migrants from the eastern seaboard arrived in the first decades of the century, hoping to capitalize on the opportunities found in the growing western outpost of St. Louis. The mobility that characterized the first half of the nineteenth century also contributed to the shifting of attorneys from the East, especially in the early years of Missouri's statehood.[5] St. Louis had thirty-one lawyers at the time of Missouri's admission to the Union in 1821, when the city had a population of only 4,700. At that time, the proportion of lawyers in the city was 6.6 per 1,000 people, higher than the ratio in Massachusetts at the same time.[6] St. Louis was a popular destination for attorneys who, like Pettibone, came to find work and rose to fill new government positions. Many lawyers heard rumors of high fees and plenty of available work, especially in debt collection. The majority of early nineteenth-century

Missouri lawyers came from the East Coast, largely from the slaveholding states of Virginia and Maryland, where a chronic oversupply of lawyers encouraged many enterprising young men to move west.[7]

Lawyers practicing in St. Louis in the early decades of the nineteenth century and throughout the antebellum years brought different kinds of training and experience to their endeavors; Pettibone's experiences attending college and reading law in the offices of other attorneys were not unusual.[8] Few of St. Louis's attorneys would have attended one of the new professional law schools cropping up in the East, and most would not have the recommended three years of apprenticeship.[9] Exams for admittance to the bar had widely varying standards because each individual judge gave the exam for his court, and attorneys needed to be certified in each town in which they planned to practice.[10] Even access to legal materials—statutes, case law, and treatises—was uneven among attorneys. Some attorneys in St. Louis possessed large legal libraries, consisting mostly of English books but also some American-authored texts and published case reports.[11] The variety of legal materials available to local attorneys provided the basis for their ability to make creative arguments in court.

When Pettibone entered the St. Louis legal community in the early years of the nineteenth century, he joined an intimate fraternity. Lawyers working on both sides of freedom suits knew each other; many attorneys worked in partnerships, allowing young novices to learn from experienced men and also facilitating the development of close relationships. The attorney Charles Drake, who worked in ten freedom suits (five for plaintiffs and five for defendants) wrote an autobiography recounting his move to St. Louis from Jacksonville, Illinois. When he arrived, Drake immediately met Hamilton Gamble (who prosecuted approximately fifteen freedom suits and defended as many as twenty-two cases), who took Drake under his wing. Drake later described Gamble as "an intimate" friend and "altogether the ablest lawyer that Missouri has had in the nearly fifty years [he had] known it."[12] Mentorship, friendship, and formal business partnerships characterized the close-knit community. For example, Pettibone formed a partnership with one prominent member of the St. Louis bar and later shared work with another local attorney, and Gamble befriended and eventually formed a successful law partnership with Edward Bates, who argued Lucy Delaney's successful freedom suit.[13]

The closeness of St. Louis's legal community could also lead to conflicts, some of which turned violent. The rough-and-tumble antebellum honor culture created an atmosphere where brawling and dueling was not unusual.[14] Lucy Delaney's attorney, Edward Bates, wrote in a letter to his brother that he wished "a plague upon George Strother—I wish he had some disease that dogs die of. He hates truth as the Devil does the piety which depopulates his kingdom."[15] George Strother (who assisted at least thirty-four enslaved plaintiffs and fourteen defendants in freedom suits) often found himself in trouble with the law for arguing with other attorneys, gambling, and "carrying a challenge" to a duel.[16] In 1825, the court suspended Strother from practicing law for six months for "his frequent interruptions of the counsel of the opposite side," including telling the opposing counsel "that he would settle the matter with him out of doors."[17] Criminal case records charged attorneys who participated in the St. Louis freedom suits with fighting, and at least two freedom suit attorneys died in duels.[18] The conflicts that escalated to violence in the streets and on "Bloody Island" (the notorious location of many St. Louis duels) influenced the behavior of these attorneys inside the courtroom and speak to some of the consequences of living and working in such a familiar community.[19]

Slavery influenced the creation, maintenance, and character of St. Louis's legal community.[20] Many St. Louis lawyers actively participated in the institution of slavery in Missouri.[21] Lawyers' claims to enslaved persons meant that they could be parties to freedom suits or have pecuniary interests in the outcomes. The same individuals who worked for enslaved plaintiffs in freedom suits sometimes found themselves having to defend a freedom suit initiated by their own alleged human property. In 1825, several enslaved plaintiffs—all part of a related claim to free status—sued Rufus Pettibone for their freedom.[22] For lawyers who worked both sides in this type of legal action, the possibility of having to defend freedom suits brought by their own slaves must have weighed on their minds.

Although the precise combination of reasons why each attorney chose to prosecute freedom suits remain largely hidden from the documentary record, a number of possible considerations contributed to lawyers' work for enslaved plaintiffs. Missouri's statute mandated that judges appoint attorneys for the enslaved plaintiff: "the court shall assign the petitioner counsel, and if they deem proper shall make an order directing the defendant or defendants to permit the petitioner to have a reasonable liberty of attending his counsel."[23] Although some plaintiffs requested particular attorneys or approached them before bringing their causes to court, many and perhaps most of them relied on whatever counsel the court appointed for them. In one enslaved plaintiff's petition, he asked for "leave to sue as a poor person, in order to establish his right to freedom, and that Trusten Polk and C. C. Carroll, Esqrs. be assigned as his counsel."[24] But this request was unusual; the vast majority of freedom suits' petitions do not specify a certain attorney. Instead, it was only after the judge appointed an attorney to prosecute the case that the lawyer began working for the plaintiff. Lawyers in these cases sometimes took freedom suits because the court assigned them to do so, much as public defenders work today.

When approaching freedom suits, St. Louis's legal community also considered the pecuniary benefits of taking on this additional type of work. White enslavers in St. Louis accused attorneys of seeking out enslaved individuals and convincing them to sue for freedom to earn the fees from this type of work. Although it is certainly possible that attorneys in freedom suits viewed enslaved plaintiffs as they did other paying clients, the low fees and uncertain nature of plaintiffs' ability to pay make this possibility seem unlikely. In most cases, the enslaved plaintiff petitioned the court to sue *au pauperis*, or as a "poor person," meaning that the person was "unable to prosecute his or her suit, and pay the costs and expenses," and therefore the court could "assign to such person, counsel who, as well as all other officers of the court, shall perform their duties in such suit without fee or reward." If the plaintiff won his or her case, the court ordered "judgment for his costs, which shall be collected for the use of the officers of the court."[25] In the early decades of Missouri's legal system, the losing party in a freedom suit was usually responsible for paying the court costs, including the attorneys' fees. By the end of the 1830s, St. Louis record books no longer listed attorneys' fees as part of a judgment for court costs, possibly because these expenses had to be covered by litigants themselves or by fees collected for hiring out enslaved plaintiffs.[26] The sheriff often hired out enslaved plaintiffs during their suits to help defray the expenses, including fees for their attorneys.

Scattered evidence remains of the fees lawyers collected for prosecuting or defending freedom suits, but a close look at the surviving documentation supports the argument that most attorneys received modest payments for their work in suits for freedom, if they received any compensation at all.[27] The best evidence for freedom suit attorneys' fees comes from the execution books, which recorded the costs for each suit and whether the responsible party paid the expenses. For example, two attorneys each received $3 in fees as part of the court costs for prosecuting two separate women's freedom suits.[28] The $3 fee matched the price mandated by a Missouri statute for lawyers working in any type of legal action.[29] The legislature raised the fee to $4 in 1835, and the fee remained the same in the 1845 and 1855 *Revised Statutes*.[30] In some instances, attorneys certainly charged enslaved clients higher fees for prosecuting freedom suits. For example, in 1833, one of the attorneys who worked in numerous St. Louis freedom suits sued a free woman of color for $125, which he claimed was his fee for prosecuting several freedom suits for the woman's children. The existing records indicate that the woman had four children who sued for their freedom, making an average charge of $31.25, although the fee may have included interest and other charges.[31] The enslaved plaintiff in an 1843 case complained that she hired her attorney, "to whom she paid at sundry times sums of money amounting in all to about fifty dollars or more, as a fee in said cause for his services."[32] The woman's complaint suggests that in at least some cases, plaintiffs not only sought out and hired an attorney but also paid these attorneys excessive fees out of their own funds, possibly obtained through hiring themselves out for wages. This woman's claim was unusual; most evidence suggests lower compensation for attorneys in freedom suits, with their earnings reliant on the losing party paying the court costs.

Evidence from other types of St. Louis–area legal actions provides context for the fees earned by attorneys in freedom suits. In a suit for damages from February 1824, Rufus Pettibone sued for a debt of $300 for his work as an attorney "in and about the prosecuting, defending and soliciting of divers causes," as well as "the drawing, copying and engrossing of divers conveyances, deeds and writing for the said defendant."[33] The suit does not list every case Pettibone handled, but a list of fees included in the case file suggests he charged $10 for most of the cases he handled. The attorney Charles Drake wrote in his autobiography that his first case when he arrived in St. Louis in the mid-1830s was for a man accused of stealing, and though his client could not afford to pay him, he wrote, "I defended him as vigorously as if he had paid me a hundred dollars; which would then have been a very large sum in such a case."[34] These bits of evidence do not provide a definitive answer to the question of what fees lawyers earned in freedom suits, but they suggest that, while most attorneys made the standard $3–$4 fee for their work in freedom suits, others charged their clients up to $50 to prosecute a suit for freedom.[35]

Scholarship on legal fees in early America suggests that fees for noncommercial cases were modest and that clients—whether free or enslaved, African or European descended—were often unable or unwilling to pay.[36] In the eighteenth century, the Virginia attorney Thomas Jefferson charged his clients according to the statute's specified amount per case (set in 1718) and only occasionally charged additional fees. He sometimes performed his work for free or on a contingent basis, and his books reveal that his clients regularly failed to pay their receipts.[37] In 1773, in response to the habitual tardiness of client payments, the general court bar in Virginia sought tighter restrictions on legal clients, requiring at least half of their fee up front before prosecuting a case.[38] In the nineteenth century, Virginia lifted the legislation limiting the specific lawyers' fees in cases, but the economic volatility of the antebellum years made steady income difficult, as financial crises kept business away and prevented clients from paying.[39] St. Louis's attorneys, like Virginia's, struggled to make ends meet: their enslaved clients proving unable or unwilling to pay their fees would not have been surprising, so pecuniary benefits were unlikely to be the primary motivation for their participation in the legal culture of slavery.

Lawyers also prosecuted freedom suits because they sympathized with the plight of enslaved plaintiffs, or at least, they may have sympathized with those whom they believed to be *illegally* enslaved. This distinction was an important one. In a slaveholding society, some attorneys may have participated in freedom suits to demonstrate the "fairness" of the slave system in Missouri. The attorney who argued Dred Scott's case pro bono before the United States Supreme Court in 1857 wrote in an 1856 letter, "In Missouri, and generally, I believe, in the Southern States, almost every lawyer feels bound to give his services when asked in *such a case* arising in the community to which he belongs."[40] Scott's attorney's letter suggests a commitment on the part of southern lawyers to prosecuting freedom suits for the purpose of ensuring the legal sanctity of slavery in their communities. Perhaps compassion is what motivated another St. Louis attorney, in an earlier case, to provide a $100 bond out of his own funds to guarantee the costs of an appeal to the Missouri Supreme Court.[41] The sympathy that some attorneys had for enslaved plaintiffs does not mean they necessarily opposed the system of slavery.

Many lawyers recognized slaves' ability to live as free persons, though they did not see this idea as threatening the legitimacy of the institution of slavery. Lucy Delaney's lawyer, Edward Bates, used his position as an enslaver to his advantage in making his argument for her freedom. In his plea to the jury, Bates stated, "I am a slave-holder myself, but, thanks to the Almighty God, I am above the base principle of holding any a slave that has as good right to her freedom as this girl has been proven to have."[42] Bates and other slaveholding attorneys may have viewed freedom suits as providing a remedy when enslavers violated the laws of slavery and illegally enslaved free people of color, so at least some enslavers did not see a contradiction in the coexistence of free and enslaved people. For them, personal status was not inherent; at least some people of African descent could and did live as legally free, and their status was worthy of protection.

Attorneys worked in freedom suits and other types of legal business to obtain experience and to solidify their status in the legal community. These suits provided the opportunity to dazzle potential clients and voters with their oratory skills, a crucial factor in any lawyer's reputation. The St. Louis attorney Charles Drake explained in his autobiography that jury trials were the best method for a young lawyer to win clients and influence others: "This gave young lawyers a capital chance for showing their ability and their eloquence, if they had any. Oftentimes the speeches before juries would attract a number of passersby; and so a single trial might make a young lawyer known to many." Drake used jury trials to build his reputation and business, and because he "had a loud voice, and talked with a great deal of force, and besides was as diligent and faithful as any young man," he began to "to attract clients in more profitable business."[13] In an article about Lucy Delaney's freedom suit, Eric Gardner suggests that Edward Bates prosecuted her case for the "game" of it, or for the challenge of trying to win the case.[44] A desire to win clients and influence through prosecuting these cases, which often included juries, may have prompted some attorneys to undertake these cases and to work hard for a successful outcome for their enslaved clients.

Although it is not possible to measure the benefits that freedom suits brought to attorneys' reputations, lawyers' efforts on behalf of enslaved plaintiffs did not irreparably damage their reputations or prevent them from pursuing their larger ambitions.[45] The lawyers who participated on both sides of freedom suits secured numerous political appointments on the local, state, and national levels, serving in a variety of judgeships, as Rufus Pettibone did, and other offices.[46] Three prominent freedom suit attorneys became judges on the Missouri Supreme Court, and one of these men also served as governor of Missouri during the Civil War. Another St. Louis freedom suit attorney served as mayor of the city (among his many political offices), and three additional attorneys who worked in freedom suits represented Missouri in the U.S. Senate. Lucy Delaney's attorney, Edward Bates, who prosecuted at least eleven freedom suits and defended at least eighteen, became Abraham Lincoln's attorney general. Freedom suit attorneys also held a number of lesser offices, including those of city attorney, county surveyor, and public administrator.[47]

Enslaved plaintiffs took a difficult step by initiating cases, but they ultimately relied on the efforts of the attorneys assigned to them to win their freedom—a lawyer could make or break an enslaved plaintiff's case simply by choosing to show up (or, conversely, by failing to appear) when court was in session. The attorney was responsible not only for filing all of the paperwork that accompanied a lawsuit but also for framing the argument in a way that would make it more acceptable to the court. Attorneys procured, prepared, and questioned potential witnesses, which sometimes required traveling far from St. Louis and incurring personal expenses. Some attorneys went to great personal expense and effort to prosecute these cases, while others destroyed plaintiffs' cases by failing to appear in court, giving bad advice, or refusing to expend personal finances for such extra necessities as traveling to take depositions. The choice to strongly pursue remedies for enslaved plaintiffs or to neglect their cases had life-altering implications for the individuals bringing these suits.

Attorneys sometimes filed additional evidence to support their enslaved clients' claims to freedom, including affidavits confirming the accuracy of enslaved plaintiffs' petitions.[48] In a group of cases filed against the administrator of the estate of the alleged owner—who was a prominent St. Louis attorney—the plaintiffs' lawyer filed affidavits supporting the petition that repeated the facts of the cases.[49] Attorneys sometimes included affidavits when they believed the defendant had removed the plaintiff from the court's jurisdiction, as one attorney did in an 1839 case, reporting that "some time in the night time on or about June last said plaintiff was taken in a clandestine manner & removed forcably from the Jurisdiction of this court." Not only did the attorney know that the plaintiff was away from the jurisdiction, but he had "good grounds to suspect & believe & does suspect & believe that Delford Benton [the defendant] aforesaid aided by others so took & removed said plaintiff."[50] These affidavits indicate lawyers' willingness to work for their clients and to protest when defendants disobeyed the court's orders. One defendant in two freedom suits even complained that while these cases were pending against him, the plaintiffs "absconded and put themselves under the protection and authority of George F. Strother and Newman, Esq. [the plaintiffs' attorneys]," where he believed them to be, and, he added, "since the Commencement of the suit of the suit [sic] for freedom I have not seen them."[51] In this instance, the attorneys may have even physically housed or protected two plaintiffs during their suits.

Attorneys in freedom suits sometimes went as far as putting up their own funds for bonds of security or to procure witness testimony, though this type of assistance was the exception rather than the rule. Plaintiffs needed monetary aid after an 1845 law required that freedom suit plaintiffs provide financial backing in order to sue. In a case brought shortly after the new requirement, the plaintiff's attorney and another St. Louis resident together provided a bond of security to cover the costs of her suit.[52] One plaintiff's attorney signed a bond for $6,000 to allow another St. Louis attorney to hire the woman and her children during her case.[53] For these attorneys, financial resources were one way they supported enslaved plaintiffs' claims and tried to win their cases for freedom.

Attorneys' interests in freedom suits could sometimes result in extra-legal maneuvering for their enslaved clients—part of the wrangling that characterized St. Louis's legal culture of slavery. For example, some attorneys consulted with witnesses before their depositions, perhaps affecting their testimony for or against enslaved plaintiffs. In one woman's freedom suit, a witness admitted on cross-examination, "I have talked with different persons about the negro woman have talked with Mr. Hastings [plaintiff's attorney] today." The witness also stated that he read depositions taken from earlier in the case, and he explained that these depositions were "showd to [him] by Mr. Hastings, the attorney in this suit for plff."[54] In a letter referencing another enslaved woman's case, the sender complained of the plaintiff's attorney interfering in the case. The letter stated that the attorney "had been up for several days fishing & killing ducks in company with one of the witnesses."[55] This line, added as an aside to the writer's primary complaint that the attorney meddled in the taking of depositions for the defense, suggests that by spending casual leisure time with the witness, the attorney may have colluded with that individual or influenced his or her testimony.

Attorneys more often appear in the case records for their negligence in their duties than for their overzealousness. Some attorneys perhaps viewed these cases as obligations, rather than opportunities, to aid enslaved plaintiffs. Several St. Louis lawyers abandoned freedom suits, leaving the enslaved plaintiff with no other recourse than to attempt to file a new case. For example, in a November 1833 case filed for the freedom of an enslaved woman and her children, the petition stated that her counsel had continued her suit for a number of years, but "finally, Mr. Bass, one of her counsel, having left the state, & the other, I. C. McGirk,

Esqr., being dead, her suit abated, for want of some person to prosecute the same."[56] After the court discontinued another woman's case because her counsel failed to appear, she filed a motion to reinstate her case, stating as one of her reasons that "her former counsel withdrew the suit without her knowledge or instructions." She also filed an affidavit explaining that "she employed Henry L. Cobb, Attorney . . . to bring suit for her freedom. . . . For his services in said suit she paid him money and did work for him as his washerwoman." When she came to court to try the case, "to her supprise her suit had been dismissed."[57] In what appears to be an instance of outright neglect of a client's business, another plaintiff complained in her 1843 suit (after the court dismissed her 1838 case) that after she paid her attorney more than fifty dollars, she learned "that the said Sproat [her attorney] had utterly neglected her business in said cause." As a result, the court issued a nonsuit in her first case, which she complained was "owing wholly to the gross neglect of said attorney and not in any manner to this petitioner."[58] Lawyers' efforts to work diligently for enslaved plaintiffs—or, conversely, their decision to ignore their responsibilities or take advantage of their vulnerable clients—had tremendous influence over the trajectory of these contests over personal status.

Arguments

In the early years of St. Louis's freedom suits, attorneys like Rufus Pettibone found little guidance in the statutes for how to successfully prove free status in court. The statutes outlined the process of freedom suits, but like other types of lawsuits, the law did not discuss particular arguments or legal strategies. The only guidelines specified that the court "may instruct the jury that the weight of proof lies on the petitioner, but to have regard not only to the written evidences of the claim to freedom, but to such other proofs either at law or in equity as the very right and justice of the case might require."[59] This instruction indicated that the plaintiffs bore the burden of proof, but it also implied an openness to the types of evidence an enslaved individual would be able to present, such as the testimony of white allies. Written proof of freedom might be difficult or impossible to produce, so the testimony of white witnesses might be given more weight than otherwise allowed in civil cases. Antebellum Americans often relied on personal connections to aid their causes in court, and slaves were no exception: personal relationships with white community members could be the difference for enslaved plaintiffs hoping to prove free status in court. For the most part, judges and juries exercised a great deal of discretion in deciding individual cases, eventually establishing basic guidelines for freedom suits.

The law allowing slaves to sue for their freedom delineated the basic parameters for a discussion over the legal definition of slavery and freedom in St. Louis, but it left many questions unanswered and open to interpretation. Freedom suits, especially those brought in the early decades of the nineteenth century, brought new issues before the inexperienced Missouri courts. Enslaved individuals pursued a variety of arguments in their cases, each forcing the courts to consider different aspects of slavery and how they defined the institution. With few precedents to guide them, early courts recognized the challenges and the importance of their decisions for guiding future case law. Like other types of litigation, state supreme court opinions often cited the opinions of appellate courts in other jurisdictions, indicating one of the ways that legal borrowing took place in antebellum America.[60]

Judges and juries allowed for a certain degree of experimentation and flexibility in response to lively debates over personal status. Enslaved plaintiffs, together with their attorneys, tried bringing different types of actions and presenting varying kinds of evidence to support their claims to freedom, while defendants, on the other hand, attempted to manipulate the system to sidestep legal determinations and to avoid forfeiting their valuable property claims. Both enslavers and enslaved plaintiffs challenged the courts to try to establish rules for these types of suits, therefore contributing to the discussion over what those rules would be. Examining early examples of the main arguments for freedom reveals the substance of this discussion and its implications for future cases. Freedom suits in St. Louis primarily involved three different arguments for freedom: that the plaintiff was free at the time of birth or descended from a free mother, that the owner had manumitted (or had agreed to manumit) the plaintiff, or that the individual became free by living or traveling in free territory. The range of arguments presented in the cases included variations on the main three mentioned here, and many freedom suits involved a combination of multiple arguments for the enslaved plaintiff's freedom.

Freedom from Birth

The argument of being free at the time of birth shifted the court's focus to the plaintiff's mother. Personal status followed the condition of the mother, under the doctrine of *partus sequitur ventrum*, literally meaning "what is born follows the womb." In other words, although the plaintiff's mother was not ordinarily a party to the suit—though there were also cases in which a mother and her children sued together—these cases tended to become disputes over the mother's status. The data on success rates for each argument in St. Louis suggest that the court most often freed those enslaved plaintiffs who claimed freedom from birth. Of the cases whose verdicts can be determined, enslaved plaintiffs won 57 out of 116 cases (49 percent successful) using the argument of freedom at the time of birth. A cluster of 1837 cases involving siblings resulted in freedom based on descent from a free mother in Virginia. In one of these cases, the petition stated of the plaintiff that "by the laws of Virginia his mother being free at the time of his birth" meant that he was "entitled to his freedom."[61] Free women of African descent could not give birth to legally enslaved children.

Arguing for freedom from birth sometimes required enslaved plaintiffs and their attorneys to engage with larger questions concerning a person's racial categorization and ancestry. In an 1848 St. Louis case, the enslaved plaintiff, Nancy, argued for freedom based on her Native American ancestors.[62] Nancy's petition stated that her "maternal grandmother was an Indian woman," that her mother "was a free woman," and that she had lived "as a free person" until "some months ago," when an enslaver claimed Nancy as a slave and transferred her to the defendant.[63] Claiming freedom based on Nancy's status as a Native American also meant using witness testimony about her racial characterization. One witness recalled how Nancy "dressed common like the Indians," though she "dressed like white people after she had come amongst them a good deal." The same witness testified that Nancy "was as much like a squaw as could be" and that "she looks like a half breed—she used to have Indian features."[64] Providing evidence of her Native American ancestry and a petition explaining that her mother's mother was an Indian, Nancy successfully proved her freedom by focusing on her descent from a free mother.

In a number of St. Louis's freedom suits, the mother of the plaintiff had either previously sued for freedom or was a party to the freedom suit of her children. These groups of cases underscore the importance of deciding a woman's status, especially if she had children, because one successful freedom suit could bring about a number of additional cases. When one enslaved mother sued for freedom in 1843, she brought suit not only for herself but also for her four children. In addition, the woman's two brothers also sued for freedom based on their mother's status as a free woman of color.[65] The freedom of all seven of these individuals rested on proving their descent from the plaintiff's mother.[66]

In a similar set of arguments, several plaintiffs also described being kidnapped or that they were free because they had been previously "living as free." One plaintiff's petition explained that "for several years she has lived as a free person" in Illinois and Missouri, until an agent of her enslaver had her imprisoned as a runaway slave. Her case file contains only a few documents, but the Circuit Court's record book indicates she won her case and $250, an unusually large sum for damages.[67] Another man's petition explained that his mother's enslaver freed her before his birth and that the man had "always from his birth enjoyed and exercised his natural freedom" until six years prior to the freedom suit, when he "was stolen and kidnapped," taken to Alabama, and sold as a slave.[68] Proving that the plaintiff's actions reflected the type of behavior expected from a free person could be pivotal to legally establishing that person's free status.

Suing for freedom based on free birth or descent from a free mother occurred frequently outside St. Louis, at the state appellate level, as well— nearly one hundred freedom suit appeals from across the country made this argument. A couple of appellate examples showcase the innovative ways that freedom suit litigants and their attorneys used the mother's status to expand or contract the court's definition of freedom. For example, in a Virginia case from 1827, one enslaver included a clause in the deed of manumission for the plaintiff's mother indicating that although the enslaver agreed to free the mother, he claimed all of her future children as slaves. The Supreme Court of Virginia refused to allow this attempt to circumvent the legal doctrine of *partus sequitur ventrum*, voided this clause, and freed the plaintiff. According to the court in this case, "a free mother cannot have children who are slaves. Such a birth would be monstrous both in the eye of reason and law."[69] One Alabama case involved a group of enslaved individuals who sued for freedom based on their birth to a free mother, although their enslaver claimed that the mother was an escaped slave from Virginia. The court's opinion stated that "in this case, notwithstanding the mother of the petitioners may be a fugitive slave . . . yet the petitioners . . . cannot be regarded as fugitives." In other words, even if the mother was legally enslaved in Virginia, her children were not fugitive slaves under the Fugitive Slave Act because of their birth in Alabama. Although the court ruled that they were not fugitive slaves, it did not sanction their argument that their birth made them free persons—their mother was a fugitive slave, and they also owed service to the person claiming their mother's labor.[70]

Prior Manumission

The second major category of arguments raised in freedom suits, arguing for prior manumission, occurred in sixty-two freedom suits (resulting in freedom in twenty-four cases, or 39 percent) and could come in several variations that reveal some of the negotiations that occurred between enslavers and their human property. Most often, cases arguing for prior manumission took the form of manumission in an enslaver's will or by a deed issued from the enslaver while he or she was still living. Many of these cases argued that the enslaved plaintiff and the enslaver reached an agreement for manumission that the alleged owner failed to honor. Sometimes these arrangements set out a plan for enslaved plaintiffs to buy their freedom, or they could include a promise by the enslaved party to serve the enslaver for a designated period of time before receiving freedom. These arrangements varied, but the courts usually failed to recognize them as legally binding because the law considered an enslaved individual to be chattel—and therefore prohibited from making contracts. Despite their classification as chattel, enslaved individuals often became parties to certain arrangements for freedom.

Enslavers frequently freed their slaves by will, perhaps attempting by this last act of mastery to clear their conscience, to reward a faithful servant, or to deprive ungrateful heirs of the value of their enslaved property. In one of the last freedom suits filed in St. Louis, in 1859, the enslaved plaintiff argued for freedom based on the will of his prior enslaver, who died in 1830. The will ordered that the plaintiff be freed at age twenty-one, so when he brought his case in 1859, the man claimed to have "long since arrived at the age of twenty one years."[71] In a similar case, an enslaved woman sued for freedom based on her former owner's will, which stated that she should serve until age twenty-one. At the time of her 1844 freedom suit, the woman's petition claimed that she was thirty-two and had since been transferred to her former enslaver's husband and then mortgaged to the defendant in her case.[72]

Freeing slaves by will could be especially complicated because it often required the cooperation of the person's heirs and the executors of the estate. One enslaved woman based her freedom suit on an agreement between her enslaver's widow and niece, whereby the niece and her husband agreed, after the death of the enslaver and his widow, to "recognize, declare & set free and will give deeds of freedom to the mulatto Peter aged about fifty years as well as to the mulatto woman Marianne and to the children whom they may have, that they may enjoy their freedom and act and contract as free and independent persons."[73] The woman claimed freedom because she was the daughter of Marianne, whom this agreement and will manumitted. Unfortunately for the enslaved plaintiff, the widow outlived the niece and her husband by fifteen years, and their heirs failed to honor this agreement and instead sold the enslaved woman. When heirs failed to honor their agreements or the agreements of their ancestors, free people of color needed the courts to uphold their right to freedom.

By the later antebellum decades, when concern over a growing free population of African descent began to supersede enslavers' wishes, Missouri shifted to the minority of slave states allowing manumission by last will; numerous states passed laws or issued judicial decisions restricting enslavers' ability to release their human property from slavery.[74] Mississippi prohibited manumission by will in an 1842 statute, though enslavers continued to attempt to free enslaved persons by will for years following the statute's passage.[75] South Carolina was another early state to adopt this restriction, passing a statute in 1841, but by the late 1850s, several additional states included these prohibitions.[76] One justification for these changes was that enslaved individuals were incapable of benefiting from a trust, so various states' courts chose to limit the power of enslavers to release their human property rather than recognize the right of an enslaved person to be a beneficiary to a trust left in a last will.[77]

Manumission by deed meant freeing an enslaved individual during the enslaver's lifetime and could happen as a result of arrangements between enslavers and their human property—such as self purchase or agreements to perform meritorious service and receive freedom in return—though increasing legal restrictions made these deals more difficult in the later antebellum years.[78] As with manumissions by will, many states were reluctant to allow these transactions because they created a population of free people of color, which legislatures increasingly feared in the later antebellum years.[79] It was common practice by the 1830s and 1840s to restrict the number of free people of color living in a state, with some states requiring licenses, prohibiting manumission, or limiting migration of freedpeople into the state. Missouri permitted manumissions by deed through the Civil War, making its laws somewhat more liberal than other slaveholding states in this regard. Although Missouri did not prohibit manumission, the legislature did pass a group of new restrictive statutes in 1835 to better "control" the growing population of free people of color in Missouri and limit their mobility. One particularly constraining piece of the 1835 legislation directed that free people of color had to have a license issued by the County Court to reside in the state.[80] Missouri's licensure laws became integral to controlling the expanding population of free people of color in St. Louis throughout the antebellum years.[81] White legislators deemed control of free people of African descent necessary to maintain the social structure and keep all black people in inferior positions to whites.

Manumission by deed often involved negotiations between the enslaved individual and the enslaver to secure freedom. Part of enslavers' authority included the power to free their slaves, and though some states restricted this ability, St. Louis's enslavers took advantage of the opportunity to sell enslaved persons their freedom, to reward favorite slaves, or to make other arrangements to free their human property. For example, when one enslaved plaintiff claimed freedom based on a deed of emancipation issued by her previous enslaver nine years prior to her suit, a witness explained that the enslaver had issued the deed of emancipation on the basis of an agreement for the woman to purchase her freedom. At the trial, the defense recounted a different series of arrangements, including multiple bills of sale between the woman's two enslavers (the first of whom issued her deed of manumission and the second of whom became the defendant in her freedom suit). The bill of sale to the defendant in her freedom suit contained the interesting qualification that, if the woman should sue for her freedom, her former enslaver was "not to be at any trouble or expense in defending the same."[82] In other words, the enslaver may have anticipated that the failed arrangement could lead to a freedom suit. Although an additional deed of manumission is available for the woman from November 1837, she lost her case in St. Louis and her appeal to the Missouri Supreme Court in 1838.[83] Freedom suits based on deeds of manumission were not unusual in St. Louis or elsewhere—occurring in more than 30 St. Louis cases and nearly 140 appellate cases from throughout the slaveholding states.[84]

Residence on Free Soil

The third major category of arguments for freedom found in St. Louis's freedom suits—based on residence on free soil—was the most common argument for freedom that enslaved plaintiffs presented in the St. Louis Circuit Court (209 cases, resulting in freedom in 79 cases, or

38 percent), and enslaved individuals usually made this claim based on time spent in Illinois. Enslaved people actively challenged the very idea of slavery as a lifelong condition by claiming that their personal status changed because they had lived in a free territory. This argument rested on the principle of an English case, *Somerset v. Stewart*, from 1772. In *Somerset*, Lord Chief Justice Mansfield found that a slave, once transported to a place where slavery did not exist, became free because slavery was "odious" to the law and therefore required the existence of positive law to support it.[85] America's courts, including the St. Louis Circuit Court, adopted this standard with some frequency in cases in which an enslaved person claimed to have lived in the Northwest Territory. When successful, these cases found that enslaved individuals having lived or traveled on "free soil" became free.

If an enslaved plaintiff could prove that he or she lived in a free state or territory, the St. Louis Circuit Court recognized this evidence as proof of lasting free status. In one example, the petitioner explained her right to freedom by drawing on her birth in Illinois as the slave of a French fur trader and her subsequent sale to a prominent St. Louis resident, who brought her to the city and claimed her as a slave. The case file clarified that the woman was born after the Northwest Ordinance of 1787 outlawed slavery in the territory.[86] In her case, not only did a jury find the French fur trader guilty (she dismissed the case against the other enslaver because he no longer claimed to own her), but the court also ordered the sheriff to pay the woman the money she earned when hired out during her freedom suit.[87] In a similar suit brought the same year, the defendant tried to circumvent a decision for freedom by focusing on the status of the plaintiff's mother prior to the Northwest Ordinance of 1787. The defense argued that if the woman's mother was a slave in the Northwest Territory prior to the Ordinance, she was not free and her daughter would also be legally enslaved. The defense in this case also included the suggestion that because the defendants were French residents of the area, the Ordinance did not apply to them. The St. Louis Circuit Court rejected this argument and found the defendant guilty, helping to establish the grounds for freedom suits based on residence in free territory.[88]

Freedom based on residence in a free territory or free state appears in twenty freedom suits in the Missouri Supreme Court and just over one hundred appellate cases from elsewhere. The majority of the appellate cases are found in northern states or states in the Upper South, though Louisiana heard twenty-eight cases using these arguments. In one Kentucky example based on a woman's birth in Pennsylvania after that state's gradual emancipation act of 1780, the lower court found for her freedom. In the appeal, the defendant complained that the lower court refused to instruct the jury that the woman's servitude for thirty years created a presumption of slavery. In the chief justice's opinion, the court recognized and explained the difficulty of bringing a freedom suit while being held as a slave. The opinion reads, "Actual slavery is a disability even greater than that of infancy or coverture, and is surely entitled to, at least, as much indulgence and protection. A person held and governed as a slave, is not either physically or intellectually a free agent. It would be unreasonable, therefore, to make the fact of constrained submission, however protracted, proof that it was rightful."[89] In other words, the fact that the woman served as a slave for thirty years did not stand as proof that she was legally enslaved. Rather, her birth and residence in the free state of Pennsylvania acted to emancipate her. In one of the few freedom suits from Mississippi, a group of enslaved plaintiffs based their freedom on residence in Indiana for more than thirty years. The Mississippi Supreme Court declared the plaintiffs free, stating the importance of following the Northwest Ordinance and the constitution of Indiana.[90]

Creativity and Negotiation

Attorneys like Rufus Pettibone and their enslaved clients worked within these categories of arguments for freedom, using different strategies to attempt to negotiate how the St. Louis courts interpreted the freedom suit statute. The pages that follow use three extended examples from the earliest years of freedom suits in St. Louis to explore the discussions that took place around contests over freedom, the creativity that enslaved plaintiffs and their attorneys brought to their legal strategies, and the tactics employed by enslavers to avoid losing enslaved property through freedom suits. When certain legal avenues failed, litigants and lawyers in freedom suits adjusted their plans and explored new methods for winning freedom. As the antebellum era continued, the creative maneuvering of these legal contests helped shape standards for future enslaved plaintiffs.

Broken promises sometimes drove enslaved individuals to ask the legal system to enforce their agreements with their enslavers, shedding light on the processes of negotiation that often happened outside the courtroom. In the case of *Winny v. Samuel Donner* (1820), a mulatto woman named Winny sued for freedom after two white men arranged to free her and one of them refused to honor the agreement. Winny worked as the slave of Jennings Beckwith until Donner made an agreement with Beckwith to purchase Winny for $300 and manumit her—after collecting $350 from Winny "by her work and labour or earning the same by being hired or otherwise."[91] This written agreement, or indenture, served as a manumission deed with the condition that Winny pay the required sum to Donner before receiving her freedom. At the time of the indenture, Winny's market value was approximately $575.[92] The arrangement prohibited Donner from selling Winny under penalty of her becoming immediately free, but it did permit him to sell her time or hire her out, a common practice in urban areas like the growing town of St. Louis. Beckwith intended to free Winny, so this indenture allowed him to receive some compensation for his benevolence. The agreement permitted Donner to make a profit and to benefit from Winny's services until she earned the required sum of money and repaid him for her purchase, but even after she paid "considerably more" than the agreed sum, her petition claimed that Donner "retains and keeps her as a slave and refuses to allow her her freedom."[93] Despite Donner's efforts to prevent her from becoming free, the court recognized Winny's indenture as binding. The jury found for Winny and awarded her legal freedom, along with token damages of one cent.[94]

Like so many of St. Louis's freedom suits, Winny's struggle did not begin or end with her legal case—her experience reveals some of the additional litigation spawned by agreements like the one between Beckwith, Donner, and Winny. Two additional Circuit Court cases demonstrate how arrangements for freedom could be contested and manipulated by white enslavers. Donner failed to pay Beckwith the agreed-on $300 for possession of Winny, so Beckwith then tried to recover this debt by reclaiming Winny and physically removing her from Donner's control. A few months after signing the indenture that transferred Winny to Donner, Donner sued Beckwith for replevin (unlawfully taking his property) for stealing Winny and asked for $1,000 in damages.[95] Beckwith defended the accusation by explaining that Donner never paid him for her sale, so Winny remained the legal property of Beckwith. Although no verdict is recorded in this action, there is a notation that the sheriff returned Winny to Donner, indicating that Donner won this case and received possession of Winny.

The conflict between Donner and Beckwith over the cost of Winny's indenture involved lengthy and escalating tensions that resulted in multiple legal actions to determine her fate. More than a year after Donner's suit against Beckwith, the latter tried a new tactic, suing Donner for debt in chancery court.[96] According to this case, by the time Beckwith realized that Donner did not intend to pay him, Donner's attorney had already recorded the indenture in court, and Beckwith had transferred Winny to Donner's possession. Beckwith also feared that several of the individuals who had testified that the debt had already been paid had conspired with Donner to deprive Beckwith of his money. All witnesses for Beckwith's side of the case were either dead or had left Missouri, so he could not obtain relief in a common law court and had to bring his case in chancery. Donner claimed that since the time of the indenture, he attempted to pay Beckwith, but Beckwith refused to accept his note as payment and exclaimed that Donner "was a rascal and that he would kill him."[97] Despite this alleged threat, the Circuit Court decided the case in Beckwith's favor for $300 plus the costs of the suit. Donner not only had to pay the cost of Winny's indenture to Beckwith but also lost possession of Winny after the Circuit Court found in her favor. In some instances, negotiations over freedom had the ability to extend far beyond a freedom suit, creating a web of interrelated legal actions. When enslavers manumitted their human property or made these types of agreements to free them, other parties could challenge the manumission or fail to honor its terms. In these instances, enslaved plaintiffs turned to the courts to win their freedom.

Failed agreements were not the only times enslaved plaintiffs needed to use the law's authority to free themselves; in other instances, agreements between enslavers and enslaved individuals were fraudulent or in violation of the law. For example, Rufus Pettibone prosecuted the freedom suit of an enslaved woman named Milly based on an arrangement with her enslaver, Mathias Rose, that violated the Northwest Ordinance. In this case, Milly argued for freedom based on her sixteen-year residence in Illinois as Rose's slave, which Rose claimed was legal because Milly had signed an indenture agreeing to serve Rose for seventy years. Prior to the 1818 Illinois constitution, the territorial laws required newcomers to the territory to register their slaves as indentured servants, a practice known as "voluntary servitude," despite the fact that there was nothing "voluntary" about these types of agreements.[98] Rose argued that the indenture was legal and that as part of this contract, he agreed to provide Milly with sufficient provisions "according to her degree and station."[99] This legal tactic allowed enslavers to move into the territory and retain their alleged slaves, effectively rendering the antislavery portion of the Northwest Ordinance meaningless.

Through the use of long-term indentures, enslavers like Mathias Rose introduced new complications to the court by creatively reconfiguring the categories of personal status. Enslavers in the Northwest Territory had to invent ways to maintain their mastery despite the federal prohibition of the Northwest Ordinance. Rose claimed that Milly voluntarily agreed to the indenture and that, because the seventy-year period had not ended, Milly remained his legal servant. Because of her indenture, Milly was technically no longer enslaved, but she was also not a free woman. When Milly brought her freedom suit, she forced the court to make a decision about categories of personal status that the legislature had not explicitly anticipated.

Enslavers' tactics expanded in response to the challenges brought by their human property. Milly's case began with a habeas corpus claim, but Rose manipulated this claim to support his defense. Milly filed a writ of habeas corpus in the Circuit Court demanding that Rose bring her before the court and explain why he held her in slavery. With this claim, Milly attempted to free herself immediately from Rose's possession. Perhaps she feared he would remove her from the court's jurisdiction or mistreat her or her children because of a freedom suit. Rose's response to her writ introduced a new defense to freedom suits in St. Louis. Rose answered the writ ordering him to bring Milly to court by stating that, a month earlier, Milly "absconded from the house and possession of the said Mathias Rose, without his consent and against his will, since which time he has neither seen nor heard of her."[100] He therefore argued that she could not continue her suit against him because the premise of her petition was that he unlawfully held her as a slave. Rose evaded prosecution by claiming Milly had run away, meaning that she was no longer in his immediate possession—perverse logic that later St. Louis defendants would use to deny possession of the enslaved plaintiff. If the defendant no longer held the plaintiff in slavery, how could the plaintiff maintain a lawsuit against the defendant to win his or her freedom? Milly responded by calling Rose's answer "evasive and insufficient," insisting that "she did not . . . abscond from the house & possession of the said Mathias Rose."[101] When enslavers, in order to avoid prosecution in freedom suits, argued that their enslaved property ran away, the local authorities sometimes intervened with criminal prosecutions to prevent these tactics. In December 1819, the U.S. government sued Rose for contempt of court for failing to produce "the body of Milly agreably to the requisition of a certain writ of Habeas Corpus issued from our said Court."[102] The Circuit Court did not free Milly, instead dismissing her suit because she failed to prosecute it sufficiently.[103] Although Rose claimed she had run away, a more likely explanation is that he prevented Milly from appearing in court and prosecuting her freedom suit against him. Milly's ability to sue Rose directly threatened his property rights to her and her children. There is no verdict in the criminal case against Rose.

The most striking example of the Missouri courts attempting to lay out a uniform doctrine in freedom suit arguments came in an early 1820s case with Rufus Pettibone as the defense attorney and eventually a defendant to the suit. In this case, an enslaved plaintiff named Winny—no relation to the Winny who sued Donner and Beckwith—sued Phebe Whitesides for freedom for herself and three of her children. Winny's other six children also filed cases against the people claiming them as slaves, all based on Winny's right to freedom.[104] The fact that the fate of such a large number of slaves rested on the decision gave the slaveholding defendants even greater motivation to fight Winny's case. According to her petition, Winny lived as the slave of John Whitesides (or Whitset); his wife, Phebe; and their son, Thomas, in Kentucky until 1792, when they moved north of the Ohio River to a place called Whitesides Station. The family lived there and claimed Winny as their slave until they moved to St. Louis in 1796. Winny continued working as the slave of Phebe and Thomas after John's death until, according to the petition in Winny's second freedom suit, Phebe sold Winny to Rufus Pettibone.[105]

While serving as Phebe Whitesides's attorney, Pettibone creatively argued to keep Winny and her family in slavery. Winny filed her original petition against Phebe Whitesides in June 1818, claiming Whitesides assaulted her and held her illegally in slavery when she was free based on her four-year residence in the Northwest Territory.[106] The defense that Pettibone crafted for Phebe Whitesides indicates the complex legal maneuvering enslavers practiced to retain their enslaved property and to manipulate the laws to their advantage. Phebe argued that Winny was not actually her slave or her husband's slave. Instead, Phebe maintained that Winny belonged to Phebe's father, who gave Winny to his infant grandchildren but ordered that Winny serve Phebe during her lifetime, then pass to her heirs. Phebe attempted to prove that Winny could not be free because she was not held in the Northwest Territory by her true owner. In essence, Phebe denied actually owning Winny in order to be able to continue holding Winny in slavery.[107] The court struggled to delineate the boundaries of legal status in response to the strategies that attorneys helped the litigants to develop.

The outcome of Winny's case is one instance when the court tried to set up a clear doctrine to deal with some of the many puzzling aspects of personal status. The court decided that Winny did actually belong to Phebe and that Phebe had held Winny in slavery while living in the Northwest Territory and thereafter; the court's explanation of the points of law to the jury introduced a new consideration into the rules for determining freedom based on the Northwest Ordinance. The judge instructed the jury that Winny's residence in the Northwest Territory with Phebe and her husband did free her under the Northwest Ordinance, "if it should appear to the satisfaction of the jury that the said defendant & her then husband resided there *with intent to make that territory the home of themselves and of the said Winne.*"[108] This case was the first use of the doctrine of the defendant *intending* to reside in the Northwest Territory, which came into wider use in later freedom suits. In later cases, judges made distinctions based on the time spent in free territory and the purpose of being there. For instance, if an enslaver passed through Illinois with his or her enslaved property, the court typically did not grant freedom to the enslaved individuals, but if an enslaver moved to Illinois and established residence there, the court usually freed any people held as slaves in Illinois. Courts did not always adhere to these distinctions, suggesting the complexity of issues at stake when deciding the personal status of plaintiffs in freedom suits. These cases were always part of a larger dialogue between Missouri and Illinois over the status of people of African descent, slave or free, in this border area.[109] Lawyers like Pettibone and defendants like Phebe Whitesides maneuvered within these contests to try to prevent the courts from freeing their valuable property, but they were not always successful.

This extraordinary verdict did not end Winny's struggle for freedom for herself and her children; negotiations over their personal status persisted when her enslavers refused to accept the court's determination. Phebe Whitesides continued to plead her case and push the issue of possession and ownership. After the jury found Winny and her children to be free, Phebe filed a list of reasons for setting aside this verdict, including the fact that she did not possess Winny when the case came to trial. Instead, she revealed to the court that her attorney, Rufus Pettibone, had purchased Winny and her family as his slaves.[110] A few years later, in 1825, Winny filed a new petition complaining that Pettibone continued to hold her and three of her children as slaves despite the court's judgment for their freedom. Her petition repeated the story behind her case and concluded that Pettibone "still refuses to liberate your Petitioner or to allow her and her said children to go at large and enjoy their natural freedom."[111] The court instituted new freedom suits for Winny and her children, assigned two attorneys to the plaintiffs, and ordered that the plaintiffs have "reasonable liberty of attending their counsel—(according to the statute on freedom, the new law)."[112] When Pettibone died during the prosecution of the 1825 freedom suit, his heirs became the defendants. The jury's verdict does not survive in this case file, but a bill of exceptions filed by the defendants indicates that Winny and her children again won their freedom in the St. Louis Circuit Court. The story of Winny and her children demonstrates the various tactics defendants and their attorneys employed to prevent the loss of their enslaved property. But in Winny's case, the judge clearly sided with her and for her freedom, instructing the jury that the Northwest Ordinance did free Winny and even suggesting that Winny should receive a similar amount of damages to any other plaintiff in a false imprisonment case.[113]

Attorneys like Rufus Pettibone shaped the strategies, arguments, and outcomes of freedom suits, contributing to the web of negotiations that took place in and around the courtroom. Attorneys became involved in freedom suits for a variety of possible reasons—for money, for experience, or on ideological grounds. Whatever their reason for participation, the body of St. Louis freedom suits includes lawyers making extraordinary efforts to secure freedom for their clients, as well as lawyers sinking their clients' chances at freedom by their lackadaisical performances. Pettibone's work crafting a unique line of reasoning for Milly's freedom or defending against Winny's claim constituted a valuable part of the process of suing for freedom. Through the tactics these attorneys designed, they and their clients helped establish legal doctrines delineating the boundaries of personal status in antebellum St. Louis. Freedom suit doctrines often focused on place; where the cases happened played a role in the arguments available as well as the litigants' access to law.

Thornton Kinney's livelihood depended on his ability to move freely from one place to another. This mobility eventually led to his capture and enslavement, though it also facilitated his suit for freedom. Born in Virginia to a Native American–descended mother, Kinney secured copies of his free papers when he turned twenty-one. Kinney took his proof of free status with him as he joined the wave of westward migration, leaving the eastern seaboard to work on steamboats traveling the Mississippi and Ohio Rivers.[1] He eventually met a member of the American Colonization Society during a stopover in St. Louis who "induced" him to travel to the colony of freed people of African descent in Liberia. Kinney stayed in Liberia only five years, but when he left the United States for the African colony, he planned to live there permanently.[2] During his years in the colony, Kinney threw away his free papers because he believed he would no longer need them and because his constant traveling had left them "so worn and mutilated that no one could decipher them."[3] Kinney did eventually return to the United States. Recognizing that his skin color left him vulnerable to enslavement, he took immediate steps to protect his freedom by approaching two separate legal arenas to secure his free status. He registered a permit proving his freedom in a Louisville, Kentucky, court and filed the same permit with a notary public in New Orleans.[4]

Free people of African descent relied on the strength of the legal system—operating through its written documents, its legal offices, and its representatives—to protect their free status, especially when traveling across borders throughout the slaveholding South. After Thornton Kinney secured legal documentation to protect his status, he resumed his work as a cook and steward on steamboats traveling the Mississippi River system. Despite his efforts, a steamboat captain claimed to own Kinney as a slave, imprisoned him in New Orleans, and offered him for sale by a slave trader. The trader's numerous attempts to sell Kinney "could not succeed, for the reason that he [Kinney] would always tell any one who spoke about buying him, that he was free."[5] Kinney made a daring escape from the window of the slave pen and resumed his business, working on steamboats on the Mississippi River. Kinney's flight suggests the limits of the law's protection for free black workers, who might find themselves unable to access legal assistance or unable to rely on legal documentation, though it also signifies his ingenuity and willingness to take risks to secure his freedom. The same steamboat captain who initially claimed Kinney as a slave eventually caught up with him in St. Louis and had Kinney arrested as a fugitive slave. Kinney sued for freedom in the St. Louis Circuit Court in November 1853.[6] On December 21, 1855, despite the many contacts Kinney made through his travels, the court dismissed his freedom suit because he failed to provide money to secure the costs, which Missouri required of enslaved plaintiffs after 1845.[7]

Thornton Kinney lived in a world in motion. The nineteenth-century United States saw countless individuals join their movements to the din of migrants traveling throughout the country and beyond it. Crossing into multiple legal jurisdictions raised a host of questions—about legal authority, evidence, and the relationship between states' laws—for antebellum courts to decide. Freedom suits highlight how individual migrations forced states to debate and to clarify definitions of personal status.

The location of suits for freedom in antebellum America mattered because not only did each jurisdiction subscribe to its own beliefs and statutory guidelines on slavery-related issues, but geography also affected freedom suits by the way each location interacted with its surrounding states' laws—what is termed "interstate comity." "Comity" refers to "the granting of rights by one nation or state to the citizens of another," and it makes up one of the legal questions that courts answered through the prosecution of freedom suits in St. Louis and elsewhere.[8] When studying slave law in the United States, "comity" refers to how nonslaveholding states dealt with citizens of slaveholding states and vice versa, as well as the relationship between different slave states. All regions of the United States faced these quandaries when enslaved and free people of African descent crossed state and national borders. In Missouri, this factor was most apparent in the state's relationship to surrounding free states, and for St. Louis, the connections between the city and the free state of Illinois raised a number of issues related to slavery and freedom.

By traveling across geopolitical borders, enslavers and enslaved individuals challenged the relationship between various local legal arenas. This chapter considers some of the ways that movement affected legal disputes surrounding slavery and freedom, including differences in state statutes but also variations in how state courts interpreted particular issues. States and regions subscribed to complex sets of attitudes and beliefs about slavery and freedom. For this reason, attempts to group together broad regions of states and territories and look for definitive patterns often mask the messiness of the web of interconnections that individuals living during this era would have recognized. Focusing on interstate comity emphasizes not only the geographic borders that existed but also how often enslaved and free persons crossed those boundaries. Though interstate comity eventually broke down in the face of mounting sectionalism, it served as a type of legal glue that bound the North and South together for much of the antebellum era, and perhaps nowhere is this more apparent than in a border region like Missouri.

St. Louis: Crossroads of Slavery and Freedom

St. Louis is an especially noteworthy place for examining the role of mobility in suits for freedom: its location as both a border city and a river city allowed enslaved individuals to exploit opportunities in the law and forced courts to respond to disputes raised by movement across geographic boundaries. St. Louis both united and separated north and south. The city connected the flow of capital from north to south and east to west; it served as a central depot for travelers to the West and up and down the Mississippi; and it brought together individuals from a wide variety of backgrounds, including large numbers of immigrants.[9] After the closing of the international slave trade in 1808, an explosion of cotton production in the Deep South fueled a massive internal slave trade, with the majority of enslaved people forced into this trade coming from Upper South states like Missouri, Maryland, and Virginia.[10] Although much of this domestic slave trade took place to the east of Missouri, St. Louis played a valuable role in facilitating the transport of enslaved individuals. By the 1820s and 1830s, steamboat travel helped to increase mobility, especially in St. Louis, and made interstate slave trading easier.[11] The city's bustling trade encompassed both legal slave trading and illegal kidnapping of free persons of color for sale from Missouri to the Deep South, especially in the 1840s and 1850s.[12] Along with St. Louis's popularity as a slave trade center and a place for travelers passing through Missouri, the vast majority of the city's freedom suit plaintiffs based their claims to freedom on questions involving movement between jurisdictions—especially residence in a free state or free territory.

As the example of St. Louis's freedom suits makes clear, Illinois and Missouri were not simply "free" and "slave" states. Both locations encompassed a broad spectrum of personal status, and their position as border states made them a critical battleground for conflicts over slavery in antebellum America. For this reason, men and women held in slavery in both states took advantage of the porous state boundary to claim freedom in a variety of ways. In an 1828 letter to a St. Louis attorney, Ninian Edwards, the governor of Illinois, complained that Illinois slaves continued to run away to St. Louis. Edwards's own human property, a woman whose name was not given, had recently absconded to St. Louis with her husband, and though Edwards claimed he held a good title to her, he wrote, "the encouragement that our negroes have received to run to St. Louis, might render it almost useless" to try to reclaim her. Edwards wanted the attorney to inform him about St. Louis's requirements for enslaved persons to carry passes and free people of color to carry free papers because he hoped to try to recover his lost property in the city. He warned that Illinois enslavers were getting "tired" of their enslaved property escaping to St. Louis, where officials failed to retrieve them. As a final protest, he chastised St. Louis enslavers who, he argued, should not complain about Illinois failing to return runaway slaves because St. Louis was also guilty of this offense: "if our negroes are to find refuge in your state, you ought not to complain if we should refuse to take up or authorize our citizens to take up yours."[13] Edwards's letter, when read alongside the evidence from St. Louis's freedom suits, demonstrates the enormity of the problem of African American mobility in the minds of Illinois enslavers.[14] St. Louis's proximity to Illinois created both opportunities and dangers for enslaved and free people of color living in the region.

In St. Louis, questions of mobility concerned the Mississippi River as well as movement across the border with Illinois. The Mississippi River provided a useful highway for the transfer of information, people, and ideas that could contribute to freedom suit litigation, as well as introduce certain dangers to the free status of people living along these routes.

River systems constituted the primary connections between regions for the vast majority of antebellum southerners until southern railroads expanded in the 1840s and 1850s.[15] For Missourians, the Mississippi River system was the economic lifeblood of the state and one of the main contributors to St. Louis's astronomical growth during the 1830s, 1840s, and 1850s. River systems also helped facilitate the spread of legal information, allowing enslaved and free people of color to learn of opportunities and legal avenues, while also introducing new challenges to the stability of black families and communities when enslavers employed the rivers to serve their nefarious purposes.

Thornton Kinney's kidnapping and attempted sale into slavery resulted from his vulnerable position as a steamboat worker of African descent. Enslavers living in St. Louis and other river cities often chose to hire their human property out to work on steamboats as cooks, laborers, and personal servants, thereby increasing the enslavers' fortunes through these valuable occupations; at the same time, people of African descent learned from their experiences working on the river. One study of African American seamen argued that work on the sea provided opportunities and relative freedom for people of color.[16] Similarly, the historian Thomas Buchanan found that working on rivers provided an increased opportunity for enslaved individuals to interact with other enslaved and free people of color, forming connections and experiencing mobility that they could use to their advantage.[17] Kinney's work experience on the Mississippi River system bolstered his ability to combat his forced migration to slavery in Louisiana and bring a lawsuit in St. Louis to prove his freedom. Throughout his life, Kinney relied on the law's authority (represented in his free papers) to protect him from the designs of those who equated his skin color with a presumption of slavery. When he began his freedom suit, Kinney sent a request for copies of his free papers in Virginia to help substantiate his claim. In addition, Kinney's case relied on affidavits of members of his riverboat community, including one witness who stated that "for near two years past he has known Thornton Kinney to be acting & passing between St. Louis & New Orleans as a free man."[18] As Kinney's story makes clear, African Americans marshaled the resources available to them—including legal documentation, geographic opportunities, and the support of their communities—to preserve or to establish their free status as they traveled the Mississippi River.

Fluid Borders

When Thornton Kinney moved west to find work, his migration was not unusual or illegal. Routine, legal movement across state and national borders contributed to freedom suit litigation throughout the United States, and Missouri was no exception. In St. Louis, the city's location meant that its residents regularly crossed political borders when they traveled for work or to visit friends and relatives. Enslaved individuals also participated in the common border crossings that characterized the region. But for enslaved men and women, these movements could allow them to sue for freedom and to ignite conflicts over the meaning of migration in local legal cultures.

The confusion surrounding the legality of slavery and other forms of servitude in Illinois, and the propensity of Missouri enslavers to travel there with their enslaved property, stretched the boundaries of legal enslavement in the region. Prior to the first Illinois constitution (passed in 1818), the federal Northwest Ordinance of 1787 prohibited slavery in areas north of the Ohio River, including Illinois, but this did not mean that slavery did not exist there. Enslavers living in the Northwest at the time of the Ordinance interpreted it to apply only to introducing new slaves into the region; they believed it did not interfere with the enslaved individuals already living in the area.[19] Also, despite legal prohibitions, many enslavers migrated to Illinois from Virginia and Kentucky in the years before statehood, and they often brought their human property along with them. Although technically the Northwest Ordinance prohibited slavery in Illinois, slavery persisted in the region prior to statehood in 1818. Legal loopholes in the new state's constitution allowed the institution to continue in only a slightly modified form through long periods of "voluntary" indentured servitude.[20] In addition, although the state's constitution outlawed slavery, it did allow for owners to hire enslaved men and women at the Saline (or Salt Lick) region of Illinois for a period of less than one year at a time. Even this exception ended in 1825.[21]

Enslavers sometimes asserted an expansive interpretation of Illinois's laws that permitted the continuation of their mastery in this border region. For example, one enslaved woman sued for her freedom in St. Louis's courts on the basis of her time spent living as a slave in Illinois. When the defendant entered his plea of not guilty, he complained to the court, "at the time of the committing the said supposed grievances . . . the said plaintiff was held to labour in the State of Illinois under the laws of said State of Illinois and had escaped into the county of Saint Louis."[22] When the defendant mentioned the "laws of said State of Illinois," he was most likely referring to the laws of indentured servitude. Illinois's law permitted any person to sign an indenture and file it in an Illinois court. Enslavers in Illinois often coerced their servants into signing these indentures, and, prior to the state constitution's limiting them to one-year terms, these terms could last for long periods of time—sometimes as long as ninety years. In this backhanded way, long-term indenture contracts allowed lifelong slavery to continue in slightly disguised form, even though these extended contracts became rarer after Illinois became a state in 1818.[23] This woman's case dealt with the laws of indentured servitude and the status of people of African descent held under long-term indentures that appeared to be of questionable legality. A more detailed example will serve to explain the complications involved in the other major exception to the prohibition on slavery in Illinois after 1818: the rule allowing enslavers to hire enslaved men and women to work at the Illinois Salt Lick (the region known as the Saline) for a period of no more than one year at a time.

The example of Vincent Duncan's struggle for freedom—as told in his multiple freedom suits in St. Louis—highlights how migrations affected personal status when enslavers tried to get around the Illinois constitution, setting up a debate over how Illinois law should apply to former Kentucky residents once they sued in Missouri.[24] Vincent Duncan was claimed as a slave by the patriarch to the Duncan family, Jesse Duncan, and, after Jesse's death, by his sons (James, John, and Coleman). The Duncan family hired Vincent out to work in Illinois from sometime in late 1817 or 1818 until 1825, although witnesses offered conflicting testimony about the exact start date of Vincent's hire (a fact that was significant when he brought his arguments to court).[25] Vincent worked for several different hirers during his time at the Salt Lick, though he enjoyed relative independence and was able to move around and conduct his own business with little interference from the Duncans. Numerous witnesses agreed that while living in Illinois, Vincent had "run about there & done as he pleased."[26] Eventually Vincent even "rented a furnace and made salt on his own account."[27] Vincent used the facts that he worked on his own, acted independent of the Duncan brothers' control, and moved around without restriction to help establish his legal freedom.

Both Vincent and his enslavers seemed to be well aware of the legal restrictions imposed by the Illinois constitution and of the dangers of Vincent's staying in Illinois after 1825. One witness recalled how, when a

Duncan brother "had Drank pretty freely and was [a] little intoxicated," he informed the witness that Vincent was to be freed at Jesse Duncan's death.[28] The witness alerted Vincent, "if you remain here [Illinois] too long, You might get your freedom," and Vincent replied "that he did not Know that he Should want it."[29] This statement implied that Vincent was not interested in becoming free, at least not while he lived a relatively independent lifestyle at the Salt Lick in Illinois, although it also indicates widespread knowledge of the legal restrictions. Vincent knew of his legal rights, even if he was unable or unwilling to take the risk to bring a suit to enforce them until his migration to St. Louis.

In a series of border crossings to Illinois, James Duncan tried to secure the Duncan brothers' property rights in Vincent and avoid the Illinois constitution's prohibition of all slave hiring after 1825. In response, Vincent began using both extralegal and eventually legal means to resist this forced migration and solidify his freedom. Several witnesses testified that Vincent became "disobedient" and refused to return with James; each time James tried to bring Vincent back to Kentucky, "of one pretense or other," he would not go. Vincent employed a number of stalling tactics to protect the limited privileges he enjoyed as an alleged slave working in the nominally free state of Illinois. One deposition recalled how Vincent would make promises to return to Kentucky but would "afterwards evade them and shirk about, and upon the whole was a trifling fellow."[30] Another witness explained that "Vincent begged very much to stay a little longer as he said to settle his business," promising to come "home as soon as that was done." The witness continued by suggesting that "it appeared that there had been a good deal of deception on the part of Vincent on this subject and that Duncan had got quite out of patience with his false pretences."[31] After several attempts by both James Duncan and a man James hired to capture Vincent, John Duncan managed to bring Vincent to Kentucky. Once John Duncan had crossed back into Kentucky, he gave Vincent to John's brother James to "hire or Dispose of as he thought proper."[32] The Duncan brothers' frustration with Vincent's efforts to assert his independence and stay in Illinois was obvious to outside observers.

Having successfully forced Vincent to travel back to Kentucky, the Duncan family must have breathed a sigh of relief, believing that they had dodged a bullet and protected their property rights. Even so, the Duncan brothers remained angry with Vincent for his insubordination; when James Duncan brought Vincent to St. Louis in 1826, he hired Vincent out and informed the hirer that Vincent was of "bad character" and so Duncan wanted someone to "keep a tight reign over him."[33] Vincent both strengthened his "bad" reputation and reclaimed his independence when, shortly after beginning his work, Vincent escaped the hirer's control and returned to hiring himself out to various masters—still sending his wages to the Duncans. A witness for Vincent described Vincent's work as a drayman in St. Louis for several years and how he worked "apparently on his own account and without the known authority and mastership of any person over him."[34] Like his years working in Illinois, Vincent's movements in St. Louis seemed relatively uninhibited by his alleged enslavement.

The Duncan family's choice to force Vincent to migrate to St. Louis ultimately resulted in the legal battle over his status. Vincent's immediate impetus for suing in 1829 is unclear, though an incident recorded in the case file suggests he may have feared that James planned to force him to travel to New Orleans for sale.[35] A witness testified that he found James in a canoe on the Mississippi River with Vincent "handcuffed and guarded by a man who had a dirk in his hand."[36] James was caught red-handed trying to evade prosecution in Vincent's freedom suit, perhaps because James recognized that Vincent's movement between Kentucky and Illinois might legally free him. After returning to court, James argued that Vincent's hiring contract was made from month to month, so he never worked in Illinois for a term of longer than a month at a time. James also believed that because Vincent had admitted to witnesses in Illinois and St. Louis that Duncan owned him, this acknowledgment proved his enslaved status. Vincent's attorney responded that even if the constitutional exception allowed Vincent to be hired monthly for a total of eight or nine years, Vincent had also been hired to work in Illinois before Congress adopted the Illinois constitution, so Vincent was free based on the Northwest Ordinance.[37]

The conflict over Vincent Duncan's status was a lengthy one, bouncing between the lower and appellate courts and requiring the Missouri Supreme Court to interpret the federal Northwest Ordinance as well as the laws of the state of Illinois. In Vincent's first trial, the St. Louis jury pronounced him a slave. Vincent filed an appeal based on the Circuit Court's failure to give the instructions he asked the judge to present to the jury and the fact that by "the Law of the land it [the judgment] should have been given for the Plaintiff."[38] The Missouri Supreme Court reversed the decision, remanding the case to the lower court for another trial. The court ruled that "if a negro were really hired to work at the Saline for five years, the fact that the negro, at the end of each year, was removed over to Kentucky, and afterwards brought back, would not cure the fraud." However, "if the negro were in good faith hired there for one year only [or, in Vincent's case, one month only], that at the end of the first year he might be again hired another year, without being taken across the line of the State."[39] The Supreme Court also pointed out, "this court has several times decided, that if the owner of slaves took them with him into Illinois, with intent to reside there, and did reside there, keeping his slaves, it was a fraud on the [Northwest] ordinance, and the slave became free. If he stay in Kentucky, and send his slave over to Illinois to reside there, it is equally a violation of the provisions of the ordinance."[40] Finally, the court determined that Vincent's statements that he belonged to James did not prove enslaved status: "Such an admission, made even by a lawyer, would be no evidence."[41] Missouri's courts refused to bend the laws of Illinois to the will of an enslaver.

The Supreme Court instructed the Circuit Court to accept Vincent's claim to freedom based on the Northwest Ordinance. Despite this directive, the Circuit Court continued to thwart Vincent's efforts, resulting in a second jury declaring Vincent a slave. Vincent again appealed the case to the Missouri Supreme Court, which issued another decision reversing the Circuit Court and remanding the case for a third trial. In April 1834, the Circuit Court called another jury to hear Vincent's case, but unfortunately, this is where the records of Vincent's freedom suit end. Although no verdict exists for the third trial in the Circuit Court, additional evidence suggests that Vincent was eventually freed.[42] Vincent's long struggle with multiple trials at various levels of the legal system reveals how difficult it was to adjudicate the complicated issues raised by living near the border of a free state whose laws remained open to interpretation.

Antebellum freedom suits provide one of the best examples for examining the legal relationship between the states because these cases raised prickly questions for judges in slave states—questions that required a certain degree of finesse and that held monumental importance to the sanctity of the federal union. By the early 1820s, Missouri's courts reacted to cases of enslavers traveling or moving to free states with their human property by drawing distinctions based on whether the enslaver *intended* to set up a permanent residence in the new locale.[43] Even so, Missouri's examples represent only a fraction of the numerous cases that arose when citizens of one state came into conflict with the laws of another state. When these conflicts surfaced, judges confronted a multitude of interests, influences, and considerations—including community beliefs and opinions, sectional tensions, and national debates. Judges in each state crafted their own careful responses to these clashing concerns when they issued their decisions, and sometimes one state's judicial traditions shifted in response to the many forces competing for its attention.

Individuals like Thornton Kinney and Vincent Duncan found that the ability to travel between regions could be beneficial, allowing them to form connections and learn of opportunities for greater freedom and autonomy. Enslaved individuals who traveled into free states or free territories with their enslavers could use their residence in free territory as a basis for a successful suit for freedom.[44] The most famous example of this argument is the *Dred Scott* case, which originated in St. Louis in 1846. In a similar case, one enslaved woman based her claim to freedom on her residence at Prairie Du Chien, a military fort on the east side of the Mississippi River in the Wisconsin Territory. Witnesses confirmed that the woman's previous owner held her in slavery at several forts along the Mississippi River in territories where slavery was prohibited.[45] The vast majority of St. Louis's freedom suit plaintiffs based their cases on the movement that resulted between Missouri and the free state of Illinois.

Enslaved persons outside Missouri also took advantage of the fact that enslavers often traveled with their human property through free states, free territories, or to foreign countries. Like the St. Louis example, residence on "free soil" was a common argument for freedom in suits in other places during the antebellum era. Residence in free territory is specifically mentioned in 209 of St. Louis's freedom suits and at least 75 appellate cases, though the issue comes up in additional appellate records even when it is not specified as the argument for freedom.[46] A number of cases based on movement arose in border areas because of how easy it was for enslavers to travel to free states; despite the prohibitions on enslavement, enslavers believed either that *their* enslaved property would never be able to take advantage of their legal rights or that the law protecting travelers would safeguard their property rights. Freedom suits based on interstate migrations are one place where the history of slave law and the history of antebellum expansion and resettlement patterns overlap.

Mobility was central to arguments for freedom based on residence or travel in a free state or free territory, which could involve jurisdictions from across the United States. One plaintiff in Virginia proved that her alleged owner took her to Ohio and immediately sold her to an Ohio resident. After two years of living in Ohio, the alleged owner sold her to the defendant, a resident of Virginia, because the first buyer realized he could not legally keep her enslaved in the free state of Ohio. Although the defendant's counsel claimed that the woman's time spent in Ohio met the requirements for "sojourning" through the free state—a distinction that allowed enslavers to travel safely in free territory without losing their enslaved property—the Virginia Supreme Court affirmed the verdict for her freedom.[47]

When Vincent Duncan convinced the Missouri Supreme Court to free him, he argued that his residence in Illinois should result in his manumission, despite his return to Kentucky. When another Kentucky resident used a similar argument in that state, he convinced the court that he had entered Illinois frequently enough to effect his emancipation—even if he afterward voluntarily returned to the slave state of Kentucky.[48] But voluntary migrations to slave states from free states did not always result in freedom. In a contrasting Kentucky opinion, one enslaved woman sued for freedom after traveling to Ohio for several weeks and returning to her enslaver in Kentucky. The Appeals Court overturned the Circuit Court's opinion for her freedom, suggesting that because the woman had voluntarily returned to Kentucky and had not sued for freedom in Ohio, the laws of Kentucky declared her enslaved. Speaking directly to the issue of comity, one judge's opinion stated,

> The appeal being to the tribunals of Kentucky is, in effect, an appeal to the laws of Kentucky, and must be decided by them; that the laws of no State have, by their own force, any operation beyond the territorial or jurisdictional limits of that State; that it pertains to the sovereignty of every independent State, to determine for itself, and according to its own interests and policy, in what cases and to what extent the foreign law shall be adopted as a part of its own, and operate upon persons and things within its territory . . . no State is bound to admit, or give effect to, a foreign law which violates its own rights or policy, and is destructive of the rights and interests of its citizens.[49]

Here is a blatant disregard for the laws of Ohio and a pledge to support Kentucky's own laws over the laws of other states. In this case, the freed person's voluntary return to a slave state voided the freedom she received by traveling to free territory.

Thornton Kinney did not argue for freedom based on his residence in the free African colony of Liberia, though the argument for freedom based on living in a free territory outside the United States did appear in appellate records from Louisiana, where Kinney spent time in a slave pen awaiting sale. In Louisiana, the argument for freedom based on residence on "free soil" often came from residence in another country where slavery was illegal—usually France or Haiti. For example, when one enslaved woman sued for freedom in Louisiana during the 1830s, she argued that the brief time she spent in France with her mistress should free her. Although the New Orleans Parish Court judge ruled that because the plaintiff's home was Louisiana, her brief stay in France did not free her, the Louisiana Supreme Court reversed the decision and declared her free based on a number of prior rulings about residence on free soil.[50] In another example, a native of Saint-Domingue (the colony that became the country of Haiti) who came to Louisiana from Cuba claimed freedom based on the general emancipation of the Haitian Revolution and because her former owner issued a manumission document to her prior to her arrival in the United States. The woman had to defend multiple attacks on her liberty, but she eventually won freedom in the Louisiana Supreme Court.[51]

Traveling with enslaved individuals into free states or free territories was a primary example of comity, when one state's laws came into conflict with another. Comity was a significant factor in each state's decisions about whether to recognize freedom when an enslaver took enslaved men and women into a free state before returning to a slave state. Some states shifted their willingness to recognize conflicting laws from other states in the later decades prior to the Civil War. The changes that occurred over time did not happen evenly or uniformly, but a discernible uneasiness with granting freedom emerged by the 1840s and 1850s.

Early in the nineteenth century, even a Deep South state like Mississippi was open to freeing enslaved individuals on the basis of residence in free territory. In one 1818 case, the Mississippi Supreme Court freed a group of enslaved persons based on their residence in the Northwest Territory (in the area that became the state of Indiana) from 1784 to 1816. The court's opinion stated, "Slavery is condemned by reason and the laws of nature. It exists and can only exist, through municipal regulations, and in matters of doubt, is it not an unquestioned rule, that courts must lean 'in favorem vitae et libertatis' [in favor of life and liberty]."[52] A statement so clearly in favor of freedom may seem strange coming from Mississippi, unless one considers the timing of the decision. By the late 1810s, Mississippi remained a sparsely settled state; only in the 1830s did cotton become king in the old southwestern states of Mississippi and Louisiana, leading the courts in these regions to tighten restrictions on freedom.[53] In 1824, the Louisiana Supreme Court freed an enslaved woman after her supposed owner moved to Ohio with her. Like Missouri's courts, the

Louisiana Supreme Court distinguished the woman's case from other cases in which an enslaver merely traveled through a free state, explaining that it was the voluntary nature of the enslaver's actions that worked freedom on the enslaved woman. The judge's opinion stated that the decision to free the plaintiff "can work injury to no one—for the principle acts only on the willing."[54] In other words, the Ohio constitution was not intended to punish enslavers; it only freed enslaved persons willingly brought to the state by their enslavers.

The exact timing of the shift varied for each state, but by the late 1840s and 1850s, comity began to break down as sectional tensions over slavery seeped into judicial opinions in both slaveholding and nonslaveholding states. These opinions reveal states' frustration with upholding the rights of citizens of states whose viewpoints on slavery opposed their own. An 1853 Ohio Supreme Court case involved an enslaver suing to recover two promissory notes issued by his enslaved man (and secured by others) for $100 each, in exchange for the man's freedom. The enslaver sued when the freed man and his securities refused to pay because, they argued, the man was already free by virtue of his residence in Ohio after the enslaver had allowed him to travel to the free state several times for "a long space of time, to wit: for the time of one day." Despite the brevity of the man's time in Ohio, which would not allow him to win freedom in slaveholding states like Missouri—though in Missouri, he would certainly have been free if he could prove a longer residence in Ohio—the Ohio Supreme Court agreed with his argument and refused to force him to pay for his freedom.[55] In an 1851 decision, Kentucky's highest court refused to free an enslaved woman on the basis of her travel to Pennsylvania. Although the court suggested that Pennsylvania law could act to free the woman while she was in that state, once she returned to Kentucky, the laws of Kentucky should decide the fate of its residents.[56]

Unsanctioned Movements

In Thornton Kinney's case, his flight from New Orleans back to St. Louis constituted an illicit action, at least in the eyes of his kidnappers. The fluidity of movement between slave and free states also allowed illicit border crossings to affect the personal status of migrants. These unsanctioned migrations resulted in conflicts over slavery and freedom that forced courts to sort out state laws and decide between the arguments of enslavers and enslaved plaintiffs.

St. Louis was a popular place for escaped slaves and for slave catchers who hoped to take advantage of the legal confusion surrounding personal status in the area. The flow of enslaved and free people of color in and out of the city, along with St. Louis's close proximity to Illinois and its location on the banks of the Mississippi River, contributed to its attractiveness for potential runaway slaves. Enslavers in St. Louis, keenly aware of the presence of runaway slaves from elsewhere who had fled to their city, feared their slaves' ability to run away. For this reason, some enslavers took precautions to prevent their property from absconding, including the preventive step of temporarily placing troublesome slaves in the St. Louis jail for "safekeeping." One freedom suit plaintiff considered running away after his former owner died and the administrator of the owner's estate claimed him as a slave. In a document filed with the court, the administrator complained that "particularly since the death of . . . Gabriel Paul [the initial enslaver], he [the plaintiff] has so comforted himself as almost to be utterly worthless, and in a great degree unmanageable, and within the past few days, gave by his actions . . . reasonable grounds for supposing that he will abscond" unless the court helped prevent this by taking him "into immediate custody" until the end of his freedom suit.[57] Because of the defendant's fear that the plaintiff would run away, he asked the court to secure the plaintiff in jail to prevent his escape. The file in this case is incomplete, but additional legal records show that the court continued it for several years until the plaintiff defaulted by failing to appear and the court granted costs to the defendant.[58] Although it is impossible to determine what happened to the plaintiff to end his freedom suit, the mobility and anonymity made possible in an urban area like St. Louis suggest that he may have eventually escaped and run away to freedom; in another potential scenario, the administrator may have prevented the plaintiff from appearing in court by removing him from St. Louis or even selling him down the river.

The Mississippi River allowed for escaped slaves to journey to St. Louis from further south. Although runaway slaves in St. Louis were most often individuals traveling from the interior of Missouri across the Mississippi into Illinois, enslaved persons traveling upriver could also stop in the city. For example, the plaintiff in an 1826 freedom suit, who based his freedom on his birth in Illinois, related to the court his story of escape up the Mississippi River. The man's alleged owner sent him to New Orleans and instructed a slave trader to sell him into slavery. While the plaintiff worked for his new enslaver in Louisiana, "being indignant at the injustice & oppression fraud & injustice thus inflicted upon him," he managed to escape—as Thornton Kinney did—and "after many hardships" returned to freedom in Illinois. The case file does not specify the "hardships" he experienced or how he managed to travel back to Illinois, but it is not difficult to imagine that the plaintiff may have stowed away on a steamboat traveling north or possibly posed as a free man of color working on a boat headed upriver.[59] Although his alleged owner transported him down the river to New Orleans for sale, the plaintiff was also able to employ knowledge of the river to journey back to Illinois and eventually to bring suit for freedom in the river city of St. Louis.

Interstate mobility brought certain advantages to enslaved and free people of African descent, but enslavers also recognized the border's opportunities; in some instances, enslavers chose to flee across that border with their enslaved property in the hopes that the fluid nature of personal status would protect their claims to enslaved men and women. When trying to avoid prosecution in St. Louis freedom suits, enslavers routinely fled the jurisdiction of the court, a fact that suggests the messiness of slavery and freedom in this region as well as the determination of enslavers to maintain their property rights. Although most enslavers removing enslaved plaintiffs from the court's jurisdiction carried them further south, St. Louis's proximity to the Northwest Territory allowed enslavers to remove their human property to areas in the North—usually this meant Illinois. Ironically, enslavers took these enslaved plaintiffs from a slave state to a free state (or free territory) to avoid losing their enslaved property. For example, when one plaintiff argued for freedom based on his birth and residence in Illinois, his enslaver tried to prevent prosecution by having the man "seized in the public streets of the City of St. Louis" and taken to the jail of St. Clair County, Illinois, where "the jail of said County refused to take Charge of your petitioner on the ground that there was no offense alledged against your petitioner."[60] It is possible that the enslaver ran to friends, relatives, or other contacts in Illinois, although her exact reasons for this move are not explained in the case file. In both Missouri and Illinois, some individuals tried to clarify their state's position in the debate over personal status. In this case, the Illinois jailer refused to help an enslaver keep her alleged slave imprisoned in a free state. After the jailer refused to hold the plaintiff, the plaintiff managed to escape during the night and return to St. Louis.[61] His choice to leave the free state of Illinois and travel to the slave state of Missouri to sue for his freedom seems peculiar unless one considers the unique situation of life in this border region or the possibility that the plaintiff returned to friends or loved ones in St. Louis.

Thornton Kinney's story demonstrates that forced migration was another possibility for people of African descent—especially individuals living and working along borders. The possibility of kidnapping could illegally shift a free person's status to permanent slavery. Kidnapping was an ever-present threat for free people of color throughout America but especially for those living in border regions, where kidnappers could more easily dispose of their human cargo.[62] Racism, a hugely profitable domestic slave trade, and a legal system designed primarily to protect slavery all combined to facilitate kidnapping of free people of color for sale as slaves. Kidnapping occurred with greater frequency in the North, and it became institutionalized in the antebellum years with the closing of the Atlantic slave trade. Kidnapping exposed the artificiality of the categories of slavery and freedom because people could be legally free and recognized as free in their community, but when forcibly removed from their homes, new communities could declare them enslaved and treat them as such. The precarious nature of freedom for free people of color becomes evident in the numerous stories of kidnapping victims found in the St. Louis Circuit Court. After removing people from their homes, kidnappers easily passed them off as enslaved because of the widespread legal presumption that all people of African descent were enslaved. This story repeated itself numerous times across the country.

Kidnappers operated all over the United States, and ironically, while the close proximity of St. Louis to the Northwest Territory provided enslaved individuals in Missouri recourse to an argument for freedom, it also rendered free blacks in the Old Northwest vulnerable to kidnappers operating out of Missouri. For example, a group of kidnappers stole a young child living in Illinois and absconded to Missouri to sell her into slavery. The young woman brought suit for freedom several years later, stating in her petition that "she was born free as she believes, in the Territory of Illinois and . . . after this Territory had been admitted into the Union as a free state, she was brought forcibly into Boonville Missouri." Her petition goes on to argue that at the time of her removal, "she was in infancy and without knowledge of her rights, and when she had no one to protect her, and since she was then brought into Missouri she has been wrongfully held as a slave."[63] In a similar group of cases, an enslaved woman and her two children sued their enslaver for kidnapping them from Illinois. The woman complained in her petition that they were "violently taken away in the night time" and brought to St. Louis as slaves, though the petition argued that she and her children were free both because of previous deeds of emancipation that had been filed for them in Indiana's courts and because of their residence for over six months in Illinois.[64] After a long and complicated legal struggle, the group of plaintiffs won their freedom in court, but this single act of kidnapping created untold misery and hardships for the young mother and her small children, separating them from their father and their home, as well as depriving them of the freedom they enjoyed in Illinois. At least twenty-seven freedom suits in St. Louis raised the argument of kidnapping as a reason for the court to grant freedom, and countless other victims of these crimes most likely failed to bring their grievances to court. St. Louis's geographic location could bring opportunities for African-descended people, but the benefits of mobility were coupled with threats to their free status.

Kidnapping not only affected free people of color in and around St. Louis; it was a national problem that raised questions about identity and presumptions about personal status. For example, a Virginia victim claimed that kidnappers stole her from her mother, a free woman of color, forty to fifty years prior to her case. Although the Lynchburg Chancery Court ruled for the woman's freedom in 1822, six years later the Virginia Supreme Court narrowly decided to reverse the decision and allow the defendant to challenge the evidence presented, specifically to impugn the character of witnesses who testified about a scar that matched the kidnapped victim.[65] Relying on witness testimony of the plaintiff's physical appearance, she hoped to prove her identity on the basis of a scar that was identical to that of a known kidnapped young woman who shared her name. Even after proving her case despite the presumption that attached after forty to fifty years in slavery, the woman returned to the County Court to defend her free status as a victim of kidnapping. When a group of South Carolina enslaved persons won freedom in 1843, the South Carolina Supreme Court's opinion specifically explained the existence of a presumption of freedom after the individuals in question had lived for over twenty years as free, and it also referenced an 1837 statute against kidnapping free people of color with the intent of depriving them of liberty.[66] These cases highlight how difficult it could be for a victim of kidnapping to bring a suit for freedom, as well as the types of evidentiary discussions that arose in cases of this nature—forcing multiple jurisdictions to sort out their positions on these complex legal questions.

Restricting Mobility

When Thornton Kinney returned from his extended sojourn in Liberia, no legal restrictions kept him from reentering the United States. He informed the court of the actions he took to secure free papers, which would allow him to resume his occupation on steamboats traveling the Mississippi River system. For much of the antebellum period, Missouri's laws permitted most travelers to move in and out of the state with few constraints. But what happened when states tried to limit interstate mobility? States sometimes limited the movement of enslavers bringing enslaved persons to their state, and other times, states tried to prevent free people of African descent from crossing their borders. State statutes that restricted or prohibited mobility held the possibility for conflict over personal status when enslavers and others flouted prohibitions and continued to move freely across borders.

One category of cases involved states that limited the importation of enslaved persons for sale, either because of a large existing slave population or because of specific fears about the types of enslaved persons brought to the state. Enslavers fleeing the Haitian Revolution often came to the United States with their enslaved property, hoping to maintain their ownership of African-descended laborers through their migration in the midst of the uprising in Saint-Domingue. Freedom suits involving Haitian refugees, while not a large percentage of freedom suits in any jurisdiction, arose in states that tried to regulate or prohibit the importation of immigrants whose slaves were viewed as "dangerous" or possibly infected with ideas about violent slave uprisings that might influence America's slave populations.[67] For example, Maryland passed a 1792 statute limiting the number of slaves brought to the state by any migrant from the "French islands" and requiring migrants to register their slaves within three months. A handful of appellate cases concerned this statute, including an example of a defendant who brought the plaintiff to Maryland to work as a domestic slave and registered him within the required period of time. The Maryland Supreme Court found for the plaintiff's freedom, most likely because the defendant was a resident of France rather than the French Islands.[68] When a group of enslaved individuals from Saint-Domingue sued for freedom after arriving in Baltimore from New York—where their alleged owner had lived before moving south for "her health"—they lost their freedom suit because the defendant claimed she never *intended* to remain in the United States. The defendant had never become a citizen of the country or of the state of Maryland, so the Maryland Supreme Court affirmed the Baltimore City Court's finding that the alleged owner's plan to return to her native country once "the troubles there had ceased" exempted her from the requirement to register her slaves within three months.[69]

States in the Chesapeake region—where soil exhaustion and the resulting diversification of agriculture meant a declining need for the large enslaved population already living there—passed laws in the 1790s and early 1800s that regulated or prohibited the importation of enslaved individuals from other states. By attempting to curb the in-migration of enslaved individuals, these border areas not only protected the property investments of their states' enslavers but also challenged the authority of enslavers to move their enslaved men and women throughout the country. Maryland's law against bringing slaves into the state after 1796 for sale within three years of arrival generated a whole body of case law in Maryland's courts (as well as in the part of that state that became the District of Columbia). For example, in 1817, the Maryland Supreme Court freed an enslaved man because his owner failed to properly register him.[70] Decades later, the Maryland Court of Appeals reversed the Circuit Court's ruling against the freedom of one enslaved mother and her children. The woman's alleged owner had taken her family to Missouri for over a year, then returned to Maryland and brought the plaintiff and her family with him. Maryland passed a new law in 1831 to limit the growth of the state's enslaved population by prohibiting the importation of enslaved persons into the state for any reason. In this case, the Court of Appeals determined that the plaintiff's alleged owner's move to Missouri for over a year did forfeit his residence in Maryland, so the appellate court required the lower court to instruct the jury that the alleged owner's state citizenship had changed. When he returned to Maryland with his human property, the law operated to free them under the provision against slave importation.[71]

Laws restricting movement continued when the United States built its new capital city out of counties from Maryland and Virginia. In response, dozens of African-descended people used Maryland's importation law to sue for freedom after their alleged owners moved to the new District of Columbia. The argument against illegal importation accounts for forty-two of the ninety-one District of Columbia freedom suits located in the appellate record (46 percent). In one of the earliest cases, an enslaved man won his freedom when his alleged owner moved from Maryland to Alexandria County in the District of Columbia.[72] A couple of years later, the D.C. Circuit Court freed the man when it determined that his supposed owner's last-minute effort to register him according to the Maryland law was insufficient. This case also set a precedent of the D.C. Circuit Court refusing to grant back wages—that is, financial restitution to persons illegally held as slaves when they should have been free and earning wages—to enslaved plaintiffs freed by the Maryland statute.[73] Like the numerous state courts that ruled that temporary residence in a free state or free territory failed to free a person held in slavery, the U.S. Supreme Court determined in an 1816 case that the plaintiff's temporary residence in D.C.—for less than a year—with the person who hired her time (not her true owner) did not free her.[74] In an 1823 case, the D.C. Circuit Court stated in its opinion that "the Maryland act was very obscure," and it determined that the plaintiff's alleged owner never intended to settle in D.C. (he moved to Virginia immediately after purchasing the plaintiff) and therefore did not violate the statute.[75] Examples abound of similar freedom suits in the courts of the District of Columbia. For these men and women, the shift in jurisdiction when the District of Columbia formed, coupled with the migrations of their alleged owners, resulted in the opportunity to seek legal freedom through the courts.[76]

State efforts to limit mobility sometimes protected the status of people of African descent. For example, Pennsylvania's Emancipation Act prohibited enslavers from removing pregnant slaves from the state, a clause intended to keep their children in the state and provide them with freedom once they reached adulthood. In a group of cases decided in Kentucky, the children of an enslaved Pennsylvania woman sued based on this protection. Kentucky's Court of Appeals ruled that they were enslaved based on their mother's status, even though the express intent of the Pennsylvania prohibition was to prevent enslavers from removing pregnant slaves to secure property rights to these children (who should have been free if born in Pennsylvania). Kentucky's court refused to enforce the Pennsylvania law, finding instead that the doctrine of *partus sequitur ventrum*—the status of the children followed that of the mother—meant that the children in this group of cases were legally enslaved.[77] Although Pennsylvania tried to protect enslaved mothers and their children from forced migrations, courts in slaveholding states did not always recognize or respect other states' laws or protections of their freedom.

Restricting mobility could also result in blocking access to freedom. Missouri allowed enslavers to manumit enslaved persons by will throughout the antebellum era, but enslavers in other states who wished to free their slaves sometimes needed to send them to another state to effect their manumission. When individuals tried to sidestep the requirements of their state's laws, the resulting conflicts brought issues of comity before the courts. In one example, the Tennessee Supreme Court decided against the validity of a North Carolina enslaver's will that directed the will's executors to take the enslaver's human property to Ohio and free them. When the executor failed to execute this bequest and instead delivered the enslaved persons to the heirs—who then brought them to Tennessee—the Tennessee Supreme Court upheld the verdict against the enslaved persons' freedom because the will was "contrary both to the law and policy of the State [of North Carolina]." In addition, the court refused freedom because Ohio's laws made it illegal to bring enslaved persons to that state for the purpose of freeing them and even required a $500 bond for bringing free people of color into the state, making it prohibitively expensive for the executor to free the fifty enslaved individuals in question in this case.[78] The fate of fifty people depended on the court's ruling in this case, making it significant not only for those individuals whose lives hung in the balance but also for the heirs, who hoped to reap a considerable financial benefit if the court included the enslaved plaintiffs in the enslaver's estate. The case forced Tennessee's judges to familiarize themselves with the laws of two states to make a decision that would follow as closely as possible their own laws and those of their sister states regarding movement of enslavers and their human property.

Conflicts over property and inheritance could bring similar questions about movement to state courts. When a Mississippi enslaver willed all of his property to his son—whom he had previously taken to Ohio and freed by issuing a deed of manumission to the man and his mother— the enslaver's heirs challenged the will. They claimed the manumission was void because it violated Mississippi's laws, and therefore the son was a slave who could not inherit the property.[79] The Mississippi Supreme Court agreed because it decided that the enslaver's actions were designed to evade the laws of the state of Mississippi. In its written opinion, the court declared that the son and his mother were enslaved, insisting that the doctrine of comity "is subject to exceptions. No state is bound to recognise or enforce a contract made elsewhere, which would injure the state or its citizens; or which would exhibit to the citizens an example pernicious and detestable." Because the court determined that "the contract had its origin in an offence against morality" and that the enslaver's will "seems to have been planned and executed with a fixed design to evade the rigor of the laws of this state," the manumission and bequest were void—a decision that reenslaved the enslaver's son and his mother, declaring them to be "a part of the estate."[80] As the Mississippi Supreme Court's language in its opinion makes clear, the enslaver's actions combined questions of comity with the violation of Mississippi's racial and sexual standards of practice: a fateful combination that resulted in his son's shift from inheriting the substantial property of the estate to being considered part of the estate's inheritable property.[81]

One additional type of convergence also affected the prosecution of suits for freedom: the meeting of personal and property law. When enslaved men, women, and children became plaintiffs in freedom suits—often the only type of lawsuit they could legally initiate—they forced courts to wade through the muddied waters of personal and property claims. The courts recognized enslaved individuals' humanity. It was no contradiction for certain categories of persons to lack particular types of legal rights. But ordinarily, enslaved individuals' involvement in lawsuits placed them into one of two categories: as persons or as property belonging to other persons. In freedom suits, these two elements of the law of slavery often combined, confusing the false distinctions that were sometimes asserted in other areas of slave law. A look at how these categories blurred together in freedom lawsuits also speaks to the ways in which enslaved individuals made arrangements with their enslavers—for freedom, for greater autonomy, or for their children—expanding the legal culture of slavery to encompass a variety of external negotiations.

5 /   Double Character

The events of the night Milton Duty died remain shrouded in suspicion. According to Duty's administrator, George Coons, Coons came to Duty's house that night at the request of one of Duty's slaves. Once Coons arrived, he "examined the corpse and observed that it looked very dark, and that there were other remarkable appearances about it."[1] Perhaps insinuating foul play, Coons told the court that he questioned several of Duty's slaves about the cause of their enslaver's death. In reply, the men and women, who later became plaintiffs in a series of freedom suits, told Coons that Duty fell ill that day and took calomel, drank some cold water, and died in the arms of one of the neighbors.

Coons's wary attitude was in response to accusations made by the enslaved plaintiffs about his own behavior that night. Duty's former slaves claimed that, on the night Duty died, Coons and another man "came into the room where the corpse was lying and without inquiring further than to ascertain that . . . Duty was certainly dead," asked one of the slaves to bring them the trunk containing Duty's personal papers. Coons and his agent then conducted a "hurried search" of these papers and, in the presence of Duty's slaves and several witnesses, "tore up and destroyed several of said papers and took others away."[2] One witness to the events recalled asking Coons "why he was disturbing the papers of the deceased before his body was entirely cold, to which he replied that he could not help it."[3] Although Coons admitted to examining Duty's papers that night, he adamantly denied that any "receipt, note, evidence of debt, memorandum, or valuable paper of any kind" was "ever destroyed, torn up, obstructed, or suppressed" by him or any of his representatives.[4]

Milton Duty was a Mississippi pork farmer who published a will freeing all of his slaves shortly before moving to St. Louis in 1836. His death in 1838 began more than a decade of contests over the manumission clause in his will. The fighting began when David Coons, the father of George Coons, made a debt claim on Duty's estate and requested permission from the court to sell several of the enslaved persons to cover this debt. These enslaved persons then filed suit for freedom, arguing that even if Duty was indebted to Coons, there were other options for paying the claim, including hiring them out or collecting money from Duty's remaining property in Mississippi. The fact that Duty's slaves were subject to sale to cover the costs of his debts reminds us of the property-like characteristics of enslaved individuals. But the subsequent freedom suits also forced the court to consider the legal personhood and actions of Duty's human property. George Coons's insistence that the slaves requested his presence that night, and his suggestion of their role in Duty's death, indicate his willingness for the court to consider them legal actors who could be held responsible for this alleged wrongdoing. At the same time, he demanded that the court consider them property subject to sale to cover the debts of the estate.

The freedom suits of Duty's slaves put their classification as legal persons and as property into direct conflict. Legal scholars have long noted the "double character" of enslaved men and women as both persons and property before the law, an idea first recorded in the Georgia jurist Thomas R. R. Cobb's 1858 treatise *An Inquiry into the Law of Negro Slavery in the United States of America*.[5] As evident from Cobb's treatise, the nineteenth-century legal community recognized and discussed the double character of slaves. Jurists, the general public, and even defendants in freedom suits rarely denied the humanity of enslaved persons because it was a fact that was too obvious to ignore. But when aspects of slaves' legal personhood combined or conflicted with enslavers' property rights, the double character of enslaved persons forced the inherent contradictions in the nature of the law of slavery into the center of public discourse.

Freedom suits flip the perspective of the historian Ariela Gross's excellent book on the double character of slaves in disputes over property transactions. In freedom suits, the primary determination was about personal status, and therefore courts had to determine whether to elevate property concerns over the legal personhood of enslaved plaintiffs. Like the property disputes in Gross's study, freedom suits were an area of law that highlighted slaves' double character, forcing judges and juries to consider slaves as people alongside their considerations of slaves as property "*at one and the same time.*"[6] While Gross's book examines property disputes between white enslavers and community members, in which enslaved men and women found indirect ways to influence the legal process, suits for freedom directly involved African Americans as litigants initiating their own legal processes. The primary question in a freedom suit was whether the alleged slave was a free *person* or enslaved *property*, with all of the implications for property law that such status conferred. When studying suits for freedom, the property aspects of slave law cannot be separated from the law's treatment of enslaved persons as legal actors. Instead, freedom suits were a type of legal action that underlined this double character and embraced its tensions.

This chapter explores interactions between enslavers and enslaved individuals that point to the central inconsistency in the law of slavery: enslaved persons could be categorized as chattel property or as legal persons, and sometimes as both, in a single lawsuit. Freedom suits, by their nature, forced courts to wrestle with these ambiguous distinctions. For this reason, all freedom suits involve the double character of slavery, but there are certain aspects of this body of case law that highlight this duality.

Manumission

As in the case of Milton Duty's slaves, freedom suits based on manumission are the most obvious example of enslaved persons' double character. This type of freedom suit raised property issues in a few significant ways. When disputes arose over manumission, the heirs of an enslaver or the enslaver's creditors often sought the property rights to the enslaved person. Sometimes these disputes resulted in the sale of the enslaved person as property of the estate, leading to the painful destruction of that person's relationships. In other instances, disputes over an enslaver's estate might deprive the person's heirs of their inheritance or lead to additional lawsuits to work out the details of promises made and broken by enslavers' choice to free their human property. The antebellum decades brought a shift in statutes concerning manumission; by the 1830s and 1840s, many states sought to limit access to freedom in order to minimize the number of free people of color in their state and to more fully secure the value of enslaved property. Limiting access to manumission was one way states handled the question of property rights versus personal status, coming down squarely on the side of the former.

Manumission by will remained legal in Missouri throughout the antebellum years, though other states sometimes restricted enslavers' ability to free their slaves by will. Milton Duty's death set off years of legal wrangling over the status of his slaves, as property that could be sold to cover debts of the estate or as free persons, per Duty's instruction in his will. Manumission by will made up about a quarter of the sixty-two manumission freedom suits in the St. Louis Circuit Court, and these disputes made up a significant portion of appellate freedom suits from elsewhere (appearing in at least 290 state supreme court freedom suits).[7] Freeing enslaved persons by will was a way for enslavers to leave freedom to their human property without losing any of their value or services during the enslaver's lifetime. The most famous example of this phenomenon is George Washington, who did not free any enslaved individuals during his life but freed them all by will.[8] Manumission by will was sometimes used as a way of confirming or solidifying earlier emancipatory acts, such as freeing an enslaved person by deed, taking enslaved individuals to free territory, or simply releasing a person from bondage and allowing him or her to live as free. When an enslaver freed an enslaved person by will, it was usually—though not always—the enslaver's heirs who contested the person's freedom because that status threatened their inheritance or the monetary value of the estate.

Heirs contested bequests of freedom because they wanted to enrich themselves through their ancestor's estate—including the estate's alleged slaves. For example, when Mary Ann Steel sued for freedom in St. Louis in 1835, she claimed freedom based on her former enslaver, Catherine Steel, setting her free in her will. Catherine claimed ownership of Mary Ann on the basis of the will of Mary Ann's initial enslaver, James Steel, and it was James's descendants who contested the manumission in Catherine Steel's will. After Catherine died, James's heirs claimed that her will was "inoperative" and asked that Mary Ann be sold and "the proceeds divided among the heirs of James Steel."[9] In response, Mary Ann's witness stated that "the Instrument of writing made by Catharine Steel . . . was good & effectual . . . to liberate your Petitioner."[10] Similarly, in an 1848 Kentucky case, the heirs of one enslaver contested the validity of the will freeing her human property and went so far as to deny their own role as witnesses to the will. One of the heirs went to court and denied that he had signed and witnessed the will as required by law, which caused the Probate Court to declare the will invalid. The woman freed by the will sued for freedom based on this attempted fraud and won. After her death, her two children found themselves enslaved by the heirs. When the Kentucky Supreme Court affirmed a decision for their freedom, it noted that the enslaved children did not "specify in their pleadings, the facts or the particular ground of relief above set forth. But they profess an ignorance which may be readily excused."[11] In other words, the court signaled its willingness to interpret the law in a manner favoring freedom over supposed property rights, even when the procedural requirements were not followed to the letter of the law.

Requirements for manumission varied widely across the slaveholding states during the antebellum period. Missouri allowed manumission by will—of enslaved persons deemed of "sound mind and body" and younger than forty-five, to prevent the freed person from becoming a public charge—throughout the antebellum years, making disputes that questioned the legality of manumissions by will more unusual in St. Louis than in other jurisdictions.[12] Some states prohibited manumission by will within the state but allowed enslavers to take enslaved persons out of their state of residence in order to free them. Other states did not have detailed statutes outlining their requirements—creating a host of problems for courts throughout the country.[13] Deciding whether to allow a manumission by will meant determining whether a particular state's laws allowed for enslavers to elevate the rights of enslaved persons over the property rights of the enslaver's heirs.

Conflicts over the interpretation of varying state manumission laws forced courts to directly confront the double character of slavery when making determinations of enslaved persons' legal status. For example, an 1852 case led the Alabama Supreme Court to decide what type of rules would govern manumissions by will in the state. In that case, an Alabama resident died and left freedom to several of his slaves, along with large monetary bequests to two former slaves who lived in Ohio. When the enslaver's heirs sued to prevent the executor from taking several of the individuals freed by the will to Ohio to legally manumit them, the County Court agreed, citing an Alabama statute prohibiting manumission by will. The Alabama Supreme Court reversed this ruling and remanded the case, determining that the monetary bequests to the freed persons living in Ohio at the time of the will were valid and that the enslaved individuals in Alabama could be taken to Ohio and freed. Once the newly freed persons arrived in Ohio, their free status—and therefore their legal personhood—allowed them to acquire property, so the court also instructed the executor to pay monetary bequests to this group of people living in slavery in Alabama at the time of the decision.[14] In an interesting interpretive twist on this line of thinking, when the Louisiana Supreme Court tried to follow Alabama's rules on manumission, it refused to *force* a legatee of an Alabama will to take the enslaver's human property to a free state to free them. The Louisiana Supreme Court concluded that this type of request must be performed voluntarily.[15]

Manumission requirements in many slaveholding states shifted in the face of rising sectional tensions and growing proslavery radicalism during the 1840s and 1850s, with rules regulating manumission and other avenues to freedom for enslaved individuals often becoming stricter.[16] Missouri continued to allow manumission but did expand other restrictions on freedom. These increasing restrictions on people of African descent are particularly evident in the written opinions of appellate courts, which strove to define the outlines of freedom and slavery and to provide a resolution to the many questions raised in complicated disputes over human property. South Carolina's laws and its ideology are perhaps the best example of the radical turnaround in thinking of a state's appellate courts. In an 1823 case, the Constitutional Court of Appeals of South Carolina affirmed the freedom of a man freed by his enslaver's will who was allowed to live as free for two years before the enslaver's creditors challenged his status. After determining that the estate held enough assets to cover its debts, the court's opinion asked, "Why should this creditor therefore have invaded the *sanctuary of freedom*, to come at his rights?"[17] Thirty years later, the South Carolina Court of Appeals of Equity, explaining the development of the state's increasingly strict manumission law, offered a blunt statement of its racial ideology: "This race, however conducive they may be in a state of slavery, to the advance of civilization, (by the results of their valuable labors,) in a state of freedom, and in the midst of a civilized community, are a dead weight to the progress of improvement."[18] This last statement contrasts sharply with the first opinion's reference to the "sanctuary of freedom," an indication of how drastically a state's legal reasoning could change during the antebellum years.[19]

Manumission by will commonly included an arrangement for an enslaved individual to be freed at some future time, either by specifying a number of years of continued service or by stating an age at which the person should be freed.[20] When manumission by will included these specifications for future freedom (what courts termed *manumission in futuro*), it consigned the person or people in question to a sort of legal limbo, a quasi-freedom that left them vulnerable to threats to their liberty.[21] Enslaved individuals who were to be free at a future date found themselves having to defend their status before they had fully realized the benefits of this freedom.[22]

When an enslaver's will granted freedom at a future date, relatives or other interested persons—hoping to capitalize on the uncertain status of people of African descent—asserted property rights that threatened the legal autonomy of manumitted individuals. In the St. Louis case of a woman and her two small children, their status as "slaves for a term" left them vulnerable to a group of individuals who claimed them as slaves for life and tried to sell them down the Mississippi River.[23] The plaintiff in this case lived in Mississippi with her enslaver, whose will specified that the woman serve the person's heir until she reached age twenty-one, after which time she would be free. The heir took the plaintiff to Illinois, where he allowed her to live with a relative. The woman eventually agreed to travel to St. Louis to attend to her enslaver's sick daughter, "with whom she was reared from early infancy" and for whom she "continued to feel a strong affection."[24] When the daughter returned to Mississippi, she left the plaintiff behind with a man who, "under some pretence of right," sold her to another man, who sold her again to the defendant in her freedom suit.[25] The woman and her children sued for freedom with the aid of an Illinois relative who acted as a next friend, or legal representative. The court returned the woman and her children to their Illinois relatives in an arrangement that included dismissing their freedom suits.[26] In this case, the court agreed to allow the plaintiff and her sons to return to their family, who most likely saw to their emancipation after the woman's twenty-first birthday.

Manumission *in futuro* raised questions about the precise status of an enslaved individual whose enslaver had freed him or her at a future date. Did manumitted persons become free, or did their status become something in between slavery and freedom? In cases of enslaved families, the answer to this question dictated the lifetime status of any children born in the interim period between the manumission's publication (either in a will or in a deed) and the point at which it took full effect. In 1836, a Kentucky resident sued for freedom based on his birth during the period between his mother's initial manumission by will and the date at which her freedom commenced. The Kentucky Supreme Court upheld the ruling for his freedom, citing language in the will indicating that because the manumission was motivated by "a clear CONVICTION of the injustice and CRIMINALITY of slavery" and because of "the fact that . . . he [the slaveholder] denominates his emancipated slaves 'the said PEOPLE,' implies that he no longer deemed them slaves, or was willing even to characterize them by a servile appellation."[27] In this instance, the court specifically mentions the use of the term "people" in the enslaver's will, elevating the plaintiff's personal status over the property rights of the enslaver's heirs.[28]

Milton Duty's slaves became involved in one of the lengthiest contests over an enslaver's will in St. Louis, with the last record dated fourteen years after Duty's death. In these suits, approximately thirty enslaved persons—the number fluctuated throughout the lengthy legal disputes, as some plaintiffs died and others had children—sued for freedom based on their manumission in Duty's will. The contest over their freedom centered on the debt claims on Duty's estate, the largest of which was made by the father of his administrator, George Coons, who served as Duty's financial agent after his arrival in St. Louis. If Duty was deeply in debt at the time of his death, his obligations could invalidate the bequest of freedom to his human property because the enslaved persons would be subject to sale to cover the estate's debts.

The complex and contradictory tales of Duty's finances that emerged through the multiple, prolonged disputes over the status of the enslaved plaintiffs highlight the double character of persons held in slavery. Preston, Braxton, Mary, and Duty's other slaves explained in their petition to the court that when Duty brought them to St. Louis, he hired them out and appointed David Coons his "financial agent." Coons controlled "all money arising from the hires" of the enslaved plaintiffs.[29] The plaintiffs admitted that Duty had borrowed "three or four thousand dollars" from Coons to cover immediate expenses in his pork business, but their petition also insisted that in 1837, Duty "must have extinguished all the claims of said Coons for money advanced" through the proceeds of a trip to Mississippi to sell Duty's pork and the funds Coons received from hiring out the plaintiffs.[30] If these funds did not cover all of the debts, the plaintiffs argued, then surely the funds Coons received from hiring them out after Duty's death would suffice to pay the obligations. Finally, the plaintiffs accused Coons of making a fraudulent claim for debt on the estate, insisting that Coons issued receipts for Duty's payments to him, but they must have been among the papers George Coons destroyed the night Duty died. Whereas the enslaved plaintiffs had emphasized Duty's solid financial standing at the time of his death, George Coons claimed that Duty was deeply in debt, that he was losing money from his pork business, and that only by selling the enslaved persons could he hope to recoup the thousands of dollars his father had lent to Duty. George

Coons recalled that Duty "met with a heavy loss in his pork business" and that when Duty traveled to Mississippi to receive the profits of the sale of his pork, he "failed to collect any of the proceeds of the sale of his pork." After detailing the advances made by David Coons to Duty, George Coons insisted that "he utterly denies each and every charge, allegation, or insinuation of fraud against him" and that "all the said charges are false."[31] The conflicting accounts of Duty's life and death also reflected an awareness of the personal responsibility of enslaved plaintiffs, even while trying to defend claims to them as property of the estate.

Missouri allowed manumission by will, as evidenced by the suits of Duty's slaves, as long as the estate did not have debts. Kentucky sometimes gave a more generous construction of the laws surrounding manumission by will—one that provided a degree of protection to the people whose enslavers wished to free them—ruling that enslaved persons manumitted by an enslaver's will were not subject to sale to satisfy the debts of the enslaver. When one man sued for freedom to prevent his sale to satisfy his prior enslaver's debts, the Kentucky Supreme Court reversed the County Court's ruling and declared that "a slave emancipated by will, is not assets in the hands of the executor, but that the title to freedom passes to the beneficiary immediately, and the assent of the executor is, consequently, in no degree necessary for the perfect consummation and instantaneous enjoyment of it."[32] Similarly, in another freedom suit brought to prevent the plaintiff's sale after his alleged owner died and left an insolvent estate, the Kentucky Supreme Court again protected a manumitted person's freedom over the enslaver's property rights, stating in its opinion, "And the slave is free, because the title to him, as a slave, has passed from his master to him. If he is emancipated by will, the title passes to him by the will."[33] This pair of decisions indicates Kentucky's willingness, in certain instances, to interpret the rights of enslavers to free enslaved persons as absolute and not subject to claims by the person's heirs or creditors.

Manumission by deed involved a slightly different—though related—set of issues from manumissions by will for enslavers and the individuals they freed. Freeing a person by a deed of manumission meant setting the individual free while the enslaver was still living. Challenges to manumissions by deed, like manumissions by will, tended to come from creditors or heirs of the enslaver, but when an alleged owner manumitted persons by deed during his or her lifetime, that same person sometimes challenged the former slaves' freedom. In both types of manumission, shifts in statutes and litigation tended to result in increasingly difficult paths for legalizing these bequests of freedom. For example, an enslaved mother and her six children sued for freedom in St. Louis based on a deed of manumission issued in Maryland for the plaintiff, her siblings, and her mother, once each of them reached the age of twenty-one. At the time of the suit, the plaintiff claimed to be fifty-five years old, and a witness for her case stated that the alleged owner was "in good health & his mind sound & unimpaired" when he presented the deed of manumission.[34] The copy of the deed of manumission helped this mother and her family win freedom in St. Louis after years of illegal enslavement. A similar group of enslaved plaintiffs filed a joint suit for freedom based on a manumission deed from their former enslaver, until agents of that person's estate seized them and committed them to jail on a property claim.[35] Disputes over manumission deeds arose in St. Louis in at least thirty-two cases, but these contests emerged in freedom suits outside Missouri as well.

Though often involving certain arrangements for freedom, enslavers freed their human property—both by deed and by will—for a variety of reasons that could result in disputes over the status of the people freed in the deed. In one striking case from the District of Columbia, the D.C. Circuit Court ruled against the freedom of a group of people when the enslaver's estranged wife argued that he freed his slaves in an attempt to defraud her of the value of his estate before the division of assets took place in her divorce suit. Although it is impossible to determine this enslaver's true motives, the suggestion that he wanted to free his enslaved persons only to cheat his wife out of their value illustrates the range of reasons enslavers might have had to relinquish their rights to their valuable human property.[36]

When deeds of manumission specified freedom at a future date (manumissions *in futuro*), states had to determine the rules governing the status of these individuals during the period after the manumission but before their freedom commenced, which, as in cases of manumission by will, was especially a concern for women and the children they bore during their interim status. A North Carolina case illustrates the confusion that ensued and the complicated issues raised in these situations. The plaintiff in this case sued for freedom based on the manumission of his grandmother. His mother was born during the interim period between the issuance of the grandmother's deed of manumission and the execution of her freedom. The North Carolina Supreme Court ruled against the plaintiff's freedom despite his arrival in North Carolina years earlier with his mother and their years

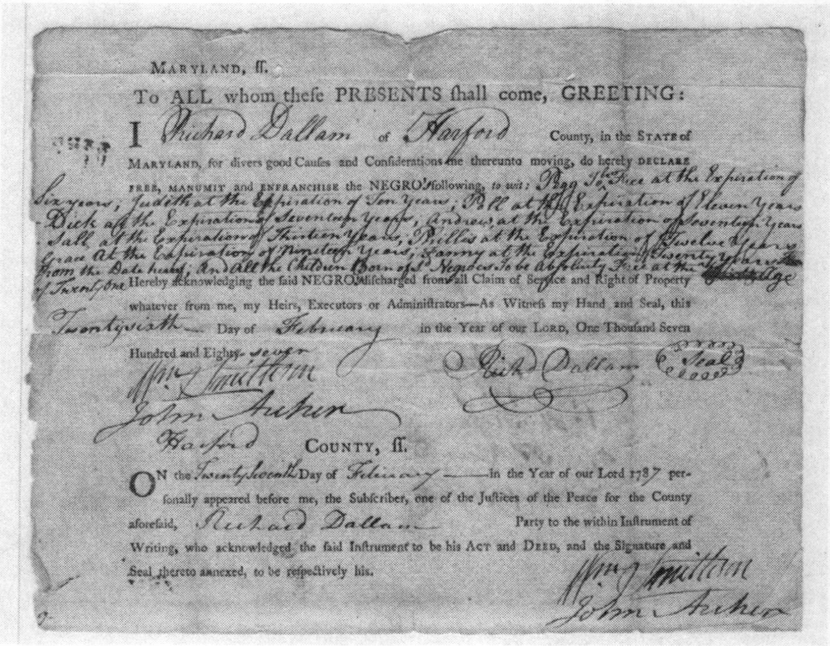

MARYLAND, ss.

To ALL whom these PRESENTS shall come, GREETING:

I Richard Dallam of Harford County, in the STATE of MARYLAND, for divers good Causes and Considerations me thereunto moving, do hereby DECLARE FREE, MANUMIT and ENFRANCHISE the NEGROS following, to wit: Peg To be Free at the Expiration of Six years, Judith at the Expiration of Ten years; Poll at the Expiration of Eleven years, Dick at the Expiration of Seventeen years, Andrew at the Expiration of Seventeen years, Sall at the Expiration of Thirteen years, Phillis at the Expiration of Twelve years, Grace at the Expiration of Nineteen years, Fanny at the Expiration of Twenty [illegible] from the Date hereof, And all the Children Born of sd Negroes to be Absolutely Free at the Age of Twenty one Hereby acknowledging the said NEGROS discharged from all Claim of Service and Right of Property whatever from me, my Heirs, Executors or Administrators—As Witness my Hand and Seal, this Twentysixth Day of February in the Year of our LORD, One Thousand Seven Hundred and Eighty-seven

Rich[d] Dallam (Seal)

Wm Smithson

John Archer

Harford COUNTY, ss.

ON the Twentyseventh Day of February in the Year of our Lord 1787 personally appeared before me, the Subscriber, one of the Justices of the Peace for the County aforesaid, Richard Dallam Party to the within Instrument of Writing, who acknowledged the said Instrument to be his ACT and DEED, and the Signature and Seal thereto annexed, to be respectively his.

Wm Smithson

John Archer

FIGURE 4. Maryland deed of manumission, which shows Jinny Jackson's mother, Peg, should be freed after six years of service, along with several other enslaved men and women. The deed also denoted that all children of these individuals should be "absolutely free" at age twenty-one. *Jinny Jackson, a woman of color v. James O. Fraser*, July 1842, Case No. 102, SLCCR, 19. Courtesy of the Missouri State Archives–St. Louis.

of residence and treatment as free people of color. The court's opinion in this case speaks volumes about the struggles faced by courts in determining how to reconcile slaves' double character when asked to determine the intermediary status of manumissions that took effect at some future date. The opinion begins, "There is a natural inclination in the bosom of every judge to favor the side of freedom, and a strong sympathy with the plaintiff . . . and, if we were permitted to decide this controversy according to our feelings, we should with promptness and pleasure pronounce our judgment for the plaintiff."[37] The judges in this case, though, felt constrained by other courts' rulings in similar cases and by the letter of the law: "the court is to be governed by a different rule, the impartial and unyielding rule of the law," and in the eyes of the law in Virginia and in "nearly all the States in the Union, in which the question could arise," the plaintiff was a slave.[38]

In cases of manumission by deed, enslavers could change their minds and try to contest or deny freedom to their former human property for any number of reasons. In one woman's St. Louis freedom suit, she explained to the court that her former enslaver had issued a deed of manumission for her and her children in January 1849, and the family had lived as free people until October 1853, when she "brought the said deed of manumission" to the former enslaver "at his request." After the former enslaver received the paper he had signed in 1849, he "destroyed the same and had [the] plaintiffs arrested," claiming he had sold them to the other defendants in the case.[39] Apparently, the enslaver had changed his mind about freeing the enslaved woman and her daughters, one of whom was "the illegitimate child of the said defendant" and the other of whom was the daughter "of her [the plaintiff's] late husband."[40] Although the case record does not elaborate on any dispute that may have taken place, the financial difficulties that may have befallen the enslaver, or any other reason that might have caused him to rescind the freedom of his former enslaved mistress and his daughter, the case represents a broader pattern of enslavers reneging on their negotiated agreements with enslaved persons.

Negotiations

Another area where the personhood of enslaved individuals came into conflict with the property demands of a slaveholding society was in the negotiations for freedom made between an enslaved person and his or her captor. The historian Ira Berlin has argued that enslaved men and women negotiated with enslavers for certain privileges and conditions beginning in the earliest years of slavery in North America and continuing into the nineteenth century.[41] Although the terms of these negotiations were always unequal and weighted toward the power of enslavers, enslaved individuals sometimes managed to convince their enslavers to enter into agreements for freedom. Freedom suits reveal some of the ways enslaved individuals continued to be able to negotiate with enslavers for freedom, though these arrangements usually came to court when an enslaver failed to honor a promise or contract with his or her enslaved person.[42] Courts throughout the South struggled with how to address conflicts that arose out of deals between enslaved persons and their enslavers: How could a piece of property enter into a legally binding contract? How could an enslaver offer a choice for certain conditions (such as choosing a new captor after the enslaver's death or offering to send the enslaved individual to Africa for freedom) to his or her property? Examining these thorny issues suggests both a recognition of enslaved individuals' legal personhood and the limits of that recognition.

Slavery was a system created and maintained through negotiations. Enslavers realized that making promises to those persons whom they claimed as property could be beneficial, especially if they had no intention of honoring those arrangements. Enslavers and enslaved persons entered into a wide variety of types of agreements that come up in the freedom suit case files, including arrangements for enslaved persons to buy their freedom, contracts for freedom after a certain period of time, manumissions with certain restrictions, and deals to allow enslaved persons a choice in their future after an enslaver's death. The contradictions inherent in the double character of slaves are perhaps nowhere as manifest as when an enslaved person entered a contract—even though the courts tended to view enslaved persons as property (therefore lacking legal standing) when determining the legitimacy and enforceability of these deals. Enslavers undoubtedly honored their agreements in some (perhaps many) instances, though these examples were less likely to appear in court.

The possibility of buying freedom was a carrot occasionally offered to enslaved persons to encourage them to work harder and earn money in their scant spare time. Enslaved individuals' ability to accumulate resources to buy freedom highlights the community's recognition that enslaved individuals were not merely property: by earning money in their spare time, enslaved individuals built their own stores of property.[43] Despite the frequency of these deals, courts rarely upheld arrangements for purchasing freedom.

Courts' frequent unwillingness to enforce these contracts reflected their interpretations of enslaved individuals as lacking legal personhood to enter a contract. The failure of these arrangements to stand up in court also (perhaps even unwittingly) emboldened more enslavers to make promises, collect the majority—or sometimes all—of the funds promised, and then renege on their promise of freedom. For example, when one St. Louis plaintiff sued for freedom, he claimed that his alleged owner made an agreement with him that he "might pass free as he pleased" to hire himself out and earn money to buy his freedom. Under the terms of their arrangement, once the plaintiff paid $200 to his enslaver, he was to be free. According to the petition, the man had "paid said Aaron Young [the defendant] Two hundred Dollars & upwards as a consideration for Petitioners' freedom & that he completed the payment . . . *more than four years ago,*" but he "holds your Petitioner in slavery & refuses to emancipate him."[44] This type of broken promise was not unusual. When another man sued for freedom in St. Louis, he claimed that his former owner had "often assured" him that he would be freed after he paid $800. The man's petition detailed payments of $246 to his enslaver before the enslaver's death, $99 to his enslaver's widow, and finally, the balance of $455 to a relative after the original enslaver's death. This second owner allegedly told the man that he would "liberate and emancipate" him, but these "promises and assurances, the said Cornelius [the relative] have broken and wholly failed to fulfil and perform."[45] Despite repeated promises to uphold the original agreement, the enslaver's creditors seized the plaintiff as payment for a debt. Even if the original enslaver had intended or planned to manumit the plaintiff, the enslaver's financial difficulties may have made this impossible; under the laws of manumission, the plaintiff remained property and could only be freed if his value was not needed to pay his enslaver's debts.[46]

Negotiated deals between enslavers and the people they held in slavery forced courts to act as mediators and sometimes directly involve themselves in orchestrating new arrangements for freedom. In one St. Louis case, the plaintiff argued that her former enslaver had manumitted her in a written deed. The defendant called the woman's deed of manumission "a forgery" and claimed he purchased her from another enslaver, so the person listed on the deed was incorrect. Although he failed to produce his bill of sale and claimed that "nor was the same [bill of sale] recorded," he *offered* to procure the original bill of sale to prove ownership. In this woman's case, the weakness of the defendant's argument may have influenced the St. Louis Circuit Court to procure a new agreement for her that allowed her to be free after paying $80 to the defendant and covering the court costs. Although it appears from the records that the defendant never legally owned her, she agreed to the terms, and the case record ends with a "stipulation of the defendant" to free her after he had received this money.[47] In this instance, the court crafted a new deal for the woman that appeased both sides in the freedom suit, shifting the court's role from interpreter of the law into a broker for freedom arrangements between persons of legal standing to enter an enforceable contract.

Occasionally recognizing these types of contracts is one area where the St. Louis Circuit Court's decisions appear to be unusual. Appellate courts in other states were less willing to uphold contracts for freedom made by enslaved plaintiffs—ruling instead that enslaved individuals lacked the legal standing to enter a contract.[48] When one Kentucky woman sued for the freedom of her daughter and three grandchildren, the Kentucky Supreme Court reversed the ruling in the Louisville Chancery Court and declared that her descendants were legally enslaved. The opinion stated that because the defendant only verbally agreed to free the enslaved persons after receiving payment for their purchase value, "this declaration cannot be construed into a *contract*. It is made with no one able to contract, nor was it made upon *consideration*."[49] In other words, the court did not view the free woman of color as able to form a contract, and the court did not believe she had given the purchase price as consideration for her descendants' freedom. In another Kentucky case a few years after this decision, the Kentucky Supreme Court laid out its doctrine more forcefully: "A slave is not competent to make a valid contract. He has no ability to enter into an agreement, nor will any promise made to him by his owner, authorize him to maintain a suit against him for his freedom."[50] The plaintiff in this case claimed he made an agreement that two men would purchase him at a discounted rate and emancipate him after he repaid the purchase price, though the court found that his enslaver did not know about the arrangement the plaintiff had made with his purchasers. The enslaver claimed that she sold him at a discounted rate only because he feigned illness. The court rejected his receipts for payments made to the men because the receipts did not directly refer to his manumission (the law required a written document). In this case, Kentucky's courts established the limits of enslaved persons' standing before the law.

Missouri's willingness to uphold some arrangements for freedom could suggest the continuing influence of the French and Spanish legal systems in the area. But in Louisiana, despite a Spanish legal heritage that allowed enslaved persons to purchase their freedom under the Spanish civil law practice of *coartación*, the state's appellate courts refused to respect these earlier arrangements once the Louisiana Civil Code took effect and officially ended *coartación*.[51] When one plaintiff sued for freedom based on an agreement for purchasing freedom, the Louisiana Supreme Court ruled that the Spanish laws allowing for enslaved persons to purchase freedom "are virtually repealed by the civil code. Slaves are incapable of making any contract for themselves, except for their freedom," excluding them from buying freedom.[52] In response to this ruling, another woman argued that she entered her agreement for purchasing freedom for herself and her children while the Spanish law was still in force. The New Orleans court and the Louisiana Supreme Court refused to recognize this earlier agreement because the courts differentiated between a contract that freed the person immediately and one that freed them *in futuro*. Because the plaintiff's alleged owner agreed to free the woman and her children only after they paid him, their contract was for future manumission and therefore could not be enforced until they paid the full amount, which did not happen until after the change in law. As the Louisiana Supreme Court explained, "Freedom must not be so favored by interpretation, as to depart entirely from the intention of the contracting parties, apparent on the contract itself."[53] In another creative twist, an enslaved man who had paid $500 of his $800 value claimed to own five-eighths of himself and therefore have the right to keep that proportion of the wages he received for hiring his time. The Louisiana Supreme Court praised "his zeal and the resources of his imagination" for having "at least, the merit of novelty."[54] But despite the court's recognition of this ingenuity, it ruled that "a slave cannot become partially free, nor can he, until legally and absolutely emancipated, own any property, without the consent of his master."[55] Although the Spanish civil code allowed for self purchase, the nineteenth-century transfer of power in Louisiana brought a swift end to these privileges.

In some appellate jurisdictions, courts used procedural matters to make determinations about an enslaved person's ability to negotiate for freedom rather than directly engaging with the central issue. When a woman sued for freedom in Washington, D.C., based on an agreement for buying freedom, the court found that she needed to bring her suit in an equity court, therefore refusing to free her because she used the incorrect legal venue. The court did insinuate that her contract for freedom was not legal, despite the fact that she paid the majority of the price, because enslaved persons lacked the status to enter a contract. The court refused to directly engage with the key issue of her case and instead dismissed her case on a technicality (despite the fact that a number of freedom suits were brought as equity cases).[56] In a similar case from Maryland, the plaintiff claimed that his enslaver allowed him to live and work as a free man to earn his purchase price, which the man paid in installments from his many jobs while living as free, some of which took him beyond the state's borders. When the enslaver refused to accept the last installment of the man's price and instead had him arrested as a runaway slave and sold, the plaintiff sued for freedom and argued that his return to Maryland from New York and subsequent sale violated Maryland's laws against importing slaves. Maryland's Court of Appeals agreed with this argument and therefore protected the plaintiff's purchase of freedom, based on his move to New York and subsequent return.[57]

Manumissions sometimes included the possibility of enslaved persons having a choice in their future. The most common example of this practice is when enslavers offered their human property the choice of either leaving their state of residence and receiving freedom or remaining in the state and in slavery. Although Missouri passed legislation limiting the migration of free people of color to the state after 1835, the state never directly required that people freed within the state must leave after receiving freedom. For this reason, cases involving an element of choice—for freedom outside the state or slavery within it—do not appear in the St. Louis freedom suits. When looking beyond Missouri, though, the issue forced courts to make determinations about enslavers' property rights while also recognizing enslaved individuals' ability to make legal decisions. The changing laws surrounding manumission in many states from the 1830s onward forced enslavers wanting to free enslaved persons to adjust the manumission clauses in their wills to adhere to their states' requirements.[58] At the same time, enslavers did not necessarily want to force manumitted persons to leave their families and their homes by requiring them to leave the state after manumission. For this reason, a number of enslavers included clauses that presented a choice to the people being freed. Freedom suits resulted when conflicts arose over the validity of these clauses; heirs and creditors of enslavers challenged the legality of offering enslaved individuals—considered property and part of the estate—the ability to choose their fate and therefore possibly deprive the heirs of their inheritance, and courts waffled on whether to recognize and uphold these arrangements.

Courts in some locations upheld clauses that granted enslaved individuals a choice of freedom outside the state or slavery within it, especially before the sectional crisis of the 1850s resulted in tighter restrictions on freedom. In Mississippi, where manumission by will was illegal, the Supreme Court upheld a will allowing the enslaved persons to choose to go to Africa (where they would be free) or to remain and be sold into slavery in Mississippi. In this case, the court determined that "the act of transporting [the slaves] to Africa, there to remain free, does not seem to be an act of manumission within the meaning of the statute [prohibiting manumissions]." The court determined that if an enslaver could legally take enslaved persons to Africa and free them prior to his death, he retained the right to do this after his death as well.[59] The court's decision in this case focused on whether the enslaver could send his enslaved persons to Africa, rather than whether the enslaved persons could choose to go to Africa or remain in slavery in Mississippi. The central issue in an 1845 North Carolina suit was whether this type of clause violated the state's prohibition on manumission by will. The North Carolina Supreme Court found that "emancipation was not prohibited for the sake merely of keeping persons in servitude in this State, and increasing the number of slaves," and therefore the trust to remove them to Liberia was valid, though it also "depends on the consent of the negroes themselves. Indeed, we are not sure that it would be proper to send them abroad *against their will,* even if there were no such restriction in the charter of the Society—since, if a slave has capacity to accept emancipation, it would seem that he must have the power also of refusing it, when the offer of his owner is upon the condition of his leaving the country."[60] By directly acknowledging the willpower of enslaved individuals in this opinion, North Carolina's highest court implicitly recognized their legal personhood as well.

Courts sometimes treated the choice of freedom as automatic, assuming that the persons in question would prefer free status, even with limitations, to a life in slavery. In an 1855 case, an enslaver's will granted freedom to several enslaved individuals if they chose to go to Liberia, but the will also designated to whom the enslaved persons would go if they refused to leave the United States for Africa. The Maryland Supreme Court granted freedom to the enslaved individuals and found, "We do not consider any *consent* to the gift of freedom necessary. The consent mentioned in the . . . act of 1831, refers to removal from the State, and not to the manumission."[61] In other words, the Maryland Supreme Court's ruling suggests that bequests of freedom that included an element of choice for the enslaved individual did not actually involve a choice about whether to be free; rather, the gift of freedom was absolute, and the determination only concerned the person's future residence—though electing not to leave could mean continuing to live in slavery. Six years after making this decision, the Maryland Supreme Court determined in a similar case that a group of enslaved individuals presented with a choice—for freedom in another state or slavery in Maryland—were not freed when they refused to leave the state, as their enslaver's will directed. Citing the intention of the enslaver in setting up this precondition for freedom, the court indicated that it must decide "the intention of the testatrix, so far as that can be done consistently with the rules of law."[62] The opinion concluded by affirming that enslaved individuals were "sentient, rational beings, and have capacity to make the election" for freedom, so the court upheld the enslaver's wishes and presented the individuals with the choice of leaving their homes for freedom or remaining in Maryland as slaves.[63]

Cases involving choice presented questions for southern courts that get at the heart of the dual nature of enslaved individuals as both persons and property before the law. These issues included not only the rights and privileges allowed to alleged slaves and free people of color but also the larger question of whether enslaved individuals possessed the free will to decide their own fate. The case that best illustrates this question is an 1858 dispute from Virginia concerning an enslaver's will with a handful of provisions that would determine the future status of approximately thirty enslaved men and women (the exact number fluctuated). The will instructed the estate to give the enslaver's human property to his widow during her lifetime (or until she remarried), and after her death, the enslaved persons should "have their choice of being emancipated or sold publicly."[64] The will specified that the enslaved persons should be hired out to pay the costs of taking them to a place where they could legally be freed because it was illegal to free them in Virginia. If they chose to remain in Virginia, the individuals would be publicly auctioned, with the proceeds divided between several heirs, who were the defendants in the legal dispute. The Circuit Court upheld the will and allowed the enslaved individuals the option of choosing freedom, but the Virginia Supreme Court reversed and remanded the case, stating in its lengthy opinion, "our slaves have no civil or social rights" and "a slave cannot take any thing under a decree or will except his freedom."[65] The court's opinion suggested that enslavers could consult enslaved persons' wishes prior to drafting a will emancipating them but said, "In the case before us, the master has endeavored to clothe his slaves with the uncontrollable and irrevocable power of determining for themselves whether they shall be manumitted. And in so doing, he has, I think, essayed the vain attempt to reconcile obvious and inherent contradictions."[66] In other words, granting enslaved persons the willpower to choose their fates meant recognizing their legal personhood, and this "vain attempt" was too threatening for the court to allow.

Reputation

In antebellum America, community relations and a person's reputation mattered. As the example of Milton Duty's slaves makes clear, the support of local, or more disparate, communities of relations could help enslaved plaintiffs win freedom or prevent them from achieving that goal. Duty's slaves relied on the testimony of multiple witnesses, in St. Louis and Mississippi, to support their account of Duty's finances, his intentions for freeing the plaintiffs, and Coons's questionable behavior on the night Duty died. Witness testimony about Duty's reputation as well as the actions of the enslaved plaintiffs and the defendants all factored into the outcome of the case. Because the purpose of a freedom suit was to determine the status of an individual, the evidence presented in many of these cases centered on the question of what made someone free: How did the individual act? How did members of the community treat the enslaved individual? What was the person's general reputation? Although some state supreme courts ruled that evidence of a person's reputation as slave or free was hearsay, and therefore inadmissible, other states' appellate courts, including the Missouri Supreme Court, specifically allowed for this type of evidence in freedom suits.

Reputation was a powerful element of interpersonal relations in early America. How others within a community viewed an enslaved plaintiff, as well as community members' willingness to testify about their impressions of the person, could have momentous consequences for determining freedom. The historian Laura Edwards has argued that in the localized legal culture of the early nineteenth century, judges and juries made determinations in a variety of types of litigation on the basis of personal reputation, or what she refers to as "credit," within the community.[67] Edwards differentiates credit from honor, which was more often the purview of the elite white men of the community.[68] Individuals earned credit by acting in their prescribed roles within the community, so enslaved plaintiffs might be able to draw on the credit they had based on their actions, their appearances, and their work lives within their communities.[69]

Reputation was particularly important for subordinated peoples, as the historian Kimberly Welch has argued, because these individuals might have limited other means or strategies for protecting themselves and their interests.[70] In local communities, people knew one another, and the ways in which enslaved and free people of color crafted interpersonal relationships and deployed these relations for their benefit constituted a valuable strategy for proving freedom to the court. People from every corner of antebellum society would have understood how important it was to establish and maintain a good reputation. White community members mobilized this knowledge and inserted their own views on character and reputation when they testified for or against the assertions of enslaved plaintiffs in freedom suits.[71]

The evidence that enslaved plaintiffs presented to the court in freedom suits often concerned the person's reputation within his or her community, including whether others treated the individual as enslaved property or as a free person. How a community viewed an enslaved person—his or her reputation and the characteristics that made that person appear to be free or enslaved—could be the difference between a successful freedom suit and a lifetime relegated to the condition of slavery. For this reason, legal status came up in many of the witnesses' descriptions of the plaintiff as either acting like a free man or woman or acting as a slave. Looking into some of the conflicts that arose over reputation and status in a community reveals another dimension to disputes over freedom; although freedom suits (and, indeed, court cases more generally) are usually considered as two-sided contests, involving an enslaved plaintiff on one side and an enslaving defendant on the other, there were multiple concerns that clashed in these disputes, including the views of the wider community. Communities helped determine what constituted free status or property rights, giving community members a voice in the body of property law and freedom suit litigation.

Community involvement could indicate that the broader public recognized the rights of enslaved individuals before the law, even if it also treated certain people as property. When one St. Louis plaintiff brought the first of his two freedom suits in 1852, his petition explained that he was born a free man in Pennsylvania and had "remained free from his birth to the present time, never having owed service nor belonged to any person whatsoever."[72] He moved to Missouri and lived as free for eight years, spending most of his time working on steamboats along the Mississippi River, before two individuals claimed him as their slave. The plaintiff drew on his relationships in Pennsylvania to make his claim to freedom. One witness testified that he first knew the plaintiff in Pennsylvania when he was "considerably smaller," that the two of them "played together many a time," and that he "was always under the impression that he [the plaintiff] was free, of course."[73] Another witness testified that his "impression was that he [the plaintiff] was a free man because he acted for himself."[74] This enslaved man relied on the testimony of the men and women he met in Pennsylvania and in his work on Mississippi River boats to bolster his arguments for freedom. The focus of these depositions was not on the man's residence in the free state of Pennsylvania, which was a common argument for freedom in the years prior to his case.[75] Rather, the testimony focused on these individuals' impressions and the opinions of the community, demonstrating the importance of the man's reputation and his relationships within the community.

Enslaved plaintiffs sometimes relied on testimony and language indicating that they *appeared* to be free and that they *acted* like a free person. In the previous example, a steamboat engineer testified that he knew the man from working on boats with him. The witness indicated that the plaintiff hired himself to one boat as a fireman, that the clerk of the boat paid him his wages, and that he worked on numerous other boats in Pennsylvania and Ohio. Although the engineer did not know if others considered the man to be free, he did add, "[The plaintiff] lived in the town where I was born & raised in a free state."[76] In another St. Louis example, a witness gave a deposition indicating that he knew the plaintiff as a slave until 1826 or 1827 and that after that point, "she did go at large and act as a free woman."[77] Both of these plaintiffs relied on their community's perception that they were free to help demonstrate that freedom to the court, though the testimony in the court records does not provide much detail about the behaviors that could prove freedom. One appellate case from New Jersey elaborated: "the uncontradicted reputation of being free, working for herself in the . . . neighborhood, marrying a freeman with whom she continues to live in a state of freedom, and by whom she has had two daughters, whom they have educated at their own trouble and expense" all served as proof of one woman's freedom (and the freedom of her daughter).[78]

Missouri's courts allowed litigants to use evidence of a person's reputation as slave or free, but not all slaveholding state courts allowed this type of hearsay evidence to reach the jury. In 1820, the Maryland Supreme Court ruled against allowing evidence of the reputation of an enslaved plaintiff's mother to determine whether the mother, and therefore her child, was free.[79] The U.S. Supreme Court weighed in on this issue in an appeal from the District of Columbia Circuit Court, stating, "However the feelings of the individual may be interested on the part of a person claiming freedom, the Court cannot perceive any legal distinction between the assertion of this and of any other right," so the Court could not "justify the application of a rule of evidence to cases of this description which would be inapplicable to general cases in which a right to property may be asserted."[80] Denoting freedom suits as property cases, in this decision, the U.S. Supreme Court explicitly ruled out the use of hearsay evidence of a person's reputation for proving freedom.

Other states' courts followed St. Louis's lead and sometimes recognized the limited ability of enslaved plaintiffs to mobilize evidence of freedom. In some instances, judges explicitly broadened the type of evidence permitted in freedom suits to accommodate these limitations. A Tennessee opinion elaborated on the challenges enslaved plaintiffs faced in procuring evidence of freedom: "How is he [the enslaved plaintiff] to show it? He may perhaps procure testimony, that he, or some ancestor, was for some time in the enjoyment of freedom; that he has acted as a freeman; that he has been received as a freeman in society." The opinion continued that an enslaved plaintiff, "for want of other evidence, [needs] to use hearsay, that he, or his ancestor, was commonly called a freeman, or commonly reputed a freeman, or, in other words, evidence of common reputation. And why should he not?"[81] When explaining the choice to broaden the rules of evidence for enslaved plaintiffs, the Tennessee judge noted, "Slavery, in our sense of the word, is not known in England. . . . The right to freedom, in this relation, as well as the mode of proceeding for its assertion, is of American growth. Courts cannot be expected to shut their eyes on this important circumstance."[82] In other words, American judges needed to adjust their reasoning to fit the circumstances of its peculiar institution, which was a uniquely American problem.

Plaintiffs in freedom suits often used evidence that they "lived as free" to support a freedom suit. When one young woman sued in St. Louis in 1831, her petition indicated that her former owner made an agreement with her in Maryland to manumit her at a future date. While in Kentucky, the enslaver set her free by custom if not by deed, "giving her complete and perfect personal liberty and power to do with herself what she pleased and requiring from her neither service nor wages for her time."[83] In an affidavit filed on her behalf, one witness stated that "she was considered a free woman" and that she "was exercising the principles of a free person." One witness's deposition indicated that she "was known by the name of 'free Jenny.'"[84] Even her nickname indicated her reputation as a free woman. If this plaintiff lived as a free woman for years without anyone questioning her status, her reputation provided powerful evidence to the court. Similar examples of the weight courts gave to evidence of a person's reputation can be found beyond St. Louis as well. One North Carolina example indicated that the plaintiff and her ancestors "have been, in the community in which they live, considered and treated as free persons. After a period of thirty years . . . in her enjoyment of her freedom, every presumption is to be made in favor of her actual emancipation."[85] The Alabama Supreme Court upheld one woman's claim to freedom by suggesting that "her deportment was that of a person having control of her own movements. On such issue, it is also permissible to show, either that she was, or was not, under the direction and control of another. Whether such evidence is sufficient, or whether it is overturned by proof of ownership, is a question for the jury."[86] In other words, the jury should make determinations about whether living independently for several years created a reputation for freedom that could be used to prove that freedom in court.

Community members reported their observations of plaintiffs' work lives and behaviors, which could be used as evidence that a person "lived as free." A witness in one St. Louis case described the plaintiff's father as a free man working as a barber in New York, stating, "He passed as a free man & kept a barber shop there. When I left there in May last, he was reputed a free man & acted as such."[87] In another case, a St. Louis woman argued for freedom based on her Native American ancestry, which she proved not solely by testimony about her skin color or physical characteristics but also through her association with Indians and the work she performed with them. One witness recalled that the woman "was as much like a squaw as could be," adding, "I used to pay her for her hire myself + so did the rest of them who hired her."[88] Receiving wages for one's work was a clear indication separating free people from the enslaved.

The community's perception of whiteness, and with it a presumption of freedom, could be used as evidence of a person's reputation as free in cases in which the plaintiffs argued for freedom based on their physical appearance. Testimony about a person's appearance, including his or her skin tone, hair texture, bone structure, or dress, was one way enslaved plaintiffs argued for freedom—arguments that spoke more to their personal status than any potential property claim. Ariela Gross argues in her study of trials of racial determination that the "performance" of whiteness was crucial to determining a person's race. This performance could include the person's appearance in court, testimony about the person's past behavior, or how the community understood the person's racial categorization.[89] When a St. Louis plaintiff argued for her freedom based on a claim to white ancestry, one witness described her as "a bright mulatto, nearly white."[90] In another example, one witness described a plaintiff as "nearly white," and another witness stated that her free mother often stated that the woman was "as free as she was" and that the witness heard her say this "one hundred times."[91] In numerous states in the antebellum years, evidence of a person's appearance could be used to argue for freedom.[92]

Evidence of reputation could also be used against enslaved plaintiffs by enslavers looking to prove that the community treated the plaintiff as a slave. Just as a person acting like a free man or woman and getting paid for work could serve to help establish freedom, defendants' witnesses could attempt to disprove a plaintiff's freedom by describing a person working as a slave or having been treated as such. In a St. Louis case, one witness testified, "Polly the plaintiff was treated as a slave, was talked [to] as such by Crickett, & was generally considered as such."[93] An alleged slave's treatment and the type of work he or she performed could also influence the verdict in a freedom suit. In an 1844 freedom suit, a witness described the plaintiff's work for a previous owner, stating that the alleged owner "ordered the boy about" and that "the boy took care of horses for Herryman [the alleged owner]." The same witness continued, "I heard Herryman say the boy was his."[94] Testimony that an enslaver treated a person as a slave reinforced the importance of the ways in which the community understood the alleged master-slave relationship to operate.

Enslavers also used testimony about a person's morals or character—aspects that related more directly to the personal status of alleged slaves, since other forms of property lacked a moral character—to attempt to discredit a claim to freedom. Some states required people of African descent to swear to uphold certain standards of behavior or good character in order to be freed and remain in the state, and this requirement allowed the state to expel or reenslave anyone who failed to maintain good behavior.[95] For this reason, attacks on a person's character could result in the loss of his or her freedom and a condemnation to slavery. The issue of character, therefore, became a powerful weapon used by enslavers against enslaved plaintiffs in freedom suits. One extreme example of an attack on a plaintiff's character from the St. Louis court records is George Relf's case. A former enslaver of Relf stated, "after he [George] had made a second attempt to commit murder on the family of this deponent[,] this deponent drove the said George from his house" and "declined having anything farther to do with him."[96] When describing these attacks, the witness recalled, "George advanced into the room where the deponent and some company were sitting with an arm elevated in a striking position meaning he would kill the rascal. This deponent sprung towards him, and with difficulty avoided the blow."[97] Three years after this incident, the witness recounted his second attack, when Relf threatened another enslaved person with a gun and then threatened to shoot the witness when he tried to intervene. After the second attack, the witness feared for the safety of his family, so he sold Relf to a slave trader. By relating these violent episodes to the court, the witness hoped to impugn Relf's character and prevent him from winning his freedom.[98] Evidence of behavior and reputation indicate the importance of the performance of personal status for enslaved plaintiffs, even if some courts rejected evidence of reputation in freedom suits.

Freedom suit contests brought together a range of legal issues and legal actors to determine the place of individual litigants in the social order, as well as to define the limits of freedom and enslavement in antebellum America. The double character of slaves—as both persons and property before the law—arose in other legal disputes, but perhaps no other type of litigation forced communities to grapple with the inherent contradictions of slave law so directly. In defending freedom suits, enslavers and their attorneys crafted legal strategies to evade prosecution, to deny enslaved individuals' personal status, and to place themselves beyond the reach of the law's power, efforts that were met with mixed success. In this way, enslavers and their attorneys brought their own interests to play in freedom suits, reacting with creative strategies, both legal and extralegal, to avoid losing their valuable enslaved property. These dealers in human flesh and powerful members of the community fought desperately to retain their privileges and wealth, enlisting courts' assistance against the formidable opposition of enslaved plaintiffs and their attorneys.

6 / Defending Suits

When Samuel T. McKinney purchased Julia and her daughter, Harriet, as slaves, he probably did not anticipate the legal trouble they would cause him. McKinney bought the two women from the Carrington family of Illinois, who maintained an active interest in their former enslaved property, especially after Julia sued McKinney for freedom in 1831. McKinney, who worked as a saddler with his brother James McKinney in St. Louis, became the defendant in a series of freedom suits in the early 1830s based on circumstances that predated his control of the enslaved plaintiffs.[1] The cases hinged on the actions of the Carringtons, who took Julia from Kentucky to Illinois and then back and forth from Illinois to Missouri, to avoid her becoming free based on Illinois's constitution.

McKinney's defense strategy was typical of many St. Louis defendants. By arguing that Julia's time in Illinois was temporary and that the Carringtons never intended to keep Julia as a slave in Illinois, McKinney's lawyer followed the legal precedent of focusing on the enslaver's intention when taking a slave to a free state or free territory. The first St. Louis jury agreed and gave a verdict for McKinney, but the Missouri Supreme Court reversed this decision and remanded the case to the Circuit Court. A second jury decided against McKinney and found for Julia's freedom in 1834. Because Harriet's case depended on Julia's status, she also won her freedom, in 1835.

McKinney was not the only person trying to prevent Julia and Harriet's freedom. Freedom suits concerned numerous other interested parties who feared prosecution or the loss of their financial investment if a defendant lost his or her suit. In McKinney's case, the Carrington family actively sought out information, suggested legal strategies, and even committed financial resources to try to prevent Julia's release from slavery. A series of letters from Mrs. Carrington and other representatives to McKinney's lawyer detail the range of tactics used by defendants and their allies by providing multiple reasons for the Carringtons to keep Julia in Illinois without it resulting in her freedom. The outcome of freedom suits had tremendous financial consequences that extended out from defendants to other interested parties. To protect their investments, enslavers like McKinney and the Carringtons wielded all of the tools available to them: hiring the best attorneys, adapting to new legal precedents, and practicing all kinds of deception.

Freedom suits provoked a range of responses from the men and women who became defendants in these cases. Fear of losing valuable property, anger and defiance at the challenges to their authority, and confidence that the law would decide in their favor were just a few examples of how defendants handled their cases. Freedom suit defendants participated in the legal culture of slavery through the negotiations they entered with enslaved plaintiffs, the arguments they presented in court, and the devious strategies they employed to avoid prosecution or to prevail in court. Like the enslaved plaintiffs who sued them, enslavers understood the laws and worked to bend the rules to their advantage.

Defendants and their attorneys worked within the confines of the law—and sometimes extralegally—to defeat enslaved plaintiffs and uphold the system of chattel slavery in antebellum America. Any enslaver could find him- or herself having to defend a lawsuit, provided his or her human property had access to legal knowledge and the means to argue for freedom. As a result, defendants drew on a variety of arguments, approaches, and methods to avoid losing their valuable enslaved property in suits for freedom. Enslavers reacted to local and appellate freedom suit decisions by crafting new strategies for defending their rights to hold human property. For the purposes of this chapter, the various approaches taken by defendants are loosely grouped into three overlapping areas: tactics for avoiding suits, defenses to plaintiffs' arguments in suits, and use of trickery and fraud.

Freedom Suit Defendants

Enslavers were always a minority in southern society, and St. Louis was no different. The men and women who defended suits for freedom varied in their occupations, their socioeconomic status, and even their racial categorization.[2] Of course, the mere fact that the defendants claimed to own human beings provided them with a more exclusive social status, but within this minority, a wide range of people held enslaved persons who managed to sue them for freedom.[3] The defendants in St. Louis's freedom suits included the city's most elite families, like the French founding family, the Chouteaus.[4] Elite defendants and their allies influenced the trajectory of freedom suits in a number of ways. For example, in one case, a member of the Chouteau family bought a group of enslaved plaintiffs shortly after his brother-in-law, the foreman of the jury, participated in the court's decision against their freedom.[5] Financiers, land speculators, and other wealthy members of the community also found themselves dragged into court to answer charges of illegal enslavement brought by the men and women they claimed to own. One pair of defendants were merchants whose dealings included a broad web of the city's elite business and steamboat owners.[6] Lawyers and judges were prominent among the city's slaveholding population—and in a couple of instances, they became defendants in freedom suits—further complicating the layers of legal influence in these suits. Looking beyond St. Louis to neighboring Kentucky, even Henry Clay, the wealthy politician known as the "great compromiser," worried about his human property suing him for freedom.[7]

It was not only the wealthiest enslavers who found themselves having to defend against these suits. Samuel McKinney was a saddler who worked with his brother and participated in the rough-and-tumble culture of violence on at least one occasion.[8] Freedom suits included accusations against the city's slave traders, jailers, and other less elite groups of people. One woman's 1832 petition described the defendant as a "regular slave trader, who follows the occupation of buying slaves in this part of the country and selling them in the lower country."[9] Another enslaver, described as a "dealer in slaves," defended at least three suits for freedom and found himself involved in numerous other civil actions relating to his profession.[10] One of the most well-known traders of human flesh in St. Louis, Bernard Lynch, was a defendant in two freedom suits in the early 1850s, but Lynch found himself peripherally involved in a number of legal actions involving enslaved persons housed at his slave pen.[11]

Because of the role of city officials like sheriffs and jailers in keeping alleged runaway slaves or serving the interests of enslavers, they also faced suits for freedom. For example, one St. Louis sheriff defended a freedom suit in 1841, and the city jailer defended multiple freedom suits and habeas corpus claims in 1844.[12] Freedom suit defendants' various economic statuses, political and geographical backgrounds, and motivations resist easy categorization, and the numerous types of strategies they adopted to prevent the loss of valuable enslaved property suggest the panoply of ways in which enslavers contributed to the local legal culture surrounding slavery and freedom.

Avoiding Freedom Suits

Freedom suit defendants approached the court with varying attitudes and levels of confidence in the law. Many defendants boldly denied their slaves' claims, asserting the right to exercise force with their human property, while others offered lengthy explanations for their treatment of enslaved plaintiffs. Taken together, the tactics employed by these defendants bolstered the development of a body of jurisprudence around this type of legal action, forcing judges and juries to consider new circumstances when making decisions. The outcomes of their struggles not only held enormous human consequences for the lives and futures of enslaved plaintiffs. The personal fortunes of the defendants hung in the balance of disputes over personal status.

The first step in defending a freedom suit, after an initial appearance in court, was to file a plea indicating whether the defendant was guilty or not guilty of the charges. The majority of these pleas, like Samuel McKinney's response to Julia's suit, simply stated that the defendant "was not guilty" of "any part" of the plaintiff's charges.[13] Some cases added the statement that the defendant was not guilty because the plaintiff "was the lawful slave" of the defendant, who was "ready to verify" his claim to ownership.[14] Sometimes defendants' pleas included a more detailed explanation of the claim, as did an 1835 example, which stated that the plaintiff was "a colored person & was born a slave and has always remained in the condition of a slave & been held and treated as such."[15] In this case, the defendant used the same kind of legal language regarding reputation that enslaved plaintiffs used to prove freedom, though he used it to defeat the plaintiff's claim. In most cases, the strategy used by an enslaver to prove ownership can be gleaned only from the defendant's evidence as presented to the court, rather than his or her plea. Though

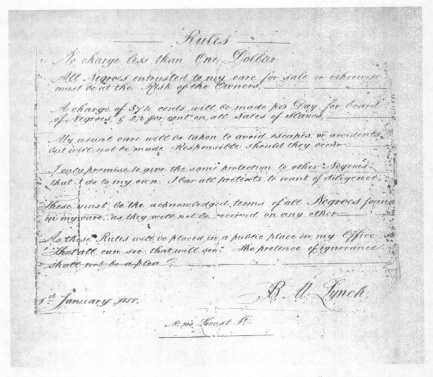

FIGURE 5. "Bernard Lynch's slave pen rules, January 1858." January 1, 1858, broadside signed Bernard Lynch, Broadsides—Slaves, Missouri History Museum, St. Louis, MO.

not always a part of the case files, the pleas and strategies in freedom suits suggest a great deal of creativity and a keen awareness of law and precedent in the St. Louis cases and in appellate records of freedom suits from elsewhere.

After defendants pled not guilty, one line of reasoning for enslavers hoping to avoid losing enslaved property was to deny owning or possessing the plaintiff in question. If the defendant did not hold the plaintiff in slavery, this argument suggests, a freedom suit against that defendant was unnecessary. When Samuel McKinney faced another, separate suit for freedom in July 1831 against his alleged slave Mariquette, his plea emphatically stated that "he had not nor claimed to have nor hath he nor doth he now claim to have but disavoweth & disclaimeth to have any title or interest in said Mariquette as a slave."[16] In one case, although a defendant claimed ownership of the plaintiff in his plea, he also answered one of the Circuit Court's orders with the explanation that the plaintiff "absconded from [his] house and possession" and that since the date he gave for her departure, "he has neither seen nor heard of her."[17] Although it is likely that some of these examples were situations in which the enslaver did not actually claim the slave, it is also true that defendants sometimes used the tactic of denying possession of an enslaved individual to avoid losing the property rights to that person in court. Courts recognized these evasive efforts and decided against them in several of the freedom suits in St. Louis.

In a desperate attempt to avoid losing defendants' financial investment in a person with a legal claim to freedom, they sometimes sold plaintiffs to a third party (who may or may not have been aware of the pending suit). In order to sue for freedom, enslaved plaintiffs had to determine who claimed ownership of them, and the maneuvering of determined enslavers made this task more difficult.[18] One St. Louis plaintiff needed to name three different defendants to make sure she sued the correct person. The first defendant quickly presented a disclaimer to the court that stated he no longer claimed the woman as a slave, whereas the second defendant—a resident of Illinois—avoided prosecution by remaining outside the court's jurisdiction. This Illinois resident avoided receiving any of the summonses of the court but managed to issue orders to the third defendant to take possession of the woman and her daughter and to remove them from the court's jurisdiction and the state of Missouri, "thus depriving them of their just and legal right to freedom, which by the law of the land they are entitled to."[19] When the third defendant received his summons in the freedom suit, he simply refused to hear it read to him. Selling enslaved plaintiffs to third parties could also mean sending the plaintiff away from the court's jurisdiction, including into Mississippi River slave-trading networks.

Denying ownership of an enslaved plaintiff to prevent a freedom suit happened infrequently outside St. Louis, appearing in only a handful of the appellate records. For example, in an 1810 case from the District of Columbia, the defendant refused to enter the required fee when he initially appeared in court because he did not own the plaintiff and therefore should not have been facing a freedom suit. Although the plaintiff's attorney charged that the defendant sold the plaintiff to avoid the freedom suit, the court ruled that he was not responsible for paying a fee if he was not claiming ownership.[20] In another example, when a group of Virginia enslaved persons sued based on their manumission in their enslaver's will, the Virginia Supreme Court refused to hear the appeal because the person named in the suit (the administrator of the will) was not the person claiming to own the plaintiffs.[21] Similarly, the Kentucky Supreme Court refused to rule on the status of a group of enslaved plaintiffs in 1848 because the defendant had sold the plaintiffs out of the state about two years prior to the institution of the suit.[22] These examples suggest that shifting control of people who might sue for freedom—or denying ownership after the enslaved person instituted suit—was a tactic that enslavers outside St. Louis at least occasionally adopted.

Defendants looking for ways to prevent enslaved plaintiffs from winning freedom in court could simply take them out of the court's jurisdiction, a strategy that led to a number of forced migrations in and out of St. Louis. When a nine-year-old girl born in Illinois sued for freedom in St. Louis in 1835, her attorney filed an affidavit stating that she "was removed out of the jurisdiction of this Court into the State of Illinois by the consent or connivance of said defendant . . . for the purpose of depriving her of the benefit of a trial of her right to freedom."[23] The girl's removal to a free state to prevent her receiving freedom is a perfect illustration of the tense relationship between slave and free states. Some enslavers fled the other direction, from Illinois to St. Louis, in hopes of protecting their property rights. An 1839 petition recalled that in April of that year, residents of Illinois, where the plaintiff lived with her enslaver for nearly a year, "signified their intention to take measures to procure the freedom" of the woman. Their threatened actions on her behalf resulted in her being "immediately sent by her master to the City of St. Louis," where she managed to take her own "measures" for freedom in the St. Louis Circuit Court.[24]

Defendants sometimes fled from St. Louis with their enslaved property, while other times they relied on slave traders to carry plaintiffs off to areas further south like New Orleans. In either instance, the court usually dealt with this phenomenon by dismissing the suit for lack of prosecution, making this an attractive strategy for defendants in freedom suits. In one St. Louis case, a defendant used trickery to assist with his efforts to sell a woman away from the city and, therefore, away from her ability to sue. The woman's attorney claimed that this defendant sold her to two other men, who became defendants and who then "did decoy the said plaintiff . . . by stating to her that they wished her to go and see her attorney and that instead of taking her to see an attorney . . . [they] did compel her . . . to go on board of the Steam Boat Isabel." So the defendants, with their agents, lied to the woman by telling her that they would take her to her attorney and instead forced her onto a steamboat. The woman's attorney accused the new defendants of coercing the plaintiff onto the boat "to be carried to New Orleans in the state of Louisiana or to some other place out of the jurisdiction of this court for the purpose of selling her as a slave."[25] He later reported to the court that he tried to determine the woman's whereabouts but that the defendants "all failed or refused to give him any information about the subject."[26] When the attorney learned in late February 1852 of the woman's removal from St. Louis, which occurred on January 10, 1852, he "received a letter from a passenger on said Steamboat Isabel or one who purports himself to have been such at the time [who] said plaintiff was taken on board and carried off on said steamer." The letter came from Memphis, suggesting that the steamboat was indeed heading for New Orleans.[27]

Missouri's enslavers were not alone in using removal from the court's jurisdiction as a strategy for avoiding freedom suits. When one woman sued for freedom in Kentucky and her enslavers removed her from the court's jurisdiction, the defendants faced an indictment for violating the Kentucky statute against removing plaintiffs during a suit for freedom. The defendants successfully avoided a conviction by claiming to have no knowledge of the woman's freedom suit—a useful tactic that was undoubtedly copied by others in that state—when the Kentucky Supreme Court ruled that "knowledge of the pendency of the suit for freedom is requisite."[28] Two enslaved women in central Tennessee brought a separate chancery case (in addition to their pending freedom suit) asking for protection to prevent their enslaver from removing them from the court's jurisdiction. When the County Court dismissed their request, suggesting that the usual protective order in their freedom suit should suffice, the Tennessee Supreme Court reversed the case, arguing that chancery allowed for broad powers that could cover the women's concerns that the defendant would flee the state before their freedom suit could be decided.[29] Separate suits asking for this type of protection were rare, but numerous examples of enslaved plaintiffs requesting protection, in Missouri and elsewhere, suggest that the choice to flee the court's jurisdiction was a widespread ploy that enslavers used to prevent losing their valuable human property.[30]

Responding to Arguments for Freedom

Samuel McKinney and the Carrington family, like the majority of St. Louis freedom suit defendants, needed to craft responses to arguments based on residence in free territories or free states. The Carringtons' letters suggest that the defense strategies evolved alongside the variations presented by enslaved plaintiffs. When a plaintiff claimed freedom based on residence on free soil, defendants often responded by claiming that the plaintiff traveled into the free state or free territory without the enslaver's permission. A jury instruction from an 1844 case directed that if the jury believed the plaintiff "was taken to Illinois + there detained without the knowledge or consent of the owner," then "the plaintiff did not . . . acquire a right to his freedom."[31] In one woman's St. Louis case, her former enslaver testified that "so far from giving any consent" to her removal to Illinois, he "positively and repeatedly forbade" his children—who at various times controlled her labor—from taking the woman away from Missouri.[32] A second witness in this case confirmed that she took the plaintiff to Illinois, "contrary to the wishes and without the permission" of her enslaver, and added that the witness "intended to return" to Missouri within four or five months but "could not in consequence of the ice in the Mississippi River."[33] As these examples show, the intention of enslavers when traveling to free territory was crucial for their cases. A defense witness in another example recalled the complicated battle over ownership that took place between two alleged owners moving back and forth across the border between slave and free territory. The witness specified, "Cross [who claimed the plaintiff at that time] did not give leave for the negro to be taken from my house [into Ohio]."[34] If the woman entered Ohio without her owner's permission, the defendant reasoned, then she did not acquire freedom based on her residence in a free state.

Defendants making these arguments, and their witnesses, sometimes inadvertently insisted on a certain degree of cunning on the part of enslaved plaintiffs. One defense witness in an 1826 St. Louis case testified that, despite the alleged owner's wishes that the enslaved woman be hired out in Missouri, she convinced the witness through her "earnest solicitations" to allow her to stay at his home on the Illinois side of the Mississippi River, "without the knowledge and contrary to the instructions of her Master." After the woman's enslaver repeated his instruction for the witness to take the woman to Missouri, the witness tried to hire her out there: "but she again enticed me to Let her return with me [to

Illinois] and refused to stay there [in Missouri]."[35] According to this testimony, it was the enslaved woman's ability to persuade the witness that led to her time in free territory—a fact that absolved his responsibility and, he hoped, prevented her from becoming free.[36] In another St. Louis example, the defendant's plea included the unusual assertion that, at the time of her complaint, the plaintiff "was held to labour in the State of Illinois . . . and had escaped into the county of Saint Louis."[37] The defendant referred to the woman's term as an indentured servant in Illinois, but the fact that she managed to escape (and chose to flee to the slave state of Missouri) suggests her awareness of the legal remedies available to her and her willingness to brave hardship to use them.

The Missouri Supreme Court sometimes affirmed decisions against freedom if an enslaver proved that a plaintiff fled to Illinois without permission.[38] Appellate decisions from other states echoed this judicial requirement that the defendant had to grant permission for the plaintiff to be in that free state or territory. A Louisiana Supreme Court case ruled that the Third Judicial Court must instruct the jury that the plaintiff's residence in Ohio, either with or without his enslaver's permission, did not necessarily result in freedom; instead, freedom in this case was a result of the laws of the state of Ohio, which freed enslaved individuals living there for an extended period of time with consent.[39] In this example, the Louisiana Supreme Court ruled that judges in freedom suits must be specific in explaining the points of law to the jury. On the other hand, the Louisiana Supreme Court ruled in another case that if an enslaver took a plaintiff to Ohio, that enslaver "must have presumed to have consented to that emancipation," given the laws of free states like Ohio.[40] According to this logic, defendants should understand the laws of free states well enough to expect the consequence that allowing an enslaved person to enter these areas for extended periods would result in freedom.

Even if defendants anticipated the consequences, there were sometimes legitimate reasons to brave the risk and keep their enslaved property in a free territory. Defendants could deflect these suits by claiming that the enslaved plaintiff was in a free state or free territory only temporarily or that something happened that required a delay in the plaintiff's return to slave territory. When Julia and Harriet sued McKinney, Julia argued that Lucinda Carrington took her to Illinois and held her there for over eight weeks in one stretch and over five weeks in another.[41] One witness for McKinney testified that Mrs. Carrington stopped at his farm in Illinois with her son and with Julia, but they did not rent his cabin for a specified period of time but instead "merely [held] it as a *temporary* shelter by his permission." The witness also added that he heard both Mrs. Carrington and her son "frequently say that they would not or had no intention of makeing a slave of Julia the plaintiff in this cause in the state of Illinois."[42] This testimony clearly reflects an awareness of the court's requirement that an enslaver intend to make his or her permanent residence in free territory. By using only a temporary shelter, Carrington tried to get around the judicial precedent that settling in a permanent home signified an established residence in free territory. In a similar defense against two enslaved women in St. Louis, one witness claimed that the defendant brought the women to Illinois temporarily. According to the witness, the defendant planned to move to Missouri, but circumstances forced him to stay and care for his wife, who was not "in a situation to move."[43] After the defendant brought the women to St. Louis, he hired them to the man who became their representative in the two suits for freedom after the defendant "informed" the representative that "he brought the said Malinda + Nelly" to St. Louis "for the purpose of preventing an application for freedom in the state of Illinois."[44] Keenly aware of the law's requirement, this enslaver's explanation of his delay in Illinois satisfied the juries in these cases and resulted in verdicts against the women's freedom.

Defendants and their attorneys sometimes offered varying interpretations of the Northwest Ordinance or the Illinois constitution of 1818 to defend their right to hold human property in a place where slavery did not legally exist. In one St. Louis case, the defense asked the court to instruct the jury that if the plaintiff's mother was enslaved in Illinois prior to the passage of the Northwest Ordinance or if she belonged to a French resident of the Illinois Territory, then the plaintiff was legally enslaved despite her birth after the passage of the Ordinance.[45] The judge in another St. Louis suit refused to give two jury instructions requested by the defense that questioned the meaning of the Ordinance: the first instruction nearly identical to the preceding case and the other stating that if the plaintiff's mother belonged to a "french inhabitant . . . who was a citizen," then the woman was not freed by the Ordinance.[46] Defendants sometimes offered alternate interpretations of the Ordinance, but the judge in this case prevented these arguments from influencing the jury's decisions.

Frequently changing locations was one way to ease defendants' fears that freedom would "catch" them or "attach" to their human property if they stayed too long in any one place. In one woman's St. Louis case, her petition recalled how her previous enslaver moved her to Illinois and kept her there "employed in the ordinary duties of a slave . . . for about the period of two months" before bringing her back to Missouri. The enslaver then returned her to his Illinois residence for nine months, eventually returning her to Missouri to avoid losing the right to her service.[47] In another case, a wealthy French resident of Kaskaskia, Illinois, who claimed he was "not interested in this suit altho it might seem that he was," recounted for the court the great pains he had taken to avoid the plaintiff's gaining freedom based on residence in Illinois.[48] Dodging freedom meant carefully moving the plaintiff across the borders of slavery: first to Ste. Genevieve, Missouri; then to "Mine La Motte," Missouri; briefly to Kaskaskia, Illinois (for "about two days"), before boarding a boat to work as a hand traveling to New Orleans; back to Kaskaskia for "a few days for the purpose of unloading the boat"; then to the "swamp in Cape Giradeau," Missouri; and finally, ending in St. Louis.[49] Undoubtedly aware of the law's restrictions on slavery in Illinois and the St. Louis court's willingness to enforce those restrictions, this witness carefully tracked his movements with the alleged slave, never allowing him to be in Illinois long enough to gain his freedom, even though the person who held claim to his labor was a resident of a free territory.[50]

Claiming to "pass through" free territories temporarily was a popular strategy for freedom suit defendants in St. Louis and throughout the antebellum United States. State supreme courts varied in their treatment of these arguments. Pennsylvania's gradual emancipation law of 1780 specified the time that a sojourner or temporary resident of that state could hold enslaved individuals before they became free as six months.[51] A Philadelphia justice referenced this specification when denying one man's request to return to South Carolina with an enslaved person he kept in Pennsylvania for longer than six months, but in another freedom suit, the Pennsylvania Supreme Court ruled that a plaintiff's argument that her enslaver moved back and forth across the Maryland border for a total period in Pennsylvania of longer than six months did not result in freedom.[52] The Louisiana Supreme Court rejected a plaintiff's argument that she became free as soon as she stepped on free soil, choosing to rule for the defendant's argument that spending only two or three months in France proved that her owner never intended to reside there.[53] As these cases make clear, the length of a person's stay on free soil was a crucial factor in determining the outcome of freedom suits. One enslaved woman failed to win freedom in a Washington, D.C., case because her enslaver claimed only a temporary residence there. The opinion stated that "the legislature must have intended to prohibit a general residence, not a special limited residence, where the slave is to remain for that portion of the year for which she was hired."[54] If defendants could prove that they held only a temporary residence in a free territory, this defense usually protected them from losing a freedom suit.[55]

On the other hand, appellate courts retained the right to determine exactly what constituted a temporary versus a permanent residence in a free territory. For example, when an enslaved woman sued in Louisiana based on her two-year residence in France, the Louisiana Supreme Court affirmed her freedom despite the defendant's claim that his residence there was only temporary and that his permanent residence was in Louisiana. The court's opinion explained that only in cases in which enslaved plaintiffs were "passing through a foreign territory on a lawful journey" could "their personal condition . . . remain unchanged. . . . This is the extent to which an immunity from the effect of the foreign law could be maintained." In the case of two years spent in France, the opinion stated, "We cannot expect that foreign nations will consent to the suspension of the operation of their fundamental laws . . . for such a length of time."[56] In other words, the Louisiana Supreme Court was willing to free enslaved persons who spent such a long, continuous time in France that the enslaver could not reasonably expect to be able to retain a property right in a country where that right did not exist. Enslavers and slave states could ask free territories (and nations) to suspend their laws for only so long.

In cases in which a plaintiff claimed freedom based on free birth, enslavers countered by casting doubt on a plaintiff's ancestry or even identity. In a St. Louis man's suit for freedom based on his birth and residence in Pennsylvania, witnesses for both sides of the case gave similar physical descriptions but entirely different versions of the man's life story. The defendant claimed that the plaintiff was a Virginia runaway slave. To prove this story, the case file includes a copy of the will of the plaintiff's alleged previous owner, which indicated that his slave should pass to his grandchildren.[57] The sworn statement of the defendant (executor of that estate) proved his version of the plaintiff's identity by claiming to have worked as an overseer at the same time the plaintiff worked as a slave. Arguing that he had known the plaintiff since he was four years old, the defendant was certain that the plaintiff in St. Louis was the same man: "for he was raised with me and I know him *as well as I know any of my family*."[58] A defense witness supported his account, adding, "he is not mistaken in his identity, that he knows him from his general appearance his size and face, and from his voice."[59] Additional defense witnesses described the man as five feet ten or eleven inches tall, of a "dark copper color with heavy beard," with "an open space in his upper front teeth" and a scar above his eye, and able to "read and write a tolerable hand but spelled badly."[60] In response, the plaintiff's witnesses also described him as "rather a brown coloured not black," about six feet tall, and "stoop shouldered when he walked." Most significantly, one plaintiff's witness testified, "[The plaintiff] always pass'd as a freeman and I never new it to be doubted."[61] Witnesses for both sides claimed to have known the plaintiff since he was a child, making the detailed descriptions of two separate African-descended men—one a free man from Pennsylvania and the other an enslaved Virginia runaway—all the more perplexing. By suggesting an alternate life history for the plaintiff and calling multiple witnesses to support this story, the defendant hoped to establish his claim to the plaintiff and disprove the plaintiff's alleged identity.[62]

Defendants often appealed to community standards of behavior, witnesses' own observations, and even scientific testimony to make racial and status determinations of enslaved plaintiffs. Appellate case files that reference identity disputes provide specific examples of this type of evidence. In a classic example, an 1839 case concerned the identity of a free man of color living in Pennsylvania with his wife and children. The defendant claimed that the plaintiff was her enslaved man, whom she believed fled from Maryland to Pennsylvania. Recognizing the difficulty of determining which side to believe, the judge stated, "If they are incompatible, as assuredly they are, if they cannot both be true, then we must take that which can be most safely relied upon."[63] For the Pennsylvania District Court, the more "reliable" set of evidence argued that the plaintiff was a free man, and the court released him from the defendant's control.

Disputes that revolved around racial classification included specific types of evidence, such as community observations based on the scientific beliefs of the day. In an example from Arkansas, an enslaved mother and her four children claimed freedom based on their white ancestry and years of treatment as free persons. One of the plaintiffs' witnesses stated that the family "visited among white folks, and went to church, parties, etc.—should suppose they were white." To combat evidence of free treatment in the community, a defense witness testified that he "did not know whether she had any negro blood in her veins or not. He only inferred so from her being treated as a slave, and from her dark color." Another defense witness testified that the plaintiff's mother was "not a dark mulatto. Her hair was about straight, might have been somewhat kinky."[64] Drawing on the stereotypes popular in the scientific racism of the time, the defense hoped to provide enough suggestive evidence of "Negro" ancestry to disprove freedom. Despite these efforts, the plaintiffs won their freedom twice in Arkansas's circuit court and faced two appeals. The appeal in the second case, decided in 1861, centered on the defendant's complaint that the family had displayed their feet to the jury to help determine their racial categorization. The defense did not object to the family being displayed in the courtroom, as the common practice in suits of racial determination was for the jury to rely on their own observations; rather, the defense complained that the family should not have removed their shoes and socks. The Arkansas Supreme Court allowed the inspection, stating, "No one, who is familiar with the peculiar formation of the *negro foot*, can doubt, but that an inspection of that member would ordinarily afford some indication of the race."[65] Defendants in these types of freedom suits played heavily on the white jury members' and judges' conceptions of and prejudices toward people of African descent, but in doing so, the defense also had to allow the courtroom members to trust their own evaluations of the visible evidence presented by the plaintiffs.

When freedom suits arose from disputed arrangements for freedom, defendants sometimes offered bold assertions of their intentions to cheat their human property out of freedom or ignore their previous agreements. For example, one St. Louis enslaver agreed to allow his enslaved man to purchase his freedom for $450. After the enslaved plaintiff paid $230 of the purchase price, the defendant set him free, allowing him to hire his own time to earn the rest of the purchase money. The petition in the case states that when the defendant seized the plaintiff in St. Louis, he "declar[ed] that it was lawful to cheat defraud, oppress + reduce" the plaintiff to "a state of slavery." A witness later recalled how the defendant informed her that "the said Negro wished to purchase his freedom" but that he "intended *to get out of the said Negro . . . all he could*, and then send him down to New Orleans," which is what happened. The plaintiff eventually managed to return to St. Louis to sue for freedom.[66] In another example, a St. Louis enslaver agreed to free his enslaved woman after four additional years of service. Although the woman lived in Illinois for long stretches (as long as six months or one year, according to her petition) and had served for longer than the four years specified in their arrangement, the enslaver sold her to the man who became the defendant in her freedom suit. The defendant's response to her claim was that he had "utter ignorance of the matter of the writ + knowledge of the plaintiff."[67] Although it is impossible to determine the defendant's role in the woman's illegal detainment, it is possible that her prior enslavers sold her to a third party unaware of their arrangement or that she sued the defendant to procure a legal judgment for her freedom. In either instance, the case ended when the plaintiff voluntarily allowed its dismissal, suggesting that perhaps she made yet another arrangement for her freedom, or the defendant could have released her from enslavement.[68]

In some instances, it was the enslaved individual who failed to uphold his or her end of the bargain for freedom, leading the enslaver to ask the court to recognize the legal agreement. For example, an enslaved man entered an agreement in Missouri to buy his freedom for $550 plus interest. The enslaver then allowed the man to hire himself out in Iowa at the salt mines to help him earn the money owed to the former owner. When the man remained in Iowa and refused to send the funds to his former enslaver, the enslaver had him arrested as a runaway slave. The Iowa Supreme Court took original jurisdiction in the imprisoned man's petition for habeas corpus, and the court ruled that because the man entered Iowa with his former enslaver's permission, he remained a free man, though the court also instructed him to pay his debt.[69] In free states like Iowa, courts could, at times, choose to ignore the requests of enslavers and protect the contracts and extralegal arrangements made between enslavers and their human property.

Legal Wrangling

Defendants and their attorneys, along with any additional interested parties, fought tooth and nail to defeat freedom suits, and occasionally, their maneuvering survives through the conversations they had in writing. The Carrington family of Illinois, while not initially named as defendants in Julia's and Harriet's freedom suits, plotted strategies with McKinney's attorney, Hamilton Gamble, demonstrating the extent of their interest in the outcome of the case. In a letter from J. G. McKinney of Illinois to Gamble, because of the Carringtons' interest, he provided an extra incentive to Gamble to win the case: "If you Succeed in gaining it, In addition to the fee which he has to give you I will add the Sum of thirty, providing the Suit is determined at the Sitting of the present Court."[70] It is unclear if he paid Gamble any extra fee for his service in this case. Nonetheless, his offer suggests the means by which a separate "interested" party would try to influence the result of a suit.

Defendants and other interested parties pushed their attorneys to pursue every available route to defeat enslaved plaintiffs' evidence. Julia appealed her freedom suit in the fall of 1833, when the Missouri Supreme Court reversed the Circuit Court and remanded the case, stating that Lucinda Carrington was not merely passing through Illinois but "went into Illinois with an avowed view to make that state her home." As a result, "these acts of the owner surely amounted to the introduction of slavery in Ill[inois]."[71] In response to this decision, another Illinois resident (whose relationship to the Carringtons is unclear) wrote a letter to Gamble explaining a possible reason for the Carringtons to keep Julia in Illinois for so long and offering a wealth of evidence to destroy the credibility of Julia's witnesses. His letter reflects not just the concern and anxiety of Lucinda Carrington over the Supreme Court's verdict but also her willingness to do whatever was necessary to win. Carrington told him she "had the negro in this state only about three or four weeks" but "was told by the neighbours & travellers that the ice was running in the Mississippi river so as to make it dangerous crossing." Poor weather could be a legitimate delay, though she also told him "that she can discredit Nancy Harris [one of Julia's witnesses] by a number of respectable witnesses who would swear that they could not from her general character believe her oath." In addition, Carrington promised evidence to discredit another witness, insisting "that those two witnesses contradicted themselves upon crossexamination" but that the opposing attorney "(who had been up for several days fishing & killing ducks in company with one of the witnesses) interfered & prevented the justice from inserting their contradictions in the depositions." Finally, the letter asked whether the Supreme Court issued a final judgment, and if the verdict included Julia's daughter, Harriet, because she could not afford to lose the value of both Julia and her daughter. Lucinda Carrington then offered Gamble an extra fee to win both cases for her, as she was "not well able to lose the woman & girl & pay the costs of suit."[72] Although McKinney was the original defendant in both cases, Carrington clearly felt a strong interest in the cases' outcomes. She had good reason: it was Carrington's actions that effected Julia's freedom, and when McKinney died in December 1835, the court named Lucinda Carrington the defendant in Harriet's suit.[73]

Enslavers complained about the minute procedures of a trial when they feared losing their cases to enslaved plaintiffs. In December 1833, when Lucinda Carrington visited St. Louis, J. G. McKinney wrote Gamble asking him to meet with her to discuss the case. McKinney wrote,

"Mrs. Carrington wishes some talk with you Relative Julias suit. She says she has never Rcd. Any notice to take deppositions." Carrington argued that the prosecuting attorney failed to present the proper notice before taking his depositions, a mistake that could have allowed the court to disregard the evidence in those depositions. In addition to this suggestion, McKinney complained that the court's rulings gave Julia unfair advantages. He grumbled to Gamble, "Burd [Julia's attorney] has had all on his side as to such matters. I consider [it] unfair."[74] McKinney's attitude, resembling that of a petulant child, is indicative of defendants' belief that their interests should supersede any procedural rulings for enslaved plaintiffs.

Carrington continued to pursue Gamble outside the courtroom, a testament to her commitment to the suit and her near obsession with winning a favorable outcome. When the case came to trial again, a new batch of letters inquiring about the case arrived at Gamble's office. One letter explained to Gamble, "[Mrs. Carrington] is anxious to hear what disposition was made of the suit in which she is interested in your court." The letter, written by Carrington's agent, went on to offer to take additional depositions in Illinois if the case carried over to the next term of court. After completing depositions for the defense, Gamble received another letter, sending the deposition of one witness who, Carrington's agent stated, "swears that he would not believe Nancy Bright from her general character" and "that she was prejudiced against Mrs. Carrington." In this letter, the agent offered yet another reason for Carrington to have kept Julia in Illinois for such a long span of time: "Mrs. Carringtons horses ran away about the time she came to this state [and] that he . . . & Mrs. Carringtons son were about one week looking for them." By the time they located the horses, "it was also understood that it was dangerous to cross the Mississippi river because of the running of ice." For this reason, Carrington kept Julia in Illinois, "during which time she manifested great anxiety to have her sent to Mo. & did send her as soon as practicable."[75] Carrington's agent offered a number of reasons for her to keep Julia in Illinois, with each excuse indicating the escalating concerns of a nervous enslaver.

The extra communications between the Carringtons and Gamble slowed after the second jury verdict in May 1834. The Circuit Court set Julia free, prompting Carrington's agent to write Gamble, "I am surprised at the result." The letter continued, "you must determine what sourse [course] to pursue in relation to the matter, if a new trial appeal or writ of error would avail anything Mrs. Carrington would be pleased to pursue

them. I am anxious to hear from you."[76] This request is the last record we
have of Carrington's and Gamble's communication, but the amount of ink
spilled outside official court proceedings to try to ascertain the course and
outcome of the case points to the presence of a large network of enslavers and agents who took an active interest in the adjudication of freedom
suits. After blaming Julia's extended stay in Illinois—and the success of
her claim to freedom—on the weather, the character of her witnesses, the
devious actions of Julia's attorney, and the loss of Carrington's horses, this
final letter searching for another way to keep Julia in slavery reveals the
desperation of defendants and their associates to prevent the loss of their
human property through suits for freedom.

Following the example of the Carringtons and the McKinneys, the
Duncan family of Kentucky used every trick in the book to protect their
financial investments in human beings. The Duncan brothers fought to
prevent Vincent Duncan from winning freedom based on his lengthy
time spent in Illinois. In addition, their struggles to keep another
enslaved man, Ralph, from winning his freedom suggest that defendants'
fighting against freedom suits sometimes resulted in the spread of legal
knowledge among the enslaved. James and Coleman Duncan employed
a series of evasive measures to avoid losing control of Ralph before he
managed to sue for freedom in 1830.[77] Ralph sought freedom based on
the two or three years he worked in Illinois and the Michigan Territory,
where he labored for James while Coleman claimed ownership of him.
Ralph sued James for freedom in Illinois while living in that free state,
but James avoided responsibility for losing Ralph by denying ownership
and claiming that his brother Coleman was Ralph's true owner. After the
Illinois court dismissed Ralph's case, Ralph chose to flee James's control
rather than use the same court to sue Coleman (an option Ralph mentioned in his St. Louis freedom suit petition). James recaptured Ralph
and "brought him to St. Louis," where Ralph feared that James or Coleman planned to take him "some place where the facts of his freedom
is unknown + sell him for a slave."[78] A similar suit brought against the
Duncan brothers by an enslaved man named Joe indicated that this
was no empty threat; Joe reported that not only did he suspect that the
Duncans wanted to sell him away from St. Louis, but the brothers did
"seize and carry away several other slaves similarly situated, but were not
able to find deponent."[79] Coleman refused Ralph's offer to purchase his
freedom for $300 ($100 of that sum in cash), adding to Ralph's fear that
the Duncan brothers wanted to sell him south to prevent his freedom.
Ralph's petition concluded with the demand, "I want such measures

taken as will secure my personal safety," a plea that echoed the concerns of many enslaved plaintiffs.[80]

Having already thwarted Ralph's multiple efforts to gain freedom, the Duncan brothers continued to search for strategies to defeat his St. Louis freedom suit. The brothers called several witnesses to testify that Coleman hired Ralph to his late father, who took Ralph to Illinois briefly and without Coleman's permission. Ralph's witness countered this story with testimony that he was in Illinois for long periods with the permission of his enslaver. The Duncan brothers responded with multiple witnesses to smear the character of Ralph's witness, whom they described as of "general bad character" and not entitled "to credit in a court of law."[81] Ralph used rebuttal witnesses, one of whom testified that Ralph's initial witness was "considered . . . a man of good character." Another witness for Ralph mentioned that a defense witness "was generally seen at horse races & his character was not good but he could not say what his character for truth was." As a result of this back and forth testimony, the court's verdict left Ralph in the hands of the Duncans.[82] Ralph appealed to the Missouri Supreme Court and won a new trial in the Circuit Court, where the jury verdict released him from slavery.[83]

The Duncans attempted one final time to prevent Ralph from obtaining his freedom. In their request for a new trial, the Duncan brothers suggested that because they did not have Ralph in their current possession, they were not guilty of the trespass. They added that Missouri law presumed that people of African descent were enslaved, and so Ralph needed to present "record evidence of his freedom" or, in the "eye of the law," he was legally enslaved.[84] After pointing out the irony of the Duncan brothers' argument that they were not guilty because Ralph had fled their custody in order to sue—a suit Ralph won after his appeal—Ralph's rejoinder concluded simply by appealing to the statute, stating emphatically that "the Statute was made to protect those who are unable to protect themselves."[85] The final judgment freed Ralph and granted him court costs, though the execution book notes that the Duncan brothers had no property available in St. Louis to seize for the costs that accrued over their four-year struggle to protect their property rights to Ralph.[86] Through this example, the Duncan brothers displayed an impressive aptitude for fighting against Ralph's efforts for freedom, though Ralph's many tactics, and his ultimate success, suggest that he also had a remarkable understanding of legal processes.

Defendants took advantage of the typical lack of literacy among enslaved men and women to trick them into agreeing to remain in virtual slavery, sometimes for as long as ninety-nine years, using laws of indentured servitude. In one St. Louis case, the plaintiff's petition recalled how at age seventeen, his former enslaver treated him as free when they moved to Illinois from Virginia. When they arrived in Illinois, the enslaver "prevailed on your petitioner to bind himself by a contract in writing to serve him" until age twenty-eight. When the enslaver offered a document, "which he represented to be" a written contract of their verbal agreement, the plaintiff signed it, "confiding in the truth of said representation" since he was "unable to read." When the plaintiff learned that the agreement allegedly bound him for ninety-nine years, the enslaver "admitted that he could not hold your petitioner in virtue thereof" and "suffered him to go at large and act as a free man" until the enslaver made an arrangement to sell the plaintiff out of the state.[87]

Controlling information was a central strategy used by enslavers, who occasionally went even further than relying on the lack of literacy among enslaved populations. Sometimes defendants' scheming crossed the line into outright lying to try to prevent their enslaved property from learning about and being able to exercise their rights. One St. Louis plaintiff sued for freedom based on two years of living in Indiana with the daughter of the defendant, who claimed ownership of him prior to his arrival in St. Louis. The defendant's plea insisted that he was not guilty and that the plaintiff was his property, but an affidavit filed by a relative of the alleged owners revealed a more duplicitous relationship between the defendant and his alleged slave. Apparently the plaintiff traveled into Indiana for two years "or upwards," and there the defendant had arranged for his daughter to take the plaintiff and continue moving around, specifying that "the residence of the boy should be changed every sixty days" to avoid any appearance of permanently residing in Indiana. The affidavit concludes with the most damning evidence: the witness claimed he had often heard the defendant say that the plaintiff "was free by the laws of Indiana, *if he but Knew it.*"[88] Withholding this valuable knowledge was part of enslavers' efforts to prevent losing their investments in human beings. The enslaver of another St. Louis woman also realized that too much time in a free state would end in her obtaining freedom, but it was "difficult to procure help" without taking her into their new state of residence. An Illinois witness testified that the woman's enslaver "sent her back to Missouri for fear she might Recover her freedom," but eventually he had to "send for her again . . . even though she should sue for her freedom."[89] This woman's enslaver weighed the risks and decided to gamble against the ability of his enslaved property to learn about and access her

legal right to freedom, which cost him when—after three hung juries—
the enslaved woman won her freedom.[90] Not all attempts to lie and cheat
enslaved individuals out of their freedom were effective.

When enslavers' usual conniving failed to prevent a freedom suit and
threatened to result in loss of property rights, in at least one instance, a
defendant went as far as witness tampering. In a suit against a member
of the wealthy, French founding family of St. Louis, one of the plaintiff's witnesses concluded his testimony with the telling confession, "Mr.
Chouteau the defendant told me if I would help him in this case he would
help me."[91] The notation in the margin of this statement suggests that
it was "not read," so perhaps the judge found it to be too prejudicial to
the case or found another reason to exclude such damning evidence of
interference on the part of this powerful defendant.

Missouri was not the only place where lying and colluding were popular tactics for defendants trying to hold onto their enslaved property. A
number of examples from the appellate records suggest the widespread
use of deception to secure the property rights of enslavers. In a Maryland freedom suit, the plaintiff recalled how the defendant, after filing
a deed of manumission for him, failed to tell the plaintiff he was free
and continued extorting his labor for an additional three years. When
the Maryland Court of Appeals ruled against the plaintiff's claim for
wages for three years of stolen labor he had performed, the judge noted
that because the deed of manumission was a public record "of which any
one is able to procure copies" and because "experience" suggested that
enslaved persons "have never failed in the recovery of their legal rights,
for the want of generous professional aid," the man could not expect to
recover lost wages.[92] This Maryland judge clearly felt that enslaved persons' access to pertinent knowledge or assistance was not as limited as
enslavers hoped. In a Kentucky example, the enslaved plaintiff claimed
that the heirs of his former enslaver had destroyed the will manumitting him.[93] In each of these cases, the pretended enslaver lied to trick the
enslaved plaintiffs out of their right to freedom.

Defrauding enslaved individuals out of agreements for freedom constituted another example of the deceit practiced by enslavers to extort
labor and cheat people out of freedom. Enslavers did not have to negotiate with the people they claimed as slaves; after all, the North Carolina Supreme Court suggested that the power of the enslaver (or a hirer)
over an enslaved person was complete, and the popular understanding
of enslavers' authority made it seem unlikely that they would surrender
any of this power or offer enslaved individuals any incentives.[94] Even so,

the absolute sovereignty of enslavers necessarily included the authority to relinquish their enslaved property however they wished.[95] The nature of the slave-master relationship involved a whole range of agreements and arrangements for freedom (or for other privileges) that imply a significant degree of negotiating.[96] Although there is no way of knowing enslavers' precise motivations in entering agreements with enslaved individuals—especially arrangements for the person to earn freedom—the numerous examples of enslavers reneging on these bargains suggest that in at least some instances, they never intended to follow through on their promises. Negotiating arrangements for freedom and then failing to complete these deals represents another form of deception that enslavers practiced to retain their enslaved property or to extort labor. When enslaved individuals recognized these schemes and turned to the legal system demanding their enforcement, enslavers boldly trusted that the law would take their side and void these extralegal arrangements.

In these fraudulent arrangements, enslavers sometimes brokered "deals" with those persons whom they realized might be entitled to freedom.[97] One St. Louis plaintiff indicated in his petition that he should have been freed, both due to his residence in Illinois and because of his former enslaver's will stating that he wanted to free the plaintiff, before the plaintiff even made any agreement. When the enslaved man "demanded his freedom," the defendant convinced him to serve for six additional years, and then "he should have his freedom."[98] After agreeing to this arrangement, the plaintiff reported that he served for six years "with honesty and fidelity," but the enslaver "still refuses" to honor his agreement.[99] Persistent negotiations did not always work out for enslaved men and women.

Agreements between white benefactors and free people of color contained similar fraudulent actions: these benefactors did not always follow through on their promises, choosing instead to extract what labor they could and deny any altruistic intentions when faced with lawsuits, as a final St. Louis example illustrates. Samuel Stokes, a free man of color, sued John and William Finney for the freedom of his two grandchildren. Several years prior to the suit, Stokes needed help to purchase his daughter, Charity, and her daughter, Mary, after their enslaver died and the estate planned to sell them at auction. Stokes and his wife "felt great anxiety to make such arrangements as to secure the freedom of their child & grand child aforesaid but they were unable at that time to buy them. that having great confidence in the responsibility & integrity & humane feelings of John and William Finney," they asked the Finneys to buy their daughter and her one-year-old child until they could pay the purchase price. The Finneys agreed to buy the family and hold them until Stokes could repay the Finney brothers. The Finneys claimed they would not make a profit off the situation, stating "that in making the contemplated purchase all they desired was to [help these slaves] be saved from sale and to serve the cause of Liberty and humanity."[100] After the arranged purchase, the young granddaughter lived with Stokes and his wife until she was old enough to serve the Finneys, so she would not become an additional mouth to feed in the Finneys' household. During Charity's pregnancy with her second child, she also lived with her parents, who "cheerfully nursed & maintained her wishing the said Finneys should be at as little trouble & expense as possible with his child & believing that they should act towards her with good faith."[101] Stokes and his wife then cared for their new grandson until he was old enough to labor for the Finneys.

Despite the Finneys' claims to benevolence, their actions revealed more nefarious motives. In a petition to the court, Stokes and his wife complained that although they paid the Finneys more than two-thirds of the initial purchase price, the Finneys "sold said Charity to one Gratiot for two hundred & fifty dollars & that she died in servitude." Despite receiving funds from Stokes and his wife and additional money for Charity's sale, the Finneys "now claim said Mary & John [Stokes's grandchildren] as slaves for life & refuse to convey them to your orator so that he may set them free or to emancipate them themselves." The Finneys also refused to refund any money to Stokes or to pay him for taking care of his grandchildren while they were young or too sick to work. Claiming the Finneys' actions to be "against equity & good conscience," Stokes asked the chancery court to remedy his situation. Because the Finneys sold the daughter "against her consent & thereby rendered it improbable that the contract between your orator & them could be performed," Stokes asked that the Finneys either convey his grandchildren to his custody or refund the money he paid to them for this purpose.[102] It is not clear if the Finneys ever did either of these things because the last record in the case file suggests that the court dismissed the case because of Stokes's failure to prosecute the suit.[103] Perhaps the Finneys had no intention of honoring their agreement with Samuel Stokes and his wife, and they used the excuse of wanting to help Stokes's family to obtain a lower price for the daughter and granddaughter at auction. Whatever the Finneys' intentions, their actions and the death of Charity while enslaved to the Finney brothers are a reminder of the fragility of the arrangements entered into between people of African descent and white enslavers.

Negotiations for freedom became increasingly difficult in the shifting political climate of the late-antebellum decades. Freedom suits took place within the broader context of increasing sectionalism, and these cases contributed to the direction of slavery politics in Missouri. By the 1840s and 1850s, changes brewing on the national and local political scenes dramatically shaped the trajectory of contests over slavery. The national crisis over the spread and retention of slavery in the United States (and, especially, in its territories) had real consequences for enslaved plaintiffs and slaveholding defendants in freedom suits. The results of freedom suits lent these contests additional significance, fueling regional and national debates over slavery, and at no time is this more apparent than in the final decades of the antebellum era. All of these changes combined to create a very different picture of freedom suits when Dred Scott and his family brought their first action for freedom.

7 /   Political Repercussions

When the St. Louis sheriff asked the court to release Elsa Hicks and her child from jail during their freedom suit, Lewis Burrell objected. According to his protests, releasing the mother and child would "hazzard and expose the rights of her owners to all unfortunate influences that abolitionists may exert upon slave property" by placing them "in the reach of those who[se] creed and religion induce them to disrespect and to prostrate . . . all rights to such property."[1] Fearing that Hicks would be secreted away by persons "tinctured with abolitionism" as soon as she left her jail cell, Burrell continuously complained about the abolitionist presence in St. Louis. Claiming to represent the interests of Hicks's true owners, a group of minors from Virginia, Burrell even suggested that the defendant named in Hicks's suit, Patrick T. McSherry, was an abolitionist who agreed to serve as a "sham defendant" merely to trick the court into issuing a legal judgment for Hicks's freedom.[2]

Burrell may have been right about McSherry's role in Hicks's suit. According to one affidavit, when the sheriff told Hicks that she would have to stay in jail during her case, Hicks denied suing McSherry. The sheriff informed her that her petition against McSherry was on file with the court, to which she replied that McSherry had never claimed her as a slave, although she had intended to sue one of the defendants in her first case. McSherry, who owned a tin, copper, and sheet-iron business in St. Louis, does not appear in any other St. Louis freedom suit, and when the sheriff tried to serve him notice of Hicks's petition, he refused to have it read to him.[3]

McSherry's actual opinions about slavery matter far less than the fact that Burrell and other enslavers *believed* in the existence of a strong abolitionist presence in St. Louis. The paranoia evident in this case and others from the last two decades of the freedom suits (1840–60) suggests how much was changing in St. Louis by the mid-1840s. The role of anti-slavery agitators in bringing freedom suits in St. Louis may never be fully appreciated because of the secretive nature of abolitionist work in a slave state like Missouri, though examples of antislavery activity do occasionally surface in freedom suits and other types of litigation.

The 1840s and 1850s were an era of increasing tensions over slavery throughout the United States, and St. Louis and Missouri were crucial to debates over slavery at the national level.[4] Several national controversies surrounding the question of slavery involved the people of Missouri, with Dred Scott's freedom suit in the U.S. Supreme Court emerging as the most well known and most significant of these events. The cases of Dred and his wife, Harriet, help uncover what was at stake when the nation argued over their freedom: the future standing of all African Americans, slave and free, in the nation.[5]

Dred Scott's case is the most direct example of the relationship between local disputes and the national political crisis over slavery, but it was not the only way in which St. Louis's story connected with national, state, or regional political trends. Freedom suits carried political implications. When plaintiffs succeeded in winning freedom through the courts, the result was an increase in the local population of free people of color, as well as a corresponding loss in property, often for the community's leading citizens. Both of these possibilities terrified the slaveholding politicians of the region, who vehemently protected their property rights and worked to limit the autonomy of enslaved and free people of African descent. Individual defendants' losses in freedom suits did not threaten the institution of slavery. In fact, the existence of a remedy for unlawful enslavement could strengthen the system and protect it from abolitionist attacks by making it appear more fair and balanced. Even so, the collective body of antebellum freedom suits could jeopardize the absolute power of enslavers by forcing them to capitulate to the authority of the law and to accept the resulting increases in the free black population.[6]

The shifting political climate in the state as well as on the national stage had implications for the laws of Missouri, and these, combined with demographic changes, paved the way for adjustments in the outcomes of freedom suits.[7] For example, a critical supplement to the law of freedom suits limited enslaved individuals' ability to bring a case for freedom. In addition, the changing atmosphere of these decades contributed to a general push for tighter legal restrictions on enslaved and free people of color in the state of Missouri, and although the courts were slow to enforce some of this legislation, eventually African-descended peoples felt the power of these new statutes through the actions of local law enforcement and the courts.

Antebellum St. Louis and National Politics of Slavery

The local atmosphere surrounding suits for freedom mattered—political conversations surrounding judges and juries influenced their lines of reasoning in suits for freedom, and in St. Louis, the city's racial climate affected political debates at the national level.[8] Key events relating to racial violence in and around St. Louis contributed to hardening attitudes toward enslaved and free people of African descent. In the late 1840s and 1850s, when enslavers pushed even harder for clear definitions of people of African descent as socially inferior and legally enslaved, the changing demographics of the city of St. Louis frustrated their designs.

The 1836 lynching of a free black steamboat steward in St. Louis pushed the issues of violence toward African-descended peoples and the place of free blacks in a slave society to the forefront of local and national attention. Eric Gardner has written of this event that it was "one of the most complex moments in St. Louis's racial history" and that it "changed the national debate on slavery," mainly because of St. Louis's response to the Reverend Elijah Lovejoy's coverage of the lynching in his newspaper editorials.[9] On April 28, 1836, Francis McIntosh tussled with the deputy sheriff and the deputy constable while these officers were attempting to arrest two other black boatmen. When the two boatmen escaped, the deputies arrested McIntosh. While en route to the St. Louis jail, McIntosh attacked the men with a knife, fatally stabbing the sheriff in the neck and wounding the constable in the abdomen. The authorities caught and arrested McIntosh, and while he was in the St. Louis jail, a mob stormed the jail, dragged McIntosh out, and burned him to death.[10] This horrific lynching drew the ire of antislavery activists and contributed to the reputation of St. Louis as a particularly violent city in its dealings with enslaved and free people of African descent.[11]

St. Louisans tried to redeem the city's reputation in an 1841 incident involving four black criminals, but the result continued to make the city a focal point for national attention to issues related to race. In May 1841, police arrested three free men of color and an enslaved man for robbing a bank and subsequently burning it down, killing two white bank tellers. The city made an effort to provide the men with a fair trial, but the court found the men guilty and sentenced them to hang. The gruesome spectacle of their execution only fed St. Louis's reputation for violence against African Americans; boats provided special transportation to witness the hangings, with an estimated attendance of twenty thousand, or "approximately three-quarters of the St. Louis population."[12] The crowds at this execution added to the infamy of St. Louis as a place where violence against African Americans, enslaved or free, was a commonly accepted part of life and even a source of entertainment.

Shortly after these executions, when Elsa Hicks first sued for freedom in the middle of the 1840s, and continuing until the outbreak of the Civil War, slavery came to dominate America's debates over western expansion. It divided Missourians as well. The debate over going to war with Mexico, as well as the new territories the United States acquired at the war's conclusion, focused discussion on the future of slavery in these new western areas. Most Missourians favored the annexation of Texas and western expansion generally, and the place of slavery in the West was of particular concern for Missourians because of their state's border with the Kansas Territory.[13] In 1854, when debates erupted over the Kansas-Nebraska Act, which allowed for popular sovereignty (allowing the settlers of these territories to vote to decide whether to have slavery), this proposal created a storm of controversy in Missouri because of its border with the territory in question. Largely surrounded by free states to the north and east, Missourians feared that the admission of Kansas to the Union as a free state would put increasing pressure on the institution in Missouri because abolitionists working in free states would entice Missouri's enslaved population to run away—a problem the state already faced with abolitionists in Illinois. Western Missourians, and those in the heavily slaveholding region of central Missouri known as "Little Dixie," pushed for slavery to expand into Kansas, and many of these individuals moved into Kansas to fraudulently vote for a proslavery legislature and representative to Congress.[14] These proslavery supporters clashed with antislavery forces moving into Missouri and into Kansas, igniting a brutal guerrilla war that left scores dead on both sides and fueled the increasing tensions within the state of Missouri.[15] This era of "Bleeding Kansas," and Missouri's involvement in it, attracted national attention.

Against the backdrop of these local and regional struggles over the slavery question and one year after Elsa Hicks filed her suit for freedom,

Dred and Harriet Scott started their fateful legal battle. Their cases thrust Missouri's freedom suits into the national spotlight and, like the Missouri Crisis of 1820, made a question about slavery in Missouri the focus of broader discussions over the fate of enslaved and free black people in antebellum America. Beginning in 1846 with two petitions filed in the St. Louis Circuit Court, the Scotts followed numerous plaintiffs like Elsa Hicks and argued for freedom based on residence in the Northwest Territory.[16] Dred and Harriet met and married at Fort Snelling, in present-day Minnesota, when Harriet's owner "gave" her to Dred.[17] Dred's petition reported that his owner held him as a slave at Fort Snelling for five years, until the owner went to Florida and left Dred and Harriet in St. Louis.[18] The Scotts did not decide to sue for freedom until after the owner's death, leaving them to sue his widow, Irene Emerson.[19]

Dred's and Harriet's freedom suits included some of the same frustrations and trickery that other enslaved plaintiffs confronted when suing for freedom, as well as new hurdles that stemmed from political tensions over slavery during the 1840s and 1850s. The Scotts lost their first case because one of the Scotts' witnesses changed his testimony at trial. The witness told the Scotts' attorney that he hired Dred Scott, but when he testified in court, he indicated that it was his wife who hired Scott. When the Scotts asked for a continuance to be able to call the wife to testify, the judge denied their motion. In a second trial, the Circuit Court granted the Scotts their freedom, but in Irene Emerson's appeal to the Missouri Supreme Court, the justices reversed years of precedent. In 1852, the Missouri Supreme Court found against the Scotts' freedom and remanded the case for further proceedings, explaining that "times now are not what they once were, when the former decisions on this subject were made."[20] This line of reasoning clearly indicated the role of political shifts on the court's deliberations: as the sectional crisis made questions of interstate comity more controversial, the Missouri Supreme Court felt less compulsion to respect the laws of free states.

The Missouri Supreme Court's ruling in the Scotts' case is momentous because it reversed years of prior decisions and led the Scotts to pursue additional legal remedies. While the proceedings against Irene Emerson continued in the Circuit Court, the Scotts also filed a federal suit in 1854 against Emerson's brother John F. A. Sanford, the executor of their owner's estate and a citizen of New York.[21] The U.S. District Court of Missouri allowed the case to proceed in federal court, meaning that the District Court recognized that if Dred Scott was a free man, he was also a citizen of the state of Missouri. The question of Scott's citizenship was to be a central concern in the decision of the U.S. Supreme Court, which ruled the opposite. The decision that Dred Scott could be a citizen of Missouri reminds us that some jurists recognized African Americans' ability to live as free persons and to enjoy the ability to sue in federal court.

When the U.S. District Court chose to follow the dictate of the Missouri Supreme Court and leave the Scotts in slavery, the parties involved pursued an appeal that thrust their arguments into the crucial national debates over the place of African Americans in society. At least some antislavery forces viewed the Scotts' freedom suit as an opportunity to press the issue before the nation's highest court. For this reason, the Scotts continued their claim with the assistance of a St. Louis family who knew Dred Scott before his freedom suit, as well as a celebrated Missouri attorney who lived in Washington, D.C., and agreed to take the case for free. Another factor involved in the Scotts' suit was the substantial sum of money collected from their hiring during their case; the winner of the federal case would also receive these funds. Most important, the outcome of this case had the potential to provide enormous support for either the pro- or antislavery cause, as well as to bring increased attention to freedom suits in Missouri.

The U.S. Supreme Court case *Dred Scott v. Sandford* is one of the most infamous decisions in the history of the Supreme Court.[22] In *Dred Scott*, Chief Justice Roger Taney attempted to resolve some of the major questions concerning slavery and its place in American society. Most significantly for the Scotts, Taney held that they were not federal citizens and therefore that the Supreme Court did not have jurisdiction to decide on Dred's freedom because his lack of citizenship prohibited him from bringing a case in federal court. This decision left the Scotts in slavery, but Taney also went on to declare the Missouri Compromise unconstitutional by finding that Congress had no power to ban slavery in the territories. These two parts of Taney's decision, that African Americans were not citizens of the United States and that Congress lacked the power to legislate over slavery in the territories, overturned established law and provoked a tempest of outrage from many northerners, even those who did not support the abolitionist cause. The Supreme Court's ruling came at a time when other events like the debate over Kansas and the question of slavery in the territories were at the apex of political attention.[23] When Kansas voted on the Lecompton Constitution, a highly disputed document that many people believed was approved in a fraudulent election (that included a multitude of Missourians who crossed into Kansas to vote), the Democratic Party divided over its authenticity.[24] It was this split in the Democratic Party, as well as the Lincoln-Douglas debates in 1858 in Illinois—debates that focused on the *Dred Scott* case—that drove the country toward civil war.

The example of Dred and Harriet Scott's case suggests the importance of the interplay between national and local political arenas, and these two interrelated sets of circumstances resulted in harsher legislation for enslaved and free people of African descent. Like other freedom suits, national events influenced the path that the Scotts' case followed and its outcome at the various levels of litigation. When Irene Emerson filed her first plea in the St. Louis Circuit Court, she did so against the backdrop of the creation of the first anti-abolitionist society in St. Louis, a society devoted to enforcing the legal restrictions against enslaved and free people of color, which her father helped to found.[25] The Scotts' first trial in St. Louis received no press coverage, both because suits for freedom were routine at this time and also because the trial took place amid celebrations of soldiers returning from the Mexican War and a celebratory speech by a Missouri senator.[26] When the Missouri Supreme Court delivered its 2–1 opinion in Emerson's appeal, the opinion described a "dark and fell spirit in relation to slavery" that had fallen across the country and "whose inevitable consequence must be the overthrow and destruction of our Government."[27] The justices recognized the enormity of this decision and chose to overturn all existing precedent to try to stem the tide of freedom suits coming into Missouri's courts. The political crisis over slavery led the Missouri Supreme Court and the U.S. Supreme Court to use Dred Scott's freedom suit to make a definitive statement about the place of slavery in antebellum America.

At the same time, conflicts over western expansion and the future of slavery ushered in a new era of two-party politics that brought the conflict to a head, culminating in the rise of the Republican Party. St. Louis quickly became a stronghold for Republicans in Missouri. In response to political changes and sectional pressures, Missouri's state legislature enacted a range of new laws attempting to stem the tide of antislavery agitation that grew stronger in and around the metropolis of St. Louis. Some of these restrictions started as early as the mid-1830s, when events outside Missouri, such as Nat Turner's 1831 rebellion, and more local events, like the lynching of Francis McIntosh in the streets of St. Louis, planted seeds of growing uneasiness in the minds of the region's proslavery lawmakers. Viewing free people of color as a menace to slavery and an orderly society, Missouri's legislators, like lawmakers in many slaveholding states, moved to restrict the growth and autonomy of the free black population.

Changes in the Law of Freedom Suits

The most dramatic changes in the laws regulating enslaved and free people of color in Missouri began in the mid-1830s. In addition to harsh punishments for harboring or concealing runaway slaves, the 1835 code also reinforced earlier restrictions against enslaved persons interrupting church services "by noise, riotous or disorderly conduct."[28] The greatest shift occurred in laws requiring free people of color to obtain a license to remain in the state, a new constraint that clearly demonstrated the legislature's fears of the growing number of free people of color in Missouri but was similar to restrictions passed throughout the slaveholding states in this period. Licensure laws severely limited the autonomy of those free people of African descent living in the state, making it more difficult for them to move within Missouri and also requiring them to pay taxes and fees for their license. These rules also made it harder for free black people to immigrate to the state without a prior connection or specific reason for moving there.[29] The 1835 code required that all free black children between ages seven and twenty-one be apprenticed by "the several county courts."[30] The new apprenticeship laws granted counties great power in deciding what trades to allow free black persons to learn to practice, which gave white officials another way to keep track of free people of African descent and control the population by controlling their children.

When Elsa Hicks brought her freedom suit in 1845, a new set of revised statutes added even greater restrictions on people of African descent. The code of 1845 dictated that not only "riots, routs and assemblies, and seditious speeches of slaves" were illegal and punishable by whipping but also "insolent and insulting language of slaves to white persons."[31] This type of legislation gave free rein to all whites to seize any enslaved person they deemed "insolent" or "insulting" to them and drag that person before a justice of the peace for corporal punishment. Because people of African descent could not testify against a white person, the accused "insolent" person would have little way to defend against these types of accusations. The 1845 code also restricted "any person" who "shall forge, for any slave, a free pass . . . by which such slave may the more readily escape from his master" and also "any person who may abduct or entice, or attempt to abduct or entice, any slave away from his master." Anyone convicted of this crime "shall be confined in the penitentiary of the state" for five to ten years.[32] These dictates, clearly aimed at abolitionists or antislavery agitators, also required the governor of Missouri "to select two newspapers in different sections of the State of Illinois, in which he shall cause this act to be published."[33] It is notable that the statute actually mandated the publication of this law in Illinois, a place Missouri legislators clearly viewed as the crux of their abolitionist problem.

The year 1845 featured a trio of laws regarding free people of color entering the state that reveal the depth of paranoia that state leaders felt about this growing population (whom they feared would be a negative influence on the enslaved population of the state), as well as their specific concerns about the border city of St. Louis. One statute directed that anyone who brought into the state "any slave entitled to freedom at a future period, shall be guilty of a misdemeanor" and face a hefty fine or six months in the county jail. A second statute specifically targeted "the harbor master of the city of St. Louis," requiring him to "report to the Recorder of said city, the arrival of any steamboat, or other vessel, having on board any free negro or mulatto, not authorized to remain in the state." The position of St. Louis on the major rivers of the state made it particularly vulnerable to entering free black people or runaway slaves. Finally, a third statute specified that "any person" who brought into the state "any free person of color . . . or who shall employ, harbor or entertain such person, after he is so introduced or brought within this state" would face a misdemeanor conviction with a fine.[34] This legislation put the onus on individuals who aided, hired, or allowed a free black person to enter the state illegally.

The events of the Mexican War and the concurrent conflicts over the spread of slavery into the western territories no doubt fed the fears of Missouri's legislators when they added restrictions to the 1847 code, as the state's position on the northern edge of slavery made it especially sensitive to anything viewed as a threat to the institution. The 1847 legislation prohibited teaching any person of African descent to read or write and was specifically aimed at schools for persons of African descent.[35] The laws required a white "sheriff, constable, marshal, police officer, or justice of the peace" to be present at all "meeting or assemblage of negroes or mulattoes, for the purpose of religious worship or preaching . . . in order to prevent all seditious speeches, and disorderly and unlawful conduct of every kind."[36] A further check on black migration passed, specifying that "no free negro or mulatto shall, *under any pretext*, emigrate to this State, from any other State or Territory."[37] This law tried to close Missouri's borders to free black migrants, but even the existence of this type of law suggests that it must have been difficult, if not impossible, to enforce. One final addition to the legal code shifted the apprenticeship laws by requiring that free black children "who would not be entitled to receive from the county court a license to remain in the State, if they were twenty-one years old, shall not be bound out as apprentices in this State."[38] The change in apprenticeship law was most likely enacted to prevent free black children from acquiring a right to a license to live in Missouri (based on living in the state for ten years) by working as apprentices.

One final piece of legislation suggests how deeply Missouri's legislators feared the population of free people of African descent living in their state. In 1859, the Missouri House and Senate passed a statute requiring that all free people of color be expelled from the state, declaring "that the presence of free negroes was a menace to slavery."[39] Passed "almost unanimously," this bill never became law. Missouri's governor knew that if he officially vetoed it, then it would pass over his veto without difficulty, so he "pocketed it, and the free negroes were left in peace."[40] Although this bill failed to become law, it both fed into and reflected the tense environment of Missouri at this time regarding the place of enslaved and free people of color in the state. With thousands of immigrants pouring into St. Louis, the state's enslaving population worried that antislavery sentiment would take over their state's politics and lead to gradual emancipation of their human property. At the heart of these fears was the presence of successful free people of color, who threw confusion on the belief that black skin should equate with slavery and that slavery was the best condition for all persons of African descent.

In the midst of the increasing restrictions on enslaved and free people of color in Missouri—as elsewhere—by the 1840s, the statute allowing enslaved persons to sue for freedom also underwent a crucial change that made bringing a suit for freedom more difficult. In 1845, the legislature passed a new restriction that required freedom suit plaintiffs to give financial "security satisfactory to the clerk, for all costs that may be adjudged against him, or her."[41] This requirement meant that the plaintiff could no longer sue "as a poor person," or without providing financial resources to secure the costs of the case.[42] In practice, this constraint meant that fewer individuals held in slavery would be able to sue for freedom because it required them either to have the financial resources to put up a bond of security themselves or to rely on the financial assistance of others.

Despite the passage of the new restriction in 1845, uneven enforcement suggests that this clause did not immediately affect the ability of all St. Louis plaintiffs suing for freedom. For example, one enslaved woman asked the court for permission to sue as a poor person in her 1848 case. Her request mirrored those of many enslaved plaintiffs who sued before 1845, but the new law made this a request for the court to make an exception and allow her to sue without security. In this case, the court agreed and granted her permission to sue as a poor person.[43] In April 1850, when an enslaved man claimed he was "unable to bear the expenses of bringing and prosecuting a suit," the court allowed him to sue only because the court also ordered the sheriff to hire him out and take $1,000 bond for his hiring.[44] Possibly recognizing the difficulties for enslaved plaintiffs to finance a suit, at least in these cases, the court appeared hesitant to enforce the new law requiring security in order to sue.

By the early 1850s, the number of freedom suits significantly decreased, suggesting that the new restriction started to be imposed for some individuals. The uptick in enforcement came, at least in part, in response to the efforts of enslavers to press the issue in court. Even in 1845, when one enslaved woman asked to sue as a poor person, the judge indicated that her case may proceed only "if the petitioner shall give security as required by law." When an attorney involved in several other freedom suits and one additional person provided security for the plaintiff, the court allowed her to sue.[45] In Elsa Hicks's second case, filed in 1847, Lewis Burrell complained that the defendant, McSherry, did not ask Hicks to provide financial security in the case.[46] Burrell used this as evidence that McSherry was not actually claiming Hicks as a slave, though his insistence on financial security was part of a pattern of enslavers and other interested parties pushing the courts to administer the new rules. One young woman faced a similar problem in her April 1848 case. She provided security for her case, but the defendant requested "a rule on the plaintiff to furnish additional security" because "the person whose name has been submitted for security is insolvent."[47] The defendant continued to complain that the person providing the plaintiff's security was unable to pay. After going back and forth several times with the defendant asking for security and the plaintiff providing the same person, the court ruled that the plaintiff failed to provide sufficient security and dismissed the case.[48] Judges may not have enforced the new law in every instance, but even in the 1840s, the court did require adequate financial resources in certain cases.

One way the courts could permit a freedom suit while meeting the law's requirements was to hire the plaintiff out to provide payment for some of the costs of the suit. Hiring out was common in many freedom suits before 1845, but the profits of the hire in those earlier suits went to the victor in the case and, sometimes, to the sheriff to cover his costs. In 1850, the court allowed the cases filed by the slaves of Milton Duty without providing security for costs. The defendant, a well-known St. Louis attorney who worked on other freedom suits, asked the court "that said petitioner be required to give security satisfactorily to the clerk of said court for all the costs that may be adjudged."[49] Despite the authority of the new law requiring security, the court overruled the defendant's motion and allowed the plaintiffs to continue their case without providing security.[50] By allowing some flexibility in the enforcement of the new law, the court kept the door open for those trying to claim legal freedom who lacked the financial resources or the support of powerful allies.

Despite the slow and uneven enforcement of the 1845 law, it, combined with other factors like the 1852 Missouri Supreme Court ruling in the *Dred Scott* case, contributed to a significant drop in the *number* of cases brought to the St. Louis Circuit Court in the last fifteen years of the freedom suits (1846–60), with only 37 cases in this period.[51] In contrast, during the five years leading up to the statute (1841–45), enslaved individuals brought 63 freedom suits. In the previous five years (1836–40), there were 38 cases, and from 1831 to 1835, there were 71 cases, for a total of 172 in the fifteen years before the 1845 statute. The drop in the overall number of cases is unsurprising. Although some enslaved individuals were able to procure security from allies with the necessary resources, many lacked this advantage and were therefore not able to sue. For this reason, the 1845 statute drastically altered the possibility of bringing a suit for freedom for many enslaved men and women in St. Louis.

Analyzing the St. Louis freedom suits brought after the passage of the 1845 statute uncovers a somewhat unexpected picture—one that raises a host of possibilities—particularly given the dominant narrative of the late 1840s and 1850s. According to this narrative, heightened political tensions over the slavery issue, on a national level and also within each of the slaveholding states, meant that legislators responded with tighter restrictions and closer monitoring of enslaved and free people of color.[52] Indeed, the 1845 requirement for financial security was an example of a new restriction on enslaved individuals, and Missouri's laws regulating enslaved and free people of color in the 1830s and 1840s also support the trend toward greater control of black autonomy. Despite these national and regional patterns, in the thirty-seven freedom suits brought from 1846 to 1860 in St. Louis, the court did not decide in favor of the defendant in a single instance, though this fact certainly did not mean the court freed all of the enslaved plaintiffs after 1845. In the thirty-seven freedom suits brought after 1845, the court found enslaved plaintiffs to be free in nine cases (24.3 percent). In addition to the nine cases directly won by the plaintiff, one case ended when the defendant defaulted by failing to appear in court. In this outcome, too, the plaintiff would likely have been set free from the defendant's control. Twelve cases (32.5 percent) resulted in either a nonsuit (seven cases), which meant that the plaintiff failed to sufficiently prosecute his or her case, or, as in Elsa Hicks's suit, a dismissal (five cases). In either of these outcomes, the plaintiff most likely failed to win freedom, although some of them may have reached arrangements with the defendant to obtain freedom through other legal means (such as purchase or later manumission). One of these dismissals happened because the plaintiff failed to provide security as required by the 1845 statute. Finally, the most common outcome in these late freedom suits occurred in sixteen cases (43.2 percent) and simply recorded that the plaintiff voluntarily allowed the case to be dismissed, agreeing not to further prosecute the case.[53]

The several cases ending in voluntary dismissal raise questions about the informal processes taking place beyond the freedom suits to determine plaintiffs' personal status, even though the lack of additional documentation in the case records makes it impossible to know for certain what happened after these litigants left the court. Why would an enslaved plaintiff ask for his or her case to be dismissed? One reason is that the plaintiff may have reached an agreement with the defendant for purchase of freedom or for freedom at some future date. For instance, less than three months after one St. Louis plaintiff voluntarily allowed her case to be dismissed in December 1847, a third party (not the defendant in her suit) manumitted her in the St. Louis Circuit Court.[54] This type of bargaining took place outside the formal legal process, but the end result was freedom for the enslaved plaintiff. Occasionally, even these informal negotiations appear in the court's records. In one woman's 1855 freedom suit, her case ended with a notation from November 1856 stating that she had reached an agreement that included the "stipulation of the defendant" for her to be set free in exchange for paying the court costs.[55] In other words, the defendant came to a type of arrangement with the plaintiff, convincing her to pay the costs of the suit. Another possible explanation for cases of voluntary dismissal—one for which no direct evidence exists but that is equally likely given the nature of the institution of slavery—is that slaveholding defendants coerced plaintiffs into dropping their cases through threats of violence or sale. Enslaved plaintiffs understood the threat of violence and sale as a real possibility. Although some cases of voluntary dismissal likely resulted in the plaintiff remaining in slavery, the existing evidence suggests that some of these examples also ended in arrangements for freedom. Negotiations for freedom took place throughout the era of St. Louis's freedom suits, and this bargaining likely continued into the late-antebellum years. What is most surprising about the post-1845 St. Louis freedom suits is that in none of the thirty-seven cases for which we know the outcome did a judge or jury find in favor of the defendant. In the cases of default by the plaintiff or nonsuit, it is likely that the ultimate outcome favored the defendant, with the plaintiff remaining in slavery. As mentioned, when enslaved plaintiffs voluntarily agreed not to further prosecute, defendants may have coerced the plaintiff into this agreement and continued to hold him or her as a slave. But another scenario in these cases is that the two parties made some other arrangement to avoid further legal action and the expense of prosecuting a freedom suit or that it was no longer necessary for the plaintiff to sue.

One possible explanation for the shifting outcomes of late-antebellum freedom suits points to the changing demographics and political preferences in St. Louis during the late 1840s and 1850s. In these decades, St. Louis's population ballooned from 16,469 in 1840 to 77,860 in 1850, and it more than doubled to 160,773 by 1860.[56] Much of this increase in the population consisted of immigrants, especially the Irish, who fled their homes to escape harvest failures in Ireland, and the Germans, who fled political upheaval in Germany in 1848.[57] These immigrants largely opposed slavery as a labor system, some on ideological grounds and others because they disliked the increased competition for jobs.[58] Although most immigrants were not abolitionists, in the mid- to late 1850s, many Germans flocked to the new Republican Party. The historian Harrison Trexler called the Germans in the 1850s "a great force in Missouri politics."[59] This growing presence among the population of St. Louis influenced the beliefs and ideas of other groups living there, perhaps contributing to an atmosphere of greater tolerance for freedom, though not necessarily for a larger population of free people of African descent. By the 1850s, the enslavers of the city remained a powerful minority, but they faced an uphill battle against an increasingly antislavery population as St. Louis shifted toward a Republican majority. This transformation in the city's politics likely affected the course of its freedom suits, though it is difficult to determine exactly how the changing political currents related to the alteration in outcomes for freedom suits during this period.

The tense political environment of the 1840s and 1850s—especially around slavery issues—led directly to the 1852 Missouri Supreme Court ruling against Dred and Harriet Scott. That decision set a precedent that altered the types of cases that were brought and eliminated the primary argument for freedom in the St. Louis cases (that a person earned freedom by living in free territory). This dramatic reversal may also help explain why the outcomes did not include verdicts for the defendants. In the eight years following the Missouri Supreme Court's surprising ruling in Dred Scott's case, freedom suits adapted to the new ruling's precedent-setting effects. Some enslaved plaintiffs continued to use the Scotts' argument, but the legal change meant that the majority of enslaved plaintiffs had to find other reasons to sue for freedom and different ways to present their cases to court. Following the U.S. Supreme Court's decision in *Scott v. Sandford* (1857), only four freedom suits appeared in the St. Louis Circuit Court, and none of these cases claimed freedom based on residence in a free state.[60] This shift suggests that the cases heard by the court, though considerably fewer than prior to *Dred Scott*, may have presented stronger arguments for freedom and therefore were more likely to be found against the defendant.

The requirement for financial security, which mandated that enslaved plaintiffs risk their own meager resources or find support from others, not only resulted in fewer cases in the later decades of St. Louis's freedom suits. This change could also help explain the higher success rates of those cases. It makes sense that wealthy benefactors would want to support the strongest potential cases for freedom, and these same financial supporters may have exerted influence on the outcomes of the cases to which they committed their resources. Just as plausible, the privileged few enslaved plaintiffs who could marshal their own resources to supply security or convince others to do so were perhaps likely to be the most legally savvy individuals, who understood the law's requirements, its risks, and the likelihood of their success in bringing an expensive legal action. Although the motivations of the individuals who agreed to provide financial resources to aid enslaved plaintiffs in freedom suits are impossible to know for certain, Elsa Hicks's suit reveals enslavers' fears that a host of abolitionists planned to threaten their property rights by supporting these cases, not only by offering financial support but also through a variety of additional efforts.

Antislavery Influences

A growing awareness of antislavery activity—in particular, anxious enslavers' belief that scheming abolitionists planned to free all of the enslaved men and women and overthrow the slave system in Missouri—formed the backdrop to the story of St. Louis's late-antebellum freedom suits. Freedom suit defendants and interested parties like Lewis Burrell (in Elsa Hicks's case) seized on these fears. However irrational these concerns may have been, Burrell and others used the tense racial climate to cast doubt on enslaved plaintiffs' claims and to stoke the suspicions of potential jurors and community members coming into the courtroom. The evidence of actual abolitionist and antislavery activity occurring in and around St. Louis's freedom suits is minimal, but these cases sometimes drew on arguments concerning antislavery activism that could and did affect the prosecution and outcome of the suits. Political tensions arose in freedom suits when antislavery activity and the suspicions of abolitionism came up in the suits, and *suggestions* of this type of action were enough to potentially influence the trajectory of these cases.

By the 1840s and 1850s, the tide was beginning to turn against slavery in St. Louis. The increasing immigrant population, especially the Germans, generally opposed slavery. In addition, the small percentage of enslaved persons in St. Louis lessened the city's dependence on their labor and made the defense of slavery the purview of a small but powerful group of wealthy enslavers.[61] Even so, openly expressing antislavery sentiment in St. Louis remained dangerous throughout the years before the Civil War, and the vitriol created by abolitionists could sometimes lead to violence. This anti-abolitionist sentiment continued to dominate public discourse in St. Louis, despite the growing presence of individuals who, though they might not actively work to end slavery, did oppose the system and favor some form of gradual emancipation or colonization.[62]

One of the most well-known examples of anti-abolitionist activism in St. Louis was the response to the Reverend Elijah P. Lovejoy. Lovejoy edited a newspaper, the *St. Louis Observer*, during the mid-1830s, and although he did not begin his career in the city as an abolitionist, his views changed in the wake of local and national events around the slavery question.[63] In 1835, he defended himself against the accusation that he sent abolitionist documents disguised in a box of Bibles to Jefferson City by claiming he had unknowingly used the newspaper the *Emancipator* as packing material for the Bibles.[64] During the trial of the ringleaders of the Francis McIntosh lynching in 1836, the aptly named Judge

Luke Lawless justified their violent actions by saying they were overcome with an "electrical frenzy" in response to the abolitionists working in St. Louis, and he cited Lovejoy and his newspaper as an example of abolitionist activity.[65] When Lovejoy retaliated with an article denouncing Judge Lawless's handling of the case, a mob destroyed his printing press and drove him out of town. His expulsion from St. Louis and the violence he witnessed at the hands of the city's mobs drove Lovejoy, within a year of his move to Alton, Illinois, to become a full-blown abolitionist, advocating for an antislavery society to form in Illinois. When he briefly returned to St. Louis in 1837, an angry mob again drove him out of town. An article in the *Missouri Republican* called for the citizens of Alton to take action against him, saying, "We had hoped that our neighbors would have ejected from amongst them that minister of mischief." Claiming that Lovejoy and other abolitionists' efforts stymied trade in the slave states, the article suggested, "Everyone who desires the harmony of the country, and the peace and prosperity of all, should unite to put them down."[66] A month later, a crowd trying to steal or destroy Lovejoy's press in Alton shot and killed the newspaperman. The St. Louis press suggested that Lovejoy got what he deserved, and many people in Alton believed the mob action that ended in his murder was the work of St. Louisans.[67] Lovejoy's murder made him a national martyr for the abolitionist cause and only fed the furor of those who were working against slavery. The violence against Lovejoy backfired against efforts to suppress antislavery agitation by providing fodder to the antislavery movement in the border states.[68]

A small but determined group of antislavery agitators began operating in Missouri in the years after Lovejoy's murder, creating a direct threat to the interests of enslavers in the state. Their rhetoric fed the persecution complex of enslavers like Lewis Burrell. Led surprisingly by former enslavers such as Thomas Hart Benton, the antislavery movement in St. Louis argued against slavery as an economic system that limited Missouri's ability to grow and affected the flow of immigration and industry to the state. Moderates whose politics aligned with the moderate wing of the new Republican Party, St. Louis's antislavery group united on the issue of preventing slavery from spreading to the western territories, which they opposed because they viewed enslaved labor as interfering with the ideal of free labor for white workers.[69] Although some politicians like Benton mostly preferred continued silence on the slavery issue in order to placate their political constituencies, other public figures began to voice their agitation against slavery through writings in the *Missouri*

Democrat newspaper. In perhaps the boldest move made by an abolition-ist in antebellum Missouri, an 1857 speech by a legislator in the Missouri House of Representatives called for slavery's immediate abolition. This speech, intended to appeal to immigrants as well as ordinary white farm-ers and laborers, instead created a backlash against antislavery agitators and forced their leaders to the background of Missouri politics until the Civil War.[70]

Elsa Hicks's freedom suit illustrates how enslavers and other proslav-ery agitators used the anxieties that many St. Louisans felt about the presence of abolitionists to their advantage. Harping on the possibility that abolitionists had crafted a new strategy—using fake freedom suits to fight the institution and threaten their property rights—Lewis Burrell argued that antislavery sympathizers set up McSherry as a "sham defen-dant." By raising the issue of abolitionism, Burrell hoped to influence the judgments within these suits, including not only the judge but also the jury and witnesses.[71] Referencing the statements Hicks made in jail while she and her child were dangerously ill, Burrell's attorney claimed that he "heard the said Elsa declare that she never authorized the said suit against McSherry." Instead, he believed she had "been harbored & Secreted" in St. Louis "for a considerable length of timme" to prevent her enslavers from taking her back to Virginia.[72] Burrell's attorney continued by claiming that the Reverend Joseph Tabour, "who has been strongly suspected of being an abolitionist," attempted to hire someone to convey Hicks in a carriage to Tabour's house. When Burrell's attorney inquired about Tabour's interest in the case, Hicks's attorney stated that Tabour "had nothing to do with the matter in any way."[73] In other words, the attorney claimed that Hicks was a passive victim in an abolitionist plot, hatched by those individuals who instituted the case in Hicks's name without her consent.

The conclusion of Burrell's charges echoed the concerns of many enslavers who feared abolitionists' scheming tactics and interventions in freedom suits. Pointing specifically to St. Louis's position on the border between slave and free states, Burrell's attorney crafted his arguments carefully, by suggesting that even the lack of open abolitionist sentiment did not forestall the possibility of secretive and conniving antislavery activists who would stop at nothing to free a legally enslaved woman like Elsa Hicks. After indicting abolitionists' influence on unsuspecting enslaved individuals like Elsa Hicks, Burrell's attorney played on the fears of unknown antislavery activism existing in St. Louis: "there are in disguise in this community as unprinsipled abolitionists as can befound disgracing that name."[74] By directly suggesting the existence of a large population of abolitionists "in disguise" within St. Louis, Burrell and his attorney appealed to the existing tensions of the late 1840s around external threats to the institution of slavery.

Complaints against St. Louis abolitionists arose in a variety of forums in the antebellum years, as evidenced by a case closely related to Hicks's freedom suit. During her second freedom suit, the state of Missouri sued Lewis Burrell to prevent him from removing Hicks and her child from the court's jurisdiction while her freedom suit continued. In Burrell's response to this charge, he again accused McSherry of creating a "collusive & fraudulent suit . . . for the purpose of cheating the owners of said slave out of their property in her."[75] Burrell defended his actions by declaring that "the frequent combinations of abolitionists to cheat the owners of Slaves out of their property in them & the frequent successes of such combinations have produced a very general practice—among slave owners, of seizing their fugitive slaves wherever they could find them."[76] In other words, it was the actions of abolitionists that led to enslavers' brash kidnappings of enslaved and free people of color, all in the name of reclaiming their property. Burrell's response to his own kidnapping charge was to denounce the kidnapping charges that often resulted from enslavers taking back their slave property, especially from free states.

St. Louis's proximity to Illinois meant that, in at least some of the existing depositions given for enslaved plaintiffs, enslavers' attorneys raised questions of witnesses' abolitionist leanings or their political persuasions. By introducing these types of questions to witnesses in freedom suits, defendants hoped to cast doubt on the witnesses' credibility, painting them as antislavery sympathizers willing to say anything to assist enslaved plaintiffs. In the 1851 case of an enslaved woman and her two children, several witnesses testified about their abolitionist beliefs. The defense attorney asked one witness if he was "a member of what is called the Abolition party," and he replied, "I do not know that I am a member but I am decidedly opposed to slavery." The defense even asked about the witness's abolitionist voting record. Well aware of the purpose of this line of questioning, the plaintiff's counsel objected that these questions were "irrelevant and illegal and otherwise informal."[77] Another witness for the plaintiff was a bit more confident in professing his abolitionist views, stating in his deposition, "I am an abolitionist as I understand it. I voted for what they call free soilers for a number of years." This witness even admitted that no one had summoned him to testify in the case; instead, he explained, "I heard they were taking deposition in regard to this negro woman . . . I wished if I could be of any benefit to the Girl by telling the truth."[78] The witness's antislavery sentiment led him to seek out the opportunity to testify on behalf of an enslaved plaintiff. One final witness in this case admitted to being paid for his testimony, but he insisted it was only for his expenses and the amount of money he would make at home during the same period of time. This last witness also added that he was not an abolitionist and said, "I allways voted the democratic ticket."[79] Although the witnesses in this case were generally forthcoming about their beliefs on slavery and abolitionism, in an 1852 case, one of the plaintiff's witnesses, when asked if he believed slavery was right or wrong, stated, "I wont answer that Question."[80] The witness simply refused to answer questions about his beliefs on slavery, perhaps realizing that the intent of the question was to discredit his opinions.

When abolitionists stepped in to help enslaved plaintiffs, their actions merely gave credence to the concerns that St. Louis's enslaving whites had about freedom suits—that these cases were instigated and perpetuated by abolitionists' desire to free enslaved individuals. In one woman's St. Louis freedom suit, her petition explained how, during her residence in Illinois (on which she based her freedom suit), "some persons in the place last aforesaid [Illinois] ha[d] signified their intentions to take measures to procure the freedom of your petitioner." In response to these antislavery offers to help the woman, she "was thereupon immediately sent by her master to the city of St. Louis."[81] Her case was not the only freedom suit that mentioned the engagement of antislavery neighbors trying to help an enslaved individual held illegally in slavery in Illinois win his or her freedom. Four years later, another plaintiff's petition explained that while his former enslaver held him to labor in Illinois for eight months, it was the interference of others in that area that caused the enslaver to send him on to St. Louis in order to retain his property rights. The plaintiff described how after eight months of laboring on his alleged owner's farm, "there began to be a good deal of talk in the neighborhood about said Prosser [the alleged owner] holding petitioner as a slave." As a result of this "talk," the enslaver, "fearing the intervention of the authorities there," brought a carriage to the farm, retrieved the man, and "drove off and brought your petitioner to St. Louis."[82] In these cases, the antislavery sentiments of enslavers' neighbors led directly to these individuals' freedom suits. Both of these enslavers chose to avoid losing their human property by sending them to the slave city of St. Louis, rather than face the possibility of legal action in Illinois. Opponents of slavery, even in areas outside St. Louis, did in some instances assist and influence freedom suits in the city.

St. Louis's proximity to Illinois, which had a small but determined abolitionist community, made it a potential hotbed for antislavery activism. One particularly rich case suggests the extent and type of antislavery activity in and around St. Louis. John Finney, a defendant in a St. Louis freedom suit, sued Calvin Kinder for taking Finney's human property across the Mississippi River into Illinois and aiding the enslaved individuals in their escape from St. Louis. The case highlights the possible consequences for those who might aid enslaved individuals in their attempts to flee to freedom. Describing several actions by whites that can be classified as abolitionist or antislavery activity, it also illustrates how the St. Louis courts dealt with these types of activities in the 1840s.

Despite the existence of a statutory provision preventing anyone from removing an enslaved person from Missouri across the Mississippi River, John Finney sued Calvin Kinder in March 1842 for breaking this law and removing his enslaved woman and her two children across the river (the charge was trespass on the case, with damages of $1,000). Finney complained in his petition that Kinder intended "to injure & defraud" him of "the price & value of the said slaves," and Kinder "did cross & transport the said slaves . . . across the Mississippi River to the State of Illinois."[83] The testimony in this case demonstrates a method for enslaved individuals trying to escape as well as how others assisted these attempts.

Suspected abolitionists denied their involvement in the attempted escape. For example, the man who drove the wagon for the family claimed innocence, reporting that the runaways' husband/father had manipulated him and others into helping the family escape to freedom. According to this witness, Nicholas Jones, "a Negro man, came to Alton [Illinois, where he lived] and contracted with . . . me, to move him and his family from the Illinois side of the Mississippi river, to Carlinsville." When the wagon driver and Jones reached the appointed spot to pick up Jones's family, they were not there, so Jones persuaded him to cross to St. Louis and retrieve his family. While crossing the river on the ferry, the driver told the captain of the ferry to collect the fare from Jones. The ferry captain then "went to the Negro, and they had some conversation together," but, the witness said, "what it was I don't know . . . and I did not see the Negro pay him any thing."[84] This testimony insinuated that the wagon driver believed the captain knowingly assisted Jones with the removal of his family from St. Louis, and it also absolved him of breaking the law against transporting enslaved persons without a pass.

To avoid responsibility for the enslaved family's attempt at escape, the wagon driver not only framed his actions in ways that indicated his ignorance of the consequences but also emphasized that several others had the opportunity to detect the escape; thus, he hoped to deflect the blame away from himself and onto these additional participants. After picking up Jones's family, the wagon driver hid the wife and three children under a cover on the back of his wagon while they traveled across the ferry, into Illinois, and all the way to Springfield. His description of this leg of the trip stated, "my waggon cover was too small and did not come down to the edge of the waggon bed by about eight inches," and therefore, "I frequently saw the heads and faces of the Negro woman & children, and I think that they might easily have been seen by any person." In other words, he should not be held responsible for his attempt to conceal the escaped persons in his wagon during the trip because they were not actually concealed. The wagon driver also claimed that when they reached Illinois, he was not familiar with the area (though he lived in Alton, Illinois), so, he said, "the Negro Jones was enabled and did, practice a trick on me, and made me hawl him all the way to Springfield instead of Carlinsville as was the bargain."[85] The wagon driver was certainly not the only potentially guilty party who tried to assign responsibility for the escape to someone else. The driver reported that a few days after he delivered the family to Springfield, a man from the ferry company approached him: "[He] told me that if he had to suffer, I would suffer too, that Finney had sued him . . . and advised me to go away."[86] The ferry official, recognizing the stakes in a suit for damages—or possibly even a criminal charge of aiding enslaved individuals in an escape—planned to blame the driver. But first, the official did him the small favor of warning him to get out of town. Another ferry-boat worker testified that he saw the wagon but did not see anyone in it. This witness then reminded the court that, even before this incident, "Negroes were in the habit of crossing on the Ferry boat without passes."[87] The escape was hardly unusual; enslaved individuals moved freely between St. Louis and Illinois without the proper authorization of their enslavers so often as to call the practice a "habit."

Enslaved persons living in St. Louis recognized that abolitionists' presence in Illinois could offer assistance in efforts to escape and could also hinder enslavers' ability to recapture runaway slaves. For example, Finney's brother-in-law John Lee, whom Finney sent to catch his escaped human property, reported to the court on the prevalence of abolitionists in Illinois and the many ways in which these antislavery activists thwarted his attempts to reclaim the enslaved family. Lee recalled the difficulty of his search for the family, stating that he "frequently heard that they were conveyed in wagons, covered, from stage to stage by abolitionists." When he finally caught them in Chicago, they were "concealed in the hold under the machinery" on the steamboat *Chicago*. Once he found the escaped family, Lee had "some difficulty" getting them off the boat because the woman was "refusing to go with him," and he also had trouble putting them in jail for safekeeping because "of the danger to which his property might be subjected by the threatened violence of the abolitionists of the place." On his return to St. Louis with the runaway slaves, Lee recounted how authorities in one Illinois town charged him with kidnapping, which forced him to hire a lawyer to defend himself from the abolitionists.[88] Lee's testimony supported St. Louis enslavers' belief that antislavery activists loomed in the region, hoping to aid enslaved individuals' escapes and ignore the property rights of enslavers. Lee's rich description of the ways that people of African descent worked to safely remove enslaved individuals from St. Louis suggests that while enslavers like Lewis Burwell or Finney may have exaggerated the extent of antislavery activism in and around the city, in at least some instances, enslaved persons in St. Louis did receive assistance with their escape efforts.

During the decade and a half prior to the Civil War, the slavery issue not only became pivotal to national debates over sectionalism and the future direction of the country but also heated up in local communities like St. Louis. These debates affected the laws of slavery and of freedom suits, as well as the operation of the laws through the local court system. Lawmakers at all levels of government struggled with how to control the increasing sectional tensions that threatened to destroy the federal union as well as the political factions within the state of Missouri. Freedom suits were integral to these debates in St. Louis, and with the *Dred Scott* case, they rose to national prominence as well. This case focused the country's attention on the plight of enslaved persons suing for freedom, arousing the anger of many fence-sitters on the slavery issue. In this direct way, freedom suits contributed to national debates over the place of enslaved and free African Americans in the country, but they also indirectly affected these debates by bringing questions of freedom before the community.

In the antebellum era, St. Louis served as a microcosm of the larger nation's political clashes; home to migrants from the Northeast, the

Midwest, and the South, as well as a massive foreign immigrant population, St. Louis vigorously debated the future of slavery in the 1840s and 1850s, with no clear outcome in sight. This explosive atmosphere meant that even the threat of abolitionist interference was enough to cast doubt on claims for freedom like that of Elsa Hicks, in part because of the vulnerability of the small and shrinking group of enslavers in the city. Despite the perceived dangers, open antislavery activism was minimal in St. Louis. Abolitionists and other antislavery sympathizers may very well have played a role in financing, encouraging, or otherwise supporting suits for freedom in St. Louis and elsewhere, but much of this activity is hidden from the historical record. In St. Louis, enslavers' paranoia over the threat of abolitionist involvement seems to be the primary way in which antislavery activism played out in the city's freedom suits.

Conclusion: After the Verdict

Determining the future of slavery in the United States was the central question of the antebellum era. Although freedom suits were disputes over the personal status of an individual enslaved plaintiff (or, occasionally, a group of plaintiffs), the various men, women, and children who participated in these cases contributed to foundational debates about the role of African Americans, enslaved and free, in local communities and in the nation. Freedom suits occurred throughout the slaveholding states—and, prior to the American Revolution, in the colonies—making these cases, while not common occurrences, certainly a well-known aspect of the law of slavery. As the initiators of these lawsuits, enslaved plaintiffs shaped the content and direction of these discussions, making their mark on the political landscape. Their lives left few traces in the historical records, and, with the exception of Dred Scott, they are largely absent from conventional histories of this era. The stories that emerge from the case files speak to the networks of interactions that took place inside and outside of the courtroom; through these efforts, enslaved plaintiffs and their supporters managed to wrestle small concessions from enslavers and set precedents for future litigants.

When enslaved individuals talked with one another, with free people of color, and with white friends, neighbors, and legal professionals about the possibility of suing for freedom, they participated in the constellation of community discussions over slavery that took place beyond the formal legal arena. Not all people of African descent interacted directly with legal institutions or with the broader deliberations surrounding freedom suits, and even for those individuals who did, knowledge of the law remained imperfect and incomplete. For many—perhaps most—enslaved individuals, suing for freedom was not an option because they lacked grounds to sue or the mobility necessary to approach the court and file a complaint. Nevertheless, the example of freedom suits in St. Louis suggests the broad dissemination of legal knowledge among enslaved and free black community members, even if the majority of these men and women never took the step of bringing a freedom suit. The history of St. Louis's legal practices created a space for enslaved and free people of color to learn about and interact with the processes of law.

Freedom suits involved a range of actors, all of whom brought their own set of interests and expectations to these contests. Lawyers were an invaluable part of the process: crafting strategies, providing support, and aiding enslaved plaintiffs with their legal actions. Attorneys joined these cases for a variety of reasons, but whatever their individual motivations were, their level of commitment to their clients had real consequences for the outcomes of these suits. In an era when the law seemed stacked against enslaved people, lawyers in freedom suits helped these plaintiffs carve out a measure of autonomy by challenging the enslavers who claimed them as human property. When faced with these provocations, enslavers had enormous financial incentives for fighting plaintiffs' claims, and many defendants fought passionately and persistently to protect their investments. In certain instances, defendants directly lied, schemed, and otherwise cheated enslaved plaintiffs out of their freedom, hoping to avoid any potential threat to their positions within their communities if the enslavers were successfully challenged in court by their human property. When community members provided testimony and support for either side of a freedom suit, they demonstrated the importance of their influence, their stakes in the outcomes of individual cases, and their concern for the development of broader legal rules for these disputes. Using freedom suits as a lens into local legal culture reveals some of the ways in which a community's views interacted with its legal actions.

Freedom suits sometimes indicated a clear path from slavery to freedom or from claiming freedom to losing free status, but more often than not, these cases were just one piece of a larger puzzle. Only by following the web of interconnected actions through the courts and behind the scenes, using additional legal actions or extralegal maneuverings, can the full picture of negotiating for freedom begin to emerge. When enslavers bargained with enslaved men and women for freedom or other privileges, they granted enslaved persons an elevated legal standing—and an ability to enter contracts and make decisions about their own lives—while often continuing to consider them property. When these arrangements ended up in court, judges and juries struggled with interpreting the strict property laws of slavery, which denied enslaved individuals the posssibility to enter legally binding contracts. When courts followed the letter of the law in these disputes, the result was that even when enslavers made promises or concessions to enslaved individuals, they retained a legal "out" for reneging on their commitments.

St. Louis sat near a confluence of rivers and legal jurisdictions that brought questions of slavery and comity to a head, making it a particularly rich place for investigating the legal implications raised by suits for freedom—especially those cases based on residence in free territory. This argument, the most common basis for freedom in St. Louis, forced each jurisdiction to decide whose laws to recognize in a dispute: the laws and customs of the slave state's court or those laws of the free territory or state. The relationship between bordering regions like the area surrounding St. Louis—what scholars have termed the "American confluence"—allowed enslaved men and women to force questions about personal status to the center of legal debates, placing the courts squarely in the middle of interstate and interregional conflicts over slavery.[1]

Closely related to the geographic location of St. Louis was its place in the mobile world of the nineteenth-century United States, where improvements in transportation made it possible for Americans to move around more easily and thus more frequently than their eighteenth-century ancestors could. The explosion of steamboat and railroad travel—as well as the increase in commerce that accompanied this expansion—contributed to the body of case law surrounding freedom suits throughout the United States. Movement across geopolitical boundaries helped to create opportunities for escape, visiting loved ones, and even temporary respite from the oppressive conditions of enslavement. When enslavers traveled or moved with enslaved men, women, and children, they risked running afoul of local laws regulating slavery and mobility, although this was a risk that many of them recognized and chose to take. On the other hand, enslaved persons' movement with their enslavers offered the possibility of suing for freedom—an opportunity that at least some enslaved individuals knew about and employed for their benefit. Freedom suits based on movement across borders signify a remarkable awareness of the intricacies of varying legal jurisdictions, speaking to the ways knowledge of law also traveled along channels of communication formed by enslaved individuals, free people of African descent, and their allies: stretching out from urban spaces to the countryside, along riverbanks and railroad stops, in church services and clandestine gatherings that took place out of view of prying eyes.

The majority of St. Louis's enslaved plaintiffs disappeared from the historical record after the verdicts in their freedom suits. For instance, the last trace of Thornton Kinney, who sued based on his free birth in Virginia, traveled to Liberia, and worked on steamboats for years before his capture as an alleged runaway slave, is the court's decision to dismiss his case in 1855 because he failed to provide financial security for his suit.[2] After the case of Elsa Hicks and her child (whose name is not listed in the case file) against Patrick T. McSherry ended because Hicks failed to show up in court, no additional evidence mentions Elsa Hicks. The defendant in Hicks's suit, Patrick T. McSherry, died in St. Louis in 1861 of what the death certificate described as a "softening of the brain," but he left no indication of what happened to Hicks or her child.[3] The conclusion of Kinney's and Hicks's freedom suits meant that they returned to relative obscurity from the historical record of their communities, perhaps working as slaves or continuing to struggle for the freedom they believed they deserved.

When lawsuits did not result in freedom, the plaintiffs in these cases occasionally appeared in additional records of their enslavers. For example, there are several references to Arch and Jack, who sued Barnabas Harris based on the manumission deed of their former enslaver, in the records of Harris's probate file and the personal papers of their former enslaver's administrator. The freedom suit files suggest that both Arch and Jack lost their applications for freedom, but while Arch appears in the distribution of his owner's estate in 1824 and 1825, Jack does not. The probate file also contains receipts for fees paid in Jack's freedom suit, including a couple of receipts for work done in 1821 and 1823, two and four years after his freedom suit case file ends.[4] These last references in the probate file imply that Jack's case continued in some fashion, perhaps for years beyond the final disposition that has survived in the case files. Jack's lack of a last name and the popularity of his first name make it difficult to know if he continued to live or work in St. Louis after this date. Although it is unclear when the sale took place, several receipts to the heirs of Jack's enslaver indicate that Peter Piant purchased Jack as a slave for $650 sometime prior to 1836 (the date of the first receipt).[5] The attorney and freedom suit defendant Rufus Pettibone died in 1825, and although there is a probate file for the defendant against his enslaved client Milly, who lost her freedom suit in 1820, Milly and her son Moses do not appear in the file's inventories of slaves of the estate.[6] Because Milly's enslaver died fourteen years after her suit, she, like many enslaved persons, may have been sold or died prior to the probate case of her enslaver's estate. Although there are few details about the daily lives of Arch, Jack, and Milly, or whether they made additional attempts for freedom, they, like numerous freedom suit plaintiffs, continued to work as slaves after their suits, and thus, the final disposition of their enslavers' estate involved fateful decisions about their futures.

Plaintiffs whose cases affirmed their free status often had additional encounters with legal institutions—leaving a trail of information about their lives after the freedom suits. For example, Missouri's licensure laws (passed in 1835) required any free person of African descent living in the state to secure a license, and these legal documents recorded certain details about the holder. After the 1843 jury verdict freed Alsey because she lived and worked in Illinois, she obtained a license in 1846 that records her age, her height, her bond of security, and her occupation as a washer.[7] Many freedom suit plaintiffs did not have a last name listed in their case file, which is part of the challenge of following plaintiffs after their cases.[8] Sometimes former slaves chose a last name for themselves, or took the surname of their enslaver. After Winny and her children's freedom suit against Phebe Whitesides (and the attorney Rufus Pettibone) established the doctrine of whether or not a defendant intended to set up residence in a free territory, Winny's son Harry adopted the last name of his former enslaver. Twenty-two-year-old Harry Whiteside, described as a "bright black mulatto," received a license in 1841 as a whitewasher.[9] In other examples, name changes make it impossible to be certain what identity the person used in later records. For instance, after the court released Julia and her daughter from the defendant Samuel T. McKinney in the mid-1830s, two women named Julia appear in the records of the 1840s. Both women were washerwomen whose ages match that of the plaintiff Julia, one a "bright mulatto" and the other described as "stout made" with a "dark complexion" and "thick lips."[10] None of the licenses for women named Harriet matched the age and description of Julia's daughter, who may have moved away from St. Louis, gotten married, or passed away before securing her license.

Lucy Delaney, the only freedom suit plaintiff to leave an account of life after her case in her 1892 narrative, recorded how the terror she felt during her long confinement in jail was only the beginning of her many personal struggles.[11] The year after Delaney celebrated her free-dom suit verdict, she married Frederick Turner and moved to Illinois; but the following year, Turner died in a steamboat explosion, and Lucy returned to St. Louis and obtained a license as a washer.[12] Delaney even-tually remarried, and although her second marriage lasted decades and resulted in four children, none of the couple's children survived past the age of twenty-four.[13] After the Civil War, like the majority of families who had endured forced separations under slavery, Delaney sought to reconnect with lost family members. She managed to reunite with her father, but "forty-five years of separation, hard work, rough times and heart longings" had prematurely aged him, and "he felt like a stranger in a strange land."[14] Delaney joined numerous other freedpeople in the decades after the Civil War as an active participant in black communal and religious organizations, including the Methodist Episcopal Church, women's Masonic groups, and the women's auxiliary to a Civil War vet-erans' association. Delaney published her life story in the 1890s, almost twenty years before she died in 1910 of "senility."[15]

Delaney's decision to publish her story came at a time when Jim Crow laws began to decimate the limited rights of people of African descent throughout the United States, and only a few short years before the U.S. Supreme Court's decision in *Plessy v. Ferguson* (1896) confirmed the doc-trine of "separate but equal."[16] Delaney opens her narrative by explain-ing that many of her friends had "urged her" to tell her story, so that "those of you who have never suffered as we have, perhaps may suppose the case."[17] The narrative is full of asides detailing the horrors of slav-ery, reminding readers of past struggles, and warning of the perils that occurred in that era of inequality. The phenomenon of freedom suits, in this late nineteenth-century context, must have seemed foreign to Afri-can Americans who found their access to legal institutions restricted by the end of Reconstruction and the reassertion of white supremacy under former enslavers. Delaney's message is clear: although she suffered unspeakable pain through the loss of family members after slavery, she clung to the satisfaction of knowing that her children were "born free and died free."[18] In her view, freedom was not the end of the struggle, but it did make the pain worth enduring. Near the conclusion of her story, Delaney informs her reader, "I have brought you with me face to face with but only a few of the painful facts engendered by slavery, and the rest can be drawn from history."[19] This book has been an effort to examine some of that history.

Appendix

Table 1. Population of St. Louis, 1820–1860

Year	Total population	White population	Free people of color	Enslaved population
1820	10,049	8,014	196	1,810
1830	14,125	11,109	220	2,796
1840	16,469	14,407	531	1,531
1850	77,890	73,806	1,398	2,656
1860	160,773	157,476	1,755	1,548

Note: No Census Data is available prior to 1820. Data from 1820 and 1830 are for St. Louis County, before St. Louis City split from the County. Adapted from the UVAHCB and Wade, *Slavery in the Cities*, 327.

Table 2. Total Cases and Outcomes in St. Louis Freedom Suits, 1810–1860

Years	Cases	Plaintiff freed	% freed	Plaintiff not freed	% not freed	Outcome unknown	% un-known	Death of plaintiff	% death of plaintiff
1810–15	2	1	50	1	50	0	0	0	0
1816–20	4	1	25	1	25	2	50	0	0
1821–25	27	20	74	5	19	2	7	0	0
1826–30	44	15	34	14	32	14	32	1	2
1831–35	71	26	36.5	9	13	31	43.5	5	7
1836–40	38	16	42	10	26	11	29	1	3
1841–45	64	22	34	25	39	17	27	0	0
1846–50	22	5	23	4	18	13	59	0	0
1851–55	11	2	18	6	55	3	27	0	0
1856–60	4	2	50	2	50	0	0	0	0
Total	287	110	38	77	27	93	32	7	3

Note: Data is collected from the St. Louis Circuit Court Case files and the Circuit Court Record Books. Cases of voluntary dismissal are counted as unknown because the status of the plaintiff cannot be determined from the records of their freedom suits.

Table 3. Arguments Presented in St. Louis Freedom Suits, 1810–1860

Years	Total cases	Residence in free territory	Free birth	Manu-mission	Unknown
1810–15	2	1	1	0	0
1816–20	4	1	0	3	0
1821–25	27	24	16	0	2
1826–30	44	40	10	10	2
1831–35	71	61	33	10	1
1836–40	38	26	22	5	0
1841–45	64	42	23	18	1
1846–50	22	8	5	10	2
1851–55	11	6	4	4	0
1856–60	4	0	2	2	0
Total	287	209	116	62	8

Note: Freedom suits frequently included multiple arguments in each case.

Table 4. Outcomes Using Residence in Free Territory, 1810–1860

Years	Cases	Plaintiff freed	% freed	Plaintiff not freed	% Not freed	Outcome unknown	% unknown	Death of plaintiff	% death of plaintiff
1810–15	1	1	100	0	0	0	0	0	0
1816–20	1	0	0	1	100	0	0	0	0
1821–25	24	19	79	4	17	1	4	0	0
1826–30	40	13	32.5	14	35	12	30	1	2.5
1831–35	61	24	39	6	10	27	44	4	7
1836–40	26	7	27	8	31	10	38	1	4
1841–45	42	12	29	21	50	9	21	0	0
1846–50	8	3	37.5	3	37.5	2	25	0	0
1851–55	6	0	0	4	66.5	2	33.5	0	0
1856–60	0	0	0	0	0	0	0	0	0
Total	209	79	38	61	29	63	30	6	3

Table 5. Outcomes Using Freedom from Birth, 1810–1860

Years	Cases	Plaintiff freed	% freed	Plaintiff not freed	% not freed	Outcome unknown	% unknown	Death of plaintiff	% death of plaintiff
1810–15	1	0	0	1	100	0	0	0	0
1816–20	0	0	0	0	0	0	0	0	0
1821–25	16	16	100	0	0	0	0	0	0
1826–30	10	3	30	1	10	6	60	0	0
1831–35	33	12	36.5	6	18	11	33.5	4	12
1836–40	22	13	59	4	18	4	18	1	5
1841–45	23	12	52	6	26	5	22	0	0
1846–50	5	1	20	3	60	1	20	0	0
1851–55	4	0	0	3	75	1	25	0	0
1856–60	2	0	0	2	100	0	0	0	0
Total	116	57	49	26	22.5	28	24	5	4.5

Table 6. Outcomes Using Prior Manumission or Agreement to Manumit, 1810–1860

Years	Cases	Plaintiff freed	% freed	Plaintiff not freed	% not freed	Outcome unknown	% unknown	Death of plaintiff	% death of plaintiff
1810–15	0	0	0	0		0	0	0	0
1816–20	3	1	33.3	2	66.6	0	0	0	0
1821–25	0	0	0	0	0	0	0	0	0
1826–30	10	6	60	2	20	2	20	0	0
1831–35	10	4	40	0	0	6	60	0	0
1836–40	5	0	0	2	40	3	60	0	0
1841–45	18	8	44.5	4	22	6	33.5	0	0
1846–50	10	1	10	0	0	9	90	0	0
1851–55	4	2	50	1	25	1	25	0	0
1856–60	2	2	100	0	0	0	0	0	0
Total	62	24	39	11	18	27	44	0	0

Table 7. Outcomes of Cases with Unknown Arguments, 1810–1860

Years	Cases	Plaintiff freed	% freed	Plaintiff not freed	% not freed	Outcome unknown	% unknown	Death of plaintiff	% death of plaintiff
1810–15	0	0	0	0	0	0	0	0	0
1816–20	0	0	0	0	0	0	0	0	0
1821–25	2	0	0	1	50	1	50	0	0
1826–30	2	1	50	0	0	1	50	0	0
1831–35	1	0	0	0	0	1	100	0	0
1836–40	0	0	0	0	0	0	0	0	0
1841–45	1	0	0	1	100	0	0	0	0
1846–50	2	0	0	0	0	2	100	0	0
1851–55	0	0	0	0	0	0	0	0	0
1856–60	0	0	0	0	0	0	0	0	0
Total	8	1	12.5	2	25	5	62.5	0	0

St. Louis Freedom Suit Case Files in Chronological Order*

Note: All cases are part of the St. Louis Circuit Court Historical Records Project unless otherwise specified.

Betty, Rachel, and Lovina v. Joseph Yoche and James McDonald, October 1810, General Court of the Territory of Louisiana, Case No. 27

William Tarleton v. Jacob Horine, February 1814, Case No. 7

Arch, a black man v. Barnabas Harris, October 1818, no case number

Jack, a black man v. Barnabas Harris, October 1818, Case No. 111

Milly, a black woman v. Mathias Rose, August 1819, Case No. 20

Winny, a woman of color v. Samuel Donner, August 1820, Case No. 70

Tempe, a black woman v. Risdon H. Price, April 1821, Case No. 181

Laban, a free person of color v. Risdon H. Price, April 1821, Case No. 182

Winny v. Phebe Whitesides (alias Pruitt), April 1821, Case No. 190

Sarah, a free girl v. Michael Hatton, April 1821, Case No. 191

Lydia, a free girl v. John Butler, April 1821, Case No. 192

Nancy, a free girl v. Isaac Voteau, April 1821, Case No. 193

Jenny, a free girl v. Robert Musick, April 1821, Case No. 194

Jerry, a free man of color v. Charles Hatton, April 1821, Case No. 195

Daniel, a free man v. John Whitesides, April 1821, Case No. 196

Hannah, a free girl v. Phebe Whitesides (alias Pruitt), April 1821, Case No. 197

Malinda, a free girl v. Phebe Whitesides (alias Pruitt), April 1821, Case No. 198

Lewis, a free boy of color v. Phebe Whitesides (alias Pruitt), April 1821, Case No. 199

Marie, a free mulatto girl v. Auguste Chouteau, April 1821, Case No. 205

Pelagie, a woman of color v. Francois Valois, February 1822, Case No. 12

Susan, a black woman v. Henry Hight, February 1822, Case No. 127

Pelagie, a person of color v. Jean P. Cabanne, June 1822, Case No. 9

Jeffrie, a mulatto boy v. Joseph Robidoux, October 1822, Case No. 39

Malinda, a free person of color v. Robert Wilburn, October 1823, Case No. 7

Nelly, a woman of color v. Robert Wilburn, October 1823, Case No. 8

Lethe Fenwick v. Samuel Abbot, October 1823, Case No. 99

Lorinda, a free girl of color v. Rufus Pettibone, Charles Hatton, Owen Wingfield, Isaac Voteau, John Butler, John Whitset, and Michael Sanford, July 1825, Case No. 11

Winny, a free woman of color v. Rufus Pettibone, Charles Hatton, Owen Wingfield, Isaac Voteau, John Butler, John Whitset, Michael Sanford, July 1825, Case No. 12

Malinda, a free girl of color v. Rufus Pettibone, Charles Hatton, Owen Wingfield, Isaac Voteau, John Butler, John Whitset, Michael Sanford, July 1825, Case No. 13

Harry, a free boy of color v. Rufus Pettibone, Charles Hatton, Owen Wingfield,

Isaac Voteau, John Butler, John Whitset, Michael Sanford, July 1825, Case No. 14

Jenny, a free woman of color v. Ephraim Musick, Charles Hatton, Owen Wingfield, Isaac Voteau, John Butler, John Whitset, Michael Sanford, July 1825, Case No. 15

Winnetta, a free girl of color v. Ephraim Musick, Charles Hatton, Owen Wingfield, Isaac Voteau, John Butler, John Whitset, Michael Sanford, July 1825, Case No. 16

Marguerite, a free woman of color v. Pierre Chouteau, Sr., July 1825, Case No. 26

State of Missouri v. John K. Walker (jailor of St. Louis), Pierre Chouteau, Bernard Pratt, Alexis Amelin, March 1826, no case number

Israel, a free man of color v. William Rector, March 1826, Case No. 21

Dorinda, a woman of color v. John Simonds Jr., March 1826, Case No. 42

Betsy Hagan v. Philip Rocheblave, July 1826, Case No. 77

John Merry, a free man of color v. Clayton Tiffin and Louis Menard, November 1826, Case No. 18

Joseph Jefferson v. William McCutchen and James McKnight, November 1826, Case No. 23

Polly Wilson, a free woman of color v. Jacob Baum, March 1827, Case No. 19

Francois LaGrange, a free man of color v. Bernard Pratte, Pierre Chouteau, Bertholemew Berthold, and Jean P. Cabanne, March 1827, Case No. 29

Milly, a free mulatto woman v. Stephen Smith, July 1827, Case No. 14

Harry Dick, a free negro man v. Stephen Smith, July 1827, Case No. 15

William, a free negro boy v. Stephen Smith, July 1827, Case No. 16

David Shipman, a free mulatto boy v. Stephen Smith, July 1827, Case No. 17

Aspasia, a free woman of color v. Francois Chouteau and Pierre Menard, July 1827, Case No. 24

Theotiste (alias Catiche), a woman of color v. Pierre Chouteau Jr., November 1827, Case No. 6

Mary, a woman of color v. Francis Menard and Andre Landreville, November 1827, Case No. 7

Elizabeth, a free girl of color v. Francis Menard and Andre Landreville, November 1827, Case No. 13

Virginia, a free girl of color v. Francis Menard and Andre Landreville, November 1827, Case No. 14

Victoire, a free girl of color v. Francis Menard and Andre Landreville, November 1827, Case No. 15

John Singleton, a free man of color v. Alexander Scott and Robert Lewis, November 1827, Case No. 23

Molly Rector, a free woman of color v. John Bivens, November 1827, Case No. 26

Aspasia, a free woman of color v. Francis Chouteau and Pierre Menard, March 1828, Case No. 5

Peter, a free man of color v. James Walton, March 1828, Case No. 12

Dolly, a free woman of color v. John Young, July 1828, Case No. 7

Suzette, a free woman of color v. John Reynolds, July 1828, Case No. 9

Angelique, a free woman of color v. John Reynolds, July 1828, Case No. 10

Edmund, a free boy of color v. John Reynolds, July 1828, Case No. 11

John, a free boy of color v. John Reynolds, July 1828, Case No. 12

George Relf, a man of color v. Thompson H. Ficklin, July 1828, Case No. 64

Matilda, a free girl of color v. Philip Rocheblave and Mary Louisa Rocheblave, November 1828, Case No. 38

Mary, a free woman of color v. Francis Menard, March 1829, Case No. 21

Elizabeth, a free girl of color v. Francis Menard, March 1829, Case No. 22

Virginia a free girl of color v. Francis Menard, March 1829, Case No. 23

Victoire a free girl of color v. Francis Menard, March 1829, Case No. 24

Vincent, a free person of color v. Jerry, a free person of color, July 1829, Case No. 14

Milly, a woman of color v. Wiley Williams, July 1829, Case No. 39

Peter, a man of color v. James Walton, July 1829, Case No. 40

Nicholas Jones, a free man of color v. John W. Honey and John Gay, July 1829, Case No. 41

Carey Ewton, a free man of color v. Benjamin Wilder, November 1829, Case No. 10

Maria Whiten, a free woman of color v. Garland Rucker, November 1829, Case No. 14

Patrick Henry, a free boy of color v. Garland Rucker, November 1829, Case No. 16

Vincent, a man of color v. James Duncan, November 1829, Case No. 110

William Henry, a black man v. David G. Bates, July 1830, Case No. 30

Ralph, a man of color v. Coleman Duncan and James Duncan, July 1830, Case No. 35

Joe, a black man v. Coleman Duncan and James Duncan, July 1830, Case No. 47

Cary, a man of color v. Benjamin Wilder, March 1831, Case No. 53

Matilda, a woman of color v. Charles St. Vrain, March 1831, Case No. 58

Julia, a woman of color v. Samuel T. McKinney, March 1831, Case No. 66

Peter, a man of color v. James Walton, March 1831, Case No. 67

Nelly Richards, a woman of color v. William Sewel, July 1831, Case No. 2

Jack, a man of color v. Charles Collins, July 1831, Case No. 3

Dunky, a colored woman v. Andrew Hay, July 1831, Case No. 12

Mariquette v. Samuel T. McKinney, July 1831, Case No. 13

Jane, a woman of color v. William Dallam, July 1831, Case No. 22

Margaret, a girl of color v. William Dallam, November 1831, Case No. 4

Sally, a girl of color v. William Dallam, November 1831, Case No. 7

Henry, a boy of color v. William Dallam, November 1831, Case No. 8

Anna, a woman of color v. Thomas Higginbotham, November 1831, Case No. 12

Louisa, a girl of color v. Sanford Calvert, November 1831, Case No. 75

Tenor Washington, a woman of color v. Henry Scott, John Scott, and Jeremiah Johnson, March 1832, Case No. 1

John, a boy of color v. William Campbell, March 1832, Case No. 6

Thenia, a woman of color v. Green Crowder, March 1832, Case No. 9

Charlotte, a colored girl v. Green Crowder, March 1832, Case No. 10

Vina, a woman of color v. Martin Mitchell, March 1832, Case No. 19

Matilda, a woman of color v. Elijah Mitchell, July 1832, Case No. 47

Anson, a boy of color v. Elijah Mitchell, July 1832, Case No. 48

Michael, a boy of color v. Elijah Mitchell, July 1832, Case No. 48 (also recorded as 49)

Sam, a person of color v. Alexander P. Field and Elijah Mitchell, July 1832, Case No. 49

Nathan, a person of color v. Alexander P. Field and Elijah Mitchell, July 1832, Case No. 50

Mary Ann, a person of color v. Alexander P. Field and Elijah Mitchell, July 1832, Case No. 51

Matilda, a woman of color v. Henry G. Mitchell and Henry Russell, July 1832, Case No. 55

Michael, a boy of color v. Henry G. Mitchell and Henry Russell, July 1832, Case No. 56

Anson, a boy of color v. Henry G. Mitchell and Henry Russell, July 1832, Case No. 57

Mahala, a free woman of color v. Martin Mitchell, November 1832, Case No. 6

Susan, a girl of color v. Lemon Parker, November 1832, Case No. 7

Tenor Washington, a woman of color v. Henry Scott and John Emerson, November 1832, Case No. 18

Jack Barton, a man of color v. William Glasgow and Ross Glasgow, November 1832, Case No. 27

Leah, a woman of color v. Arthur Mitchell, November 1832, Case No. 68

Susan, a girl of color v. Lemon Parker, March 1833, Case No. 5

Sarah, a girl of color v. Thomas Johnson and Janus Johnson, July 1833, Case No. 9

Harriet, an infant v. Samuel T. McKinney and James Walker, July 1833, Case No. 17

Milly, a woman of color v. Wiley Williams, July 1833, Case No. 28

Harriet v. Samuel T. McKinney, July 1833, Case No. 54

Ralph, a free man of color v. Robert Duncan and James Duncan, July 1833, Case No. 99

James Wilkinson, a man of color v. Aaron Young, July 1833, Case No. 102

Mary, a woman of color v. Francis Menard and Daniel Busby, November 1833, Case No. 34

Adolphe Vincent, a boy of color v. Marie P. Leduc, November 1833, Case No. 49

Marcelline Vincent v. Marie P. Leduc, November 1833, Case No. 50

Louise Vincent, a woman of color v. Marie P. Leduc, November 1833, Case No. 52

Henry, a man of color v. William Morrisson and John C. Swan, July 1834, Case No. 19

Reuben, a man of color v. William Morrisson and John C. Swan, July 1834, Case No. 20

Andrew Dutton, a free boy of color v. John Paca, July 1834, Case No. 114

Abraham Dutton, a free boy of color v. John Paca, July 1834, Case No. 115

Lemon Dutton, a free girl of color v. John Paca, July 1834, Case No. 116

Mary Ann (also known as Julia), an infant of color v. Robert Duncan, November 1834, Case No. 46

Rachel, a woman of color v. William Walker, November 1834, Case No. 82

James Henry, a boy of color v. William Walker, November 1834, Case No. 83

Nelson Kerr, a free man of color v. Mathew Kerr, July 1834, Case No. 104

Judy (also known as Julia Logan) v. John Berry Meachum, March 1835, Case No. 11

Hetty, a woman of color v. Arthur L. Magenis, March 1835, Case No. 43

Nancy Ligon, a woman of color v. Daniel Ligon and William Myers, March 1835, Case No. 67

Lewis, a man of color v. James Newton and Jacob Cooper, July 1835, Case No. 7

Daniel Wilson, a man of color v. Edmund Melvin, July 1835, Case No. 10

Sally Melvin, a woman of color v. Robert Cohen, July 1835, Case No. 12

Daniel Wilson v. Robert Cohen, July 1835, Case No. 13

Eliza Tyler, a woman of color v. Nelson Campbell, July 1835, Case No. 35

Mary Farnham v. Samuel D. Walker, July 1835, Case No. 48

Mary Johnson (also known as Bevinue) v. Michael Menard, July 1835, Case No. 66

Paul Auguste Allard, an infant of color v. Bazil Auguste Allard and Arend Rutgers, July 1835, Case No. 67

Mary Ann Steel v. Curtis Skinner, July 1835, Case No. 96

Mary Ann Steel v. William Walker, July 1835, Case No. 97

Sally, a person of color v. Henry Chouteau, July 1835, Case No. 101

Agnis (also known as Agathe), a woman of color v. Pierre Menard, November 1835, Case No. 3

Michael Edwards, a colored lad v. J. J. Birdsong, November 1835, Case No. 11

Josephine LaCourse, an infant of color v. George Mitchell, November 1835, Case No. 22

Milly, a woman of color v. James Duncan, November 1835, Case No. 63

Courtney, a woman of color v. Samuel Rayburn, March 1836, Case No. 10

Ben, a man of color v. Thomas J. White and William L. Woods, March 1836, Case No. 50

Green Berry Logan, an infant of color v. John Berry Meachum, a free man of color, July 1836, Case No. 22

Delph (also known as Delphy), a mulatress v. Stephen Dorris, November 1836, Case No. 4

Aspisa, a woman of color v. Joseph Rosati, March 1837, Case No. 39

Judy, a woman of color v. John Berry Meachum, March 1837, Case No. 40

Celeste, a woman of color v. Laforce Papin, March 1837, Case No. 41

Celestine, a woman of color v. Laforce Papin, March 1837, Case No. 42

Andrew, a boy of color v. John B. Sarpy, March 1837, Case No. 43

Lewis Stubbs v. William Burd, July 1837, Case No. 132

William Stubbs v. William Burd, July 1837, Case No. 133

Aspisa, a woman of color v. Hardage Lane, July 1837, Case No. 263

Jack, a man of color v. Absalom Link, November 1837, Case No. 38

James alias James Haskins v. Charles Haskins, November 1837, Case No. 169

Nancy Stubbs v. William Burd, November 1837, Case No. 521

Robert Stubbs v. William Burd, November 1837, Case No. 522

Phebe Stubbs v. William Burd, November 1837, Case No. 523

Stepney, Tarlton, Cassy, Lucy Jane, George Louis, Marquetta, and Huriah v. Duff Fields, March 1838, SLCCF, Case No. 46

Rebecca, a colored girl v. James Black and Louis Matlock, July 1838, Case No. 237

Samuel Stokes, a man of color v. John Finney and William Finney, November 1838, Case No. 501

James Talbot v. Delford Benton, James C. Musick, and Prudence Musick, March 1839, Case No. 92

Ann Davis v. James F. Symington, March 1839, Case No. 515

Charles Endicott v. Benjamin Clapp, July 1839, Case No. 116

Lewis, a boy of color v. John Stacker, July 1839, Case No. 185

Celeste, a woman of color v. Alexander Papin, July 1839, Case No. 335

Aspasia (also known as Aspisa) v. Hardage Lane, July 1839, Case No. 347

Andrew, a person of color v. Peter Sarpy, November 1839, Case No. 20

Polly Wash v. Joseph M. Magehan, November 1839, Case No. 167

Eliza Briscoe v. William Anderson, November 1839, Case No. 219

Seyton (also known as Sydney), a woman of color v. William Littleton, March 1840, Case No. 3

Charles, a man of color v. Peter Verhagen, July 1840, Case No. 203

Brunetta Barnes, of color v. John Berry Meachum, November 1840, Case No. 40

Archibald Barnes, of color v. John Berry Meachum, November 1840, Case No. 41

Archibald Barnes, of color v. John Berry Meachum, November 1840, Case No. 120

Brunetta Barnes, of color v. John Berry Meachum, November 1840, Case No. 121

Pierre, a mulatto v. Therese Cerre Chouteau, November 1840, Case No. 192

Diana Cephas, a woman of color v. James Scott, November 1840, Case No. 254

Josiah Cephas, a colored boy v. James Scott and Murray McConnell, November 1840, Case No. 361

Richard Tompson, a man of color v. James Blount and Leakin Baker, March 1841, Case No. 161

James Talbot v. Delford Benton, James Musick, and Prudence Musick, March 1841, Case No. 162

Alsey, a woman of color v. William Randolph, March 1841, Case No. 305

Charles, a man of color v. Belina Christy, March 1841, Case No. 343

Louis Scott, a man of color v. William Burd, March 1841, Case No. 362

Diana Cephas, a woman of color v. James Scott, July 1841, Case No. 5

Squire Brown, a man of color v. William C. Anderson, July 1841, Case No. 119

Charles, a man of color v. Peter Verhagen, August 1841, Case No. 75

Mary Robertson, a person of color v. Ringrose D. Watson, November 1841, Case No. 30

Jonathan, a man of color v. Marshall Brotherton, Joel Danah, and Aza Willoughby, November 1841, Case No. 32

Peter, a man of color v. John Richardson, November 1841, Case No. 84

Preston, Braxton, Mary, Nat, Beverly, et al. v. George W. Coons, Administrator of Duty, et al., November 1841, Case No. 674

Charles, a man of color v. Belina Christy, February 1842, Case No. 359

Mary, a colored woman v. James alias E. C. Dougherty and Richmond Curle, July 1842, Case No. 23

Vica, a woman of color v. Samuel Hobart, July 1842, Case No. 31

Thadeus Alonzo, a boy of color v. John Sparr, Samuel Hobart, James Mellody, and George Charles, July 1842, Case No. 32

Musa Ben Abel Gazen, a boy of color v. John Sparr, Samuel Hobart, James Mellody, and George Charles, July 1842, Case No. 33

Jinny Jackson, a woman of color v. James O. Fraser, July 1842, Case No. 102

Henry Jackson, a person of color v. James O. Fraser, July 1842, Case No. 103

Ann Maria, a person of color v. James O. Fraser, July 1842, Case No. 104

Sally Jackson (also known as Sarah), a person of color v. James O. Fraser, July 1842, Case No. 105

Margaret Jackson, a person of color v. James O. Fraser, July 1842, Case No. 106

William Henry, a person of color v. James O. Fraser, July 1842, Case No. 107

Smith, a person of color v. James O. Fraser, July 1842, Case No. 108

Pierre, a mulatto v. Gabriel Chouteau, November 1842, Case No. 125

Thomas Jefferson, a man of color v. Milton W. Hopkins, March 1843, Case No. 14

Rebecca, a negro woman v. James Black, Thomas Horine, and George Melody, March 1843, Case No. 24

Emily Davenport v. Rene Paul, March 1843, SLCCF, Case No. 239

Squire Brown, a man of color v. Charles Anderson, April 1843, Case No. 232

Mary Charlotte, a woman of color v. Gabriel Chouteau, November 1843, Case No. 13

Catherine, Felix, William, & Minta, persons of color v. Thomas Hundley, D. Pattison, and William Russell, November 1843, Case No. 20

Squire Brown, a man of color v. Charles Anderson and S. Israel, November 1843, Case No. 328

Samuel, a man of color v. John Howdeshell, April 1844, Case No. 6

Louis Chouteau, a man of color v. Gabriel Chouteau, April 1844, Case No. 51

Michel Paul, a man of color v. Gabriel Paul, April 1844, Case No. 151

Adrian Paschal, a man of color v. Richard W. Ulrici, April 1844, Case No. 340

Mary Ann Speaks v. John M. Jameson, April 1844, Case No. 386

Thomas Jefferson, a man of color v. Milton W. Hopkins, September 1844, Case No. 219

James, a person of color v. Hiram Cordell, November 1844, Case No. 8

Martha Ann, a person of color v. Hiram Cordell, November 1844, Case No. 9

Celestine, a woman of color v. Julia Dumont, November 1844, Case No. 15

Hannah, a woman of color v. John Pitcher, November 1844, Case No. 16

Lucy Ann Britton v. David D. Mitchell, November 1844, Case No. 18

Hannah, a woman of color v. John Pitcher, November 1844, Case No. 28

Jesse, a man of color v. George W. Coons, Administrator, November 1844, Case No. 32

Preston, a man of color v. George W. Coons, Administrator, November 1844, Case No. 34

Nat, a person of color v. George W. Coons, Administrator, November 1844, Case No. 35

Ann, a person of color v. William Wilson and John M. Jamison, November 1844, Case No. 39

Cloe Ann Smith, a woman of color v. Franklin Knox, November 1844, Case No. 120

Jane Brown (also known as Jinny), a woman of color v. Francis I. Steigers, November 1844, Case No. 173

Amy Moore v. Robert N. Moore, November 1844, Case No. 174

Jim Brown v. William Head, November 1844, Case No. 229

Mary Brown v. William Head, November 1844, Case No. 230

Stephen Brown v. William Head, November 1844, Case No. 231

Martha Drusella v. Richmond L. Curle, November 1844, Case No. 252

Mary, a negro woman v. James Clemens, Sr., November 1844, Case No. 346

Mary Robinson, a woman of color v. Ringrose D. Watson and Amos Corson, April 1845, Case No. 11

Elsa Hicks, a mulatto girl v. S. Burrell and James Mitchell, April 1845, Case No. 55

Michel Paul v. Adolph Paul, Administrator, April 1845, Case No. 143

Rachel Steele, a colored woman v. Thomas Taylor, April 1845, Case No. 187

Thomas Jefferson, a man of color v. George A. Colton and Jonathan Moulton, November 1845, Case No. 24

Sarah, a colored woman v. William Waddingham, November 1845, Case No. 81

Jane McCray, a mulatto woman v. William R. Hopkins, William Miller, Eliza Oliver, et al., November 1845, Case No. 162

Malinda, a woman of color v. George W. Coons, Administrator, November 1845, Case No. 220

Caroline Bascom, a free mulatto woman v. John H. Ferguson, April 1846, Case No. 20

Dred Scott, a man of color v. Irene Emerson, November 1846, Case No. 1

Harriet Scott, a woman of color v. Irene Emerson, November 1846, Case No. 2

Matilda Thomas (also known as Matilda Cunningham), person of color v. William Littleton, November 1846, Case No. 28

Missouri Littleton v. William Littleton, November 1846, Case No. 29

Gabriel, a man of color v. Andrew Christy, Executor, and Mary Coons, Executrix, November 1846, Case No. 324

Elsa Hicks, a mulatto girl v. Patrick T. McSherry, November 1847, Case No. 121

Nancy, a free woman of color v. Enoch Steen, April 1848, Case No. 4

Jane Cotton, a free person of color v. James A. Little, April 1848, Case No. 37

Thomas Scott, a man of color v. James Harrison, November 1848, Case No. 90

Alfred Taylor, a free man of color v. Cornelius Van Houten, Lewis Martin, and Samuel Conway, November 1848, Case No. 93

Peggy Perryman, a woman of color v. Joseph Philibert, November 1848, Case No. 255

Patsy Curd v. William H. Barksdale, April 1850, Case No. 1

Harry Duty v. John F. Darby, Administrator, April 1850, Case No. 17

Ellen Duty v. John F. Darby, Administrator, April 1850, Case No. 18

Nelly Duty v. John F. Darby, Administrator, April 1850, Case No. 19

Jordan Duty v. John F. Darby, Administrator, April 1850, Case No. 20

Preston Duty v. John F. Darby, Administrator, April 1850, Case No. 21

Lucinda Duty v. John F. Darby, Administrator, April 1850, Case No. 22

Caroline Duty v. John F. Darby, Administrator, April 1850, Case No. 23

Mary Duty v. John F. Darby, Administrator, April 1850, Case No. 24

David McFoy v. William Brown, April 1850, Case No. 37

Mary, of color, and her children Samuel & Edward v. Launcelot H. Calvert, April 1851, Case No. 2

Samuel, infant of color v. Bernard T. Lynch, November 1851, Case No. 29

Henry Lohre v. Gayers Duty, April 1852, no case number

Gabriel, of color v. Michael Wiles, April 1852, Case No. 16

Laura, a woman of color v. Henry Belt, April 1852, Case No. 22

George Johnson, a man of color v. Henry Moore, April 1852, Case No. 36

George Johnson, a man of color v. Reuben Bartlett, November 1852, Case No. 281

Thornton Kinney, a man of color v. John F. Hatcher and Charles C. Bridges, November 1853, Case No. 35

Hester Williams, Ella Williams & Priscilla Williams v. A. B. McAfee, Frederick Norcum, Glanville Blakey, and William Moore, November 1853, Case No. 119

Mount St. Mary's College (to the use of Louisa, a woman of color) v. Francis B. Jameson and Edmond McCabe, April 1854, Case No. 107

Mary (also known as Mary Davis), a woman of color v. Samuel B. Bellis, April 1855, Case No. 96

Richard Clinton, a man of color v. John Blackburn, Edward Blackburn, Martha A. Blackburn, Charles A. Blackburn, Rufus C. Blackburn, and Edward Hall, Curator, September 1859, Case No. 111

Louisa (also known as Louisa Lewis) v. Henry N. Hart, Administrator, February 1860, Case No. 12

Isham Shaw v. Augustus H. Evans, February 1860, Case No. 456

Julia Shaw v. Augustus H. Evans, February 1860, Case No. 457

Notes

Abbreviations

A Letter Signed. ALS
Missouri History Museum, St. Louis. MHM
Missouri State Archives–St. Louis. MSA-STL
Missouri Supreme Court Database. MOSCD
St. Louis Circuit Court Historical Records Project Files. SLCCR
St. Louis Circuit Court Case Files. SLCCF
St. Louis Circuit Court Record Book. CCRB
St. Louis Circuit Court Execution Book. SLEB
St. Louis Criminal Court Case Files. SLCRCF
St. Louis Probate Files. SLPF
University of Virginia, Historical Census Browser. UVAHCB
Western Historical Manuscripts Collection, Columbia, MO. WHMC

Introduction

1. "Constitution of 1818," in Verlie, *Illinois Constitutions*, 38–39.

2. Cross's daughter Rachel claimed that her husband, Robert Funkhouser, had "borrowed" Alsey from her father and that, when Funkhouser owed money to a third party who seized Alsey as payment, she tried to stop the transaction. *Alsey, a woman of color v. William Randolph*, March 1841, Case No. 305, SLCCR, 51–55 (page numbers of case files correspond to the order of documents in each file).

3. Ibid., 23.

4. It is not clear when Alsey had her son, Moses, and her other children; Moses is listed as seven years old in 1843, and Judge Wash later makes reference to two other, older children that are likely Alsey's children as well. *William S. Randolph, to the use of Alfred Tracy v. Robert Wash*, November 1843, Case No. 155, SLCCF.

5. *Alsey, a woman of color v. William Randolph*, March 1841, Case No. 305, SLCCR, 30–32. For more on the freedom suits of the witness, James Duncan, see chap. 2.

6. Ibid.; CCRB No. 14, September 13, 1843, 170; *Randolph v. Alsey*, July 1844, Case No. 28, MOSCD.

7. Randolph demanded $1,500 in damages for the $850 he paid for Alsey and Moses, plus the court costs (just over $20) and damages he suffered. *William S. Randolph, to the use of Alfred Tracy v. Robert Wash*, November 1843, Case No. 155, SLCCF; CCRB No. 14, December 4, 1843, 251.

8. In the first case, the Missouri Supreme Court remanded the suit for further proceedings in the Court of Common Pleas, and in the second case, the Supreme Court affirmed the Court of Common Pleas' decision in favor of Randolph. *Robert Wash v. William Randolph, to the use of Alfred Tracy, Trustee for Francis Randolph*, January 1845, Case No. 56, MOSCD; *Robert Wash v. W. S. Randolph*, March 1846, Case No. 38, MOSCD.

9. Robert M. Funkhouser (son of the elder Robert Funkhouser, Cross's son-in-law, who took Alsey to Illinois) wrote an 1851 letter to Wash indicating that he had heard that "the negro woman he [Cross] had sold to you [Wash] had sewed for her freedom." He reassured Wash that he would not help Alsey's case because he "cant remember any thing about her." Alsey's freedom suit ended several years prior to his letter, so Wash was likely not worried about Funkhouser helping her in the 1850s. It is unclear why he included this information, but perhaps he had not heard about the lawsuit, or he wanted to feign ignorance. Robert M. Funkhouser to Robert Wash, ALS, May 5, 1851, Folder 3, "Misc., Land + Legal Records, 1840–1899," Link Collection, MHM. Funkhouser explained in his letter that he was only a small child when his father had possession of Alsey in the 1810s.

10. Robert Wash to J. T. Barbour, ALS, January 30, 1852, Folder 4, Goode Papers, MHM. Burrie and Louisa may have also been Alsey's older children, referenced briefly in the case file, though not by name.

11. Ibid.; E. B. Webb to J. T. Barbour, ALS, September 28, 1852, Folder 4, Goode Papers, MHM.

12. This definition is culled from the extensive scholarship on legal culture, which begins with Lawrence Friedman's definition. See Friedman, "Legal Culture and Social Development." For additional elements, particularly the idea that legal culture is "about who we are not just what we do," see Nelken, "Using the Concept of Legal Culture," 1. For more on legal culture, in the United States and elsewhere, see for example, Edwards, *People and Their Peace*; Welch, "People at Law"; Cutter, *Legal Culture of Northern New Spain*; Sharafi, *Law and Identity in Colonial South Asia*; Bryen, *Violence in Roman Egypt*.

13. The existing legal consciousness literature is vast, but the ideas presented here are most heavily influenced by Susan Silbey's scholarship. See Silbey, "Legal Consciousness"; Silbey, "Legal Culture and Legal Consciousness"; and Silbey, "After Legal Consciousness."

14. For a recent book making a similar argument for the importance of free people of African descent in Virginia, see Maris-Wolf, *Family Bonds*, Introduction, esp. 5, 17. See also von Daacke, *Freedom Has a Face*.

15. See for example, Watson, *Slave Law in the Americas*; Hartog, *Man and Wife in America*; Cottrol, *Long, Lingering Shadow*; Middleton, *Black Laws*; Schafer, *Slavery,*

the Civil Law, and the Supreme Court of Louisiana; Schafer, *Becoming Free, Remaining Free*; Dayton, *Women before the Bar*; Edwards, *People and Their Peace*; Gross, *Double Character*; Gigantino, *Ragged Road to Abolition*; and Maris-Wolf, *Family Bonds*. A number of promising dissertations on this area of study suggest that the field is on the verge of an explosion in scholarship that examines slavery and the law, in particular. For example, Schoeppner, "Navigating the Dangerous Atlantic"; Twitty, "Slavery and Freedom in the American Confluence"; Welch, "People at Law"; and Nasta, "Making Slavery's Border."

16. For a work that examines black involvement in suits against whites after the Civil War and Reconstruction, see Milewski, "From Slave to Litigant."

17. Gross, *Double Character*; Edwards, *People and Their Peace*; M. Jones, "Case of Jean Baptiste, un Créole de Saint-Domingue."

18. See also Maris-Wolf, *Freedom Bonds*, 11, 14; Sheppard Wolf, "Manumission and the Two-Race System," 320; and Condon, "Slave Owner's Family and Manumission," 344.

19. See also Schoeppner, "Peculiar Quarantines."

20. The literature on Dred and Harriet Scott's freedom suits is considerable, but for a couple of representative works, see Fehrenbacher, *Dred Scott Case*; Konig, Finkelman, and Bracey, *Dred Scott Case*; VanderVelde, *Mrs. Dred Scott*. The only book-length survey of appellate freedom suits is Fede, *Roadblocks to Freedom*. Fede's work is a deeply researched overview that stresses the increasing restrictions on enslaved individuals' ability to win freedom through the courts. Focused largely on procedure and manumission, Fede's book has been enormously useful in suggesting resources on particular aspects of appellate case law. For two recent works on St. Louis's freedom suits that include case studies of particular suits in the city and its surrounding region, see VanderVelde, *Redemption Songs*; and Twitty, *Before* Dred Scott.

21. For a few exceptions, see Schafer, *Becoming Free, Remaining Free*; Fede, *Roadblocks to Freedom*; Schweninger, "Freedom Suits, African American Women, and the Genealogy of Slavery"; Brana-Shute and Sparks, *Paths to Freedom*; Aslakson, *Making Race in the Courtroom*; Twitty, *Before* Dred Scott; and VanderVelde, *Redemption Songs*. *Redemption Songs* begins to situate St. Louis's suits in the context of national expansion, specifically westward migration. VanderVelde focuses on several cases that established precedents or highlight significant issues within the freedom suit files, with a final chapter that provides a brief overview of the cases.

22. On the adaptability of slavery, see, for example, Oakes, *Slavery and Freedom*.

23. There are notable exceptions, such as Edwards, *People and Their Peace*; Bryen, *Violence in Roman Egypt*; and Sharafi, *Law and Identity in Colonial South Asia*.

24. Nader, *Life of the Law*.

25. The two themes of mobility and geography are explored in more detail in Kennington, "Geography, Mobility, and the Law."

26. Nader, *Life of the Law*.

27. For a recent treatment of the importance of slavery and freedom along the border regions of the country, see Salafia, *Slavery's Borderland*. Although not a strictly legal history, Salafia's book contributes valuable information on slave life along the border. Many of the topics he discusses—such as kidnapping, movement, and the significance of geography—are echoed in this study of suits for freedom.

28. On the messiness of local legal verdicts, see Edwards, *People and Their Peace*. VanderVelde's work on St. Louis freedom suits echoes this conclusion, noting how the

St. Louis Circuit Court's verdicts were relatively consistent until the *Dred Scott* case. See VanderVelde, *Redemption Songs*, 20.

29. For a further breakdown of the number of cases and their outcomes, as well as a list of all suits for freedom in St. Louis analyzed in this study, see the appendix.

30. This outcome is counted as unknown because additional evidence suggests that several of these cases resulted in arrangements for freedom. If these 49 cases are counted as the plaintiff failing to win freedom, the breakdown of percentages is the following: plaintiffs freed in 110 cases (38.3 percent), plaintiffs not freed in 133 cases (46.3 percent), and unknown in 44 cases (15.3 percent).

31. For a survey of the number of cases, see the appendix. Plaintiffs often presented multiple arguments for freedom in a single case, so the numbers do not correspond to the total number of cases (287).

32. For a breakdown of the St. Louis cases using these groups, see Twitty, *Before Dred Scott*, table 2 of appendix. VanderVelde also discusses the role of family groups in *Redemption Songs*.

33. See Grinberg, "Manumission, Gender, and the Law in Nineteenth-Century Brazil," tables on 226–27. Grinberg's 400 cases are drawn from the years 1806–88, though the majority of the cases in her study occurred around the time of St. Louis's freedom suits (308 cases from 1823 to 1870), providing an interesting point of comparison.

34. See table 1 in the appendix.

35. The work on enslaved persons' communication networks is also a growing field. See, for example, J. Scott, "Common Wind"; Cecelski, *Waterman's Song*; Buchanan, *Black Life on the Mississippi*; Schoeppner, "Navigating the Dangerous Atlantic"; Kaye, *Joining Places*; and O'Donovan, "Universities of Social and Political Change."

36. On the importance of black movement across state and national borders to making law, see Schoeppner, "Status across Borders"; and M. Jones, "Time, Space, and Jurisdiction."

37. In *Somerset*, Lord Chief Justice Mansfield found that a slave, once transported to a place where slavery did not exist, became free because slavery was "odious" to the law and therefore required the existence of positive law to support it. America's courts, including the St. Louis Circuit Court, adopted this standard with some frequency in cases in which a person claimed to have lived in the Northwest Territory. When successful, these cases found that enslaved persons having lived or traveled on "free soil" became free. For more information on the *Somerset* case, see Cotter, "Somerset Case and the Abolition of Slavery in England"; and "Forum: *Somerset's Case* Revisited," *Law and History Review* 24, no. 3 (2006): 601–72.

38. Gross, *Double Character*.

39. For discussions of the dangers of the free black population in another context, see Schoeppner, "Peculiar Quarantines"; and Maris-Wolf, *Family Bonds*.

1 / Setting the Scene

1. *Arch, a black man v. Barnabas Harris*, October 1818, no case number, SLCCR; *Jack, a black man v. Barnabas Harris*, October 1818, Case No. 111, SLCCR.

2. *Arch, a black man v. Barnabas Harris*, October 1818, no case number, SLCCR, 1–4.

3. For a few of the many existing examples of disputes that arose over life estates from other jurisdictions, see *South v. Solomon and Others*, 20 Va. 12 (1817); *The Executors of Charles James v. William B. Masters*, 7 N.C. 110 (1819); *E. O. Hawkins v. P. F.*

Hawkins, Jackson Hawkins, James F. Hawkins, Harriet C. Hawkins, and George W. Hawkins, Persons of Color, 52 Ky. 245 (1852); *T. L. Philleo v. Holliday and Others,* 24 Tex. 38 (1859).

4. *Jack, a black man v. Barnabas Harris,* October 1818, Case No. 111, SLCCR, 21.

5. "Docket Book, 1818–1827," Folder 5, Box 1, Gamble Papers, MHM.

6. The heirs, George Hubbard, Thomas Ballus, and John Proctor, openly admitted to knowing about the deed in a letter written after the cases began. *Jack, a black man v. Barnabas Harris,* October 1818, Case No. 111, SLCCR, 1–2.

7. State statutes outlined the format for bringing a freedom suit, establishing the parameters of the discussion over slavery and freedom that took place in antebellum courtrooms throughout the slaveholding states. Statutes are useful guides for studying the outlines of freedom suit litigation, but law in action often added complexity to the law as recorded in statutes, appellate records, and treatises—what is sometimes referred to as law on the books. For a brief discussion of the externalist versus internalist views on law and legal history, see Hall and Karsten, *Magic Mirror,* esp. 1–2; Friedman, *History of American Law,* esp. 688–89. For an example that uses these ideas to compare customary law with case law, see Hartog, "Pigs and Positivism." For an excellent analysis of these issues in relation to the law of race and slavery, see Gross, "Beyond Black and White," esp. 688–89.

8. Foley, *Genesis of Missouri,* 8, 26. For a recent treatment of colonial St. Louis, see also Cleary, *World, the Flesh, and the Devil.*

9. Billon, *Annals of St. Louis,* 21.

10. Foley, *Genesis of Missouri,* 28.

11. *Jack, a black man v. Barnabas Harris,* October 1818, Case No. 111, SLCCR, 3–4.

12. Billon, *Annals of St. Louis,* 36, quoting the inventory of Joseph Lefevre d'Inglebert, Deputy of the Orderer of Louisiana and Judge of the Royal Jurisdiction of the Illinois.

13. Ibid., 63.

14. Ibid., 78.

15. According to some estimates, from St. Louis's founding to 1818, the Church baptized "582 negroes," performed one black marriage, and buried 362 blacks. Newspaper clipping dated January 1, 1868, located in Folder 2, Primm Papers, MHM.

16. Billon, *Annals of St. Louis,* 242–43 (emphasis added).

17. Christian, *Before Louis and Clark,* 30–33.

18. Foley, *Genesis of Missouri,* 244.

19. Foley, *Genesis of Missouri,* 253, 293.

20. Michael Holt argues that the system of two-party politics managed to contain the slavery question throughout the antebellum years or, at least, until the system broke down in the early 1850s. I agree with Holt that the system of national (rather than sectional) parties helped contain some of the tensions inherent in debates over slavery for much of the antebellum period. Where I differ slightly from Holt's analysis is in the primacy of slavery to the national political crisis of the 1850s. Slavery came to dominate political debate in the wake of the Mexican War, when the question of whether the institution would spread into new territories became increasingly divisive in national politics, and I argue that it became the primary issue in American politics during the 1850s with the *Dred Scott* decision, the Kansas-Nebraska Act, the publication of *Uncle Tom's Cabin,* and John Brown's raid on Harpers Ferry. See Holt, *Political Crisis of the 1850s.*

21. UVAHCB. See also Robinson, "St. Louis," 2378.

22. UVAHCB; Foley, *Genesis of Missouri*, 253.

23. *U.S. v. Elijah, Slave of John B. Smith*, 1818, MOSCD.

24. Foley, *Genesis of Missouri*, chap. 14.

25. Civil law was a system based on written legal codes, whereas common law was based on judicial decisions and interpretation of legislation.

26. Foley, *Genesis of Missouri*, 98–99; Missouri State Archives, "Abstract of the St. Louis Court System."

27. From March 26, 1804, to July 3, 1805, St. Louis became part of the Louisiana District of the Indiana Territory, which consisted of the area north of the thirty-third parallel. On July 4, 1805, Congress created the Louisiana Territory and divided it into five administrative districts, including the district of St. Louis. This division continued until the creation of the Missouri Territory on June 4, 1812, and of St. Louis County on October 1, 1812. Missouri State Archives, "Abstract of St. Louis Court System," 2–3.

28. Ibid., 3–4. Civil cases involved conflicts between individuals, such as trespass or debt. Criminal cases involved breaking the criminal laws, including cases of theft, murder, and arson. Chancery courts provided equity jurisdiction, which gave people a remedy when the common law solution was insufficient in some way. For example, when someone failed to follow his or her end of a contract, a chancery court could order the person to fulfill the agreement. Probate courts dealt with the execution of wills and estate settlements. After the County Court took over probate in 1820, the Circuit Court continued to perform these other functions until the end of the 1830s.

29. Schafer, *Slavery, the Civil Law, and the Supreme Court of Louisiana*, 1–2.

30. *Coartación* began in Spanish Cuba before Spanish Louisiana adopted the practice, which ended in Louisiana with the Black Code of 1807. Aslakson, *Making Race in the Courtroom*, 58–60, 62–63.

31. Foley, *Genesis of Missouri*, 114–15. See Foley, "Slave Freedom Suits before Dred Scott."

32. Foley, *Genesis of Missouri*, 154; *Laws of a Public and General Nature, of the District of Louisiana*, 28–29. An interesting exception to the rule of allowing enslaved individuals to carry firearms stated that "all negroes or mulattoes, bond or free living at any frontier plantation, may be permitted to keep and use guns," as long as they had a license from a justice of the peace (*Laws of a Public and General Nature, of the District of Louisiana*, 28).

33. *Laws of a Public and General Nature, of the District of Louisiana*, 28.

34. Ibid., 30.

35. Ibid., 31. When a sheriff sold a slave for self hiring, 25 percent of the sale went to "lessening the district levy," 5 percent to the sheriff for his trouble, and, after deducting the jailor's fees, the remainder of the sale price went to the owner.

36. Ibid., 31–32. Lawmakers included age limits so that older freed persons would not become public charges and younger enslaved persons would be old enough to support themselves.

37. For a recent work on revolutionary-era South Carolina and Massachusetts freedom suits, see Blanck, *Tyrannicide*.

38. The historian Bradley J. Nicholson has observed how the slave law of the first American colonies came from borrowing related English legal traditions. See Nicholson, "Legal Borrowing and the Origins of Slave Law in the British Colonies."

39. P. Morgan, "Virginia's Other Prototype," esp. 377.

40. Foley, *Genesis of Missouri*, 154.

41. For discussion of enslavers' fears of rebellion and outside influences that threatened the system of slavery, see, for example, Ford, *Deliver Us from Evil*; Ashworth, *Slavery, Capitalism, and Politics in the Antebellum Republic*, vol. 2; J. Rothman, *Flush Times and Fever Dreams*.

42. *Laws of the State of Delaware*, 380–81.

43. Cobb, *Digest of the Laws of the State of Georgia*, 1007.

44. *Collection of All Such Acts of the General Assembly of Virginia*, 347.

45. *Barnabas Harris v. Joseph McClurg*, June 1818, Case No. 45, SLCCF; *Barnabas Harris v. Joseph McClurg*, June 1818, Case No. 67, SLCCF; *United States v. Joseph McClurg*, August 1818, Superior Court Case Files, Reel F/1/4, MSA-STL.

46. *Revised Code of the Laws of Mississippi*, 387.

47. McCord, *Statutes at Large of South Carolina*, 448.

48. The role of antislavery activists is discussed in chap. 7.

49. *Laws of a Public and General Nature, of the District of Louisiana*, 96.

50. Of the fourteen slaveholding jurisdictions with explicit freedom suit statutes, the six discussed here provided the legal form for suing for freedom, and eight failed to dictate the type of legal case that an illegally enslaved plaintiff should bring.

51. For Missouri and Arkansas, see *Laws of a Public and General Nature, of the District of Louisiana*, 96–97; Steele and M'Campbell, *Laws of the Arkansas Territory*, 268–69.

52. Watkins and Watkins, *Digest of the Laws of the State of Georgia*, 163–65; McCord, *Statutes at Large of South Carolina*, 371, 385, 398.

53. *Acts of the Legislative Council of the Territory of Florida*, 289.

54. *Laws of the State of Delaware*, 380–83.

55. The jurisdictions whose freedom suit statutes did not specify a particular legal form were Alabama, Kentucky, Louisiana, Maryland, Mississippi, Tennessee, Virginia, and the District of Columbia.

56. *Glover v. Millings*, 2 Stew. & P. 28 (1832).

57. McCord, *Statutes at Large of South Carolina*, 398; Watkins and Watkins, *Digest of the Laws of the State of Georgia*, 164.

58. Chapter 2 more fully enumerates these considerations.

59. *Laws of a Public and General Nature, of the District of Louisiana*, 96–97; *Acts of the Legislative Council of the Territory of Florida*, 289; Steele and M'Campbell, *Laws of the Arkansas Territory*, 269; Watkins and Watkins, *Digest of the Laws of the State of Georgia*, 164.

60. Equity developed as a parallel system of justice to arrive at fairer results when following outcomes at law would be unjust.

61. Scott and M'Cullough, *Maryland Code*, 467–68.

62. For example, see O'Donovan, "Universities of Social and Political Change." The spread of legal information in freedom suits is discussed at greater length in chap. 2.

63. For more on the significance of court day to southern communities, see Isaac, *Transformation of Virginia*, esp. chaps. 5 and 13; Roeber, *Faithful Magistrates and Republican Lawyers*, chap. 5; Shepard, "This Being Court Day"; Gross, *Double Character*, chap. 1; and Edwards, *People and Their Peace*, chap. 3.

64. *Arch, a black man v. Barnabas Harris*, October 1818, no case number, SLCCR, 7 (emphasis added). Tucker was the son of the legal scholar St. George Tucker, of Virginia, and the half brother of the Roanoke jurist John Randolph.

65. Ibid., 9–10.

66. Ibid.

67. Ibid., 5–6.

68. The role of attorneys in freedom suits is discussed in more detail in chap. 3.

69. See *Laws of a Public and General Nature of the State of Missouri,* chap. 42, p. 86.

70. See *Laws of a Public and General Nature, of the District of Louisiana,* 96; *Collection of All Such Acts of the General Assembly of Virginia,* 346; *Code of Laws for the District of Columbia,* 302; Steele and M'Campbell, *Laws of the Arkansas Territory,* 268–69; and Herty, *Digest of the Laws of Maryland,* 390–91.

71. For a discussion of the procedures in criminal trials of the enslaved, see Morris, *Southern Slavery and the Law,* chap. 9.

72. *Revised Statutes of Missouri,* 1845, 283–84. Persons thought to be slaves rarely received monetary awards. The 1845 law prohibited plaintiffs from recovering monetary damages even if their suit succeeded.

73. See *Laws of a Public and General Nature, of the District of Louisiana,* 96; Steele and M'Campbell, *Laws of the Arkansas Territory,* 268; and *Collection of All Such Acts of the General Assembly of Virginia,* 346.

74. *Code of Laws for the District of Columbia,* 275–76. In the District of Columbia example, defendants who won freedom suits had to pay for the costs of the case before the sheriff would release the enslaved property to them. Likewise, successful freedom suit plaintiffs had to work off the costs of the suit (either through their hired labor or through any other resources available to them) before the sheriff set them free. A more detailed description of the costs of freedom suits in Missouri can be found in chap. 3.

75. *Tempe, a black woman v. Risdon H. Price,* April 1821, Case No. 181, SLCCR, 3.

76. *Polly Wilson, a free woman of color v. Jacob Baum,* March 1827, Case No. 19, SLCCR, 1.

77. Dorinda to Hamilton Gamble, ALS, April 1, 1827, Folder 2, Box 2, Gamble Papers, MHM. In another example, Margaret's 1831 case against William Dallam, her petition complained that Dallam and his agents were preparing to take Margaret and her family away from the reach of assistance and where it will be "impossible for them to assert their right to freedom." *Margaret, a girl of color v. William Dallam,* November 1831, Case No. 4, SLCCR, 1.

78. *Laws of a Public and General Nature, of the District of Louisiana,* 96–97; McCord, *Statutes at Large of South Carolina,* 398; Haywood and Cobbs, *Statute Laws of the State of Tennessee,* 328–29; *Collection of All Such Acts of the General Assembly of Virginia,* 346; Watkins and Watkins, *Digest of the Laws of the State of Georgia,* 164; and *Revised Code of the Laws of Mississippi,* 387.

79. Toulmin, *Digest of the Laws of the State of Alabama,* 632; *Code of Laws for the District of Columbia,* 275–76; Alden and Van Housen, *Digest of the Laws of Mississippi,* 761–62; *Code of Virginia,* 464–65; and *Revised Statutes of the State of Delaware,* 256. In one South Carolina case, the court specified that a judge could issue orders of protection at any point during a freedom suit. *Daniel Carpenter v. Matthew Coleman,* 2 Bay 436 (1802).

80. *Sylvia and Phillis, by Next Friend v. Covey,* 12 Tenn. 297 (1833).

81. Loughborough, *Digest of the Statute Laws of Kentucky,* 225–26. One appeal of an indictment brought under this statute included an interpretation of the purpose of the law: "The evil that the Legislature intended to guard against, by the passage of

this law, was the removal of persons of color from this State, with a view to prevent the successful prosecution of a suit instituted by them for their freedom." In the same appeal, the Kentucky Supreme Court found that an enslaver who claimed to have no knowledge of the pending suit for freedom could not be found guilty under the statute, a decision that created a fairly convenient defense for enslavers charged with illegally removing enslaved plaintiffs. See *Commonwealth v. Stout*, 46 Ky. 247 (1847). In St. Louis, evidence like Dorinda's letter suggests that enslavers sometimes ignored these protections and sold or removed enslaved plaintiffs from the court's jurisdiction.

82. *Harriet v. Samuel T. McKinney*, July 1833, Case No. 54, SLCCR, 1; *Leah, a woman of color v. Arthur Mitchell*, November 1832, Case No. 68, SLCCR, 6.

83. *Jack, a black man v. Barnabas Harris*, October 1818, Case No. 111, SLCCR, 31.

84. *Marie, a free mulatto girl v. Auguste Chouteau*, April 1821, Case No. 205, SLCCR, 11–12.

85. For more on the limitations and uses of court records, see especially W. Johnson, *Soul by Soul*, introduction, in which Johnson explains that court records and testimony, though not necessarily a good indicator of what actually happened, when "given in support of a high-stakes legal action, must be believable" (12). Johnson treats all of the court docket's testimony as "lies" that had to be "believable" and therefore have meaning for historians as descriptions of plausible events. For analysis of using the WPA narratives, see Blassingame, "Using the Testimony of Ex-Slaves"; Baptist, *Creating an Old South*, 82, 84.

86. *Jack, a black man v. Barnabas Harris*, October 1818, Case No. 111, SLCCR, 21–24.

87. A notation on one of the depositions, taken April 10, 1819, indicates that Barnabas Harris had died, making Frederick Hyatt, his administrator, the defendant in the case. There is a notation near the end of the case file that Carr became the attorney for Hyatt after Harris died. This does not mean for certain that Carr was Harris's attorney from the start of the case.

88. *Jack, a black man v. Barnabas Harris*, October 1818, Case No. 111, SLCCR, 25–28.

89. States whose statutes mention juries in freedom suits are Arkansas, Georgia, Louisiana, Maryland, Mississippi, Missouri, South Carolina, and Virginia. See Steele and M'Campbell, *Laws of the Arkansas Territory*, 269; Hotchkiss, *Codification of the Statute Law of Georgia*, 803–4; Phillips, *Revised Statutes of Louisiana*, 1856; Herty, *Digest of the Laws of Maryland*, 390; *Revised Code of the Laws of Mississippi*, 387; *Laws of a Public and General Nature, of the District of Louisiana*, 96; McCord, *Statutes at Large of South Carolina*, 385; and *Revised Code of the Laws of Virginia*, 481.

90. *Revised Code of the District of Columbia*, 169–70. The code specified that each side in the case could have up to twelve preemptory challenges to potential jurors.

91. *Revised Statutes of the State of Delaware*, 255–56.

92. *Revised Code of the Laws of Virginia*, 481; *Revised Code of the Laws of Mississippi*, 387.

93. The role of the broader community in freedom suits in Missouri, partly through community members' jury service, is discussed at greater length in chap. 5.

94. For more on the role of juries in nineteenth-century legal cases, see McDermott, "Gentleman of the Jury"; and Blinka, "Trial by Jury in Revolutionary Virginia."

95. *Martha Drusella v. Richmond L. Curle*, November 1844, Case No. 252, SLCCR, 39.

96. Ibid., 24. The jury verdict freeing Drusella is found in CCRB No. 17, February 12, 1846, 95.

97. *Jack, a black man v. Barnabas Harris*, October 1818, Case No. 111, SLCCR, 33.

98. Ibid., 35.

99. Ibid., 31.

100. The historian Laura F. Edwards has argued that verdicts in local lawsuits are so dependent on community variables that it is impossible to generalize from them. In the St. Louis example, although the verdicts can be a good starting point for thinking about the outcomes of freedom suits, they did not always represent the end of the struggle between enslavers and enslaved individuals over personal status. See Edwards, *People and Their Peace*, esp. 65.

101. For the verdict in *Judy (also known as Julia Logan) v. John Berry Meachum*, March 1835, Case No. 11, see CCRB No. 8, March 23, 1836, 24. After an appeal, Rachel won her case and freedom for herself and her son. See *Rachel, a woman of color v. William Walker*, November 1834, Case No. 82, SLCCR, 19–24, and *James Henry, a boy of color v. William Walker*, November 1834, Case No. 83, SLCCR. CCRB No. 8, December 13, 1836, 164, records the changed verdict for Rachel and her son.

102. See McCord, *Statutes at Large of South Carolina*, 398; *Laws of a Public and General Nature, of the District of Louisiana*, 96; Loughborough, *Digest of the Statute Laws of Kentucky*, 225; *Code of Virginia*, 465; and Watkins and Watkins, *Digest of the Laws of the State of Georgia*, 164. Missouri amended its freedom suit statute to prohibit damages. See *Revised Statutes of the State of Missouri*, 1841, 286. Additional states included damages awards, even if their statutes did not specify whether plaintiffs could collect monetary damages.

103. Clark, Cobb, and Irwin, *Code of the State of Georgia*, 760.

104. *Revised Statutes of the State of Missouri*, 1841, 286; Ball and Roane, *Revised Statutes of the State of Arkansas*, 418.

105. *Marguerite, a free woman of color v. Pierre Chouteau, Sr.*, July 1825, Case No. 26, SLCCR, 13.

106. For a brief discussion of the representativeness of state supreme court records in Louisiana, see Schafer, *Slavery, the Civil Law, and the Supreme Court of Louisiana*, xi–xii.

107. Barnabas Harris to Overton Harris, ALS, June 29, 1818, in "Barnabas Harris Papers and Estate, 1818–1836," Folder 4, Hyatt-Hume Papers, MHM, 1–2.

108. Thomas Ballus to Barnabas Harris, ALS, August 5, 1818, ibid., 1.

109. Ibid. (emphasis added)

2 / Bringing Suit

1. Delaney, *From the Darkness Cometh the Light*, 39, 47.

2. Ibid., 48. The trial documents record Lucy as Lucy Ann Britton, but her lawyer, Judge Bates, refers to her as Lucy Berry in her memoir. This variation in names demonstrates the precarious state of enslaved persons' identities under slavery because they often adopted their owners' last names. In 1849, Lucy changed her name to Delaney after marrying her second husband, Zachariah Delaney.

3. Ibid., 49.

4. Lucy Delaney is the only freedom suit plaintiff known to have written a description of the experience.

5. On the hegemonic function of the law, see Genovese, *Roll, Jordan, Roll*, 25–48.

6. Delaney, *From the Darkness Cometh the Light*, 12, 14, 21–24.

7. Even so, we do know that the presence of African Americans in local antebellum courts was not unusual. See Edwards, "Status without Rights"; Gross, *Double Character*; and Welch, "Black Litigants in the Antebellum American South."

8. For recent work that highlights African American legal knowledge among free people of color in Virginia, see Maris-Wolf, *Family Bonds*, esp. 48; and von Daacke, *Freedom Has a Face*.

9. Susan O'Donovan has argued that the lack of access to reading and writing meant that enslaved individuals placed special importance on spoken communication. See O'Donovan, "Universities of Social and Political Change," 138. For more on how the urban landscape made information accessible to slaves, see Wade, *Slavery in the Cities*, esp. 56–57. Ira Berlin also emphasizes the efficacy and pervasiveness of what he calls the "grapevine telegraph." See Berlin, *Generations of Captivity*, chap. 4.

10. Scholars of numerous other slave societies have argued for the existence of considerable channels of communication among enslaved communities. In a study of freedom suits in France, Sue Peabody found that enslaved individuals learned of their rights to sue for freedom through informal networks, and they also used these networks to secure funds and assistance in their suits. See Peabody, "*There Are No Slaves in France*," 48. See also J. Scott, "Common Wind," for a discussion of how enslaved individuals spread information throughout the Caribbean and to the United States, including information about potential uprisings and also changes in French and English slave law. For a closer look at the antebellum slave community, see Kaye, *Joining Places*, esp. chap. 1; and Schermerhorn, *Money over Mastery, Family over Freedom*, chap. 1. For a mention of this network by a former enslaved man, see the testimony of Robert Glen, as found in Yetman, *When I Was a Slave*, 47.

11. Delaney, *From the Darkness Cometh the Light*, 23–24. Delaney's claim is in contrast to the process explained by Lea VanderVelde, who describes freedom suit plaintiffs as initiating cases with a justice of the peace or the clerk of court, who then assigned the attorney to represent the plaintiff. See VanderVelde, *Redemption Songs*, 2; for VanderVelde's specific claim that the court assigned Polly Wash's attorney, see VanderVelde, *Redemption Songs*, 252n45.

12. *Daniel Wilson, a man of color v. Edmund Melvin*, July 1835, Case No. 10, SLCCR; *Rebecca, a colored girl v. James Black and Louis Matlock*, July 1838, Case No. 237, SLCCR. Sproat is listed in the city directories from 1838–39, 1840–41, 1842, and 1852, though the last two directories only list his residence, rather than a law office address. See Keemle, *St. Louis Directory for the Years 1838-9*, 45; *St. Louis Directory for the Years 1840-1*, 56; *Saint Louis Directory for the Year 1842*, 26; *Morrison's St. Louis Directory, for 1852*, 243.

13. *Rebecca, a negro woman v. James Black Thomas Horine, and George Melody*, March 1843, Case No. 24, SLCCR, 2.

14. Schafer, *Becoming Free, Remaining Free*, chap. 2. Schafer also describes the attorney, Jean Charles David, encouraging cases that were not contested and engaging in other dubious activities, suggesting perhaps that working for enslaved clients was the best kind of employment a lawyer of his questionable ethics could expect.

15. See ibid.

16. Byars, "Dred Scott—Life of the Famous Fugitive and Missouri Litigant," T. W. Chamberlin Collection, MHM, 1. According to Robert Moore Jr., Byars took this

description of Bird and Risque from a contemporary newspaper report. See Moore, "Ray of Hope, Extinguished," 8. Moore also emphasizes the important role of slave communication systems in the urban setting of St. Louis in informing enslaved men and women of their right to sue.

17. Gustavus A. Bird prosecuted thirty-four suits for freedom, and Ferdinand Risque worked for an enslaved plaintiff in twenty-two cases. English, *Pioneer Lawyer and Jurist in Missouri*, 49–66. Bird's motivation may have been pecuniary, as suggested by his July 1833 suit against Lydia Titus for the fees incurred in prosecuting at least eight suits for freedom for Lydia's children. See *Gustavus Bird v. Lydia Titus, a free woman of color*, July 1833, Case No. 44, SLCCF.

18. See Wade, *Slavery in the Cities*; Schafer, *Becoming Free, Remaining Free*; Rasmussen, *American Uprising*; Blackett, *Making Freedom*; Hahn, *Nation under Our Feet*.

19. Morris, *Southern Slavery and the Law*, chap. 16.

20. The statute levied a fine of three dollars for each offense or twenty lashes if the accused could not pay. See *Laws of a Public and General Nature, of the District of Louisiana*, 29. See ibid., 28–30, for other laws restricting slaves' gatherings. See also *Revised Statutes of the State of Missouri*, 1835, 585; Casselberry, *Revised Statutes of the State of Missouri*, 530; and Hardin, *Revised Statutes of the State of Missouri*, vol. 2, 1474–75.

21. *Jack, a man of color v. Absalom Link*, November 1837, Case No. 38, SLCCR, 1. See also *Susan, a black woman v. Henry Hight*, February 1822, Case No. 127, SLCCR; and *Seyton (also known as Sydney), a woman of color v. William Littleton*, March 1840, Case No. 3, SLCCR.

22. Welch, "Black Litigants in the Antebellum American South," chaps. 1 and 6; Kaye, *Joining Places*, chaps. 1 and 5.

23. Wade, *Slavery in the Cities*, 249.

24. *St. Louis Daily Evening Gazette*, August 18, 1841, quoted in Trexler, *Slavery in Missouri*, 177–78.

25. Olmsted, *Journey in the Seaboard Slave States*, 591.

26. *Missouri Argus*, January 20, 1837, quoted in Wade, *Slavery in the Cities*, 257.

27. The number of manumissions is based on a study conducted by Bob Moore and Kris Zapalac, which can be accessed on the National Parks Service website for the St. Louis Arch. Accessed February 13, 2016, http://www.nps.gov/jeff/learn/historyculture/emancipations.htm.

28. The most complete study of escaped slaves is Franklin and Schweninger, *Runaway Slaves*. Franklin and Schweninger found that slaves living in many of the areas they studied fled slavery to urban centers or possibly even to areas farther south, since reaching freedom in the North was difficult for most enslaved individuals. See ibid., 120–22. For more on the prevalence of runaway slaves in and around Missouri, see Burke, *On Slavery's Border*, esp. 175; Harris, *History of Negro Servitude in Illinois*; Wade, *Slavery in the Cities*, chap. 8; and Frazier, *Runaway Missouri Slaves and Those Who Helped Them*.

29. For more on the everyday resistance of the enslaved, see Berlin, *Generations of Captivity*; and especially Camp, *Closer to Freedom*.

30. For more information on the considerations made by enslaved men and women before attempting to escape slavery, see Franklin and Schweninger, *Runaway Slaves*, esp. 137; and Camp, *Closer to Freedom*, esp. chap. 2. Lea VanderVelde argues that Delaney's description of her mother's flight is "unlikely" to be true because it took place

before the Fugitive Slave Act and because it is not mentioned in Wash's affidavit. See VanderVelde, *Redemption Songs*, 150. It would be highly unusual to mention running away in an affidavit during a freedom suit, though it is certainly possible that Delaney's memory of the events when writing her memoir fifty years later had faded.

31. Delaney, *From the Darkness Cometh the Light*, 18.

32. Ibid., 20.

33. Ibid., 23; *Polly Wash v. Joseph M. Magehan*, November 1839, Case No. 167, SLCCR.

34. Missouri's relationship with Illinois, and particularly the role of runaway slaves moving between the two states, is discussed in more detail in chap. 4.

35. *Laws of a Public and General Nature, of the District of Louisiana*, 32; *Revised Statutes of the State of Missouri*, 1835, 588–90; Casselberry, *Revised Statutes of the State of Missouri*, 531–35; Hardin, *Revised Statutes of the State of Missouri*, vol. 2, 1098, 1479–87.

36. The many ads in St. Louis newspapers for runaway slaves suggest both the existence of large numbers of runaways from St. Louis and that St. Louis was a popular place for runaways to pass through on their way to free states or to Canada. See, for example, the *Missouri Republican*, September 17, 1823, 1; February 28, 1825, 4; October 12, 1826, 3; November 29, 1827, 3; September 27, 1831, 3; June 6, 1835, 3; July 3, 1835, 3.

37. *Samuel Slaughter, a negro, in the matter of habeas corpus*, November 1854, Case No. 253, SLCCR, 7. CCRB No. 24, November 23, 1854, 340, shows that the jailer brought Slaughter to court and the court discharged him from custody.

38. Most records of justices of the peace—at least those in St. Louis—have not survived. The informal nature of these procedures meant that justices did not always record them or keep their records for posterity. For another example from St. Louis, see *David McFoy v. William Brown*, April 1850, Case No. 37, SLCCR, 19.

39. *Mary Ann Steel v. Curtis Skinner*, July 1835, Case No. 96, SLCCR, 1. The case records do not say exactly what happened to Mary Ann Steel after her petition for freedom. She sued both Curtis Skinner and William Walker for her freedom, and in both cases, the record indicates that she voluntarily agreed not to further prosecute her suits.

40. For more information on the restrictions faced by indentured servants and other nominally free people of African descent living in antebellum Illinois, which is discussed at greater length in chap. 3, see Finkelman, *Imperfect Union*, chap. 3.

41. *Vincent, a man of color v. James Duncan*, November 1829, Case No. 110, SLCCR, 33. The petition is most likely referring to Gustavus A. Bird, an attorney and justice of the peace in St. Louis. He served as both Vincent's and Ralph's attorney in their freedom suits. Bird was a St. Louis attorney who prosecuted a high number of freedom suits (thirty-four), though several of these suits were related to one another, including at least three enslaved plaintiffs who brought multiple suits for freedom. See SLCCR.

42. *Vincent, a man of color v. James Duncan*, November 1829, Case No. 110, SLCCR, 33–34. Both Ralph and Joe sued James and Coleman Duncan. Ralph's case went on for years, with at least one appeal to the Missouri Supreme Court before Ralph won his case and his freedom. Joe died during the prosecution of his case.

43. For an essay on forum shopping in colonial South Asia, see Sharafi, "Marital Patchwork of Colonial South Asia."

44. *Revised Code of the Laws of Virginia*, 419, as cited in *Ratcliff v. Polly & als.*, 53 Va. 528 (1855).

45. *Butler et al. v. Duvall*, 3 Cranch C.C. 611 (1829).

46. Ibid. In a related scenario, when an alleged slaveholder wanted to return to his previous home state of Maryland with his alleged slaves—perhaps hoping to receive a more favorable verdict—the D.C. court refused to allow this strategy. Because the enslaver and his human property had lived in the District of Columbia for over a year, the plaintiffs' right to freedom arose in the District and the defendant could not take them back to Maryland. *Simon v. Paine's Administrator*, 4 Cranch C.C. 99 (1830).

47. Delaney, *From the Darkness Cometh the Light*, 30–31.

48. Ibid., 33.

49. Ibid., 29–34.

50. *Laws of a Public and General Nature, of the District of Louisiana*, 96. See also *Revised Statutes of the State of Missouri*, 1835, 285–86; Casselberry, *Revised Statutes of the State of Missouri*, 283–84; Hardin, *Revised Statutes of the State of Missouri*, vol. 1, 809–12.

51. *Cary, a man of color v. Benjamin Wilder*, March 1831, Case No. 53, SLCCR, 1.

52. *Mary, a woman of color v. Francis Menard and Andre Landreville*, November 1827, Case No. 7, SLCCR, 3.

53. *Pelagie, a person of color v. Jean P. Cabanne*, June 1822, Case No. 9, SLCCR, 13–14. Pelagie's case file ends with this petition, so perhaps her alleged owner succeeded in selling her away from her ability to sue for freedom.

54. Delaney, *From the Darkness Cometh the Light*, 31.

55. *Elsa Hicks, a mulatto girl v. S. Burrell and James Mitchell*, April 1845, Case No. 55, SLCCR, 7.

56. See *Laws of a Public and General Nature, of the District of Louisiana*, 31, 33; *Revised Statutes of the State of Missouri*, 1835, 586; Casselberry, *Revised Statutes of the State of Missouri*, 530; and Hardin, *Revised Statutes of the State of Missouri*, vol. 2, 1476–77. One case demonstrating boat owners' fear of prosecution for helping enslaved individuals escape is the November 1842 case of *John Finney v. Calvin Kinder*, Case No. 17, SLCCF. There are also a handful of references in the criminal record books to "slave stealing" and "allowing a slave to escape," though unfortunately the criminal case files have mostly been lost for this period. See Criminal Court Record Books 2 and 3, MSA-STL.

57. The recipient of her letter, Hamilton Gamble, was a wealthy St. Louis attorney who eventually became governor of Missouri during the Civil War. For more on Gamble, see Boman, *Lincoln's Resolute Unionist*.

58. Eugene Genovese estimates that perhaps only 5 percent of slaves could read. See Genovese, *Roll Jordan Roll*, 561–65, but he finds that the percentage was higher in cities. Thomas Morris, however, argues that the laws against teaching slaves to read and write were mostly symbolic and not actually enforced. See Morris, *Southern Slavery and the Law*, 348. Plaintiffs in the St. Louis freedom suits almost universally signed their petitions with only a mark, suggesting a low level of literacy.

59. *Dorinda, a woman of color v. John Simonds Jr.*, March 1826, Case No. 42, SLCCR.

60. Dorinda to Hamilton R. Gamble, ALS, April 1, 1827, Folder 2, Box 2, Gamble Papers, MHM.

61. Delaney, *From the Darkness Cometh the Light*, 27.

62. For more on the role of violence in the master-slave relationship, see, for example, Patterson, *Slavery and Social Death*, introduction; D. Davis, *Inhuman Bondage*;

Genovese, *World the Slaves Made*; and W. Johnson, *River of Dark Dreams*, esp. chaps. 6–7.

63. The historian Vincent Brown has convincingly argued that the idea of a slave being "socially dead," as the sociologist Orlando Patterson theorized, has been used too literally in recent studies of enslavement, and thus Brown argues for the importance of including the lived experience of the enslaved. See V. Brown, "Social Death and Political Life in the Study of Slavery." See also the literature on the North Carolina Supreme Court case *State v. Mann* (1829), in which Justice Thomas Ruffin's opinion was that "the power of the master must be absolute to render the submission of the slave perfect." See *State v. Mann*, 13 N.C. Reports 263 (1829). For more on the *State v. Mann* case, see, for example, Tushnet, *Slave Law in the American South*; Hadden, "Judging Slavery"; and Greene, "Thomas Ruffin and the Perils of Public Homage."

64. On the issue of violence in the antebellum South, see, for example, Wyatt-Brown, *Honor and Violence in the Old South*; Ayers, *Vengeance and Justice*; Courtwright, *Violent Land*; and Baptist, *Creating an Old South*. The best recent study on the role of violence in maintaining and strengthening the system of slavery in the antebellum South is W. Johnson, *River of Dark Dreams*, esp. chap. 6–7.

65. *Hannah, a woman of color v. John Pitcher*, November 1844, Case No. 28, SLCCR, 2. She sued for freedom on the basis of living in Boston, Massachusetts, but the jury decided against her and she remained Pitcher's slave.

66. *Laws of a Public and General Nature, of the District of Louisiana*, 96.

67. For the argument that court testimony should be approached with caution and even the assumption that it is all "lies" but lies that have to be "believable," see W. Johnson, *Soul by Soul*, 12.

68. *Tempe, a black woman v. Risdon H. Price*, April 1821, Case No. 181, SLCCR, 3.

69. Ibid., 27 (emphasis added). Tempe and her husband, Laban, both sued Price for freedom on the basis of their residence in the Northwest Territory; juries in both cases found Price guilty and declared Tempe and Laban free.

70. *Matilda, f.w.c. v. Autrey, et ux.*, 10 La. Ann. 555 (1855).

71. Ibid.

72. On the role of law in limiting the absolute power of enslavers, see Genovese, *Roll, Jordan, Roll*, 25–48.

73. *Milly, a black woman v. Mathias Rose*, August 1819, Case No. 20, SLCCR, 9 (emphasis added).

74. *Lethe Fenwick v. Samuel Abbot*, October 1823, Case No. 99, SLCCR, 1–2 (emphasis added).

75. As Susan O'Donovan has pointed out, however, jails could also be subversive spaces and a place where information spread among the enslaved population. See O'Donovan, "Universities of Social and Political Change." O'Donovan also found that, given enslaved persons' value as laborers, they rarely spent much time in jail. The exception was enslaved individuals involved in property disputes. Freedom suit plaintiffs certainly fell into this latter category, and while jailers usually tried to hire plaintiffs out during their suits, sheriffs and jailers were not always able to do so. See ibid., 131.

76. Delaney, *From the Darkness Cometh the Light*, 34–35.

77. CCRB No. 13, December 13, 1842, 341.

78. Frazier, *Slavery and Crime in Missouri*, 17.

79. See, for example, *Molly, a free woman of color v. Charles Mullikin and John Mullikin*, August 1825, no case number, SLCCR; *Ann, a woman of color v. John M. Jamison*, April 1844, Case No. 394, SLCCR; and *Mary Ann Speaks v. John M. Jameson*, April 1844, Case No. 386, SLCCR.

80. Protective custody for enslaved persons suing for freedom was common in many slave societies. See Blumenthal, "Promise of Freedom in Late Medieval Valencia," 56; and Mamigonian, "Conflicts over the Meanings of Freedom," 242.

81. *Sam, a person of color v. Alexander P. Field and Elijah Mitchell*, July 1832, Case No. 49, SLCCR, 6.

82. *Pierre, a mulatto v. Gabriel Chouteau*, November 1842, Case No. 125, SLCCR, 241.

83. Ibid., 227.

84. St. Louis Criminal Court Record Book 1, 57, 68, 79, 85–86, 101, 123. See also English, *Pioneer Lawyer and Jurist in Missouri*, 66.

85. St. Louis Criminal Court Record Book 1, 166, 226, 248, 259, 440.

86. Wines and Dwight, *Report on the Prisons and Reformatories*, 318.

87. Ibid.

88. The freedom suit statute specified that the sheriff should hire out freedom suit plaintiffs. The sheriff's fees came from the money earned from the person's hire, and the sheriff turned over the remainder of profits from the plaintiff's hire to the winning party in each suit. See *Laws of a Public and General Nature, of the District of Louisiana*, 95–96; *Revised Statutes of the State of Missouri*, 286; Casselberry, *Revised Statutes of the State of Missouri*, 283–84; and Hardin, *Revised Statutes of the State of Missouri*, vol. 1, 811.

89. *Sarah (a woman of colour) v. Henry*, 12 Va. 19 (1808).

90. *Jones v. Covey*, 26 Ala. 464 (1855). When a Louisiana plaintiff—freed by the court in his freedom suit—sued for wages and damages for the months he spent in jail during his case, the state supreme court affirmed a decision awarding him twenty-five dollars for his time in jail, plus the costs of his freedom suit. *Coby v. Kock*, 3 La. Ann. 439 (1848).

91. Jordan, *Frontier Law and Order*, 146.

92. *Revised Statutes of the State of Missouri*, 1841, 269.

93. *Louis Chouteau, a man of color v. Gabriel Chouteau*, April 1844, Case No. 51, SLCCR, 49.

94. *Isham Shaw v. Augustus H. Evans*, February 1860, Case No. 456, SLCCR, 41.

95. Wines and Dwight, *Report on the Prisons and Reformatories*, 319–20.

96. *Elsa Hicks, a mulatto girl v. Patrick T. McSherry*, November 1847, Case No. 121, SLCCR, 15.

97. Ibid., 16 (emphasis added).

98. Ibid.

99. Ibid.

100. *Louis Chouteau, a man of color v. Gabriel Chouteau*, April 1844, Case No. 51, SLCCR, 46–47.

101. Ibid., 53.

102. For more on slave hiring in the South, see Martin, *Divided Mastery*.

103. *Polly Wash v. Joseph M. Magehan*, November 1839, Case No. 167, SLCCR, 39–40.

104. See Martin, *Divided Mastery*.

105. Ted Maris-Wolf also discusses the faith that free people of color in Virginia had in the law to recognize and respond to their demands. See Maris-Wolf, *Family Bonds*, 3.

106. For more on the restrictions placed on free people of color in antebellum America, see, for example, Berlin, *Slaves without Masters*; Schweninger, *Black Property Owners in the South*; Schermerhorn, *Money over Mastery, Family over Freedom*; and esp. West, *Family or Freedom*; and Maris-Wolf, *Family Bonds*.

107. But freedom could hold a variety of different meanings for people of African descent. For examples of the varying definitions of freedom for African Americans before and after Emancipation, including elements like family and community, economic opportunity, the ability to move about freely, and the right to political participation, see Maris-Wolf, *Family Bonds*, 119, 150; Kantrowitz, *More than Freedom*; Hunter, *To 'Joy My Freedom*; Romeo, *Gender and the Jubilee*; and Hahn, *Nation under Our Feet*.

108. Delaney, *From the Darkness Cometh the Light*, 58. The desire for freedom and appreciation of it, despite its limitations, has most readily been described at the moment of Emancipation and in studies of Reconstruction. See, for example, Hunter, *To 'Joy My Freedom*; Frankel, *Freedom's Women*; Schwalm, *Hard Fight for We*; and Schermerhorn, *Money over Mastery, Family over Freedom*.

109. Delaney, *From the Darkness Cometh the Light*, 29. Another enslaved woman, named Seyton, sued for freedom in March 1840 when she was "informed and believe[d]" her alleged owner was preparing to sell her to "a distant place where she will be unable to procure the evidence of her freedom." *Seyton (also known as Sydney), a woman of color v. William Littleton*, March 1840, Case No. 3, SLCCR, 2.

110. In the 287 cases for freedom identified in St. Louis, at least 110 of them (38 percent) resulted in freedom for the enslaved plaintiff, and an additional 49 cases (17.1 percent) resulted in voluntary dismissals, suggesting that these individuals, too, may have eventually received freedom after filing suit for freedom. See the appendix.

111. Delaney, *From the Darkness Cometh the Light*.

3 / Crafting Strategy

1. Bay, *Reminiscences of the Bench and Bar of Missouri*, 98–100. Pettibone joined the law practice of Colonel Rufus Easton. Pettibone worked on preparing the state's *Revised Statutes* in 1824–25 with Henry S. Geyer, the future U.S. senator from Missouri. Pettibone's admission to the St. Louis bar is dated June 8, 1818. See CCRB No. 1, June 8, 1818, 190. When another prominent St. Louis attorney arrived in town the same year as Pettibone, he described the town as having "even then a striking and imposing appearance." See Darby, *Personal Recollections*, 2.

2. Bay, *Reminiscences of the Bench and Bar of Missouri*, 99. Pettibone lived in St. Louis until 1821, when he moved to the neighboring town of St. Charles.

3. For more information on negotiations among African Americans and white slaveholders, see Berlin, *Many Thousands Gone*; W. Johnson, *Soul by Soul*; Penningroth, *Claims of Kinfolk*; D. Davis, *Inhuman Bondage*.

4. Ted Maris-Wolf's recent book echoes many of the findings of this chapter about attorneys' work for free people of African descent in Virginia, pointing out that not only were attorneys willing to take on black clients but doing so did not hurt their

careers or affect their views on slavery. See Maris-Wolf, *Family Bonds*, chap. 3, esp. 48, 50, 61.

5. Lawyers came to Missouri in the early nineteenth century, intermingling with the largely French population and bringing ideas and experience from the eastern states. Most of Missouri's lawyers moved to the area in the 1810s, and no lawyers lived in Missouri prior to the Louisiana Purchase. After the Purchase, the implementation of American governmental institutions created opportunities for enterprising attorneys to migrate to the new territory. In the first two decades of the nineteenth century, the population of lawyers exploded. See Banner, *Legal Systems in Conflict*, 38.

6. Ibid., 104. This percentage also surpasses the percentage in the United States in the twenty-first century, when complaints about having more than enough lawyers are frequent. See American Bar Foundation, "Legal Profession Statistics," accessed February 20, 2016, http://www.americanbar.org/resources_for_lawyers/profession_statistics.html.

7. Banner, *Legal Systems in Conflict*, esp. chap. 6.

8. English, *Pioneer Lawyer and Jurist in Missouri*, chap. 7.

9. Shepard, "Breaking into the Profession."

10. Banner, *Legal Systems in Conflict*, 108.

11. William Francis English notes that Charles Lucas, Rufus Easton, William C. Carr, and Edward Bates all had large law libraries. See English, *Pioneer Lawyer and Jurist in Missouri*, 125. When the St. Louis attorney Beverly Allen died in 1845, his law library included the complete laws of Missouri, as well as volumes by Joseph Story on partnership, Willard Phillips on insurance, and Simon Greenleaf on evidence. Ibid., 124; "Account Books," Records of the Estate of Beverly Allen, 1849–1869, MHM.

12. Charles Drake Autobiography, WHMC, 475–76.

13. Other St. Louis law partnerships included Pettibone and Rufus Easton, Thomas Hudson and James Bowlin, Charles Lord and Miron Leslie, and Lewis Bogy and Logan Hunton, to name a few examples. Bay, *Reminiscences of the Bench and Bar of Missouri*, 99, 193, 289–90, 304, 577.

14. Joanne Freeman locates the roots for this culture of honor in early national politics, when duels often involved lawyers and lawmakers. See Freeman, *Affairs of Honor*, esp. chap. 4.

15. Edward Bates to Frederick Bates, ALS, August 24, 1824, Box 6, 1817–1824, Bates Family Papers, MHM.

16. See *State v. George Strother*, November 1827, Case No. 71, SLCRCF; *State v. George Strother*, March 1828, Case No. 34, SLCRCF; Criminal Court Record Book 5, 374, MSA-STL; Criminal Court Record Book 1, 282, MSA-STL.

17. Transcript of Missouri Supreme Court appeal, found in *State v. George Strother*, July 1825, SLCRCF. The Missouri Supreme Court approved the fine but found that the court lacked the authority to suspend Strother for six months.

18. See *State v. Horatio Cozens* (charge of assault and battery), April 1820, SLCRCF; *State v. Joseph Charless Jr.* (charge of starting an affray and fighting in public), July 1825, SLCRCF; *State v. Charless* (charge of assault and battery), November 1827, SLCRCF. For the two killed in duels, see SLCRCF; and copy of article from the *Missouri Intelligencer*, July 8, 1823, Folder 1, Duels Collection, MHM, which details Joshua Barton's death in a duel with Thomas Rector; and Edward Dobyns, "Account of the Duel of Spencer Pettis and Major Thomas Biddle on Bloody Island," November 10,

1866, Folder 2, Duels Collection, MHM. Luke Lawless fought in a duel and received a wound that left him with a permanent limp. Thomas B. Hudson fought a duel with Colonel A. B. Chambers in 1840. But according to the nineteenth-century historian W. V. N. Bay, in his *Reminiscences of the Bench and Bar of Missouri*, the incident did not make Hudson a "duelist." Instead, Bay explains that in that time "the custom was sanctioned by long usage and a perverted public opinion; and no young man, particularly if he belonged to the profession of the law, could live in this country without acknowledging its obligation." Bay, *Reminiscences of the Bench and Bar of Missouri*, 440, 194. See also English, *Pioneer Lawyer and Jurist in Missouri*, chap. 5.

19. For more on the importance of honor and reputation among early Americans, especially lawyers and politicians, see Freeman, *Affairs of Honor*; and for the argument that violence and honor were particularly pronounced among southerners because there the tradition of honor combined with the existence of slavery, see Wyatt-Brown, *Honor and Violence in the Old South*.

20. Slavery was integral to legal communities throughout the antebellum South. See Gross, *Double Character*, esp. chap. 1.

21. An 1845 tax receipt reveals that Edward Bates paid taxes on seven slaves valued at $1,400. An 1821 receipt from Bates to John B. C. Lucas shows that Bates hired out his enslaved woman Chloe to Lucas at the rate of $8 per month. John F. Darby's papers contain numerous letters about buying and selling slaves. In 1844, Gouveneur Morris of New York wrote to ask Darby to sell his slave Cecilia, who was about twenty-two years old, "a likely looking mulatto," and "a first rate servant." He insisted that "she is worth about $500, at least She cost me about that sum." Beverly Allen's estate record indicates that he owned eleven slaves worth over $2,000 at his death, and the attorney Hamilton Gamble's papers contain numerous bills of sale for slaves he purchased. "Receipt for hire of slave Chloe," April 10, 1821, Folder 1, Correspondence 1794–1841, William H. Semsrott Papers; and "Tax Receipt," 1845, Box 6, Bates Family Papers, both in MHM. Gouveneur Morris to John F. Darby, November 1, 1844, Box 3, Darby Family Papers, MHM. "Account Books," Records of the Estate of Beverly Allen, 1849–1869, MHM. And for examples of Gamble's slave purchases, see "Bill of Sale of Priscilla, and her children William Henry and Jane for $650," January 8, 1835, Folder 4, Box 5; "Bill of Sale of Simon Bolivar for $550," August 25, 1847, and "Bill of Sale of Sukey and her daughters Ellen, Martha, and Mary for $1050," September 10, 1847, both in Folder 4, Box 8, Gamble Papers, MHM.

22. *Malinda, a free girl of color v. Rufus Pettibone, Charles Hatton, Owen Wingfield, Isaac Voteau, John Butler, John Whitset, Michael Sanford*, July 1825, Case No. 13, SLCCR; *Lorinda, a free girl of color v. Rufus Pettibone, Charles Hatton, Owen Wingfield, Isaac Voteau, John Butler, John Whitset, and Michael Sanford*, July 1825, Case No. 11, SLCCR; *Winny, a free woman of color v. Rufus Pettibone, Charles Hatton, Owen Wingfield, Isaac Voteau, John Butler, John Whitset, Michael Sanford*, July 1825, Case No. 12, SLCCR; *Harry, a free boy of color v. Rufus Pettibone, Charles Hatton, Owen Wingfield, Isaac Voteau, John Butler, John Whitset, Michael Sanford*, July 1825, Case No. 14, SLCCR. For additional examples, see Sam's case against the attorneys Alexander P. Field and Elijah Mitchell, and in 1835, Hetty's suit against the attorney Arthur Magenis. *Sam, a person of color v. Alexander P. Field and Elijah Mitchell*, July 1832, Case No. 49, SLCCR; *Hetty, a woman of color v. Arthur L. Magenis*, March 1835, Case No. 43, SLCCR.

23. *Laws of a Public and General Nature, of the District of Louisiana*, 96.

24. *Charles, a man of color v. Peter Verhagen*, July 1840, Case No. 203, SLCCR, 1.

25. "An Act Concerning Costs," in *Revised Statutes of the State of Missouri*, 128.

26. In St. Louis, the court recorded the costs of each case, once paid, in a set of execution books that specify the fees for each element of the case and the date on which the losing party paid these costs. For example, see SLEB No. 4, July 3, 1837, 35, for a notation showing the costs satisfied in the case of *Rachel, a woman of color v. William Walker*, November 1834, Case. No. 82, SLCCR. No attorneys' fees appear in the record books after the book covering 1837.

27. Lea VanderVelde claims that most St. Louis freedom suit attorneys did not receive compensation. See VanderVelde, *Redemption Songs*, 9. Evidence from execution books suggests that perhaps more attorneys received compensation than previously realized.

28. SLEB No. 4, 35 (*Rachel, a woman of color v. William Walker*, November 1834, Case. No. 82, SLCCR); SLEB No. 4, 28 (*Sally, a person of color v. Henry Chouteau*, July 1835, Case No. 101, SLCCR). This translates to around $59.95 in 2012 figures. Estimates are based on "The Inflation Calculator," accessed January 19, 2014, http://www.westegg.com/inflation/.

29. See *Laws of a Public and General Nature of the State of Missouri*, 86.

30. See Geyer, *Digest of the Laws of Missouri Territory*, 186; *Revised Statutes of the State of Missouri*, 1835, 263; Casselberry, *Revised Statutes of the State of Missouri*, 490; and Hardin, *Revised Statutes of the State of Missouri*, vol. 1, 756. See also English, *Pioneer Lawyer and Jurist in Missouri*, 51.

31. *Gustavus Bird v. Lydia Titus*, July 1833, Case No. 44, SLCCF. Other charges included costs such as travel or fees associated with taking depositions, filing motions, or other similar expenses. When Bird sued to recover his fees, the court awarded him a $125 fee, plus costs, because Lydia Titus failed to appear in court. The records indicate that Titus was not a resident of St. Louis, and after she was arrested to pay the fees, the court released her as an insolvent debtor. This case suggests that, even when attorneys charged higher fees to enslaved or free black clients, they were not always able to collect.

32. *Rebecca, a negro woman v. James Black, Thomas Horine, and George Melody*, March 1843, Case No. 24, SLCCR, 2.

33. *Rufus Pettibone v. Charles Fremon Delauriere*, February 1824, Case No. 48, SLCCF, 3–4.

34. Chap. 15, Drake Autobiography, WHMC, 486.

35. This translates to around $50–$830 in today's figures. Estimates are based on "The Inflation Calculator," accessed April 28, 2008, http://www.westegg.com/inflation/, by looking at the figures for $10 and $30 in 1830. The numbers range slightly up over the course of the antebellum years, but this gives a sense of comparable amounts today.

36. See, for example, Dewey, *Thomas Jefferson, Lawyer*, chap. 9; Shepard, "Lawyers Look at Themselves"; Shepard, "Breaking into the Profession," 409.

37. Dewey, *Thomas Jefferson, Lawyer*, 88–91; Roeber, *Faithful Magistrates and Republican Lawyers*, 68.

38. Shepard, "Lawyers Look at Themselves," 2–3.

39. Shepard, "Breaking into the Profession," 408–9.

40. Montgomery Blair to the editors of the *National Intelligencer*, ALS, December 24, 1856, typescript copy, Folder 6, Box 1, Dred Scott Papers, MHM (emphasis added).

41. *Susan, a black woman v. Henry Hight*, February 1822, Case No. 127, SLCCR, 15–16. It is also possible that, given the early date of the case, St. Louis attorneys might expect compensation as part of the court costs.

42. Delaney, *From the Darkness cometh the Light*, 42.

43. Chap. 16, Drake Autobiography, WHMC, 511.

44. Gardner, "You Have No Business to Whip Me," 41. See also English, *Pioneer Lawyer and Jurist in Missouri*, 118.

45. Even so, work in freedom suits could sometimes bring repercussions from enslavers and their allies. A St. Louis newspaper reported one example of a physical assault in Illinois against an attorney who worked for an enslaved client in a St. Louis freedom suit. See "Below, we give the account promised yesterday of the mob of lynching, which lately took place in Kaskaskia," *Daily Missouri Republican*, August 24, 1841, col. C. For the editorials from Kaskaskia residents responding to this piece, see *Daily Missouri Republican*, September 1, 1841, col. B, and *Daily Missouri Republican*, September 15, 1841, col. B.

46. Banner, *Legal Systems in Conflict*, 103. Banner finds that it was not unusual for lawyers to be "overrepresented" in politics, and this was certainly the case with St. Louis's attorneys. See also English, *Pioneer Lawyer and Jurist in Missouri*, 127–30.

47. Matthias McGirk, Robert Wash, and Hamilton Gamble served on the Missouri Supreme Court; Hamilton Gamble became governor of Missouri; John F. Darby was mayor of St. Louis; Spencer Pettis, Henry Geyer, and David Barton became U.S. senators. English, *Pioneer Lawyer and Jurist in Missouri*, 127–30; Bay, *Reminiscences of the Bench and Bar of Missouri*, 126–29, 203, 244–46, 288–96, 314–15, 474, 536.

48. *Ralph, a man of color v. Coleman Duncan and James Duncan*, July 1830, Case No. 35, SLCCR, 4.

49. *Ellen Duty v. John F. Darby, Administrator*, April 1850, Case No. 18, SLCCR, 1–2; *Lucinda Duty v. John F. Darby, Administrator*, April 1850, Case No. 22, SLCCR, 1–2; *Caroline Duty v. John F. Darby, Administrator*, April 1850, Case No. 23, SLCCR, 1–2; *Mary Duty v. John F. Darby, Administrator*, April 1850, Case No. 24, SLCCR, 1–2.

50. *James Talbot v. Delford Benton, James C. Musick, and Prudence Musick*, March 1839, Case No. 92, SLCCR, 9. In a similar example, the attorney reported in his affidavit that the defendant had sold the plaintiff to slave traders who took her out of St. Louis on a steamboat. *Laura, a woman of color v. Henry Belt*, April 1852, Case No. 22, SLCCR, 7–10.

51. *Maria Whiten, a free woman of color v. Garland Rucker*, November 1829, Case No. 14, SLCCR, 8.

52. *Malinda, a woman of color v. George W. Coons, Administrator*, November 1845, Case No. 220, SLCCR, 9. In the same term of court, another attorney helped to provide a bond of security in an enslaved woman's case against several defendants. *Jane McCray, a mulatto woman v. William R. Hopkins, Eliza Oliver, et al.*, November 1845, Case No. 162, SLCCR, 10.

53. *Mary Charlotte, a woman of color v. Gabriel Chouteau*, November 1843, Case No. 13, SLCCR, 107–8.

54. *Mary, of color, and her children Samuel & Edward v. Launcelot H. Calvert*, April 1851, Case No. 2, SLCCR, 27.

55. Archibald Williams to Archibald Gamble, ALS, October 28, 1833, Folder 1, Box 5, Gamble Papers, MHM.

56. *Mary, a woman of color v. Francis Menard and Daniel Busby*, November 1833, Case No. 34, SLCCR, 2.

57. *Mary Robertson, a person of color v. Ringrose D. Watson*, November 1841, Case No. 30, SLCCR, 25–27. Robertson won her motion to reinstate her case, but the jury found for Watson and left her in slavery. She brought a second case in 1845, which ended when she voluntarily agreed not to prosecute her suit. This outcome could mean that she made other arrangements with Watson and Amos Corson (who also claimed her as his slave) to become free or that Watson and Corson no longer held her in slavery.

58. *Rebecca, a negro woman v. James Black, Thomas Horine, and George Melody*, March 1843, SLCCR, 2. Unfortunately for Rebecca, in her second case, although a jury found in her favor, the court set aside this verdict, and a second jury found the defendant not guilty. See CCRB No. 15, December 15, 1844, 389; and CCRB No. 16, December 5, 1845, 432.

59. *Laws of a General and Public Nature of the District of Louisiana*, 97.

60. For a few examples of state supreme courts citing laws and decisions of other states, see *William Edwards v. John P. M'Connel*, 3 Tenn. 304 (1813); *Joseph Jarrot v. Julia Jarrot*, 7 Ill. 1 (1845); *Samuel S. Sibley v. Maria*, 2 Fla. 553 (1849).

61. *Lewis Stubbs v. William Burd*, July 1837, Case No. 132, SLCCR, 2.

62. For more on Native American slavery in Missouri, see Trexler, *Slavery in Missouri*, 81; Foley, "Slave Freedom Suits before Dred Scott"; Foley, *Genesis of Missouri*, chap. 6.

63. *Nancy, a free woman of color v. Enoch Steen*, April 1848, Case No. 4, SLCCR, 1.

64. Ibid., 11–12.

65. *Pierre, a mulatto v. Gabriel Chouteau*, November 1842, Case No. 125, SLCCR; *Louis Chouteau, a man of color v. Gabriel Chouteau*, April 1844, Case No. 51, SLCCR.

66. *Mary Charlotte, a woman of color v. Gabriel Chouteau*, November 1843, Case No. 13, SLCCR. Lucy Delaney sued in 1844 based on her mother's successful 1839 freedom suit, winning freedom based on her birth to a free mother. Delaney, *From the Darkness Cometh the Light*. See also the case files: *Polly Wash v. Joseph M. Magehan*, November 1839, Case No. 167, SLCCR; and *Lucy Ann Britton v. David D. Mitchell*, November 1844, Case No. 18, SLCCR.

67. *Vina, a woman of color v. Martin Mitchell*, March 1832, Case No. 19, SLCCR; CCRB No. 6, May 4, 1833, 492.

68. In April 1828, a jury found John Singleton's enslavers guilty and set him free. *John Singleton, a free man of color v. Alexander Scott and Robert Lewis*, November 1827, Case No. 23, SLCCR, 1; CCRB No. 5, April 3, 1828, 121.

69. *Fulton v. Shaw*, 25 Va. 597 (1827).

70. *Fields v. Walker et al.*, 23 Ala. 155 (1853).

71. *Richard Clinton, a man of color v. John Blackburn, Edward Blackburn, Martha A. Blackburn, Charles A. Blackburn, Rufus C. Blackburn, and Edward Hall, Curator*, September 1859, Case No. 111, SLCCR, 2. The court set Richard free on December 13, 1859. See CCRB No. 29, December 13, 1859, 207.

72. *Mary, a negro woman v. James Clemens, Sr.*, November 1844, Case No. 346, SLCCR. The record book notation indicates that Mary agreed not to further prosecute her suit, suggesting that perhaps Clemens no longer claimed her as a slave. See CCRB No. 15, November 19, 1844, 297.

73. *Sally, a person of color v. Henry Chouteau*, July 1835, Case No. 101, SLCCR, 3–4.

74. For more on the specific concerns raised by manumissions by will, see Morris, *Southern Slavery and the Law*, chap. 18, esp. 373–80, 398–99. In an 1848 case, the Alabama Supreme Court judge J. Dargon declared a will freeing enslaved individuals invalid, even when that question was not the central issue involved in the dispute. *Welch's Heirs v. Welch's Administrators*, 14 Ala. 76 (1848).

75. Hutchinson, *Code of Mississippi*, 539; *Ira D. Read v. Reuben S. Manning*, 30 Miss. 308 (1855).

76. Years after passage of the 1841 South Carolina statute prohibiting manumission by will in that state, a South Carolina Supreme Court judge quoted it, writing, "Every devise or bequest to a slave or slaves, or to any person upon a trust or confidence, secret or expressed, for the benefit of any slave or slaves, shall be null and void." *John Jolliffe v. Fanning & Phillips & Others*, 10 Rich. 186 (1856). See also Morris, *Southern Slavery and the Law*, 398, which mentions Arkansas's and Maryland's statutes.

77. See also B. Jones, *Fathers of Conscience*.

78. For more on the various types of manumission by deed, see Morris, *Southern Slavery and the Law*, chap. 18.

79. Ira Berlin discusses the fear of a growing free black population and how this fear contributed to legal restrictions on freeing slaves and on the lives of free people of color, in *Slaves without Masters*, chap. 11. See also Stevenson, *Life in Black and White*; D. Davis, *Inhuman Bondage*, chap. 10; Fede, *Roadblocks to Freedom*; and Maris-Wolf, *Family Bonds*.

80. *Revised Statutes of the State of Missouri*, 1841, 414. Beginning with the 1835 *Revised Statutes*, Missouri's law also required people of African descent to obtain a license to carry weapons, a common restriction found in laws of other states.

81. In 1847, Missouri added new restrictions prohibiting teaching any black person to read or write, requiring all black gatherings (including church services) to have white supervision, and forbidding any black person from immigrating to the state. Hardin, *Revised Statutes of the State of Missouri*, vol. 2, 1100–1101.

82. *Delph (also known as Delphy), a mulatress v. Stephen Dorris*, November 1836, Case No. 4, SLCCR, 72.

83. Deed of Emancipation, November 19, 1837, from Jefferson Clark to Delph, in St. Louis, Folder 40, "Slave Emancipation and Fugitive Slave Legal Papers," in Missouri Collection, WHMC; *Delph v. Stephen Dorris*, June 1838, Case No. 14, MOSCD.

84. These disputes are discussed in more detail in chap. 5.

85. For more information on the *Somerset v. Stewart* case, see Cotter, "Somerset Case and the Abolition of Slavery in England"; and "Forum: *Somerset's Case* Revisited," *Law and History Review* 24, no. 3 (2006): 601–72.

86. *Aspasia, a free woman of color v. Francois Chouteau and Pierre Menard*, March 1828, Case No. 5, SLCCR, 3.

87. CCRB No. 5, December 6, 1828, 176; and CCRB No. 5, December 23, 1828, 199.

88. *Matilda, a free girl of color v. Philip Rocheblave and Mary Louisa Rocheblave*, November 1828, Case No. 38, SLCCR; CCRB No. 5, January 25, 1830, 480–81.

89. *Gentry v. Polly McMinnis*, 33 Ky. 382 (1835).

90. *Harry and Others v. Decker & Hopkins*, 1 Miss. 36 (1818).

91. *Winny, a woman of color v. Samuel Donner*, August 1820, Case No. 70, SLCCR, 6.

92. This figure is determined by taking the average of the figure of $650, which Beckwith argued was Winny's value, and $500, which is the value Donner claimed for Winny. In either case, Winny's value clearly exceeded the figure of $300, which is the price of her sale to Donner.

93. *Winny, a woman of color v. Samuel Donner*, August 1820, Case No. 70, SLCCR, 7.

94. Ibid., 41. The verdict is signed by Obediah Reynolds, the foreman, who worked as a stone mason and hired slaves to help with his business.

95. In this suit, Donner claimed Winny's value was $500. *Samuel Donner v. Jennings Beckwith*, February 1818, Case No. 16, SLCCF.

96. *Jennings Beckwith v. Samuel Donner*, June 1819, Case No. 80, SLCCF. Chancery courts provided equity jurisdiction, which gave people a remedy when they could not prove their case in a common law proceeding or when the common law solution was lacking in some way.

97. Ibid., response of Donner. According to Donner, Beckwith first called him and one of his witnesses "rascals" when Donner tried to pay him with a note from the witness, but Beckwith repeated the charge and added that he "would kill him" after Donner received the money from the witness and tried again to pay Beckwith.

98. For more on the nature of and debates over voluntary servitude in Illinois, see Simeone, *Democracy and Slavery in Frontier Illinois*, esp. 19–21. The 1818 Illinois Constitution restricted future indentures to one-year terms.

99. *Milly, a black woman v. Mathias Rose*, August 1819, Case No. 20, SLCCR, 6–9 (quote on 9). This is an interesting qualification on the type of provisions Rose had to provide for Milly because it demonstrates how slaves' livelihoods required a different "degree and station" of care.

100. Ibid., 11.

101. Ibid., 18.

102. *United States v. Mathias Rose*, December 1819, no case number, SLCRCF, 1.

103. CCRB No. 2, April 17, 1820, 111.

104. *Winny, a free woman v. Phebe Whitesides (alias Pruitt)*, April 1821, Case No. 190, SLCCR; see also *Sarah, a free girl v. Charles Hatton*, April 1821, Case No. 191, SLCCR; *Lydia, a free girl v. John Butler*, April 1821, Case No. 192, SLCCR; *Nancy, a free girl v. Isaac Voteau*, April 1821, Case No. 193, SLCCR; *Jenny, a free girl v. Robert Musick*, April 1821, Case No. 194, SLCCR; *Jerry, a free man of color v. Charles Hatton*, April 1821, Case No. 195, SLCCR; *Daniel, a free man v. John Whitesides*, April 1821, Case No. 196, SLCCR; *Hannah, a free girl of color v. Phebe Whitesides (alias Pruitt)*, April 1821, Case No. 197, SLCCR; *Malinda, a free girl of color v. Phebe Whitesides (alias Pruitt)*, April 1821, Case No. 198, SLCCR; and *Lewis, a free boy of color v. Phebe Whitesides (alias Pruitt)*, April 1821, Case No. 199, SLCCR.

105. *Winny v. Rufus Pettibone et al.*, July 1825, Case No. 12, petition, found in "Slaves Papers," MHM.

106. The court dismissed this petition, but Winny continued to argue for her freedom, with hers and her children's cases finally appearing in court in the April 1821 term. *Winny, a free woman v. Phebe Whitesides (alias Pruitt)*, April 1821, Case No. 190, SLCCR, 9. The reason the court dismissed Winny's first petition is not given in the records.

107. But Phebe also claimed that at the time of the freedom suit, she no longer held Winny or her children as her slaves. Ibid., 21–22, 29–30. A similar argument was popular in defense of freedom suits in late medieval Valencia, when alleged owners argued that the person who promised to free an enslaved individual did not have the title to that person's labor. See Blumenthal, "Promise of Freedom in Late Medieval Valencia"; and Blumenthal, *Enemies and Familiars*.

108. *Winny, a free woman v. Phebe Whitesides (alias Pruitt)*, April 1821, Case No. 190, SLCCR, 28 (emphasis added). A notice in the *Missouri Republican*, November 29, 1824, explained the ruling on this doctrine of intent.

109. The relationship between Missouri and Illinois is discussed in chap. 4.

110. *Winny, a free woman v. Phebe Whitesides (alias Pruitt)*, April 1821, Case No. 190, SLCCR, 21–22. This document is signed by Pettibone and his attorney.

111. *Winny v. Rufus Pettibone et al.*, July 1825, Case No. 12, petition, found in Folder 1, "Slaves Collection," MHM, 2.

112. *Winny, a free woman of color v. Rufus Pettibone, Charles Hatton, Owen Wing-field, Isaac Voteau, John Butler, John Whitset, Michael Sanford*, July 1825, Case No. 12, SLCCR, 27. This language references the fact that the territorial statute on freedom suits became state law in 1824.

113. Winny's case is a clear example of the court's struggles to determine the rules for freedom suits. In later cases, large damage awards for enslaved plaintiffs became extremely rare.

4 / A World in Motion

1. *Thornton Kinney, a man of color v. John F. Hatcher and Charles C. Bridges*, November 1853, Case No. 35, SLCCR, 5; *In the Matter of Thornton Kinney*, Writ of Habeas Corpus, SLCRCF; St. Louis Criminal Court Book 7, July 12, 1853, 463; July 23, 1853, 476; and July 25, 1853, 478.

2. For more on African Americans' decisions to move to Liberia and, sometimes, to return to the United States, see Maris-Wolf, *Family Bonds*, chap. 5.

3. *Thornton Kinney, a man of color v. John F. Hatcher and Charles C. Bridges*, November 1853, Case No. 35, SLCCR, 9–10.

4. Ibid., 10. On the significance of paper documentation of legal status for people of African descent, see R. Scott, "Slavery and the Law in Atlantic Perspective," 924; and, especially, R. Scott, "Paper Thin."

5. *Thornton Kinney, a man of color v. John F. Hatcher and Charles C. Bridges*, November 1853, Case No. 35, SLCCR, 11.

6. Ibid., 9.

7. CCRB No. 25, December 21, 1855, 253. In February 1856, Kinney asked the court to set aside the dismissal, but on April 9, 1856, the court overruled this motion. CCRB No. 25, February 19, 1856, 314; and CCRB No. 25, April 9, 1856, 362.

8. Finkelman, *Imperfect Union*, 34.

9. Other scholars have noted the significance of St. Louis as a central slave city connecting regions and welcoming travelers from all parts of the country. See, for example, Wade, *Slavery in the Cities*; Foley, *Genesis of Missouri*; Banner, *Legal Systems in Conflict*; Christian, *Before Lewis and Clark*; Towers, *Urban South and the Coming of Civil War*; Konig, "Long Road to *Dred Scott*"; Arenson, *Great Heart of the Republic*.

10. For more on the internal slave trade, see Bancroft, *Slave-Trading in the Old South*; A. Rothman, *Slave Country*; W. Johnson, *Soul by Soul*; W. Johnson, *Chattel Principle*; Deyle, *Carry Me Back*; W. Johnson, *River of Dark Dreams*; and Baptist, *Half Has Never Been Told*.

11. For more on the rise and significance of steamboat commerce, see especially W. Johnson, *River of Dark Dreams*.

12. Missouri remained a net slave importing state through the 1830s because many travelers from the East brought their slaves with the expectation of being able to re-create a plantation society in the West. The majority of these new migrants found that conditions in Missouri were not suitable for staple crop production, leading many of them to sell their slaves out of the state in the 1840s and 1850s. St. Louis was the center of this slave trading, with more than thirty traders listed in the 1851 city directory. See Bancroft, *Slave-Trading in the Old South*, chap. 6 and esp. 138. Bancroft finds that "St. Louis was, indeed, one of the five or six cities that sent the most negroes to the insatiable 'Southern market.'" Ibid., 139.

13. Ninian Edwards, Belleville, Illinois, to William Carr Lane, St. Louis, Missouri, ALS, September 21, 1828, William Carr Lane Papers, MHM.

14. For more on the complexity of slavery in a border region, see Salafia, *Slavery's Borderland*.

15. For more on the transformation from steamboats and river travel to railroads, see W. Johnson, *River of Dark Dreams*, 124–25, 293–96.

16. Bolster, *Black Jacks*. The historian David S. Cecelski has argued that African Americans working on boats were "key agents of antislavery thought and militant resistance to slavery," through their autonomous, egalitarian culture as much as through their direct resistance. See Cecelski, *Waterman's Song*, xvi.

17. Buchanan, *Black Life on the Mississippi*, 25.

18. *Thornton Kinney, a man of color v. John F. Hatcher and Charles C. Bridges*, November 1853, Case No. 35, SLCCR, 13.

19. One early nineteenth-century governor of Illinois believed the Ordinance only applied to new residents of the state. See Arthur St. Clair to the president, in St. Clair, *St. Clair Papers*, 176.

20. Finkelman, *Imperfect Union*, chap. 3. See also Simeone, *Democracy and Slavery in Frontier Illinois*; Dexter, *Bondage in Egypt*; Heerman, "In a State of Slavery."

21. "Constitution of 1818," in Verlie, *Illinois Constitutions*, 38–39.

22. *Dunky, a colored woman v. Andrew Hay*, July 1831, Case No. 12, SLCCR, 5. Dunky won her freedom from Hay in 1834 by a jury verdict.

23. For more on slavery and indentured servitude in Illinois, see Gorsuch, "To Indent Oneself"; Gorsuch, "Legacies of Empire"; Finkelman, *Imperfect Union*, esp. chap. 3; J. Davis, *Frontier Illinois*, 20, 22, 161, 165; Simeone, *Democracy and Slavery in Frontier Illinois*; and Harris, *History of Negro Servitude in Illinois*.

24. For a more detailed chapter on the Duncan family, see VanderVelde, *Redemption Songs*, chap. 8.

25. Vincent's petition stated that he began his hire in 1815 or 1816, most witnesses put the date at 1817, and James Duncan argued that the date was after his father's death in November 1818.

26. *Vincent, a man of color v. James Duncan*, November 1829, Case No. 110, SLCCR, 8–15. Vincent's jobs included work at the Saline Tavern but he also worked in the

salt business, laid tubes for conducting salt water, chopped wood for the furnace, and operated the furnace.

27. Defendant's brief, *Vincent v. James Duncan and Coleman Duncan*, September 1830, Case No. 68, MOSCD, 1. Sometimes Vincent's hirers would pay him with salt, so James Duncan traveled often to Illinois to get his salt as payment for Vincent's work.

28. *Vincent, a man of color v. James Duncan*, November 1829, Case No. 110, SLCCR, 39.

29. Ibid., 113.

30. Ibid., 19.

31. Ibid., 20.

32. Ibid., 14.

33. Ibid., 62. The man who hired Vincent was a brick maker who found himself in court numerous times for slave stealing and other crimes. Keemle, *St. Louis Directory for the Years 1836-7*; for examples of Letcher's legal difficulties, see *Enoch Steen v. Isaac Letcher*, July 1827, Case No. 25, SLCCF; *Robert Simpson v. Isaac Letcher and James Lyle*, March 1831, Case No. 11, SLCCF; and *Isaac Letcher v. Steamboat "Far West,"* July 1836, Case No. 16, SLCCF.

34. Transcript, *Vincent v. James Duncan and Coleman Duncan*, September 1830, Case No. 68, MOSCD. For more on slave hiring, see Martin, *Divided Mastery*. Martin argues that the practice of slave hiring fueled social conflicts among southern whites by pitting the property rights of two individuals against each other. He also argues that slaves could sometimes play hirers and owners off each other for their own advantage. For two nineteenth-century newspaper articles denouncing the practice of slaves hiring themselves, as Vincent did, see "To the Public: Disorderly Negroes," *Missouri Republican*, July 12, 1824, 1; and "Slaves," *Missouri Republican*, July 19, 1824, 2.

35. It was common for owners to threaten enslaved persons in the border states or Upper South with being "sold South," or "sold to New Orleans," a threat that meant being separated from family and friends and may also have implied a harsher form of slavery.

36. *Vincent, a man of color v. James Duncan*, November 1829, Case No. 110, SLCCR, 63.

37. This argument is why the date of the start of Vincent's hire was so important. James claimed that Vincent was not hired to the Salt Lick until immediately following his father's death, in November 1818. Illinois approved the new constitution in August 1818, but Congress did not adopt the constitution until December 1818, so James claimed that Vincent should not be freed by the Northwest Ordinance because the Illinois constitution took effect as soon as the state approved it in August.

38. Plaintiff's statement and brief, *Vincent v. James Duncan and Coleman Duncan*, September 1830, Case No. 68, MOSCD.

39. Decision, ibid.

40. Ibid.

41. Ibid.

42. In 1835, Missouri passed a law requiring all free blacks living in the state to apply for a license to remain there. See *Revised Statutes of the State of Missouri*, 1841, 413–17. The St. Louis County Court handled all licensing for the city, and in December 1835, this court granted Vincent Duncan, a forty-seven-year-old drayman, a license to continue living in St. Louis as a free man. For the filing of the license, see Vincent Duncan,

application for license, St. Louis County Court Records, roll SLCCRR-2, Volume 1, Special Collections Department, St. Louis County Library, 460. Additional court cases also indicate Vincent's freedom because only a free person could sue (for anything other than a freedom suit) and be sued in the St. Louis Circuit Court. See *Thornton Tyler v. Vincent Duncan*, November 1837, Case No. 478, SLCCF; *Vincent Duncan v. Andrew Fifer*, July 1838, Case No. 29, SLCCF. The last records mentioning Vincent Duncan are two cases from March and July 1839, in both of which the court found against Vincent because he failed to appear. *Daniel Chapman v. Vincent Duncan*, March 1839, Case No. 21, SLCCF; *James L. Wood v. Vincent Duncan*, July 1839, Case No. 305, SLCCF.

43. See *Winny, a free woman v. Phebe Whitesides (alias Pruitt)*, April 1821, Case No. 190, SLCCR.

44. See the special issue of *Slavery & Abolition* on the concept of "free soil," which was used by slaves to establish freedom in a wide variety of historical contexts. "Free Soil," special issue, *Slavery & Abolition* 32, no. 3 (2011), especially the introductory essay: Peabody and Grinberg, "Free Soil."

45. *Rachel, a woman of color v. William Walker*, November 1834, Case No. 82, SLCCR, 1, 15–18. These forts included Fort Snelling, which is where Dred and Harriet Scott lived before suing for freedom based on residence in free territory. In another example, witness testimony recounted how a plaintiff's alleged owner took him from Tennessee to Madison County, Illinois, four miles from the Mississippi River. *Jonathan, a man of color v. Marshall Brotherton, Joel Danah, and Aza Willoughby*, November 1841, Case No. 32, SLCCR, 9–14.

46. "Free Soil," *Slavery & Abolition*.

47. *Griffith v. Fanny*, 21 Va. 143 (1820). See also *Lunsford v. Coquillon*, 2 Mart. (n.s.) 401 (1824); and *Blackmore and Hadley v. Negro Phil*, 7 Yeager 452 (1835). Mississippi's Supreme Court made a similar decision in 1818, upholding the Northwest Ordinance's provision against slavery and explicitly stating the court's willingness to favor freedom whenever possible. *Harry & others v. Decker & Hopkins*, 1 Miss. 36 (1818).

48. *Ben Mercer v. Gillman*, 20 Ky. 210 (1850). The opinion in this case elaborates on the facts, explaining that the alleged owner of Mercer had spoken frequently about his intention to free Mercer in his will. Chief Justice Marshall found that, although this intention was not enough to free Mercer, it did speak to the supposed owner's willingness to allow Mercer to travel to a free state often enough to effect his freedom.

49. *Collins, &c. v. America, a woman of color*, 48 Ky. 565 (1849).

50. *Priscilla Smith, f.w.c. v. Smith*, 13 La. 441 (1839). For a discussion of Priscilla Smith's case, see Schafer, *Slavery, the Civil Law, and the Supreme Court of Louisiana*, 273–74; for a more general discussion of the law of slavery in France, see also Peabody, "*There Are No Slaves in France.*"

51. For more on this woman's incredible story, see Scott, "She . . . Refuses to Deliver Up Herself as the Slave of Your Petitioner"; and Scott and Hébrard, *Freedom Papers*, 69–70.

52. *Harry and Others v. Decker & Hopkins*, 1 Miss. 36 (1818).

53. For more on the changes that swept the Mississippi Valley during the 1830s, 1840s, and 1850s, see W. Johnson, *River of Dark Dreams*.

54. *Lunsford v. Coquillon*, 2 Mart. (n.s.) 401 (1824).

55. *John Anderson v. Henry Poindexter and Others*, 6 Ohio St. 622 (1856). Judge J. Bowen, in his opinion, described Ohio's stance on the question of comity as harking

back to the Northwest Ordinance. According to Judge Bowen, slavery's "manacles instantly break asunder and crumble to dust, when he who has worn them obtains the liberty from his oppressor, and is afforded the opportunity by him of placing his feet upon our shore, and of breathing the air of freedom."

56. *Maria v. Kirby*, 51 Ky. 542 (1851).

57. *Michel Paul v. Adolph Paul, Administrator*, April 1845, Case No. 143, SLCCR, 5–6.

58. See CCRB No. 22, November 22, 1852, 285.

59. *John Merry, a free man of color v. Clayton Tiffin and Louis Menard*, November 1826, Case No. 18, SLCCR.

60. The defendant was actually the widow of the former alleged owner. See *Charles, a man of color v. Belina Christy*, March 1841, Case No. 343, SLCCR, 9.

61. The case lasted two years, and after a change of venue from the Circuit Court to the Court of Common Pleas, the plaintiff received his freedom.

62. Berlin writes in *Slaves without Masters* that "kidnappers acted with impunity" (99), and when slave prices rose, they sometimes worked "with the tacit consent of local officials" (160). Hundreds, perhaps thousands, of men and women suffered at the hands of a growing number of professional kidnapping gangs. See also Wilson, *Freedom at Risk*.

63. *Jane Cotton, a free person of color v. James A. Little*, April 1848, Case No. 37, SLCCR, 1–8, 3. There are not exact dates or ages recorded in Jane's case file, so it is not possible to determine her exact age at the time of her kidnapping or when she brought suit. The case file only indicates that she was a minor at the time of her kidnapping and that only after a number of years was she old enough to act for herself and sue for her freedom. The court dismissed Cotton's case because she failed to provide security for costs.

64. *Milly, a free mulatto woman v. Stephen Smith*, July 1827, Case No. 14, SLCCR, 16.

65. *Arthur v. Chavis*, 27 Va. 142 (1828).

66. *The State v. William Hill*, 29 S.C.L. 150 (1843). The statute can be found at McCord, 6 *Stat. at Large*, 674.

67. On the issue of the individuals who fled the conflict in Saint-Domingue, see White, *Encountering Revolution*.

68. *Boisneuf v. Lewis*, 4 H. & McH. 414 (1799).

69. *Baptiste, et al. v. De Volunbrun*, 5 H. & J. 86 (1820). See also M. Jones, "Case of Jean Baptiste, un Créole de Saint-Domingue."

70. *Henderson v. Negro Tom*, 4 Harr. and John. 282 (1817).

71. *Rebecca Ringgold and others, Negroes v. David Barkley*, 5 Md. 186 (1853).

72. *Loudon v. Scott*, 1 Cranch C.C. 264 (1805).

73. See the three cases concerning Ben's freedom: *Ben v. Scott*, 1 Cranch C.C. 350 (1806); *Ben v. Scott*, 1 Cranch 365 (1806); and *Ben v. Scott*, 1 Cranch 407 (1807). As an interesting side note, Ben's attorney in all three cases is listed as F. S. Key, a D.C.-area lawyer made famous years later for his songwriting talents.

74. *Negress Sally Henry, by William Henry, Her Father and Next Friend v. Ball*, 14 U.S. 1 (1816).

75. *Jordan v. Sawyer*, 2 Cranch C.C. 373 (1823). The court reports indicate that this case was "settled by parties," though it is not clear what that settlement entailed.

76. A collection of freedom suits brought in the District of Columbia is now available online through the project "O Say Can You See: Early Washington D.C., Law & Family," http://earlywashingtondc.org/.

77. *Frank v. Milam's executor*; *Tom v. Smith*; *Mary v. Shannon*; and *Betsey v. Shannon*, 4 Ky. 615 (1809).

78. *Nancy et als. v. Wright et als.*, 28 Tenn. 597 (1848).

79. John Monroe Brazealle's case became a freedom suit when the heirs argued that he was a slave, forcing him to defend his freedom to the court. See *Hinds et al. v. Brazealle et al.*, 3 Miss. 837 (1838).

80. Ibid.

81. For an example of a published work discussing *Hinds v. Brazealle* in the context of interstate comity and inheritance issues, see B. Jones, *Fathers of Conscience*, 54–55.

5 / Double Character

1. *Preston, Braxton, Mary, Nat, Beverly, et al. v. George W. Coons, Administrator et al.*, November 1841, Case No. 674, SLCCR, 90.

2. Ibid., 9–10.

3. Ibid., 34.

4. Ibid., 90–91. Preston and the other slaves of Milton Duty received an injunction preventing their sale in their 1841 case, though they had to bring multiple additional lawsuits to try to secure their freedom. The last records of Preston are from his 1850 case against Duty's second administrator, John F. Darby, when Preston voluntarily allowed his case to be dismissed. See *Preston, a man of color v. George W. Coons, Administrator*, November 1844, Case No. 34, SLCCR; and *Preston Duty v. John F. Darby, Administrator*, April 1850, Case No. 21, SLCCR.

5. Cobb, *Inquiry into the Law of Negro Slavery*.

6. Gross, *Double Character*, 3.

7. Hardin, *Revised Statutes of the State of Missouri*, vol. 2, 1478–79. Because of the frequency of these cases in the appellate records, this section often draws on particularly illustrative examples from outside Missouri to flesh out the range of issues raised when these property transfers went awry.

8. Washington's will specified that his slaves should serve his widow, Martha Washington, until her death, at which point the slaves would be free. Martha Washington, realizing that this bequest—what is termed a life estate—made her death desirable for her slaves, freed them by deed. For this story and an explanation of Washington's motives, see Riley, "Written with My Own Hand," 171.

9. *Mary Ann Steel v. William Walker*, July 1835, Case No. 97, SLCCR, 1. Mary Ann filed a corresponding freedom suit against the second man claiming her as a slave; see *Mary Ann Steel v. Curtis Skinner*, July 1835, Case No. 96, SLCCR.

10. *Mary Ann Steel v. William Walker*, July 1835, Case No. 97, SLCCR, 1. It is not clear if James Steel's heirs gave up their claim or if Mary Ann reached another arrangement for freedom, but the records indicate that, in 1836, she agreed not to prosecute her case against either of the two men she sued. For this verdict, see CCRB No. 8, August 25, 1836, 117.

11. *Mullins et al. v. Wall et al.*, 47 Ky. 445 (1848).

12. See Hardin, *Revised Statutes of the State of Missouri*, vol. 2, 1478–79. For Virginia, see Condon, "Slave Owner's Family and Manumission in the Post-Revolutionary Chesapeake Tidewater," 346.

13. For an excellent discussion of the distinctions made in state regulations of manumission, see Morris, *Southern Slavery and the Law*, chap. 18.

14. *Atwood's Heirs v. Beck, Administrator*, 21 Ala. 590 (1852).

15. "To treat this trust as compulsory, would be, to enable a testator to do indirectly, and *in fraudem legis*, that which he could not have done directly." In trying to interpret the Alabama will as the Alabama Supreme Court and the statutes of Alabama dictated, the Louisiana Supreme Court issued a decision that denied freedom to an enslaved person whose enslaver attempted to follow Alabama's requirements for manumitting by will. *Young, f.m.c. v. Egan, et al.*, 10 La. Ann. 415 (1855).

16. For more on this point, see Fede, *Roadblocks to Freedom*.

17. *Richard Rice v. Samuel Spear and James Galbreatu*, Harp 20 (1823) (emphasis added).

18. *The Heirs of David Morton v. Thompson and Another, Executors*, 6 Rich. Eq. 370 (1854).

19. For more on the shift in South Carolina's racial attitudes during the antebellum years, see Ford, *Origins of Southern Radicalism*; and Sinha, *Counter-revolution of Slavery*.

20. Manumission practices from numerous slave societies included similar arrangements, making them, in essence, what the scholar Orlando Patterson describes as a "gift exchange." See Patterson, "Three Notes of Freedom." See also Blackburn, introduction to *Paths to Freedom*, 9; Phillips, "Manumission in Metropolitan Spain and the Canaries," 32; Blumenthal, "Promise of Freedom in Late Medieval Valencia," 51; Klooster, "Manumission in an Entrepôt," 167; and Condon, "Slave Owner's Family and Manumission in the Post-Revolutionary Chesapeake Tidewater," 340.

21. For a treatment of this topic in relation to gradual emancipation, see Gigantino, *Ragged Road to Abolition*.

22. An 1838 Tennessee Supreme Court case declared that "if there be any doubt of the meaning of the will, the power of disposition, must be construed to be subordinate, to the higher, and more important right of freedom." Tennessee's highest court therefore affirmed the right to free enslaved persons *in futuro*, though not all southern courts followed suit. *Jacob v. Sharp*, 19 Tenn. 114 (1838). In this case, Tennessee's highest court elaborated on the intentions of an owner who freed a slave by will and denied the right of the widow—who held a life estate in Jacob, after which point he was to be freed—to deny freedom to Jacob on the basis of alleged bad behavior: "The liberty which a testator intends to bestow, is of so high a value to the objects of his benevolence,—and must be supposed so to occupy his thoughts, and so strongly to fix his purposes, that a devise of freedom is not to be defeated by any right of disposition (not exercised) which may be given to a devisee for life."

23. For more on "slaves for a term" in New Jersey, see Gigantino, *Ragged Road to Abolition*.

24. *Vica, a woman of color v. Samuel Hobart*, July 1842, Case No. 31, SLCCR, 1. For Vica's children, see *Thadeus Alonzo, a boy of color v. John Sparr, Samuel Hobart, James Mellody, and George Charles*, July 1842, Case No. 32, SLCCR; *Musa Ben Abel Gazen,*

a boy of color v. John Sparr, Samuel Hobart, James Mellody, and George Charles, July 1842, Case No. 33, SLCCR.

25. *Vica, a woman of color v. Samuel Hobart*, July 1842, Case No. 31, SLCCR, 2.

26. For the verdict of the case, see CCRB No. 13, July 22, 1842, 227, which states that Vica's and her children's cases were dismissed and that the defendants released the plaintiffs to their relative and next friend, Christy Evans.

27. *Hudgens v. Spencer*, 34 Ky. 589 (1836).

28. In the same opinion, the court stated that "the question as to his right to freedom was sufficiently doubtful to authorize the presumption that he had been held in slavery in good faith," meaning that the man won only the wages of his hire during his court case but no damages from his time in slavery, a wrong the court excused because it was done "in good faith." Ibid.

29. *Preston, Braxton, Mary, Nat, Beverly et al. v. George W. Coons, Administrator of Duty, et al.*, November 1841, Case No. 674, SLCCR, 8.

30. Ibid., 9.

31. Ibid., 88.

32. *Caleb v. Field and Others*, 39 Ky. 346 (1840).

33. *Snead v. David*, 39 Ky. 350 (1840).

34. *Jinny Jackson, a woman of color v. James O. Fraser*, July 1842, Case No. 102, SLCCR, 14. See also the cases of Jackson's children: *Henry Jackson, a person of color v. James O. Fraser*, July 1842, Case No. 103, SLCCR; *Ann Maria, a person of color v. James O. Fraser*, July 1842, Case No. 104, SLCCR; *Sally Jackson (also known as Sarah), a person of color v. James O. Fraser*, July 1842, Case No. 105, SLCCR; *Margaret Jackson, a person of color v. James O. Fraser*, July 1842, Case No. 106, SLCCR; *William Henry, a person of color v. James O. Fraser*, July 1842, Case No. 107, SLCCR; and *Smith, a person of color v. James O. Fraser*, July 1842, Case No. 108, SLCCR.

35. *Catherine, Felix, William, & Minta, persons of color v. Thomas Hundley, D. Pattison, and William Russell*, November 1843, Case No. 20, SLCCR. The record book indicates that this group of enslaved plaintiffs voluntarily agreed not to prosecute their case. See CCRB No. 15, June 6, 1844, 95. It is not clear why Jinny Jackson's family sued in separate cases and Catherine and her family sued in a joint case.

36. *Clagett et al. v. Gibson*, 5 F. Cas. 808 (1828).

37. *William Mayho, by his next friend v. Edward Sears*, 25 N.C. 224 (1842). For more on how antebellum southern judges shaped the law of slavery, see Brophy, *University, Court, and Slave*.

38. *William Mayho, by his next friend v. Edward Sears*, 25 N.C. 224 (1842).

39. *Hester Williams, Ella Williams & Priscilla Williams v. A. B. McAfee, Frederick Norcum, Glanville Blakey, and William Moore*, November 1853, Case No. 119, SLCCR, 3.

40. Ibid., 3. Hester Williams's case ended with the court finding the defendants guilty and setting Williams and her daughters free. See CCRB No. 25, April 18, 1855, 372.

41. Berlin, *Many Thousands Gone*; Berlin, *Generations of Captivity*.

42. For examples of broken promises of manumission in earlier slave societies, see Phillips, "Manumission in Metropolitan Spain and the Canaries," 43; and Blumenthal, "Promise of Freedom in Late Medieval Valencia," 53–54.

43. Dylan Penningroth details the world of slave property ownership in the nineteenth century. See Penningroth, *Claims of Kinfolk*.

44. *James Wilkinson, a man of color v. Aaron Young*, July 1833, Case No. 102, SLCCR, 1 (emphasis added). The case record in this instance is brief, and the man won his freedom when the defendant defaulted by refusing to appear in court to defend the charges. CCRB No. 7, August 12, 1844, 35.

45. *Alfred Taylor, a free man of color v. Cornelius Van Houten, Lewis Martin, and Samuel Conway*, November 1848, Case No. 93, SLCCR, 2.

46. Although this plaintiff's fate is not revealed in the court records, his suit for freedom ended when he allowed it to be dismissed at his own costs. This conclusion could have been because he had already been freed or because someone forced him to abandon his case. See CCRB No. 19, September 11, 1849, 175.

47. *Mary (also known as Mary Davis), a woman of color v. Samuel B. Bellis*, April 1855, Case No. 96, SLCCR, 11; CCRB No. 26, November 12, 1856, 52.

48. See Fede, *Roadblocks to Freedom*, esp. 46.

49. *Throckmorton and Russell v. Jinny Lewelin et al.*, 44 Ky. 585 (1845) (emphasis in original).

50. *Willis (of color) v. Bruce and Warfield*, 47 Ky. 548 (1848).

51. Aslakson, *Making Race in the Courtroom*, 62–63.

52. *Victoire v. Dussuau*, 4 Mart. (o.s.) 212 (1816).

53. *Cuffy v. Castillon*, 5 Mart. (o.s.) 494 (1818).

54. *Francois v. Jacinto Lobrano*, 10 Rob. 450 (1845).

55. Ibid.

56. *Letty et al. v. Lowe*, 15 F. Cas. 411 (1825).

57. *Bland and Woolfolk v. Negro Beverly Dowling*, 9 G. & J. 19 (1837).

58. Virginia's statute was one of the earliest, passed in 1806. See Maris-Wolf, *Family Bonds*, chap. 1.

59. *Jane B. Ross et al. v. Vertner et al.*, 6 Miss. 305 (1840).

60. *John Cox, Executor of Mary Bissell v. William J. H. B. Williams & al.*, 39 N.C. 15 (1845) (emphasis added).

61. *Thomas Tongue v. Negroes Crissy, Rhody and Others*, 7 Md. 453 (1855).

62. *James T. N. Maddox, Executor of Eleanor W. Turner v. Negroes Price and Others*, 17 Md. 413 (1861).

63. Ibid.

64. *Bailey & als. v. Poindexter's Executor*, 55 Va. 132 (1858).

65. Ibid.

66. Ibid. Supreme courts in Florida and Alabama followed the same logic and voided clauses in enslavers' wills that presented enslaved individuals with a choice between freedom in a free state (or in Liberia) and slavery within the state of residence. See, for example, *Charles K. Miller v. James M. Gaskins*, 11 Fla. 73 (1864–65), which cites *Bailey & als. v. Poindexter's Executor* as precedent; and *Carroll and Wife v. Brumby, Administrator*, 13 Ala. 102 (1848).

67. Edwards, *People and Their Peace*, 101.

68. Ibid. Joanne Freeman explains how the meaning of terms like "rank, credit, fame, character, name, and honor" could shift within a particular historical context and how these terms also overlapped in their meanings. Freeman writes of the difference between honor and reputation, "Reputation was not unlike honor, and indeed, early Americans often used these words interchangeably. *Honor* was reputation with a moral dimension and an elite cast." See Freeman, *Affairs of Honor*, xix–xx. For the

purposes of this study of enslaved plaintiffs, the word "reputation" refers to Edwards's conception of "credit," which encompassed both the ways in which an individual's community viewed that individual and how individuals could use that understanding to their benefit in court.

69. As Edwards notes, "Far more than white men, dependents and subordinates lived and died by the good words of others, including the words of other dependents and subordinates." See Edwards, *People and Their Peace*, 130.

70. Welch, "Black Litigiousness and White Accountability." Welch highlights a multitude of examples of enslaved and free people of color calling on what she terms the "politics of reputation" when presenting evidence in court.

71. This practice began to shift by the later antebellum years, as cities expanded and communities became larger and less intimate. In areas like St. Louis and other growing cities, it became increasingly difficult for people to know each other and earn this type of credit. As the historian Karen Halttunen has observed, "Surface impressions were essential to success in the world of strangers . . . because appearances revealed character." Halttunen, *Confidence Men and Painted Women*, 40. For a longer discussion of reputation in the context of middle-class young men, see ibid., 46–50.

72. *George Johnson, a man of color v. Henry Moore*, April 1852, Case No. 36, SLCCR, 1.

73. *George Johnson, a man of color v. Reuben Bartlett*, November 1852, Case No. 281, SLCCR, 36. Witness testimony for freedom suit plaintiffs came through either depositions taken by the parties' attorneys or a witness appearing in open court. The freedom suit case files primarily contain depositions, with few if any references made to court testimony.

74. Ibid., 34.

75. The Missouri Supreme Court decision in *Dred Scott* in 1852 also contributed to the shift in focus of this type of testimony.

76. Ibid. One newspaper notice threatened to sell any enslaved persons found hiring themselves out because of the threat to enslavers' control posed by self-hire and free people of African descent. *Missouri Republican*, July 12, 1824, 1. Another piece stated that self-hire allowed slaves to "take upon themselves . . . the airs of freemen." *Missouri Republican*, July 17, 1824, 2.

77. *Delph (also known as Delphy), a mulatress v. Stephen Dorris*, November 1836, Case No. 4, SLCCR, 45.

78. *The State v. Lyon*, 1 N.J.L. 462 (1789).

79. *Walkup v. Pratt*, 5 H. & J. 51 (1820).

80. *Mima Queen and Child, Petitioners for Freedom v. Hepburn*, 11 U.S. 290 (1813).

81. *Abraham Vaughn v. Phebe, a Woman of Color*, 8 Tenn. 5 (1827).

82. Ibid. Despite allowing the hearsay evidence, the court reversed the verdict for freedom and remanded the case, stating that the evidence of a prior freedom suit needed to be proven by copies of the records themselves.

83. *Jane, a woman of color v. William Dallam*, July 1831, Case No. 22, SLCCR, 2.

84. Ibid., 1.

85. *May Stringer v. Shepherd W. Burcham*, 34 N.C. 41 (1851).

86. *Farrelly v. Maria Louisa (Woman of Color)*, 34 Ala. 284 (1859).

87. *Charles Endicott v. Benjamin Clapp*, July 1839, Case No. 116, SLCCR, 9.

88. *Nancy, a free woman of color v. Enoch Steen*, April 1848, Case No. 4, SLCCR, 11, 14. For additional testimony about a person's work demonstrating freedom, see *Becton v. Ferguson*, 22 Ala. 599 (1853).

89. Gross, "Litigating Whiteness."

90. *Martha Drusella v. Richmond L. Curle*, November 1844, Case No. 252, SLCCR, 25.

91. *Louisa (also known as Louisa Lewis) v. Henry N. Hart, Administrator*, February 1860, Case No. 12, SLCCR, 30–31. A jury found the defendant guilty and set Louisa Lewis free shortly after she brought her initial petition for freedom. See CCRB No. 30, April 27, 1860, 33.

92. See, for example, *Gobu v. E. Gobu*, 1 N.C. 188 (1802); *Hudgins v. Wrights*, 1 Va. 134 (1806); *Adelle v. Beauregard*, 1 Mart. (o.s.) 183 (1810); *Chancellor v. Milly*, 39 Ky. 23 (1839); *Spalding v. Taylor et al.*, 11 La. Ann. 195 (1846); *Gatliff's Administrator v. Rose et al.*, 47 Ky. 629 (1848); *George S. Gaines v. Ann*, 17 Tex. 211 (1856); *Guilford v. Hicks*, 36 Ala. 95 (1860); *Alexina Morrison v. James White*, 16 La. Ann. 100 (1861). An 1845 Louisiana Supreme Court case raised a similar argument, and the court upheld a different standard of proof for persons of mixed-race parentage, stating, "Considering how much probability there is in favor of the liberty of these persons, they ought not to be deprived of it upon mere presumptions." *Sally Miller v. Louis Belmonti*, 11 Rob. La. 339 (1845).

93. *Polly Wash v. Joseph M. Magehan*, November 1839, Case No. 167, SLCCR, 22.

94. *Samuel, a man of color v. John Howdeshell*, April 1844, Case No. 6, SLCCR, 29. For additional examples, see *Phillis v. Pierre Gentin*, April 1834, Case No. 11262, First Judicial District Court, Orleans Parish, Louisiana Division and City Archives, New Orleans Public Library, 19; and *Ralph, a man of color v. Coleman Duncan and James Duncan*, July 1830, Case No. 35, SLCCR, 25.

95. For example, see Missouri's requirement for free people of color to obtain licenses to live in Missouri; the statute states that the person must "make application to a county court . . . that he is of good character and behavior." *Revised Statutes of the State of Missouri*, 1841, 415.

96. *George Relf, a man of color v. Thompson H. Ficklin*, July 1828, Case No. 64, SLCCR, 12–13.

97. Ibid., 14.

98. Ibid., 14–15. For another example of testimony impugning an enslaved plaintiff's character, see *Caroline Sampson v. George W. B. Burgwin*, 20 N.C. 21 (1838). A similar example is found in a Louisiana Supreme Court case from 1843 denying freedom when the woman in question, according to the opinion, was "of a bad reputation, thievish, and insolent." *Nole v. Charles de St. Romes and Wife*, 3 Rob. 484 (1843).

6 / Defending Suits

1. *Julia, a woman of color v. Samuel McKinney*, March 1831, Case No. 66, SLCCR; *Mariquette v. Samuel T. McKinney*, July 1831, Case No. 13, SLCCR; *Harriet, an infant v. Samuel T. McKinney and James Walker*, July 1833, Case No. 17, SLCCR; *Harriet v. Samuel T. McKinney*, July 1833, Case No. 54, SLCCR. Just prior to purchasing Julia and Harriet, McKinney also found himself defending a civil suit and criminal charges for assaulting another St. Louis saddler. *State of Missouri v. Samuel T. McKinney*, March 1829, SLCRCF; and *Thornton Grimsley v. Samuel T. McKinney*, July 1829, Case No. 16, SLCCF.

2. Missouri law had no ban on free black slave ownership, although only one black defendant, John Berry Meachum, appeared in the St. Louis Circuit Court freedom suits.

3. In 1860, 497 slaveholders lived in the city of St. Louis. See Trexler, *Slavery in Missouri*, 18n42.

4. The members of the Chouteau family were defendants in at least eleven freedom suits in the St. Louis Circuit Court. For more on the Chouteaus, see Hoig, *Chouteaus*; and especially Foley and Rice, *First Chouteaus*.

5. Foley, "Slave Suits for Freedom before Dred Scott," 10–12.

6. For a sampling of the legal cases that resulted from their business ventures, see *John Finney and William Finney v. Rockwood W. Keys*, November 1835, Case No. 15, SLCCF; *John Finney and William Finney v. Steamboat Cygnet*, July 1837, Case No. 333, SLCCF; *The Boston Iron Company v. John Finney and William Finney*, July 1840, Case No. 422, SLCCF; and *William E. Rogers v. John Finney and William Finney*, April 1845, Case No. 146, SLCCF (case for failing to pay rent on their store).

7. See Clay's response to his slaves' petition for freedom in 1829 and the bond he put up to take them to Kentucky while their suit continued in the District of Columbia, found in Folder 1, Box 1, Henry Clay Papers, David M. Rubenstein Rare Book and Manuscript Library, Duke University, Durham, NC.

8. *State of Missouri v. Samuel T. McKinney*, March 1829, SLCRCF; and *Thornton Grimsley v. Samuel T. McKinney*, July 1829, Case No. 16, SLCCF.

9. *Thenia, a woman of color v. Green Crowder*, March 1832, Case No. 9, SLCCR, 2.

10. For William Walker's three freedom suits, see *Rachel, a woman of color v. William Walker*, November 1834, Case No. 82, SLCCR; *James Henry, a boy of color v. William Walker*, November 1834, Case No. 83, SLCCR; and *Mary Ann Steel v. William Walker*, July 1835, Case No. 97, SLCCR. For a few examples of Walker's other legal troubles relating to slave sales, see *William Russell v. William Walker*, Nov. 1831, Case No. 42, SLCCF; *George Freyschlay v. William Walker*, July 1835, Case No. 84, SLCCF; and *Benjamin Roach v. William Walker*, November 1837, Case No. 62, SLCCF.

11. *Samuel, infant of color v. Bernard T. Lynch*, November 1851, Case No. 29, SLCCR; *Thornton Kinney, a man of color v. John F. Hatcher and Charles C. Bridges*, November 1853, Case No. 35, SLCCR; *Mary, of color, and her children Samuel & Edward v. Launcelot H. Calvert*, April 1851, Case No. 2, SLCCR; and *Laura, a woman of color v. Henry Belt*, April 1852, Case No. 22, SLCCR.

12. *Jonathan, a man of color v. Marshall Brotherton, Joel Danah, and Aza Willoughby*, November 1841, Case No. 32, SLCCR; *Mary Ann Speaks v. John M. Jameson*, April 1844, Case No. 386, SLCCR; *Ann, a woman of color v. John M. Jameson*, April 1844, Case No. 394, SLCCR; and *Anderson Steward, a free man of color v. John M. Jameson*, April 1844, Case No. 390, SLCCR.

13. *Julia, a woman of color v. Samuel McKinney*, March 1831, Case No. 66, SLCCR, 9–10.

14. *Marie, a free mulatto girl v. Auguste Chouteau*, April 1821, Case No. 205, SLCCR, 11.

15. *Mary Ann Steel v. Curtis Skinner*, July 1835, Case No. 96, SLCCR, 3.

16. *Mariquette v. Samuel T. McKinney*, July 1831, Case No. 13, SLCCR, 9. Although the argument was not unusual, the Missouri Supreme Court refused to accept a similar denial in the 1821 case of *Winny v. Whitesides. Winny, a free woman v. Phebe*

Whitesides (alias Pruitt), April 1821, Case No. 190, SLCCR; *Winny v. Whitesides*, 1 Mo. 472 (1824).

17. *Milly, a black woman v. Mathias Rose*, August 1819, Case No. 20, SLCCR, 11. Milly's attorney responded to this claim by calling it "evasive and insufficient" because Milly "did not at the time . . . or at any time since abscond from the person or possession" of the defendant. See ibid., 18.

18. *Pelagie, a woman of color v. Francois Valois*, February 1822, Case No. 12, SLCCR, 8. In a second case, Pelagie sued Jean P. Cabanne, the person to whom Valois claimed to sell her. See *Pelagie, a woman of color v. Jean P. Cabanne*, June 1822, Case No. 9, SLCCR.

19. *Mary, a woman of color v. Francis Menard and Daniel Busby*, November 1833, Case No. 34, SLCCR, 3.

20. *Thomas v. Scott*, 2 Cranch C.C. 2 (1810).

21. *Emory and Others, Paupers v. Erskine*, 34 Va. 267 (1836).

22. *John, James, &c. (of Color) v. Walker, Executor of Bates*, 47 Ky. 605 (1848). When another Kentucky plaintiff sued for freedom based on his illegal importation after spending more than a year in Virginia and then returning to D.C., the defendant claimed that the plaintiff traveled to Virginia with a temporary enslaver and so should remain in slavery. The court agreed. *Kennedy v. Purnell*, 5 Cranch 552 (1839).

23. *Josephine LaCourse, an infant of color v. George Mitchell*, November 1835, Case No. 22, SLCCR, 5.

24. *Eliza Briscoe v. William Anderson*, November 1839, Case No. 219, SLCCR, 1.

25. *Laura, a woman of color v. Henry Belt*, April 1852, Case No. 22, SLCCR, 7.

26. Ibid., 8.

27. Ibid., 9.

28. *Commonwealth v. Stout, &c.*, 46 Ky. 247 (1847).

29. *Sylvia and Phillis, by Next Friend v. Covey*, 12 Tenn. 297 (1833).

30. Examples of this phenomenon, in St. Louis and elsewhere, are widespread. For a handful of examples from St. Louis, see *Malinda, a free person of color v. Robert Wilburn*, October 1823, Case No. 7, SLCCR, 6; *Margaret, a girl of color v. William Dallam*, November 1831, Case No. 4, SLCCR, 2; *Anna, a woman of color v. Thomas Higginbotham*, November 1831, Case No. 12, SLCCR, 2–3; and *Peter, a free man of color v. James Walton*, March 1828, Case No. 12, SLCCR, 9. For examples outside Missouri, see *Warfield v. Davis*, 53 Ky. 33 (1853); *Ex Parte Letty*, 15 Fed. Cas. 411 (1806); *Daniel Carpenter, Guardian of Sundry Free Negroes v. Matthew Coleman*, 2 Bay 436 (1802); and *Graham v. Alexander*, 10 F. Cas. 916 (1840).

31. *Samuel, a man of color v. John Howdeshell*, April 1844, Case No. 6, SLCCR, 70. See also *Diana Cephas, a woman of color v. James Scott*, July 1841, Case No. 5, SLCCR, 23, which states that it was not sufficient evidence of freedom for Cephas to establish that her residence in Illinois was with the knowledge of her owner but not necessarily with his consent.

32. *Rebecca, a colored girl v. James Black and Louis Matlock*, July 1838, Case No. 237, SLCCR, 14.

33. Ibid., 22.

34. *Alsey, a woman of color v. William Randolph*, March 1841, Case No. 305, SLCCR, 45.

35. *Dorinda, a woman of color v. John Simonds, Jr.*, March 1826, Case No. 42, SLCCR, 8.

36. The court eventually dismissed her suit when her attorney failed to appear in court, and her enslaver removed her from the court's jurisdiction to prevent her from doing anything to protect her case. Dorinda to Hamilton R. Gamble, ALS, April 1, 1827, Folder 2, Box 2, Gamble Papers, MHM.

37. *Dunky, a colored woman v. Andrew Hay*, July 1831, Case No. 12, SLCCR, 5.

38. *Nat (a Man of Color) v. Ruddle*, 3 Mo. 400 (1834).

39. *Louis, f.m.c. v. Cabarrus et als.*, 7 La. 170 (1834).

40. *Frank, f.m.c. v. Powell*, 11 La. 499 (1838).

41. *Julia, a woman of color v. Samuel McKinney*, March 1831, Case No. 66, SLCCR, 3.

42. Ibid., 17 (emphasis added).

43. *Malinda, a free person of color v. Robert Wilburn*, October 1823, Case No. 7, SLCCR, 13. See also *Nelly, a woman of color v. Robert Wilburn*, October 1823, Case No. 8, SLCCR. The "situation" referred to here was most likely pregnancy or sickness related to pregnancy.

44. *Nelly, a woman of color v. Robert Wilburn*, October 1823, Case No. 8, SLCCR, 3.

45. *Aspasia, a free woman of color v. Francis Chouteau and Pierre Menard*, March 1828, Case No. 5, SLCCR, 19.

46. *Matilda, a free girl of color v. Philip Rocheblave and Mary Louisa Rocheblave*, November 1828, Case No. 38, SLCCR, 16. In another example, the defense requested a jury instruction that the plaintiff's residence in the Northwest Territory "did not render" her or her mother, whose freedom she relied on in her argument, "free under and in virtue of the Ordinance." *Jenny, a free girl v. Robert Musick*, April 1821, Case No. 194, SLCCR, 9.

47. *Hetty, a woman of color v. Arthur L. Magenis*, March 1835, Case No. 43, SLCCR, 1–2.

48. *Francois LaGrange, a free man of color v. Bernard Pratte, Pierre Chouteau, Bertholemew Berthold, and Jean P. Cabanne*, March 1827, Case No. 29, SLCCR, 33. After the plaintiff's previous enslaver requested that the defendant purchase the plaintiff, the defendant at first refused, citing the fact that he lived in Illinois. He eventually capitulated to the request of his close associate, because the seller did not want to sell to a St. Louis resident. The defendant agreed to help his friend by buying the plaintiff, taking him down the Mississippi River for a few months and eventually delivering him to the St. Louis resident.

49. Ibid.

50. Both the witness's and his associate's families appeared as defendants in a long list of St. Louis freedom suits in the 1820s and 1830s. A witness in another example specified that the plaintiff lived in Illinois for one or two years, until "the owners of slaves becoming alarmed at the prospect of loosing their slaves when Indiana should become a free state [in 1816], a great number were run off." *Judy, a woman of color v. John Berry Meachum*, March 1837, Case No. 40, SLCCR, 7.

51. See "An Act for the Gradual Emancipation of Slavery," passed March 1, 1780.

52. *Ex parte Simmons*, 22 Fed. Cas. 151 (1823); *Butler and Others v. Delaplaine*, 7 Serg. & Rawle 378 (1821). If the woman's enslaver had been in Pennsylvania for six *consecutive* months, she would have been free, but the court did not allow her to add up the total time she had spent in the state in order to prove freedom. The Connecticut Supreme Court rejected this argument and refused to allow an enslaver to claim temporary residence after moving back and forth between Connecticut and Georgia for two years with his alleged slave. *Nancy Jackson v. Bulloch*, 12 Conn. 38 (1837).

53. *Liza, c.w. v. Dr. Puissant et al.*, 7 La. Ann. 80 (1852). In a similar Louisiana Supreme Court appeal, the court again refused to free a plaintiff because her enslaver argued that she spent only a few days in Cincinnati before returning voluntarily to the South. *Sarah Haynes (alias Mielkie) v. Henry Forno et al., C. Y. Hutchinson, and H. R. W. Hill, Curator*, 8 La. Ann. 35 (1853).

54. *Negress Sally Henry, by William Henry, Her Father and Next Friend v. Ball*, 14. U.S. 1 (1816).

55. In all of these instances, appellate courts had to wade through a growing flood of legal doctrine that stretched back to English law and raised issues of comity that became increasingly important in the years prior to the Civil War. By 1860, when the South Carolina Supreme Court chose to free a group of enslaved individuals taken to Ohio by their enslaver, who intended to free them but died just days after arriving, the opinion traced the history of the doctrine of free soil in painstaking detail but managed to base the decision on a lack of specific South Carolina statutory prohibitions against freeing slaves in a free state. The decision in *Willis v. Jolliffe* (1860) suggests that, even in a Deep South state like South Carolina on the eve of the Civil War, questions remained over the length of time a person could spend (or had to spend, in this case) in a free territory before the person's enslaved property became free. *Michael Willis and Others v. John Jolliffe and Others*, 11 Rich. Eq. 447 (1860).

56. *Arsene v. Pigneguy*, 2 La. Ann. 620 (1847).

57. *David McFoy v. William Brown*, April 1850, Case No. 37, SLCCR, 3–6.

58. Ibid., 30 (emphasis added)

59. Ibid., 29.

60. Ibid., 66–67.

61. Ibid., 41, 50.

62. McFoy's case ended in 1851, when he appeared in court and voluntarily allowed his case to be dismissed. This verdict could indicate that he managed to work out another arrangement for freedom or that Brown simply stopped claiming McFoy as a slave. CCRB No. 21, May 12, 1851, 76.

63. *In re. Williams*, 29 F. Cas. 1334 (1839).

64. *Daniel v. Guy et al.*, 19 Ark. 121 (1857). Testimony quoted is from the reported opinion of Judge English. For a more in-depth analysis of Abby Guy's case and a discussion of a variety of issues in trials of racial determination, see Gross, *What Blood Won't Tell*, esp. 32–47.

65. *Daniel v. Guy et al.*, 23 Ark. 50 (1861) (emphasis in original).

66. *John Merry, a free man of color v. Clayton Tiffin and Louis Menard*, November 1826, Case No. 18, SLCCR, 20 (emphasis added). The plaintiff won his freedom but only after an appeal to the Missouri Supreme Court.

67. *Molly Rector, a free woman of color v. John Bivens*, November 1827, Case No. 26, SLCCR, 6.

68. Ibid.; CCRB No. 5, December 11, 1827, 88.

69. *In re. Ralph*, 1 Morris 1 (1839).

70. J. G. McKinney to Hamilton R. Gamble, ALS, December 12, 1831, Folder 6, Box 4, Gamble Papers, MHM. The court rendered its decision for McKinney in 1833, so Gamble did not meet the second stipulation in McKinney's letter.

71. *Julia, a woman of color v. Samuel T. McKinney*, March 1831, Case No. 66, SLCCR, 78.

72. Archibald Williams to Hamilton R. Gamble, ALS, October 28, 1833, Folder 1, Box 5, Gamble Papers, MHM.

73. CCRB No. 7, December 1, 1835, 482.

74. Sam. T. McKinney to Hamilton R. Gamble, ALS, December 26, 1833, Folder 2, Box 5, Gamble Papers, MHM.

75. Archibald Williams to Hamilton Gamble, ALS, March 20, 1834, Folder 3, Box 5, Gamble Papers, MHM.

76. Archibald Williams to Hamilton Gamble, ALS, May 8, 1834, Folder 3, Box 5, Gamble Papers, MHM.

77. For purposes of clarity, the Duncan family members are referred to by their first names.

78. *Ralph, a man of color v. Coleman Duncan and James Duncan*, July 1830, Case No. 35, SLCCR, 3–4.

79. *Joe, a black man v. Coleman Duncan and James Duncan*, July 1830, Case No. 47, SLCCR, 5.

80. *Ralph, a man of color v. Coleman Duncan and James Duncan*, July 1830, Case No. 35, SLCCR, 7.

81. Ibid., 83–85. For more on the issue of "credit" in local legal proceedings, see Edwards, *People and Their Peace*, 101.

82. *Ralph, a man of color v. Coleman Duncan and James Duncan*, July 1830, Case No. 35, SLCCR, 115–16.

83. *Ralph v. James and Coleman Duncan*, 3 Mo. 194 (1833).

84. *Ralph, a man of color v. Coleman Duncan and James Duncan*, July 1830, Case No. 35, SLCCR, 183.

85. Ibid., 184.

86. SLEB No. 3, 227. Ralph brought a separate suit for the wages he earned through being hired out during his freedom suit, and when he appealed this case to the Missouri Supreme Court, it awarded him $153 in back wages. There is no indication of whether Ralph ever received this money.

87. *George Relf, a man of color v. Thompson H. Ficklin*, July 1828, Case No. 64, SLCCR, 1–2. The plaintiff eventually won his freedom based on his extended residence in Illinois. See CCRB No. 5, April 3, 1829, 264. A similar fraud occurred in a Pennsylvania appellate case, when one enslaver tricked a man into working as a slave until 1810, then convinced him that his manumission agreement included a requirement to serve the enslaver for one additional year. *Thomas Ferris v. Samuel Henderson and Wife*, 12 Pa. 49 (1849).

88. *Peter, a man of color v. James Walton*, March 1831, Case No. 67, SLCCR, 5 (emphasis added).

89. *Martha Ann, a person of color v. Hiram Cordell*, November 1844, Case No. 9, SLCCR, 13.

90. Ibid., 59; CCRB No. 17, January 21, 1846, 47; CCRB No. 17, May 5, 1847, 278; CCRB No. 17, May 13, 1847, 592; CCRB No. 19, December 12, 1849, 265.

91. *Pierre, a mulatto v. Gabriel Chouteau*, November 1842, Case No. 125, SLCCR, 159.

92. *Negro Andrew Franklin v. Freeborn G. Waters, Executor of Charles Waters*, 8 Gill 322 (1849). It should be noted that the Court of Appeals dismissed Franklin's suit for back wages because, it argued, he should have used the freedom suit statute to establish his status and claim damages. Even so, the court's unwillingness to allow

Franklin's claim despite his enslaver's obvious fraud speaks to the judges' understanding of enslaved persons' knowledge of the law and their ability to procure help in using the legal system.

93. *Barnes and Wife v. Edward (of Color)*, 56 Ky. 632 (1856).

94. *State v. Mann*, 13 N.C. 263 (1829).

95. See Blackburn, introduction to *Paths to Freedom*, 5, 9; Mamigonian, "Conflicts over the Meanings of Freedom," 241; Sheppard Wolf, "Manumission and the Two-Race System in Early National Virginia," 333.

96. Berlin, *Many Thousands Gone*; Camp, *Closer to Freedom*. Walter Johnson discusses some of the types of negotiations and wrangling that went on in the slave market in *Soul by Soul*, and Berlin also discusses negotiations taking place during the antebellum years in *Generations of Captivity*.

97. For a similar example of making arrangements to negotiate the best possible circumstances, see Hartog, *Someday All This Will Be Yours*.

98. *James alias James Haskins v. Charles Haskins*, November 1837, Case No. 169, SLCCR, 3.

99. Ibid., 4; CCRB No. 10, January 9, 1840, 64. The freedom suit concluded with a notation that the plaintiff would no longer prosecute his case, so perhaps he entered yet another arrangement for freedom.

100. *Samuel Stokes, a man of color v. John Finney and William Finney*, November 1838, Case No. 501, SLCCR, 1–2.

101. Ibid., 3–4.

102. Ibid., 4–5.

103. St. Louis Chancery Court Record Book 2, September 6, 1842, 153.

7 / Political Repercussions

1. *Elsa Hicks, a mulatto girl v. Patrick T. McSherry*, November 1847, Case No. 121, SLCCR, 20. The sheriff requested their release because he believed their health was in danger. The court responded to his request by sending them to the County Farm to work. See ibid., 21–23; CCRB No. 18, June 12, 1848, 342. Hicks based both of her freedom suits on her residence in Wisconsin for six years before her alleged owners brought her to St. Louis. The court dismissed her first case when the sheriff was unable to locate the defendants. The second case, filed against Patrick McSherry more than a year later, continued until 1850, when Hicks failed to appear in court. CCRB No. 17, November 25, 1846, 375; and CCRB No. 20, December 23, 1850, 226.

2. *Elsa Hicks, a mulatto girl v. Patrick T. McSherry*, November 1847, Case No. 121, SLCCR, 19, 13.

3. Ibid., 8; Sloss, *St. Louis Directory for 1848*, 155.

4. Potter, *Impending Crisis*; Holt, *Political Crisis of the 1850s*; Foner, *Politics and Ideology in the Age of the Civil War*; Freehling, *Road to Disunion*, vols. 1 and 2; Ashworth, *Slavery, Capitalism, and Politics in the Antebellum Republic*; Morrison, *Slavery and the American West*; Varon, *Disunion!*; Foner, *Free Soil, Free Labor, Free Men*; and Wilentz, *Rise of American Democracy*.

5. For more on the coming of Civil War in a border state, see Salafia, *Slavery's Borderland*, esp. chap. 8; and Epps, *Slavery on the Periphery*.

6. On this point, see Grinberg, "Manumission, Gender, and the Law in Nineteenth-Century Brazil," 220–21, 232.

7. Towers, *Urban South and the Coming of the Civil War*, chap. 3.

8. St. Louis and Missouri were often at the heart of the nation's debates over the slavery issue, from the Missouri Compromise to Bleeding Kansas to *Dred Scott*. St. Louis witnessed a number of other episodes, such as the lynching of Francis McIntosh and the attacks on and martyrdom of the abolitionist Elijah Lovejoy, which surely factored into discussions surrounding slavery in the city and also into the outcomes of freedom suits.

9. Gardner, "You Have No Business to Whip Me," 35.

10. Ibid.; Gerteis, *Civil War St. Louis*, chap. 1.

11. Holland, "African Americans in Henry Shaw's St. Louis," 60.

12. Ibid.

13. McCandless, *History of Missouri*, vol. 2, 233; Winn, "Gods in Ruins," 24.

14. "Little Dixie" refers to several counties lining the Missouri River where most of Missouri's slaves lived. The area was the leading agricultural region of the state and a magnet for settlers from the Upper South states of Virginia, Kentucky, and Tennessee. For more on this region, see Hurt, *Agriculture and Slavery in Missouri's Little Dixie*.

15. Gerteis, *Civil War St. Louis*, 68. This struggle also had consequences for Missouri's economy, as northern investors and businessmen worried about the violence and began to view St. Louis as perhaps more southern than western. See Primm, "Economy of Nineteenth-Century St. Louis," 126–27.

16. Dred and Harriet Scott filed separate petitions for freedom in 1846; but shortly after, Harriet's case joined with Dred's, and her fate became dependent on the outcome of her husband's case. Dred also spent time in Rock Island, Illinois, bolstering his claim for freedom. For a detailed commentary on Harriet's life and her case, including the argument that she had a stronger claim to freedom than Dred did, see VanderVelde and Subramanian, "Mrs. Dred Scott"; VanderVelde, *Mrs. Dred Scott*.

17. Lawrence Talioferro noted in his journal that he "gave" Harriet to Dred. Talioferro, *Auto-biography of Maj. Lawrence Talioferro*, 235. The exact meaning of this statement is unclear: it could mean he granted her freedom to allow her to marry Dred or that he gave her to Dred's owner or perhaps even sold her to Dred's owner. VanderVelde and Subramanian argue that Talioferro's giving Harriet to Dred made her claim to freedom even stronger than his, making it strange that his case subsumed hers. VanderVelde and Subramanian, "Mrs. Dred Scott."

18. *Dred Scott, a man of color v. Irene Emerson*, November 1846, Case No. 1, SLCCR, 1–12.

19. The issue of why the Scotts decided to sue when they did is a matter of debate among scholars. Some scholars argue that perhaps Dred or Harriet only recently learned of their right to sue for freedom. See Finkelman, *Dred Scott v. Sandford*, 19. See also Fehrenbacher, *Dred Scott Case*, 252, suggesting that Dred Scott learned of this right from the Blow family or from talking to other slaves in St. Louis; and VanderVelde and Subramanian, "Mrs. Dred Scott," 1083.

20. *Scott v. Emerson*, 15 Mo. 576 (1852).

21. The U.S. Supreme Court clerk misspelled Sanford's name, so the Supreme Court case is *Dred Scott v. John F. A. Sandford*.

22. For more information on the *Dred Scott* case and its implications for federal law, see Fehrenbacher, *Dred Scott Case*; Ehrlich, *They Have No Rights*; Fehrenbacher,

Slavery, Law, and Politics; Finkelman, *Dred Scott v. Sandford*; Graber, *Dred Scott and the Problem of Constitutional Evil*; and Maltz, *Dred Scott and the Politics of Slavery*.

23. For the relationship between Kansas and Missouri in this era, see Epps, *Slavery on the Periphery*.

24. Fehrenbacher, *Dred Scott Case*, 485.

25. Gerteis, *Civil War St. Louis*, 22.

26. Ibid., 24.

27. *Scott v. Emerson*, 15 Mo. 576, 586 (1852), reprinted in Finkelman, *Dred Scott v. Sandford*, 22.

28. *Revised Statutes of the State of Missouri*, 1835, 584, 586; *Laws of a Public and General Nature of the State of Missouri*, 354. Punishment for this crime increased in the later statute.

29. *Revised Statutes of the State of Missouri*, 1835, 414–15.

30. Ibid., 1835, 414.

31. Casselberry, *Revised Statutes of the State of Missouri*, 529.

32. Ibid., 534.

33. Ibid., 534–35.

34. Ibid., 394.

35. Hardin, *Revised Statutes of the State of Missouri*, vol. 2, 1100.

36. Ibid., 1101.

37. Ibid. (emphasis added).

38. Ibid.

39. Galusha Anderson discusses this law in *The Story of a Border City during the Civil War*, 11. Similar legislation appeared throughout the South at the end of the 1850s. See West, *Family or Freedom*, 46–51.

40. Anderson, *Story of a Border City during the Civil War*, 14.

41. Casselberry, *Revised Statutes of the State of Missouri*, 283.

42. *Revised Statutes of the State of Missouri*, 1841, 285.

43. *Peggy Perryman, a woman of color v. Joseph Philibert*, November 1848, Case No. 255, SLCCR, 2, 14.

44. *David McFoy v. William Brown*, April 1850, Case No. 37, SLCCR, 19; CCRB No. 19, December 14, 1849, 268.

45. *Jane McCray, a mulatto woman v. William R. Hopkins, William Miller, Eliza Oliver, et al.*, November 1845, Case No. 162, SLCCR, 4, 10. In another St. Louis case, the defendant asked the court to dismiss the case not only because he claimed the plaintiff as a slave and his own property but also because the plaintiff had "not filed security for the costs as the law of the land in such case made and provided, requires." *Matilda Thomas (also known as Matilda Cunningham), person of color v. William Littleton*, November 1846, Case No. 28, SLCCR, 7. In her case, Matilda Thomas voluntarily allowed her case to be dismissed less than two weeks after the defendant filed his objection. See CCRB No. 17, November 28, 1846, 387.

46. Burrell made this complaint to suggest that McSherry was aiding Hicks with her case. *Elsa Hicks, a mulatto girl v. Patrick T. McSherry*, November 1847, Case No. 121, SLCCR, 14.

47. *Jane Cotton, a free person of color v. James A. Little*, April 1848, Case No. 37, SLCCR, 11.

48. Ibid., 11–12, 27–28; CCRB No. 18, April 20, 1848, 218; CCRB No. 18, April 29, 1848, 255; CCRB No. 18, May 1, 1848, 260; CCRB No. 18, May 2–3, 1848, 266; CCRB No. 18, May 6, 1848, 279; CCRB No. 18, June 28, 1848, 369, 389; CCRB No. 18, December 4, 1848, 421.

49. *Ellen Duty v. John F. Darby, Administrator*, April 1850, Case No. 18, SLCCR, 9.

50. CCRB No. 20, June 12, 1850, 82.

51. See the appendix for a complete breakdown of the cases during this period.

52. For examples of this literature, see West, *Family or Freedom*; and D. Davis, *Inhuman Bondage*.

53. The Circuit Court Record Books use the term "voluntarily" to describe these dismissals, though it is important to recognize that there may have been coercion or other arrangements happening outside of the court's records. For example, see CCRB No. 4, December 29, 1829, 453, in which Robert Simpson voluntarily agreed to his case's dismissal.

54. See CCRB No. 17, December 17, 1847, 437; and CCRB No. 18, March 8, 1848, 199. For an example from the earlier decades of St. Louis's freedom suits, see *Daniel Wilson v. Robert Cohen*, July 1835, No. 13; and CCRB No. 8, November 20, 1837, 367. Studies of freedom suits in other locations also found that legal actions initiated by enslaved men and women could result in manumission or other arrangements for freedom. See, for example, Grinberg, "Manumission, Gender, and Law in Nineteenth-Century Brazil," 220; and Sheppard Wolf, "Manumission and the Two-Race System in Early National Virginia," 310.

55. *Mary (also known as Mary Davis), a woman of color v. Samuel B. Bellis*, April 1855, Case No. 96, SLCCR; CCRB No. 26, November 12, 1856, 52.

56. Wade, *Slavery in the Cities*, 327.

57. Kamphoefner, "Learning from the 'Majority-Minority' City," 82.

58. Winn, "Gods in Ruins," 34–36. Walter Kamphoefner argues that Germans had less interaction with people of African descent, slave or free, than did the Irish. Germans were generally more skilled and able to work in industries dominated by successful German immigrants, such as brewing, whereas the Irish were more rural and lacked the skills necessary to move beyond the most menial jobs. For this reason, Irish found themselves competing with enslaved and free people of color for unskilled work. See Kamphoefner, "Learning from the 'Majority-Minority' City," 93. Walter Johnson has argued that in New Orleans, the tensions over immigrants' views on slavery erupted into violence and led to increasing mistreatment of the immigrant segment of the city's population. See W. Johnson, "Slave Trader, the White Slave, and the Politics of Racial Determination in the 1850s," esp. 32–33.

59. Trexler, *Slavery in Missouri*, 165.

60. Two of these cases argued for prior manumission, and the other two claimed freedom from birth.

61. Towers, *Urban South and the Coming of the Civil War*, 95.

62. Hoffman, "If I Fall, My Grave Shall Be Made in Alton," 12.

63. Merkel, "Abolition Aspects of Missouri's Antislavery Controversy."

64. *St. Louis Observer*, November 5, 1835, cited ibid., 239.

65. *Missouri Republican*, May 26, 1836, cited ibid., 239–40; Gerteis, *Civil War St. Louis*, 14.

66. *Missouri Republican*, August 17, 1837, quoted in Hoffman, "If I Fall, My Grave Shall Be Made in Alton," 14.

67. Ibid., 19; Dempsey, *Searching for Jim*, 29–30.

68. Merkel, "Abolition Aspects of Missouri's Antislavery Controversy," 240; Gerteis, *Civil War St. Louis*, 7.

69. Winn, "Gods in Ruins," 37–39.

70. Ibid., 39–40. In the late 1850s, the American Missionary Association (AMA) also tried to convince Missouri's enslavers to consider abolishing slavery, but instead slaveholders drove the organization out of the state until the Civil War. See Holland, "African Americans in Henry Shaw's St. Louis," 67.

71. *Elsa Hicks, a mulatto girl v. Patrick T. McSherry*, November 1847, Case No. 121, SLCCR, 13.

72. Ibid., 19.

73. Ibid., 19–20.

74. Ibid., 20.

75. *State of Missouri v. Lewis Burrell*, November 1847, Case No. 237, SLCCF, 9.

76. Ibid., 9–10. Antonio F. Holland has argued that Missouri's geographic location makes it seem likely that there was some Underground Railroad activity in the state: "it is unlikely that it had the effect on Missouri slavery that contemporary masters believed." See Holland, "African Americans in Henry Shaw's St. Louis," 59.

77. *Mary, of color, and her children Samuel & Edward v. Launcelot H. Calvert*, April 1851, Case No. 2, SLCCR, 41.

78. Ibid., 43.

79. Ibid., 55.

80. *George Johnson, a man of color v. Reuben Bartlett*, November 1852, Case No. 281, SLCCR, 17.

81. *Eliza Briscoe v. William Anderson*, November 1839, Case No. 219, SLCCR, 1.

82. *Thomas Jefferson, a man of color v. Milton W. Hopkins*, March 1843, Case No. 14, SLCCR, 3–4.

83. *John Finney v. Calvin Kinder*, March 1842, Case No. 113, SLCCF; *John Finney v. Calvin Kinder*, November 1842, Case No. 17, SLCCF, petition of John Finney. An 1835 statute ordered that "any ferryman, or other person, who shall cross any slave, from this state across the Mississippi river, unless such slave have a pass, . . . shall forfeit and pay to the owner or employer . . . all damages and costs which may accrue to the owner or employer of such slave, and the value of such slave in addition thereto." A similar law forbade any "master, commander or owner of a steamboat, or any other vessel" from transporting enslaved persons, with a penalty of $150 "to be recovered by action of debt, without prejudice to the right of such owner to his action at common law." See *Revised Statutes of the State of Missouri*, 1835, 586.

84. *John Finney v. Calvin Kinder*, November 1842, Case No. 17, SLCCF, deposition of William Smith Wallace, 2–3.

85. Ibid., deposition of Wallace, 4–6.

86. Ibid.

87. Ibid., deposition of Robert McEvan.

88. Ibid., deposition of John Lee. Lee also recounts how as payment for his services for four weeks to return the slaves to Finney, he received the eldest daughter of Jones and Ritter, whom he sold for $200.

Conclusion

1. Aron, *American Confluence*; Twitty, "Slavery and Freedom in the American Confluence."

2. CCRB No. 25, December 21, 1855, 253.

3. P. T. McSherry, Roll C 10364, Missouri Birth and Death Records Database Collection, Missouri Digital Heritage website.

4. Estate of Barnabas Harris, 1819, Case No. 322, SLPF. See especially 11, 15, 146, 159, 172.

5. "Receipt to Durrett Patterson for $202.89," May 20, 1836, and "Receipt to Madison Harris for $143.07," September 26, 1839, both in Folder 4, "Barnabas Harris Papers and Estate, 1818-1836," Hyatt-Hume Papers, MHM.

6. Estate of Mathias Rose, 1834, Case No. 1116, SLPF.

7. St. Louis County Court Record Book 4, December 22, 1846, 399, available at National Park Services, "Freedom Licenses," accessed March 20, 2016, http://www.nps.gov/jeff/learn/historyculture/freedom-licenses.htm.

8. Alsey does not have a last name in the County Court books, as in her freedom suit, but matching details from both records strongly suggest the same person.

9. St. Louis County Court Record Book 3, December 8, 1841, 54, available at National Park Services, "Freedom Licenses," accessed March 20, 2016, http://www.nps.gov/jeff/learn/historyculture/freedom-licenses.htm.

10. Julia Essex, St. Louis County Court Record Book 3, April 1, 1842, 15; and Julia, St. Louis County Court Record Book 3, June 17, 1842, 158, both available at National Park Services, "Freedom Licenses," accessed March 20, 2016, http://www.nps.gov/jeff/learn/historyculture/freedom-licenses.htm.

11. Delaney, *From the Darkness Cometh the Light*.

12. Ibid.; St. Louis County Court Record Book 4, December 23, 1846, 401, available at National Park Services, "Freedom Licenses," accessed March 20, 2016, http://www.nps.gov/jeff/learn/historyculture/freedom-licenses.htm. Delaney's designation as a washer seems ironic considering that the argument with her enslaver's wife, which led to her sale and subsequent freedom suit, was over her inability to do washing.

13. Delaney, *From the Darkness Cometh the Light*, 57–58.

14. Ibid., 61.

15. Ibid., 62–63; Death Certificate in Missouri Death Certificates Collection, Missouri Digital Heritage website.

16. For more information on the Jim Crow era and *Plessy v. Ferguson*, see Gilmore, *Gender and Jim Crow*; Hale, *Making Whiteness*; Kelley, *Right to Ride*; R. Scott, "Public Rights, Social Equality, and the Conceptual Roots of the *Plessy* Challenge"; Lofgren, *The Plessy Case*; Welke, "When All the Women Were White, and All the Blacks Were Men."

17. Delaney, *From the Darkness Cometh the Light*, vii.

18. Ibid., 58.

19. Ibid., 62.

Bibliography

Archival Sources

David M. Rubenstein Rare Book and Manuscript Library, Duke University, Durham, North Carolina.
Clay, Henry. Papers.
Louisiana Division and City Archives, New Orleans Public Library, New Orleans, Louisiana.
First Judicial District Court Records, Orleans Parish.
Missouri Digital Heritage website. Missouri Office of the Secretary of State, http://s1.sos.mo.gov/records/archives/archivesdb/deathcertificates/.
Missouri Birth and Death Records Database Collection.
Missouri Death Certificates Collection.
Missouri Judicial Records Database Collection.
St. Louis Probate Court Records.
Missouri History Museum, St. Louis, Missouri.
Allen, Beverly. Estate Records.
Bates, Edward. Papers.
Bates Family. Papers.
Broadsides—Slaves.
Chamberlin, T. W. Collection.
Darby Family. Papers.
Duels Collection.
Gamble, Hamilton R. Papers.
Goode, George R. Papers.
Hyatt-Hume. Papers.
Lane, William Carr. Papers.

Link, Theodore C. Collection.
Lucas, John B. C. Papers.
Primm, Wilson. Papers.
Scott, Dred. Papers.
Semsrott, William C. Papers.
Slaves Papers.
Missouri State Archives, Office of the Secretary of State, Jefferson City, Missouri.
Missouri Supreme Court Case Files.
National Archives and Records Administration, Kansas City Branch, Kansas City, Missouri.
United States District Court Record Volume A, 1822–56.
National Park Service, Online Collections. http://www.nps.gov/jeff/learn/historyculture.htm.
Emancipations.
Freedom Licenses.
Office of the Circuit Clerk, Missouri State Archives, Office of the Secretary of State, St. Louis, Missouri.
General Court for the Territory of Louisiana Case Files.
St. Louis Chancery Court Case Files.
St. Louis Circuit Court Case Files
St. Louis Circuit Court Execution Books.
St. Louis Circuit Court Record Books.
St. Louis Court of Common Pleas Case Files.
St. Louis Criminal Court Case Files.
Superior Court Case Files.
Special Collections Department, St. Louis County Library, St. Louis, Missouri.
St. Louis County Court Case Files.
The University of Virginia Geospatial and Statistical Data Center, http://fisher.lib.virginia.edu/collections/stats/histcensus
Historical Census Browser.
Western Historical Manuscripts Collection, Columbia, Missouri.
Drake, Charles. Manuscript Autobiography.
Missouri Collection.

Newspapers

Daily Missouri Republican
Missouri Argus
Missouri Democrat
Missouri Republican
St. Louis Observer

Published Primary Sources

"Act for the Gradual Emancipation of Slavery, An." March 1, 1780. Record Group 26. Records of the Department of State. Available at Black History in Pennsylvania, published by the Pennsylvania Historical and Museum Commission, accessed August 17, 2013, http://www.portal.state.pa.us/portal/server.pt/community/empowerment/18325/gradual_abolition_of_slavery_act/623285.

Acts of the Legislative Council of the Territory of Florida, Passed at Their Third Session, 1824. Tallahassee: Printed at the Office of the Florida Intelligencer, 1825.

Alden, T. J. Fox, and J. A. Van Housen. *A Digest of the Laws of Mississippi . . .* New York: Alexander S. Gould, 1839.

American Bar Foundation. "Legal Profession Statistics." Accessed February 20, 2016, http://www.americanbar.org/resources_for_lawyers/profession_statistics.html.

Anderson, Galusha. *The Story of a Border City during the Civil War.* Boston: Little, Brown, 1908.

Ball, William McK., and Sam C. Roane. *Revised Statutes of the State of Arkansas . . .* Boston: Weeks, Jordan, 1838.

Bay, W. V. N. *Reminiscences of the Bench and Bar of Missouri, with an Appendix, Containing Biographical Sketches of Nearly All of the Judges and Lawyers Who Have Passed Away, Together with Many Interesting and Valuable Letters Never Before Published of Washington, Jefferson, Burr, Granger, Clinton, and Others, Some of Which Throw Additional Light upon the Famous Burr Conspiracy.* St. Louis: F. H. Thomas, 1878.

Brackenridge, Henry Marie. *Views of Louisiana: Together with a Journal of a Voyage up the Missouri River in 1811.* Pittsburgh: Cramer, Spear and Eichbaum, 1814.

Casselberry, Evans. *The Revised Statutes of the State of Missouri, Revised and Digested by the Thirteenth General Assembly . . .* St. Louis: printed by Chambers and Knapp, 1845.

Catterall, Helen Tunnicliff. *Judicial Cases Concerning American Slavery and the Negro.* 5 vols. Washington, DC: Carnegie Institution of Washington, 1926.

Clamorgan, Cyprian. *The Colored Aristocracy of St. Louis.* Edited by Julie Winch. Columbia: University of Missouri Press, 1999.

Clark, R. H., T. R. R. Cobb, and D. Irwin. *The Code of the State of Georgia.* Atlanta: John H. Seals, 1861.

Cobb, Thomas R. R. *A Digest of the Laws of the State of Georgia . . .* Vol. 1. Athens, GA: Christy, Kelsea, and Burke, 1851.

———. *An Inquiry into the Law of Negro Slavery in the United States of America: To Which Is Prefixed, a Historical Sketch of Slavery.* Philadelphia: T. and J. W. Johnson, 1858.

Code of Laws for the District of Columbia . . . Washington, DC: printed by Davis and Force, 1819.

Code of Virginia, The: With the Declaration of Independence and Constitution of the United States, and the Declaration of Rights and Constitution of Virginia. Richmond, VA: printed by William F. Ritchie, 1849.

Collection of All Such Acts of the General Assembly of Virginia of a Public and Permanent Nature, A . . . Vol. 1. Richmond, VA: printed by Samuel Pleasants, Jun. and Henry Pace, 1803.

Darby, John F. *Personal Recollections of Many Prominent People Whom I Have Known, and of Events—Especially of Those Relating to the History of St. Louis—During the First Half of the Present Century.* St. Louis: G. I. Jones, 1880.

Delaney, Lucy A. *From the Darkness Cometh the Light; or, Struggles for Freedom.* St. Louis: Publishing House of J. T. Smith, 1892. Electronic edition by Documenting the American South, University of North Carolina, Chapel Hill, 2001, http://docsouth.unc.edu/neh/delaney/delaney.html.

Geyer, Henry S. *A Digest of the Laws of Missouri Territory.* St. Louis: printed for the publisher, by Joseph Charless at the Missouri Gazette Office, 1818.

Hardin, Charles H. *The Revised Statutes of the State of Missouri, Revised and Digested by the Eighteenth General Assembly* . . . 2 vols. Jefferson City, MO: printed for the state, by James Lusk, 1856.

Haywood, John, and Robert L. Cobbs. *The Statute Laws of the State of Tennessee, of a Public and General Nature.* Vol. 1. Knoxville, TN: P. S. Heiskell, 1831.

Herty, Thomas. *A Digest of the Laws of Maryland.* Baltimore: printed for the editor, 1799.

Hotchkiss, William A. *A Codification of the Statute Law of Georgia Including the English Statutes of Force.* Savannah, GA: published by John M. Cooper, 1845.

Hutchinson, A. *Code of Mississippi, Being an Analytical Compilation of the Public and General Statutes of the Territory and State.* Jackson, MS: Price and Fall, 1848.

Keemle, Charles. *The St. Louis Directory for the Years 1836–7: Containing the Names of the Inhabitants, Their Occupations* . . . St. Louis: printed by Keemle, 1836.

———. *The St. Louis Directory for the Years 1838–9: Containing the Names of the Inhabitants, Their Occupations* . . . St. Louis: printed by Keemle, 1838.

Laws of a Public and General Nature, of the District of Louisiana, of the Territory of Louisiana, of the Territory of Missouri, and of the State of Missouri up to the Year 1824. . Jefferson City, MO: W. Lusk and Son, 1842.

Laws of a Public and General Nature of the State of Missouri, Passed between the Years 1824 & 1836, Not Published in the Digest of 1825, nor in the Digest of 1835. Jefferson City, MO: W. Lusk and Son, 1842.

Laws of the State of Delaware . . . New Castle, DE: printed by Samuel and John Adams, 1797.

Loughborough, Preston S. *A Digest of the Statute Laws of Kentucky, of a Public and Permanent Nature* . . . Frankfort, KY: printed by Albert G. Hodges, 1842.

McCord, David J. *The Statutes at Large of South Carolina.* Vol. 7. Columbia, SC: printed by A. S. Johnston, 1840.

Meachum, John Berry. "An Address to All the Colored Citizens of the United States." Philadelphia: Printed for the author by King and Baird, 1846. Electronic edition by Documenting the American South, University of North Carolina, Chapel Hill, 2001, http://docsouth.unc.edu/neh/meachum/meachum.html.

Morrison's St. Louis Directory, for 1852, Containing the Names of the Inhabitants, Their Occupations . . . St. Louis: Missouri Republican Office, 1852.

Olmsted, Frederick Law. *A Journey in the Seaboard Slave States, with Remarks on Their Economy.* New York: Dix and Edwards, 1856. Electronic edition by Documenting the American South, University of North Carolina, Chapel Hill, 2001, http://docsouth.unc.edu/nc/olmsted/menu.html.

Phillips, U. B. *The Revised Statutes of Louisiana.* New Orleans: J. Claiborne, 1856.

Revised Code of the District of Columbia, The . . . Washington, DC: printed by A. O. P. Nicholson, 1857.

Revised Code of the Laws of Mississippi, The: In Which Are Comprised All Such Acts of the General Assembly, of a Public Nature . . . Natchez, MS: printed by Francis Baker, 1824.

Revised Code of the Laws of Virginia, The: Being a Collection of All Such Acts of the General Assembly of a Public and Permanent Nature . . . Vol. 1. Richmond, VA: printed by Thomas Ritchie, 1819.

Revised Statutes of Missouri, The. St. Louis: Chambers and Knapp, 1845.

Revised Statutes of the State of Delaware. Dover, DE: S. Kimmey, 1852.

Revised Statutes of the State of Missouri, The: Revised and Digested by the Eighth General Assembly during the Years One Thousand Eight Hundred and Thirty-Four, and One Thousand Eight Hundred and Thirty-Five, Together with the Constitutions of Missouri and of the United States. St. Louis: printed at the Argus Office, 1835.

Revised Statutes of the State of Missouri, The: Revised and Digested by the Eighth General Assembly, during the Years One Thousand Eight Hundred and Thirty-Four and One Thousand Eight Hundred and Thirty-Five, Together with the Constitutions of Missouri and of the United States. 3rd ed. St. Louis: printed by order of the Secretary of State, by Chambers and Knapp—Republican Office, 1841.

Saint Louis Directory for the Year 1842, The: Containing the Names of the Inhabitants . . . St. Louis: printed by Chambers and Knapp, 1842.

Scott, Otho, and Hiram M'Cullough. *The Maryland Code: Public General Laws and Public Local Laws*. Vol. 1. Baltimore: John Murphy, 1860.

Sloss, J. H. *The St. Louis Directory for 1848*. St. Louis: printed for Charles and Hammond, 1848.

St. Clair, Arthur. *St. Clair Papers, The: The Life and Public Services of Arthur St. Clair*. Cincinnati, OH: Robert Clarke, 1882.

Steele, J., and J. M. M'Campbell. *Laws of the Arkansas Territory, Compiled and Arranged*. Little Rock, AR: printed by J. Steele, 1835.

St. Louis Directory for the Years 1840–1, The: Containing the Names of the Inhabitants, Their Occupations . . . St. Louis: printed by C. Keemle, 1840.

Talioferro, Lawrence. *Auto-biography of Maj. Lawrence Talioferro (Written in 1864), in 6 Collections of the Minnesota Historical Society*. St. Paul, MN: Pioneer, 1894.

Toulmin, Harry. *A Digest of the Laws of the State of Alabama* . . . Cahawba, AL: Ginn and Curtis, 1823.

Verlie, Emile Joseph, ed. *Illinois Constitutions*. Springfield: Illinois State Historical Library, 1919.

Watkins, Robert, and George Watkins. *A Digest of the Laws of the State of Georgia from Its First Establishment as a British Province down to the Year 1798* . . . Philadelphia: printed by R. Aitken, 1800.

Wines, E. C., and Theodore W. Dwight. *Report on the Prisons and Reformatories of the United States and Canada*. Albany, NY: Van Benthuysen and Sons' Steam Printing House, 1867.

Yetman, Norman R., ed. *When I Was a Slave: Memoirs from the Slave Narrative Collection*. Mineola, NY: Dover, 2002.

Secondary Works

Arenson, Adam. *The Great Heart of the Republic: St. Louis and the Cultural Civil War*. Cambridge, MA: Harvard University Press, 2011.

Aron, Stephen. *American Confluence: The Missouri Frontier from Borderland to Border State*. Bloomington: Indiana University Press, 2005.

Ashworth, John. *Slavery, Capitalism, and Politics in the Antebellum Republic*. Cambridge: Cambridge University Press, 1995.

———. *Slavery, Capitalism, and Politics in the Antebellum Republic*. Vol. 2, *The Coming of the Civil War, 1850–1861*. New York: Cambridge University Press, 2007.

Aslakson, Kenneth R. *Making Race in the Courtroom: The Legal Construction of Three Races in Early New Orleans*. New York: New York University Press, 2014.

Ayers, Edward L. *Vengeance and Justice: Crime and Punishment in the 19th Century American South*. New York: Oxford University Press, 1984.

Bancroft, Frederic. *Slave-Trading in the Old South*. Baltimore: J. H. Furst, 1931.

Banner, Stuart. *Legal Systems in Conflict: Property and Sovereignty in Missouri, 1750–1860*. Norman: University of Oklahoma Press, 2000.

Baptist, Edward E. *Creating an Old South: Middle Florida's Plantation Frontier before the Civil War*. Chapel Hill: University of North Carolina Press, 2002.

———. *The Half Has Never Been Told: Slavery and the Making of American Capitalism*. New York: Basic Books, 2014.

Berlin, Ira. *Generations of Captivity: A History of African-American Slaves*. Cambridge, MA: Harvard University Press, 2003.

———. *Many Thousands Gone: The First Two Centuries of Slavery in North America*. Cambridge, MA: Harvard University Press, 1998.

———. *Slaves without Masters: The Free Negro in the Antebellum South*. New York: Pantheon Books, 1974.

Berlin, Ira, Joseph P. Reidy, and Leslie S. Rowland, eds. *The Black Military Experience*. Cambridge: Cambridge University Press, 1982.

Billon, Frederic L. *Annals of St. Louis in Its Early Days under the French and Spanish Dominations*. St. Louis: G. I. Jones, 1886.

Blackburn, Robin. Introduction to *Paths to Freedom: Manumission in the Atlantic World*, edited by Rosemary Brana-Shute and Randy J. Sparks, 1–13. Columbia: University of South Carolina Press, 2009.

Blackett, R. J. M. *Making Freedom: The Underground Railroad and the Politics of Slavery*. Chapel Hill: University of North Carolina Press, 2013.

Blanck, Emily. "Seventeen Eighty-Three: The Turning Point in the Law of Slavery and Freedom in Massachusetts." *New England Quarterly* 75 (2002): 24–51.

———. *Tyrannicide: Forging an American Law of Slavery in Revolutionary South Carolina and Massachusetts*. Athens: University of Georgia Press, 2015.

Blassingame, John W. "Using the Testimony of Ex-Slaves: Approaches and Problems." *Journal of Southern History* 41, no. 4 (1975): 474–92.

Blinka, Daniel D. "Trial by Jury in Revolutionary Virginia: Old-Style Trials in the New Republic." Ph.D. diss., University of Wisconsin, 2001.

Blumenthal, Debra G. *Enemies and Familiars: Slavery and Mastery in Fifteenth-Century Valencia*. Ithaca, NY: Cornell University Press, 2009.

———. "The Promise of Freedom in Late Medieval Valencia." In *Paths to Freedom: Manumission in the Atlantic World*, edited by Rosemary Brana-Shute and Randy J. Sparks, 51–68. Columbia: University of South Carolina Press, 2009.

Bolster, W. Jeffrey. *Black Jacks: African American Seamen in the Age of Sail*. Cambridge, MA: Harvard University Press, 1997.

Boman, Dennis K. *Lincoln's Resolute Unionist: Hamilton Gamble, Dred Scott Dissenter and Missouri's Civil War Governor*. Baton Rouge: Louisiana State University Press, 2006.

Brophy, Alfred L. *University, Court, and Slave: Pro-Slavery Thought in Southern*

Colleges & Courts and the Coming of the Civil War. New York: Oxford University Press, 2016.

Brown, Kathleen M. *Good Wives, Nasty Wenches, and Anxious Patriarchs: Gender, Race, and Power in Colonial Virginia.* Chapel Hill: University of North Carolina Press, 1996.

Brown, Vincent. "Social Death and Political Life in the Study of Slavery." *American Historical Review* 114, no. 5 (2009): 1231–49.

Bryen, Ari Z. *Violence in Roman Egypt: A Study in Legal Interpretation.* Philadelphia: University of Pennsylvania Press, 2013.

Buchanan, Thomas C. *Black Life on the Mississippi: Slaves, Free Blacks, and the Western Steamboat World.* Chapel Hill: University of North Carolina Press, 2004.

Burke, Diane Mutti. *On Slavery's Border: Missouri's Small Slaveholding Households, 1815–1865.* Athens: University of Georgia Press, 2010.

Bushnell, Eleanore. "The Impeachment and Trial of James H. Peck." *Missouri Historical Review* 74 (1979–80): 137–65.

Camp, Stephanie M. H. *Closer to Freedom: Enslaved Women and Everyday Resistance in the Plantation South.* Chapel Hill: University of North Carolina Press, 2004.

Cecelski, David S. *The Waterman's Song: Slavery and Freedom in Maritime North Carolina.* Chapel Hill: University of North Carolina Press, 2001.

Christian, Shirley. *Before Lewis and Clark: The Story of the Chouteaus, the French Dynasty That Ruled America's Frontier.* New York: Farrar, Straus and Giroux, 2004.

Cleary, Patricia. *The World, the Flesh, and the Devil: A History of Colonial St. Louis.* Columbia: University of Missouri Press, 2011.

Condon, Sean. "The Slave Owner's Family and Manumission in the Post-Revolutionary Chesapeake Tidewater: Evidence from Anne Arundel County Wills, 1790–1820." In *Paths to Freedom: Manumission in the Atlantic World,* edited by Rosemary Brana-Shute and Randy J. Sparks, 339–62. Columbia: University of South Carolina Press, 2009.

Cotter, William R. "The Somerset Case and the Abolition of Slavery in England." *History* 79 (February 1994): 31–56.

Cottrol, Robert J. *The Long, Lingering Shadow: Slavery, Race, and Law in the American Hemisphere.* Athens: University of Georgia Press, 2013.

Courtwright, David T. *Violent Land: Single Men and Social Disorder from the Frontier to the Inner City.* Cambridge, MA: Harvard University Press, 1996.

Cramer, Clayton. *Black Demographic Data, 1790–1860: A Sourcebook.* Westport, CT: Greenwood, 1997.

Cutter, Charles R. *The Legal Culture of Northern New Spain, 1700–1810.* Albuquerque: University of New Mexico Press, 1995.

Davis, David Brion. *Inhuman Bondage: The Rise and Fall of Slavery in the New World.* New York: Oxford University Press, 2006.

———. *The Problem of Slavery in the Age of Revolution, 1770–1823*. Ithaca, NY: Cornell University Press, 1975.

Davis, James E. *Frontier Illinois*. Bloomington: Indiana University Press, 1998.

Dayton, Cornelia Hughes. *Women before the Bar: Gender, Law, and Society in Connecticut, 1639–1789*. Chapel Hill: University of North Carolina Press, 1995.

Dempsey, Terrell. *Searching for Jim: Slavery in Sam Clemens's World*. Columbia: University of Missouri Press, 2003.

Dewey, Frank L. *Thomas Jefferson, Lawyer*. Charlottesville: University of Virginia Press, 1986.

Dexter, Darrell. *Bondage in Egypt: Slavery in Southern Illinois*. Cape Girardeau, MO: Center for Regional History, Southeast Missouri State University, 2011.

Deyle, Steven. *Carry Me Back: The Domestic Slave Trade in American Life*. New York: Oxford University Press, 2005.

Durst, Dennis L. "The Reverend John Berry Meachum (1789–1854) of St. Louis: Prophet and Entrepreneurial Black Educator in Historiographical Perspective." *North Star: A Journal of African American Religious History* 7, no. 2 (2004). http://northstar.vassar.edu/volume7/durst.pdf.

Edwards, Laura F. *Gendered Strife and Confusion: The Political Culture of Reconstruction*. Urbana: University of Illinois Press, 1997.

———. *The People and Their Peace: Legal Culture and the Transformation of Inequality in the Post-Revolutionary South*. Chapel Hill: University of North Carolina Press, 2009.

———. "Status without Rights: African Americans and the Tangled History of Law and Governance in the Nineteenth-Century U.S. South." *American Historical Review* 112, no. 2 (2007): 365–93.

Ehrlich, Walter. *They Have No Rights: Dred Scott's Struggle for Freedom*. Westport, CT: Greenwood Press, 1979.

English, William Francis. *The Pioneer Lawyer and Jurist in Missouri*. Columbia: University of Missouri Press, 1947.

Epps, Kristen. *Slavery on the Periphery: The Kansas-Missouri Border in the Antebellum and Civil War Eras*. Athens: University of Georgia Press, 2016.

Fede, Andrew. *Roadblocks to Freedom: Slavery and Manumission in the United States South*. New Orleans: Quid Pro Books, 2011.

Fehrenbacher, Don E. *The Dred Scott Case: Its Significance in American Law and Politics*. New York: Oxford University Press, 1978.

———. *Slavery, Law, and Politics: The Dred Scott Case in Historical Perspective*. New York: Oxford University Press, 1981.

Fields, Barbara Jeanne. *Slavery and Freedom on the Middle Ground: Maryland during the Nineteenth Century*. New Haven, CT: Yale University Press, 1985.

Finkelman, Paul. *Dred Scott v. Sandford: A Brief History with Documents*. Bedford Series in History and Culture. Boston: Bedford Books, 1997.

———. *An Imperfect Union: Slavery, Federalism, and Comity*. Chapel Hill: University of North Carolina Press, 1981.

Foley, William E. *The Genesis of Missouri: From Wilderness Outpost to Statehood*. Columbia: University of Missouri Press, 1989.

———. "Slave Freedom Suits before Dred Scott: The Case of Marie Jean Scypion's Descendants." *Missouri Historical Review* 79 (1984–85): 1–23.

Foley, William E., and David C. Rice. *The First Chouteaus: River Barons of Early St. Louis*. Urbana: University of Illinois Press, 2000.

Foner, Eric. *Free Soil, Free Labor, Free Men: The Ideology of the Republican Party before the Civil War*. New York: Oxford University Press, 1970.

———. *Politics and Ideology in the Age of the Civil War*. New York: Oxford University Press, 1980.

Ford, Lacy K. *Deliver Us from Evil: The Slavery Question in the Old South*. New York: Oxford University Press, 2009.

———. *Origins of Southern Radicalism: The South Carolina Upcountry, 1800–1860*. New York: Oxford University Press, 1988.

"Forum: *Somerset's Case* Revisited." *Law and History Review* 24, no. 3 (2006): 601–72.

Frankel, Noralee. *Freedom's Women: Black Women and Families in Civil War Era Mississippi*. Bloomington: Indiana University Press, 1999.

Franklin, John Hope, and Loren Schweninger. *In Search of the Promised Land: A Slave Family in the Old South*. New York: Oxford University Press, 2006.

———. *Runaway Slaves: Rebels on the Plantation*. New York: Oxford University Press, 1999.

Frazier, Harriet C. *Runaway and Freed Missouri Slaves and Those Who Helped Them, 1763–1865*. Jefferson, NC: McFarland, 2004.

———. *Slavery and Crime in Missouri, 1773–1865*. Jefferson, NC: McFarland, 2001.

Freehling, William W. *The Road to Disunion*. Vol. 1, *Secessionists at Bay, 1776–1854*. New York: Oxford University Press, 1990.

———. *The Road to Disunion*. Vol. 2, *Secessionists Triumphant, 1854–1861*. New York: Oxford University Press, 2007.

Freeman, Joanne B. *Affairs of Honor: National Politics in the New Republic*. New Haven, CT: Yale University Press, 2001.

"Free Soil." Special issue, *Slavery & Abolition* 32, no. 3 (2011).

Friedman, Lawrence M. *A History of American Law*. 2nd ed. New York: Simon and Schuster, 1985.

———. "Legal Culture and Social Development." *Law & Society Review* 4, no. 1 (1969): 29–44.

Gardner, Eric. "'You Have No Business to Whip Me': The Freedom Suits of Polly Wash and Lucy Ann Delaney." *African American Review* 41, no. 1 (2007): 33–50.

Genovese, Eugene D. *Roll, Jordan, Roll: The World the Slaves Made*. New York: Pantheon Books, 1974.

———. *The World the Slaveholders Made*. 1972. Reprint, New York: Vintage Books, 1974.

Gerteis, Louis S. *Civil War St. Louis*. Lawrence: University Press of Kansas, 2001.

Gigantino, James J., II. *The Ragged Road to Abolition: Slavery and Freedom in New Jersey, 1775–1865*. Philadelphia: University of Pennsylvania Press, 2015.

Gilmore, Glenda Elizabeth. *Gender and Jim Crow: Women and the Politics of White Supremacy in North Carolina, 1896–1920*. Chapel Hill: University of North Carolina Press, 1996.

Gorsuch, Allison Mileo. "Legacies of Empire: Race and Labor Contracts in the Upper Mississippi River Valley." In *The Legal Histories of the British Empire*, edited by John McLaren and Shaunnagh Dorsett, 189–202. New York: Routledge, 2014.

———. "To Indent Oneself: Ownership, Contracts, and Consent in Antebellum Illinois." In *The Legal Understanding of Slavery: From the Historical to the Contemporary*, edited by Jean Allain, 131–41. New York: Oxford University Press, 2012.

Graber, Mark A. *Dred Scott and the Problem of Constitutional Evil*. Cambridge: Cambridge University Press, 2006.

Greene, Sally. "Thomas Ruffin and the Perils of Public Homage: *State v. Mann* Exhumed." *North Carolina Law Review* 87 (March 2009): 702–55.

Grinberg, Keila. "Manumission, Gender, and the Law in Nineteenth-Century Brazil." In *Paths to Freedom: Manumission in the Atlantic World*, edited by Rosemary Brana-Shute and Randy J. Sparks, 219–34. Columbia: University of South Carolina Press, 2009.

Gross, Ariela. "Beyond Black and White: Cultural Approaches to Race and Slavery." *Columbia Law Review* 101 (April 2001): 640–90.

———. *Double Character: Slavery and Mastery in the Antebellum Southern Courtroom*. Princeton, NJ: Princeton University Press, 2000.

———. "Litigating Whiteness: Trials of Racial Determination in the Nineteenth Century South." *Yale Law Journal* 108, no. 1 (1998): 109–89.

———. *What Blood Won't Tell: A History of Race on Trial*. Cambridge, MA: Harvard University Press, 2008.

Hadden, Sally. "Judging Slavery: Thomas Ruffin and *State v. Mann*." In *Local Matters: Race, Crime, and Justice in the Nineteenth-Century South*, edited by Christopher Waldrep and Donald G. Nieman, 1–28. Athens: University of Georgia Press, 2001.

———. *Slave Patrols: Law and Violence in Virginia and the Carolinas*. Cambridge, MA: Harvard University Press, 2001.

Hahn, Steven. *A Nation under Our Feet: Black Political Struggles in the Rural*

South from Slavery to the Great Migration. Cambridge, MA: Harvard University Press, 2003.

Hale, Grace Elizabeth. *Making Whiteness: The Culture of Segregation in the South, 1890–1940.* New York: Vintage Books, 1999.

Hall, Kermit L., and Peter Karsten. *The Magic Mirror: Law in American History.* 2nd. ed. New York: Oxford University Press, 2009.

Halttunen, Karen. *Confidence Men and Painted Women: A Study of Middle-Class Culture in America, 1830–1870.* New Haven, CT: Yale University Press, 1982.

Harris, N. Dwight. *The History of Negro Servitude in Illinois, and of the Slavery Agitation in That State.* Chicago: A. C. McClurg, 1904.

Hartog, Hendrik. *Man and Wife in America: A History.* Cambridge, MA: Harvard University Press, 2000.

———. "Pigs and Positivism." *Wisconsin Law Review,* July–August 1985, 899–935.

———. *Someday All This Will Be Yours: A History of Inheritance and Old Age.* Cambridge, MA: Harvard University Press, 2012.

Heerman, Scott. "In a State of Slavery: Black Servitude in Illinois: 1800–1830." *Early American Studies* 14 (Winter 2016): 114–39.

Hoffman, Judy. "'If I Fall, My Grave Shall Be Made in Alton': Elijah Lovejoy, Martyr for Abolition." *Gateway Heritage: Quarterly Journal of the MHM* 25 (2005): 10–21.

Hoig, Stan. *The Chouteaus: First Family of the Fur Trade.* Albuquerque: University of New Mexico Press, 2008.

Holland, Antonio F. "African Americans in Henry Shaw's St. Louis." In *St. Louis in the Century of Henry Shaw: A View beyond the Garden Wall,* edited by Eric Sandweiss, 51–78. Columbia: University of Missouri Press, 2003.

Holt, Michael F. *The Political Crisis of the 1850s.* New York: Wiley, 1978.

Hunter, Tera. *To 'Joy My Freedom: Southern Black Women's Lives and Labors after the Civil War.* Cambridge, MA: Harvard University Press, 1997.

Hurt, R. Douglas. *Agriculture and Slavery in Missouri's Little Dixie.* Columbia: University of Missouri Press, 1992.

Isaac, Rhys. *The Transformation of Virginia, 1740–1790.* 1982. Reprint, Chapel Hill: University of North Carolina Press, 1999.

Johnson, Michael P., and James L. Roark. *Black Masters: A Free Family of Color in the Old South.* New York: Norton, 1984.

Johnson, Walter, ed. *The Chattel Principle: Internal Slave Trades in the Americas.* New Haven, CT: Yale University Press, 2004.

———. *River of Dark Dreams: Slavery and Empire in the Cotton Kingdom.* Cambridge, MA: Harvard University Press, 2013.

———. "The Slave Trader, the White Slave, and the Politics of Racial Determination in the 1850s." *Journal of American History* 87 (June 2000): 13–38.

———. *Soul by Soul: Life Inside the Antebellum Slave Market.* Cambridge, MA: Harvard University Press, 1999.

Jones, Bernie. *Fathers of Conscience: Mixed-Race Inheritance in the Antebellum South.* Athens: University of Georgia Press, 2009.

Jones, Martha S. "The Case of *Jean Baptiste, un Créole de Saint-Domingue*: Narrating Slavery, Freedom, and the Haitian Revolution in Baltimore City." In *The American South and the Atlantic World*, edited by B. Ward, M. Bone, and W. A. Link, 104–28. Gainesville: University Press of Florida, 2013.

———. "Time, Space, and Jurisdiction in Atlantic World Slavery: The Volunbrun Household in Gradual Emancipation New York." *Law & History Review* 29, no. 4 (2011): 1031–60.

Jordan, Philip D. *Frontier Law and Order.* Lincoln: University of Nebraska Press, 1970.

Kamphoefner, Walter D. "Learning from the 'Majority-Minority' City: Immigration in Nineteenth-Century St. Louis." In *St. Louis in the Century of Henry Shaw: A View beyond the Garden Wall*, edited by Eric Sandweiss, 79–102. Columbia: University of Missouri Press, 2003.

Kantrowitz, Stephen. *More than Freedom: Fighting for Black Citizenship in a White Republic, 1829–1889.* New York: Penguin Books, 2012.

Karsten, Peter. *Heart versus Head: Judge-Made Law in Nineteenth-Century America.* Chapel Hill: University of North Carolina Press, 1997.

Kaye, Anthony E. *Joining Places: Slave Neighborhoods in the Old South.* Chapel Hill: University of North Carolina Press, 2007.

Kelley, Blair L. M. *Right to Ride: Streetcar Boycotts and African American Citizenship in the Era of* Plessy v. Ferguson. Chapel Hill: University of North Carolina Press, 2010.

Kennington, Kelly Marie. "Geography, Mobility, and the Law: Suing for Freedom in Antebellum St. Louis." *Journal of Southern History* 80, no. 3 (2014): 575–604.

Klooster, William Wubbo. "Manumission in an Entrepôt: The Case of Curaçao." In *Paths to Freedom: Manumission in the Atlantic World*, edited by Rosemary Brana-Shute and Randy J. Sparks, 161–74. Columbia: University of South Carolina Press, 2009.

Kolchin, Peter. *American Slavery, 1619–1877.* New York: Hill and Wang, 1993.

Konig, David Thomas. "The Long Road to *Dred Scott*: Personhood and the Rule of Law in the Trial Court Records of St. Louis Slave Freedom Suits." *University of Missouri–Kansas City Law Review* 75 (2006): 53–79.

Konig, David Thomas, Paul Finkelman, and Christopher Alan Bracey, eds. *The Dred Scott Case: Historical and Contemporary Perspectives on Race and Law.* Athens: Ohio University Press, 2010.

Lebsock, Suzanne. *The Free Women of Petersburg: Status and Culture in a Southern Town, 1784–1860.* New York: Norton, 1984.

Lofgren, Charles A. *The Plessy Case: A Legal-Historical Interpretation*. New York: Oxford University Press, 1988.

Maltz, Earl M. *Dred Scott and the Politics of Slavery*. Lawrence: University Press of Kansas, 2007.

Mamigonian, Beatriz Gallotti. "Conflicts over the Meanings of Freedom: The Liberated Africans' Struggle for Emancipation in Brazil, 1840s–1860s." In *Paths to Freedom: Manumission in the Atlantic World*, edited by Rosemary Brana-Shute and Randy J. Sparks, 235–64. Columbia: University of South Carolina Press, 2009.

March, David D. *The History of Missouri*. 2 vols. New York: Lewis, 1967.

Maris-Wolf, Ted. *Family Bonds: Free Blacks and Re-enslavement Law in Antebellum Virginia*. Chapel Hill: University of North Carolina Press, 2015.

Martin, Jonathan D. *Divided Mastery: Slave Hiring in the American South*. Cambridge, MA: Harvard University Press, 2004.

McCandless, Perry. *A History of Missouri*. Vol. 2, *1820 to 1860*. Columbia: University of Missouri Press, 1972.

McCurry, Stephanie. *Masters of Small Worlds: Yeoman Households, Gender Relations, and the Political Culture of the Antebellum South Carolina Lowcountry*. New York: Oxford University Press, 1995.

McDermott, Stacy Pratt. "'Gentlemen of the Jury': The Status of Jurors and the Reputation of the Jury in the Midwest, 1830–1860." Ph.D. diss., University of Illinois, Urbana-Champaign, 2007.

Merkel, Benjamin C. "The Abolition Aspects of Missouri's Antislavery Controversy 1819–1865." *Missouri Historical Review* 44 (1949–50): 232–53.

Middleton, Stephen. *The Black Laws: Race and the Legal Process in Early Ohio*. Athens: Ohio University Press, 2005.

Milewski, Melissa. "From Slave to Litigant: African Americans in Court in the Postwar South, 1865–1920." *Law and History Review* 30 (August 2012): 723–69.

Missouri State Archives. "An Abstract of the St. Louis Court System, 1804 to 1875." St. Louis: Missouri State Archives, 2004.

Moore, Robert, Jr. "A Ray of Hope, Extinguished: St. Louis Slave Suits for Freedom." *Gateway Heritage* 14 (1993–94): 4–15.

Morgan, Edmund S. *American Slavery, American Freedom: The Ordeal of Colonial Virginia*. New York: Norton, 1975.

Morgan, Philip D. "Virginia's Other Prototype: The Caribbean." In *The Atlantic World and Virginia, 1550–1624*, edited by Peter C. Mancall, 342–80. Chapel Hill: University of North Carolina Press, 2007.

Morris, Thomas D. *Southern Slavery and the Law, 1619–1860*. Chapel Hill: University of North Carolina Press, 1996.

Morrison, Michael A. *Slavery and the American West: The Eclipse of Manifest Destiny and the Coming of the Civil War*. Chapel Hill: University of North Carolina Press, 1997.

Nader, Laura. *The Life of the Law: Anthropological Projects*. Berkeley: University of California Press, 2002.

Nasta, Jesse. "Making Slavery's Border: Legal Culture and the Transformation of Slavery's Northwestern Frontier, 1787–1860." Ph.D. diss., Northwestern University, 2016.

Nelken, David. "Using the Concept of Legal Culture." *Australian Journal of Legal Philosophy* 29, no. 1 (2004): 1–27.

Nicholls, Michael L. "'The Squint of Freedom': African-American Freedom Suits in Post-Revolutionary Virginia." *Slavery & Abolition* 20 (1999): 47–62.

Nicholson, Bradley J. "Legal Borrowing and the Origins of Slave Law in the British Colonies." *American Journal of Legal History* 38, no. 1 (1994): 38–54.

Oakes, James. *Slavery and Freedom: An Interpretation of the Old South*. New York: Knopf, 1990.

O'Donovan, Susan Eva. "Universities of Social and Political Change: Slaves in Jail in Antebellum America." In *Buried Lives: Incarcerated in Early America*, edited by Michele Lise Tarter and Richard Bell, 124–48. Athens: University of Georgia Press, 2012.

Oubre, Claude F., and Keith P. Fontenot, "Liber Vel Non: Selected Freedom Cases in Antebellum St. Landry Parish." *Louisiana History* 39 (1998): 319–45.

Patterson, Orlando. *Slavery and Social Death: A Comparative Study*. Cambridge, MA: Harvard University Press, 1982.

———. "Three Notes of Freedom: The Nature and Consequences of Manumission." In *Paths to Freedom: Manumission in the Atlantic World*, edited by Rosemary Brana-Shute and Randy J. Sparks, 15–30. Columbia: University of South Carolina Press, 2009.

Peabody, Sue. *"There Are No Slaves in France": The Political Culture of Race and Slavery in the Ancien Régime*. New York: Oxford University Press, 1996.

Peabody, Sue, and Keila Grinberg. "Free Soil: The Generation and Circulation of an Atlantic Legal Principle." *Slavery & Abolition* 32, no. 3 (2011): 331–39.

Penningroth, Dylan. *The Claims of Kinfolk: African American Property and Community in the Nineteenth-Century South*. Chapel Hill: University of North Carolina Press, 2003.

Phillips, William D., Jr. "Manumission in Metropolitan Spain and the Canaries in the Fifteenth and Sixteenth Centuries." In *Paths to Freedom: Manumission in the Atlantic World*, edited by Rosemary Brana-Shute and Randy J. Sparks, 31–50. Columbia: University of South Carolina Press, 2009.

Potter, David. *The Impending Crisis 1848–1861*. New York: Harper and Row, 1976.

Primm, James Neal. "The Economy of Nineteenth-Century St. Louis." In *St. Louis in the Century of Henry Shaw: A View beyond the Garden Wall*, edited by Eric Sandweiss, 103–35. Columbia: University of Missouri Press, 2003.

Rasmussen, Daniel. *American Uprising: The Untold Story of America's Largest Slave Revolt*. New York: HarperCollins, 2012.

Riley, John P. "Written with My Own Hand: George Washington's Last Will and Testament." *Virginia Cavalcade* 48, no. 4 (1990): 168–77.

Robinson, Greg. "St. Louis." In *Encyclopedia of African-American Culture and History*, vol. 5, edited by Jack Salzman, David Lionel Smith, and Cornel West, 2378–82. New York: Simon and Schuster, 1996.

Roeber, A. G. *Faithful Magistrates and Republican Lawyers: Creators of Virginia Legal Culture, 1680–1810.* Chapel Hill: University of North Carolina Press, 1981.

Romeo, Sharon. *Gender and the Jubilee: Black Freedom and the Reconstruction of Citizenship in Civil War Missouri.* Athens: University of Georgia Press, 2016.

Rothman, Adam. *Slave Country: American Expansion and Origins of the Deep South.* Cambridge, MA: Harvard University Press, 2005.

Rothman, Joshua D. *Flush Times and Fever Dreams: A Story of Capitalism and Slavery in the Age of Jackson.* Athens: University of Georgia Press, 2012.

———. *Notorious in the Neighborhood: Sex and Families Across the Color Line in Virginia, 1787–1861.* Chapel Hill: University of North Carolina Press, 2003.

Salafia, Matthew. *Slavery's Borderland: Freedom and Bondage along the Ohio River.* Philadelphia: University of Pennsylvania Press, 2013.

Sandweiss, Eric, ed. *St. Louis in the Century of Henry Shaw: A View beyond the Garden Wall.* Columbia: University of Missouri Press, 2003.

Saville, Julie. *The Work of Reconstruction: From Slave to Wage Labor in South Carolina, 1860–1870.* Cambridge: Cambridge University Press, 1994.

Schafer, Judith Kelleher. *Becoming Free, Remaining Free: Manumission and Enslavement in New Orleans, 1846–1862.* Baton Rouge: Louisiana State University Press, 2003.

———. *Slavery, the Civil Law, and the Supreme Court of Louisiana.* Baton Rouge: Louisiana State University Press, 1994.

Schermerhorn, Calvin. *Money over Mastery, Family over Freedom: Slavery in the Antebellum Upper South.* Baltimore: Johns Hopkins University Press, 2011.

Schoeppner, Michael. "Navigating the Dangerous Atlantic: Racial Quarantines, Black Sailors, and United States Constitutionalism." Ph.D. diss., University of Florida, 2010.

———. "Peculiar Quarantines: The Seamen Acts and Regulatory Authority in the Antebellum South." *Law and History Review* 31 (August 2013): 559–86.

———. "Status across Borders: Roger Taney, Black British Subjects, and a Diplomatic Antecedent to the Dred Scott Decision." *Journal of American History* 100, no. 1 (2013): 46–67.

Schwalm, Leslie. *A Hard Fight for We: Women's Transition from Slavery to Freedom in South Carolina.* Urbana: University of Illinois Press, 1997.

Schweninger, Loren. *Black Property Owners in the South, 1790–1915.* Urbana: University of Illinois Press, 1990.

———. "Freedom Suits, African American Women, and the Genealogy of Slavery." *William and Mary Quarterly* 71, no. 1 (2014): 35–62.

Scott, Julius Sherrard, III. "The Common Wind: Currents of Afro-American Communication in the Era of the Haitian Revolution." Ph.D. diss., Duke University, 1986.

Scott, Rebecca J. "Paper Thin: Freedom and Re-enslavement in the Diaspora of the Haitian Revolution." *Law and History Review* 29, no. 4 (2011): 1061–87.

———."Public Rights, Social Equality, and the Conceptual Roots of the *Plessy* Challenge." *Michigan Law Review* 106 (March 2008): 774–804.

———. "'She . . . Refuses to Deliver Up Herself as the Slave of Your Petitioner': Émigrés, Enslavement, and the 1808 Louisiana Digest of the Civil Laws." *Tulane European & Civil Law Forum* 24 (2009): 115–36.

———. "Slavery and the Law in Atlantic Perspective: Jurisdiction, Jurisprudence, and Justice." *Law and History Review* 29 (November 2011): 915–24.

Scott, Rebecca J., and Jean M. Hébrard. *Freedom Papers: An Atlantic Odyssey in the Age of Emancipation*. Cambridge, MA: Harvard University Press, 2012.

Sharafi, Mitra. *Law and Identity in Colonial South Asia: Parsi Legal Culture, 1772–1947*. New York: Cambridge University Press, 2014.

———. "The Marital Patchwork of Colonial South Asia: Forum Shopping from Britain to Baroda." *Law and History Review* 28 (2010): 979–1009.

Shepard, E. Lee. "Breaking Into the Profession: Establishing a Law Practice in Antebellum Virginia." *Journal of Southern History* 48, no. 3 (1982): 393–410.

———. "Lawyers Look at Themselves: Professional Consciousness and the Virginia Bar, 1770–1850." *American Journal of Legal History* 25 (1981): 1–23.

———. "'This Being Court Day': Courthouses and Community Life in Rural Virginia." *Virginia Magazine of History and Biography* 103, no. 4 (1995): 459–70.

Sheppard Wolf, Eva. "Manumission and the Two-Race System in Early National Virginia." In *Paths to Freedom: Manumission in the Atlantic World*, edited by Rosemary Brana-Shute and Randy J. Sparks, 309–38. Columbia: University of South Carolina Press, 2009.

Silbey, Susan. "After Legal Consciousness." *Annual Review of Law and Social Sciences* 1 (2005): 323–68.

———. "Legal Consciousness." In *New Oxford Companion to Law*, edited by Peter Cane and Joanne Conaghan. Oxford: Oxford University Press, 2008. http://www.oxfordreference.com/view/10.1093/acref/9780199290543.001.0001/acref-9780199290543-div1-1665.

———. "Legal Culture and Legal Consciousness." In *International Encyclopedia of Social and Behavioral Sciences*, edited by Neil J. Smelser and Paul B. Baltes, 8624–28. New York: Elsevier, Pergamon, 2001.

Simeone, James. *Democracy and Slavery in Frontier Illinois: The Bottomland Republic*. DeKalb: Northern Illinois University Press, 2000.

Sinha, Manisha. *Counter-revolution of Slavery: Politics and Ideology in Antebellum South Carolina*. Chapel Hill: University of North Carolina Press, 2000.

Stampp, Kenneth M. *The Peculiar Institution: Slavery in the Ante-Bellum South*. New York: Vintage Books, 1956.

Stevenson, Brenda E. *Life in Black and White: Family and Community in the Slave South*. New York: Oxford University Press, 1996.

Towers, Frank. *The Urban South and the Coming of the Civil War*. Charlottesville: University of Virginia Press, 2004.

Trexler, Harrison Anthony. *Slavery in Missouri: 1804–1865*. Baltimore: Johns Hopkins University Press, 1914.

Tushnet, Mark V. *Slave Law in the American South*: State v. Mann *in History and Literature*. Lawrence: University Press of Kansas, 2003.

Twitty, Anne Silverwood. *Before* Dred Scott: *Slavery and Legal Culture in the American Confluence, 1787–1857*. Cambridge: Cambridge University Press, 2016.

———. "Slavery and Freedom in the American Confluence, from the Northwest Ordinance to Dred Scott." Ph.D. diss., Princeton University, 2010.

VanderVelde, Lea. *Mrs. Dred Scott: A Life on Slavery's Frontier*. New York: Oxford University Press, 2009.

———. *Redemption Songs: Suing for Freedom before Dred Scott*. New York: Oxford University Press, 2014.

VanderVelde, Lea, and Sandhya Subramanian. "Mrs. Dred Scott." *Yale Law Journal* 106, no. 4 (1997): 1033–1122.

Varon, Elizabeth R. *Disunion! The Coming of the American Civil War, 1789–1859*. Chapel Hill: University of North Carolina Press, 2008.

von Daacke, Kirt. *Freedom Has a Face: Race, Identity, and Community in Jefferson's Virginia*. Charlottesville: University of Virginia Press, 2012.

Wade, Richard C. *Slavery in the Cities: The South, 1820–1860*. New York: Oxford University Press, 1964.

Watson, Alan. *Slave Law in the Americas*. Athens: University of Georgia Press, 1989.

Welch, Kimberly M. "Black Litigiousness and White Accountability: Free Blacks and the Rhetoric of Reputation in the Antebellum Natchez District." *Journal of the Civil War Era* 5, no. 3 (2015): 372–98.

———. "People at Law: Subordinate Southerners, Popular Governance, and Local Legal Culture in Antebellum Mississippi and Louisiana." Ph.D. diss., University of Maryland, 2012.

———. "Black Litigants in the Antebellum American South." Unpublished manuscript.

Welke, Barbara Y. "When All the Women Were White, and All the Blacks Were Men: Gender, Class, Race, and the Road to *Plessy*, 1855–1914." *Law and History Review* 13, no. 2 (1995): 261–316.

West, Emily. *Family or Freedom: People of Color in the Antebellum South.* Lexington: University Press of Kentucky, 2012.

White, Ashli. *Encountering Revolution: Haiti and the Making of the Early Republic.* Baltimore: Johns Hopkins University Press, 2010.

Wilentz, Sean. *The Rise of American Democracy: Jefferson to Lincoln.* New York: Norton, 2005.

Wilson, Carol. *Freedom at Risk: The Kidnapping of Free Blacks in America, 1780–1865.* Lexington: University Press of Kentucky, 1994.

Winn, Kenneth. "Gods in Ruins: St. Louis Politicians and American Destiny, 1764–1875." In *St. Louis in the Century of Henry Shaw: A View beyond the Garden Wall*, edited by Eric Sandweiss, 19–50. Columbia: University of Missouri Press, 2003.

Woodman, Harold. *New South-New Law: The Legal Foundations of Credit and Labor Relations in the Postbellum Agricultural South.* Baton Rouge: Louisiana State University Press, 1995.

Wyatt-Brown, Bertram. *Honor and Violence in the Old South.* New York: Oxford University Press, 1986.

INDEX

Page references in italics indicate references to illustrative material

abolitionism: and freedom suits, effect on, 167–68, 170, 177, 181, 182–83, 184–90; growth of, 168, 183; and paranoia about, 167–68, 181, 182–83; pro-slavery response to, 173–74; as threat to enslavers, 27
Allen, Beverly, 232n11, 233n21
Alsey (enslaved woman), 1–5, 195
Alsey, a woman of color v. Randolph (1841), 215–16nn1–11, 251n34
American Colonization Society, 93, 132–33
Arch (enslaved man), 17–18, 20, 30–31, 35, 38–40, 194–95
Arch, a black man v. Harris (1818), 20, 24, 35, 38–40, 218nn1–2, 221–22nn64–67
arguments for freedom in freedom suits: born free argument, 79–82, 90, 107–8, 109–10, 113, 136–37; Native American ancestry, 139; prior manumissions, 82–84, 86–88, 105, 109–10, 118–27, 163–66; and reputation, 134–41; residence on free soil, 3, 7, 84–86, 88–92, 98–99, 103–4, 109–10, 142–43, 160–61, 162, 193 (*see also* *Dred Scott v. Sandford*); residence on free soil argument, elimination of, 181
Aspasia, a free woman of color v. Chouteau and Menard (1828), 237nn86–87, 252n45
attorneys. *See* lawyers

Bailey & als. v. Poindexter's Executor (1858), 247nn64–66

Barton, Joshua, 31, 232n18
Bates, Edward, 70–71, 74–76, 224n2, 232n11, 233n21
Beckwith, Jennings, 87–88
Beckwith, Jennings v. Donner (1819), 238nn96–97
Benton, Thomas Hart, 183
Berlin, Ira, 127, 237n79, 243n62
Bird, Gustavus A., 45, 50, 159, 234n31
Blair, Montgomery, 74
Bland and Woolfolk v. Negro Beverly Dowling (1837), 247n57
Bleeding Kansas, 170
"Bloody Island": dueling, 70–71
Braxton (enslaved man), 123–24, 134–35
Brazealle, John Monroe, 244nn79–81
Brazil, 10
Briscoe, Eliza v. Anderson (1839), 251n24, 259n81
Britton, Lucy Ann. *See* Delaney, Lucy
Burd, Gustavus A., 45, 50, 159, 234n31
Burrell, Lewis, 167, 177, 182, 184–85
Butler et al. v. Duvall (1829), 228nn45–46

Campbell, William, 1–3
Carr, William C., 223n87, 232n11
Carrington, Lucinda, 151–52, 158–60
Carrington family, 142–43, 157–60
Charity (enslaved woman), 164–66
Chouteau, Louis, a man of color v. Chouteau (1844), 230nn100–101, 236nn65–66

Chouteau family, 144; Auguste, 19; Gabriel, 163; Marie-Thérèse, 20

Clay, Henry, 144

Code Noir, 23–24

comity. *See* interstate comity

commandants, 22

common law, 25

Commonwealth v. Stout (1847), 251n28

communication networks: enslavers' fears of, 45, 229n75; and legal knowledge, spread of, 43–47, 97, 191–94; and rivers, 46, 96–97

community members: as assisting in freedom suits, 27; and reputation, 134–41; as witnesses, 80, 97, 192

Compromise of 1820, 21, 172

contracts for freedom, 82–84, 127–32, 192–93. *See also* manumissions

Coons, David, 117, 123–24

Coons, George, 116–17, 123–24, 135

costs, of freedom suits, 62, 72–74, 94, 176–78, 179, 243n63

Cotton, Jane, 243n63

Cotton, Jane, a free person of color v. Little (1848), 243n63, 257–58nn47–48

courthouses, role of in communities, 30

court system, 101–2

Cross, Robert, 1–3

Cuffy v. Castillon (1818), 247n53

damages, in freedom suits, 38, 81, 87, 92, 230n90, 246n28

Daniel v. Guy et al. (1857), 253n64

Daniel v. Guy et al. (1861), 253n65

Darby, John F., 233n21, 235n47, 244n4

defendants. *See* defense arguments in freedom suits; enslavers; freedom suits

defense arguments in freedom suits: deception, use of, 156–57, 162–66; deny ownership defense, 90, 160 (*see also Winny, a free woman v. Whitesides* (1821); *Winny v. Whitesides* (1824)); deny possession of, 146–48; identity of enslaved defense, 154–56; manumissions, reneging of, 156–57; removal of plaintiffs from jurisdictions, 33–34, 52–55, 76, 89–90, 108, 147–49, 222n81; and reputation, 134–41; residence on free soil, 105–6, 142, 150–54; selling of plaintiffs, 147–49

Delaney, Lucy, 195–96; argument for freedom, 41–42; *From the Darkness Cometh the Light*, 41–43; decision to bring suit, 42–43, 52, 64–65; freedom of, 64; freedom suit of, 74–75; jailed, 58, 60, 63; legal argument, 236n66; legal process, knowledge of, 42; on mother's freedom suit, 43–44; runs away, 52; on sister's running away, 48; verdict of case, 41, 70; and violence, 55; and white sympathizer, 53–54

Delph (also known as Delphy), a mulatress v. Dorris (1836), 237nn82–83, 248n77

Donner, Samuel, 87–88

Dorinda (enslaved woman), 54–55, 222n77

Dorinda, a woman of color v. Simonds (1826), 228nn57–60, 251–52nn35–36

double character, 82, 192–93; defined, 116–18; and manumissions, 118–27; and negotiations, 127–34; and reputation, 134–41

Drake, Charles, 70, 73, 75

Dred Scott, a man of color v. Emerson (1846), 256nn18–19

Dred Scott, a man of color v. Emerson (1852), 256n20, 257n27

Dred Scott v. Sandford, 217n20; and citizenship of enslaved persons, 171–72, 189; and freedom suits following decision, 181; historiography of, 6; lawyers' reputations, 45; moves through courts, 171–72, 173; and politics, influences on case, 172–73, 180–81; as pro bono case, 74; residence on free soil argument, 103; significance of, 168

Drusella, Martha, 223–24nn95–96

Drusella, Martha v. Curle (1844), 223–24nn95–96, 249n90

dueling, 70–71

Duncan, Coleman, 99–102, 160–61, 227nn41–42

Duncan, James, 99–102, 160–61, 227nn41–42

Duncan, Jesse, 99–100

Duncan, John, 99–102

Duncan, Vincent, 99–102, 104, 160

Dunky, a colored woman v. Hay (1831), 240nn22–23, 252n37

Duty, Ellen v. Darby (1850), 258nn49–50

Duty, Milton, 116–17, 119, 123–24, 134–35, 178

Easton, Rufus, 231n1, 232n11
education, 175
Edwards, Laura, 135, 224n100
Edwards, Ninian, 96
Emerson, Irene, 171, 173
Emory and Others, Paupers v. Erskine
(1836), 251n21
enslaved persons: as *au pauperis*, 31–32,
72, 176–78; as chattel, 82 (*see also*
double character); and communication
networks, 193–94; and contracts,
127–34, 130–31, 134, 192–93; decisions
to bring freedom suits, 42, 49, 64–65,
65–66, 101; and everyday resistance, 48;
and lawyers, choice of, 71–72, 73; and
legal knowledge, 5, 43–47, 51, 54–55,
65–66, 97, 100, 191–92, 193–94; legal
personhood of (*see* double character);
literacy of, 31, 43, 54, 161–62, 175, 237n81;
mobility of, 103, 131–32; and reputation,
134–41; restrictions on, 169, 174, 178; and
running away, 48–52, 58, 89, 174–75;
surnames as problematic, 194–95,
224n2. *See also* individual plaintiffs
enslavers: attempts to protect selves from
freedom suits, 39, 84, 145–49; and
deception used by, 156–57, 162–66;
as defendants, 192 (*see also* defense
arguments in freedom suits); property
rights of, 26, 89–90, 100–103, 108, 113,
147 (*see also* double character); removal
of enslaved persons from jurisdictions,
33–34, 52–55, 76, 89–90, 108, 147–49,
222n81; and selling of plaintiffs, 147–49.
See also individual defendants
Farrelly v. Maria Louisa (Woman of Color)
(1859), 248n86
fees: attorney fees, 31–32, 44, 72–74, 157–58;
bonds of security, 32–33, 60–64, 77, 176;
court fees, 147; licensure for free people
of color, 174; suing as *au pauperis*, 31–
32, 72, 176–78
Fields v. Walker et al. (1853), 236n70
Finney, John, 164–66, 187, 188
Finney, John v. Kinder (1842), 228n56,
259nn83–88
Finney, William, 164–66
Fort Snelling, 171, 242n45
forum shopping, 50–52. *See also* interstate
comity
France, 104–5, 111

Francois v. Lobrano (1845), 247nn54–55
freedom statutes: ability to bring suits,
168–69, 176; and burdens of proof, 29,
78; and community involvement, 26–
27; and court-appointed prosecutors,
71–72; and expenses associated with,
31–32, 181; and financial backing, 77;
and free people of color, protections for,
26; and initial jurisdiction of freedom
suits, 29–32; in jurisdictions outside
Missouri, 26–29, 31, 32, 33–34, 36, 38;
legal borrowing, 25; and legal definition
of slavery, 79; and legal process of
freedom suits, 32–40; and legislation of,
25–26; and orders of protection, 33–34;
protection against retaliation, 52–55; as
trespass cases, 27–28, 30–31; and white
allies' testimony, 78–79
freedom suits: and abolitionism's effect
on, 167–68, 170, 177, 181, 182–83, 184–90;
appeals of, 38; and *au pauperis*, 31–32,
72, 176–78; and Brazil, comparison to,
10; and community involvement, 35–38,
136–37; and contracts for manumissions,
127–32; costs of, 62, 72–74, 94, 176–78,
179, 243n63; as courts superseding
enslavers, 59, 65; and damages awarded,
38, 81, 87, 92, 230n90, 246n28; as debate
over slavery, 42, 191–92, 193 (*see also*
Dred Scott v. Sandford); deception,
enslavers' use of, 162–66; decisions to
bring suit, 42, 49, 64–65, 65–66, 101;
defendants, status of, 50–52, 144–45;
defendants' attempts to avoid, 39, 84,
145–49; definition of, 4, 18; enslavers
challenge verdicts of, 91–92; enslavers'
legal wrangling in, 157–66; and forum
shopping, 50–52; and fraud, use of, 192;
and free people of color, population
growth, 168; habeas corpus claim, 49,
89; and Haitian Revolution, 111; and
imprisonment of plaintiffs, 107, 167;
and judges' discretionary powers,
36–38, 86, 101–2; and juries, 35–38; and
kidnappings, 57; and legal culture of
slavery, 6–9; legal process of, 18, 32–40,
179–81; legal strategies, changes in,
68–69; length of, 18, 41, 52, 58, 59, 61–62,
107, 123, 243n61; numbers of, 10–11,
168–69, 177–78; outcomes of, 10–11,
65, 80, 82, 84–85, 178–80, 181, 194–96;

records incomplete, 34–35; removal from jurisdictions, 33–34, 52–55, 76, 89–90, 108, 147–49, 222n81; role of in society, 168 (*see also* slavery:national debates over); and running away, initiation of, 49–50; and violence, 55–58; and voluntary dismissal of, 179–80; and white sympathizers, 53–54. *See also* arguments for freedom in freedom suits; defense arguments in freedom suits; freedom statutes; individuals involved in cases

free people of color: and apprenticeship laws, 174, 176; communication networks, 193–94; expulsion from Missouri, 176; and free papers, 94, 110; and kidnappings, 96, 97, 108–10, 136; and legal knowledge of, 43, 65, 97, 191–92, 193–94; and licensure laws, 174, 195–96; literacy of, 43, 175, 237n81; mobility of, 93–94, 98, 103, 106, 110, 111–13, 114, 132, 175–76; population growth of, 83–84, 168; protections for, 26; relationship with legal system, 93–94; and reputation, 135–41; restrictions on, 24, 26, 64, 83–84, 114, 132, 140–41, 169, 173–74, 175, 178, 241n42; as threat to slavery, 46, 173–74, 175, 176

free soil: as argument in freedom suits, 3, 7, 84–86, 88–92, 98–99, 103–4, 109–10, 142–43, 160–61, 162, 181, 193 (*see also Dred Scott v. Sandford*); as defense in freedom suits, 105–6, 142, 150–54. *See also* Northwest Ordinance of 1787

Fugitive Slave Act, 81–82, 226n30

Funkhouser, Robert, 215n2

Funkhouser, Robert M, 216n9

Gamble, Hamilton, 70, 157–60, 222n77, 228n57, 233n21, 235n47

Gentry v. McMinnis (1835), 237n89

Geyer, Henry S., 231n1, 235n47

Griffith v. Fanny (1820), 242n47

Grimsley, Thornton v. McKinney (1829), 249n1, 250n8

Grinberg, Keila, 10

Gross, Ariela, 5–6, 13, 117–18, 139

Haiti, 104–5, 111

Haitian Revolution, 105, 111

Harriet (enslaved child), 142–43, 151–52, 157–60, 195

Harriet, an infant v. McKinney and Walker (1833), 249n1

Harriet v. McKinney (1833), 249n1

Harris, Barnabas, 17–18, 27, 30–31, 34, 35, 39, 194

Harry and Others v. Decker & Hopkins (1818), 237n90, 242n47, 242n52

Hay, Andrew, 240nn22–23

Henry, James, a boy of color v. Walker (1834), 224n101, 250n10

Henry, Sally, Negress, by William Henry, Her Father and Next Friend v. Ball (1816), 243n74, 253n54

Hetty, a woman of color v. Magenis (1835), 233n22, 252n47

Hicks, Elsa, 61–62, 167, 177, 181, 184–85, 194

Hicks, Elsa, a mulatto girl v. Burrell and Mitchell (1845), 228n55

Hicks, Elsa, a mulatto girl v. McSherry (1847), 230nn96–99, 255nn1–3, 259nn71–74

Hinds et al. v. Brazealle et al. (1838), 244nn79–81

hiring out: to cover court costs, 61–63, 177–78; of imprisoned plaintiffs, 60, 61–62, 72, 85; jobs assigned, 63; profits from, 123; to purchase freedom, 87, 128–29, 157; restrictions on, 24; as seamen laborers, 97; self-hiring out, 248n76

historiography, 5–6

honor, definition of, 135

Hubbard, Eusebius, 17–21, 30–31, 35, 37

Hubbard, George, 35, 219n6

Hudgens v. Spencer (1836), 246nn27–28

Hyatt, Frederick, 34, 223n87

Illinois: and indentured servitude, 88, 98–99; and St. Louis, relationship with, 94, 96, 175, 185–89; slavery in, 98–102. *See also* arguments for freedom in freedom suits: residence on free soil argument

immigrants, 8, 95, 180, 182

indentured servitude, 50; in Illinois, 88, 98–99

interstate comity, 102–3, 104, 105, 114, 193, 253n55; definition of, 13, 94–95; and sectional crisis, 105–6, 171. *See also* mobility

Jack (enslaved man), 17–18, 20, 27, 30–31, 34–35, 37–40, 194–95

Jack, a black man v. Harris (1818), 20–21, 24, 34–35, 37, 38–40, 218–19nn1–6, 222n68

Jack, a man of color v. Link (1837), 226n21

Jackson, Jenny, *126*, 246n34

jails, 58–63; and imprisonment of plaintiffs, 107

James alias James Haskins v. Haskins (1837), 255nn98–99

Jane, a woman of color v. Dallam (1831), 248nn83–84

Jefferson, Thomas, 74

Jenny, a free girl v. Musick (1821), 238n104, 252n46

Jim Crow laws, 196

John (enslaved child), 165–66

Johnson, George, 248nn72–76

Johnson, George, a man of color v. Bartlett (1852), 248nn73–76, 259n80

Jonathan, a man of color v. Brotherton, Danah, and Willoughby (1841), 242n45, 250n12

Jones, Nicholas, 187–88

judges: discretionary powers of, 36–38, 42, 51–52, 79, 86, 91–92, 101–2; as enslavers, 144; and legal culture, 9, 25–26, 135, 169; and the legal process, 32–40; and orders for protection for plaintiffs, 52–53; protect slavery, 10, 102–3

Judy, a woman of color v. Meachum (1837), 252n50

Judy (also known as Julia Logan) v. Meachum (1835), 224n101

Julia (enslaved woman), 142–43, 145, 151–52, 157–60, 195

Julia, a woman of color v. McKinney (1831), 249n1, 250n13, 252nn41–42, 253n71

juries: choosing of jury members, 36; discretion of, 38–39, 42, 78–79, 156; and jury instructions, 36–38, 86, 101–2, 150, 152; and legal culture, 135, 169

Kansas-Nebraska Act, 170, 172–73, 219n20

Key, Francis Scott, 243n73

kidnappings: and free people of color, 57, 96, 97, 108–10, 136–37

Kinney, Thornton, 93–94, 97–98, 104, 106, 110–11, 194

Kinney, Thornton, a man of color v. Hatcher and Bridges (1853), 239nn1–7, 240n18, 250n11

Lacléde, Pierre, 19, 20

LaGrange, Francois, a free man of color v. Pratte, Chouteau, Berthold, and Cabanne (1827), 252nn48–49

Laura, a woman of color v. Belt (1852), 250n11, 251nn25–27

Lawless, Luke, 182–83, 232n18

law schools, 70

lawyers: and attorney fees, 72–74; and bonds of security, payment of, 77; as defendants in freedom suits, 71; as enslavers, 71, 75; and freedom suits, power over, 76–78; negligence of, 77–78; network of, 70–71; and political appointments, 75–76; reasons for taking freedom suits, 69, 71–76, 92; reputations of, 44–45, 75; role of, 192; in St. Louis, 69–71; violence against, 235n45; and witnesses, interactions with, 77. *See also* Pettibone, Rufus

Lecompton Constitution, 172–73

Lee, John, 188–89

legal borrowing, 79

legal community, 71, 192

legal consciousness: defined, 4–5

legal culture, 69, 102–3, 192; defined, 4–5; and freedom suits, 6–9; and legal culture of slavery, 6–9

legal knowledge: of enslaved persons, 5, 43–47, 51, 54–55, 65–66, 97, 100, 191–92, 193–94; of free people of color, 43, 65, 97, 191–92, 193–94

life estates: defined, 17. *See also* manumissions

Lincoln-Douglas debates, 173

literacy: of enslaved persons, 31, 43, 54, 161–62, 175, 237n81; of free people of color, 43, 175, 237n81

Loudon v. Scott (1805), 243nn72–73

Louisiana Civil Code, 130–31

Louisiana Purchase, 19, 232n5

Lovejoy, Elijah P., 169, 182–83, 256n8

Lunsford v. Coquillon (1824), 242n54

Lynch, Bernard, 144, *146*

lynchings, 169

Maddox, James T., Executor of Turner v. Negroes Price and Others (1861), 247nn62–63

Malinda, a free girl of color v. Pettibone, Hatton, Wingfield, Voteau, Butler, Whitset, Sanford (1825), 233n22

Malinda, a free girl of color v. Whitesides (1821), 238n104

Malinda, a free person of color v. Wilburn (1823), 252n43

Mansfield, 1st Earl of (William Murray), 85, 218n37

manumissions: challenged, 17–18, 119–20, 125–27, 129, 132; as contracts, 127–32; by deed, 83–84, 87, 124–27, *126*, 129, 244n8; and double character, 118–27; and estate debt, 124, 129 (*see also* Duty, Milton); *in futuro*, 121–23, 125–27, 130–31, 134, 138; and life estates, 244n8, 245n22; means of, 47–48; motivations for, 125; restrictions on, 24, 83–84, 113–14, 118–19, 120–21, 132–34; "slave for a term," 122; through purchasing own freedom, 128–32; violations of, 24–25, 39, 81, 82–84, 86–88, 105, 113–14; by will, 82–83, 117, 119, 123–24, 132–34; as written document, 130

Marguerite, a free woman of color v. Chouteau (1825), 224nn105–6

Maria Whiten, a free woman of color v. Rucker (1829), 235n51

Marie, a free mulatto girl v. Chouteau (1821), 223n84, 250n14

Mariquette v. McKinney (1831), 249n1, 250n16

Martha Ann, a person of color v. Cordell (1844), 254nn89–90

Mary (enslaved woman), 123, 134–35, 164–66

Mary, a woman of color v. Menard and Busby (1833), 236n56, 251n19

Mary, a woman of color v. Menard and Landreville (1827), 228n52

Mary, of color, and her children Samuel & Edward v. Calvert (1851), 235n54, 250n11, 259nn77–79

Mary (also known as Mary Davis), a woman of color v. Bellis (1855), 247n47, 258n55

Matilda, a free girl of color v. Rocheblave and Rocheblave (1828), 237n88, 252n46

Matilda, f. w. c. v. Autrey, et ux. (1855), 229nn70–71

Mayho, William v. Sears (1842), 246nn37–38

McFoy, David v. Brown (1850), 253nn57–62, 257n44

McGirk, Isaac C., 77–78

McGirk, Mathias, 235n47

McIntosh, Francis, 169, 182, 256n8

McKinney, Samuel T., 142–47, 151–52, 157–60, 195

McSherry, Patrick T., 167–68, 177, 184–85, 194

Meachum, John Berry, 224n101, 250n2, 252n50

mental illness, 59

Merry, John, a free man of color v. Tiffin and Menard (1826), 243n59, 253n66

Mexican War, 170, 173, 219n20

Milly (enslaved woman), 88–90, 195

Milly, a black woman v. Rose (1819), 229n73, 238nn98–103, 251n17

Mississippi River: and escaped slaves, 107–8; and free people of color, 93–94, 96–97, 136; location of (*see under* St. Louis); steamboats, 52, 64–65, 149. *See also* mobility

Missouri Compromise, 21, 172

Missouri slave law, 23–24

Mitchell, David, 52, 60

Mitchell, Martha, 55, 64–65

mobility: of enslaved persons, 103, 131–32; of free people of color, 93–94, 98, 103, 106, 110, 111–13, 114, 132, 175–76; and kidnappings, 57, 96, 97, 108–10, 136; removal of plaintiffs from jurisdictions, 33–34, 52–55, 76, 89–90, 108, 147–49, 222n81; and rivers as opportunity for, 52, 64–65, 93–94, 96–98, 104, 106, 107–8, 110–11, 136, 149, 189, 193–94. *See also* free soil; interstate comity

Moses (Alsey's son), 3–4, 195, 215nn1–4

Mullins et al. v. Wall et al. (1848), 244n11

Murray, William (1st Earl of Mansfield), 85, 218n37

Nader, Laura, 7

Nancy, a free woman of color v. Steen (1848), 236nn62–64, 249n88

Nancy et als. v. Wright et als. (1848), 244n78

Native Americans: enslaved, 23; and heritage and freedom suits, 80, 139; Missouri, 19; Osage, 19

negotiations, of institution of slavery: and double character, 127–34; through court systems, 4, 6–7, 18, 39, 42, 68, 86–92, 191–92, 193; through everyday maneuverings, 48; through extralegal wrangling, 77, 147, 192–93. *See also* enslaved persons; freedom suits

Newman, John, 76–77

Northwest Ordinance of 1787, 85–86, 98; circumventions of, 88; as defense in freedom suits, 152; doctrine of intent to reside, 90–91, 102; and Illinois, 101–2. *See also* arguments for freedom in freedom suits: residence on free soil argument

Paul, Michel v. Paul (1845), 243nn57–58

Pelagie, a person of color v. Cabanne (1822), 228n53, 251n18

Pelagie, a woman of color v. Valois (1822), 251n18

Pennsylvania Emancipation Act, 113

Pettibone, Rufus: and attorney fees, 73; career of, 67; death of, 92, 194–95; as defendant in freedom suits, 71, 90–92, 194–95; and early St. Louis law, 69; legal career, 70; prosecutes freedom suit, 88–90, 92, 194–95; and slavery debates, 67–68

Pettis, Spencer, 232n18, 235n47

Pierre, a mulatto v. Chouteau (1842), 230nn82–83, 236nn65–66, 254n91

plaintiffs. *See* arguments for freedom in freedom suits; enslaved persons; freedom suits

Plessy v. Ferguson (1896), 196

Preston (enslaved man), 123–24, 134–35, 244nn1–4

Preston, Braxton, Mary, Nat, Beverly, et al. v. Coons, Administrator of Duty et al. (1841), 244nn1–4, 246nn29–31

Price, Risdon H., 229nn68–69

Proctor, John, 35, 39, 219n6

Rachel, a woman of color v. Walker (1834), 224n101, 234n28, 242n45, 250n10

racial categorization, 80

racial violence, 169–70, 182–83

Ralph (enslaved man), 50, 160–61

Ralph, a man of color v. Duncan (1833), 254n83

Ralph, a man of color v. Duncan and Duncan (1830), 254n78, 254nn80–82, 254nn84–86,

Randolph, William, 3–4

Randolph, William S., to the use of Alfred Tracy v. Wash (1843), 215n4, 216n7

Randolph v. Alsey (1844), 216n6

Rebecca, a colored girl v. Black and Matlock (1838), 225n12, 251n32

Rebecca, a negro woman v. Black, Horine, and Melody (1843), 225n13, 234n32, 236n58

Rector, Molly, a free woman of color v. Bivens (1827), 253nn67–68

Relf, George, 140–41

Relf, George, a man of color v. Ficklin (1828), 249nn96–98, 254n87

Republican Party, 173, 180

reputation, 134–41

Rose, Mathias, 88–90

Ruffin, Thomas, 229n63

runaway slave advertisements, 49

running away, 48–52, 58, 89, 107–8, 174–75, 193–94. *See also* mobility

Saint-Domingue, 104–5, 111

St. Louis: and abolitionism, 183–84, 190; and debates over slavery, 169–70, 189–90; as destination for escaped slaves, 106–8; early settlement of, 19–22, 21–22, 69–70; and French law, legacy of, 130–31; and Illinois, relationship with, 94, 96, 175, 185–89; and immigrants, 180, 182; and lawyers, numbers of, 69–70; legal system of, 22–25; location of, *xx*, 2, 7–8, 8, 95, 98, 106, 175, 193; and Native Americans, relationship with, 19; population of, 19–22, 21–22, 180; population of enslaved persons, 21, 182; population of free people of color, 20, 21; and racial violence, 169–70, 182–83; and Republican Party, 173, 180, 183; slave ownership, rates of, 250n3; and slave trade, role in, 95–96; and Spanish law, legacy of, 130–31

Sally, a person of color v. Chouteau (1835), 234n28, 237n73

Sam, a person of color v. Field and Mitchell (1832), 230n81, 233n22

Samuel (enslaved man), 249n94

Samuel, a man of color v. Howdeshell (1844), 249n94, 251n31

Sanford, John F. A. *See Dred Scott v. Sandford*

Schafer, Judith Kelleher, 44

Scott, Dred, 242n45. *See also Dred Scott v. Sandford*

Scott, Harriet, 171, 242n45. *See also Dred Scott v. Sandford*
Seven Years' War, 19
Singleton, John, a free man of color v. Scott and Lewis (1827), 236n68
slave codes, 45
slave insurrections, fear of, 22, 25–26, 45, 111
slavery: communication networks within, 29–30; national debates over, 18, 21, 170, 172–75, 178, 189, 219n5; negotiated through courts, 4, 6–7, 68 (*see also* freedom suits); and violence, 55–58. *See also* enslaved persons; enslavers; freedom suits
slave trade, domestic, 95–96, 109
Smith, Priscilla, f.w.c. v. Smith (1839), 242nn50–51
Somerset v. Stewart (1772), 13, 85
Spanish slave law, 23–24; *coartación*, 130–31
Sproat, Harris L., 44, 78
State of Missouri v. Burrell (1847), 259nn75–76
State of Missouri v. McKinney (1829), 249n1, 250n8
State v. Mann (1829), 229n63, 255n94
Steel, Mary Ann, 119, 227n39
Steel, Mary Ann v. Skinner (1835), 227n39, 244n9, 250n15
Steel, Mary Ann v. Walker (1835), 244nn9–10, 250n10
Stokes, Samuel, 164–66
Stokes, Samuel, a man of color v. Finney and Finney (1838), 255nn100–103
Strother, George, 71, 76–77
Sylvia and Phillis, by Next Friend v. Covey (1833), 222n80, 251n29

Taney, Roger, 172
Taylor, Alfred, 247nn45–46
Taylor, Alfred, a free man of color v. Van Houten, Martin, and Conway (1848), 247nn45–46
Tempe, a black woman v. Price (1821), 222n75, 229nn68–69
Tucker, Nathaniel Beverly, 30–31
Tucker, St. George, 221n64

Underground Railroad, 259n76

VanderVelde, Lea, 225n11, 226n30, 234n27
Vaughn, Abraham v. Phebe, a Woman of Color (1827), 248nn81–82
Vica, a woman of color v. Hobart (1842), 245–46nn24–26
Vincent, a man of color v. Duncan (1829), 227nn41–42, 240–41nn24–42
Vincent v. Duncan and Duncan (1830), 240–41nn24–42

Wallace, William Smith, 259nn84–86
War of 1812, 20–21
Wash, Polly, 43–44, 48, 52, 58, 140; decision to bring suit, 65; hired out, 63
Wash, Polly v. Magehan (1839), 227n33, 230n103, 249n93
Wash, Robert, 2–3, 5, 235n47
Wash, Robert v. Randolph (1846), 216n8
Wash, Robert v. Randolph, to the use of Alfred Tracy, Trustee for Francis Randolph (1845), 216n8
Welch, Kimberly, 135
Whitesides, Phebe, 90–92, 195
Wilkinson, James, 247n44
Wilkinson, James, a man of color v. Young (1833), 247n44
Williams, Hester, 246nn39–40
Williams, Hester, Ella Williams, & Priscilla Williams v. McAfee, Norcum, Blakey, and Moore (1853), 246nn39–40
Winny (enslaved woman), 86–88
Winny (another enslaved woman), 90–92, 195
Winny, a free woman of color v. Pettibone, Hatton, Wingfield, Voteau, Butler, Whitset, Sanford (1825), 233n22, 239n112
Winny, a free woman v. Whitesides (1821), 238–39nn104–113, 242n43, 250n16
Winny v. Donner (1820), 86–88
Winny v. Pettibone et al. (1825), 238–39nn104–113
Winny v. Whitesides (1824), 250n16

Young, Aaron, 128–29

EARLY AMERICAN PLACES

On Slavery's Border: Missouri's Small Slaveholding Households, 1815–1865
by Diane Mutti Burke

*Sounding America: Identity and the Music Culture of the Lower Mississippi
River Valley, 1800–1860*
by Ann Ostendorf

*The Year of the Lash: Free People of Color in Cuba and the Nineteenth-
Century Atlantic World*
by Michele Reid-Vazquez

*Ordinary Lives in the Early Caribbean: Religion, Colonial Competition, and
the Politics of Profit*
by Kirsten Block

Creolization and Contraband: Curaçao in the Early Modern Atlantic World
by Linda M. Rupert

*An Empire of Small Places: Mapping the Southeastern Anglo-Indian Trade,
1732–1795*
by Robert Paulett

*Everyday Life and the Construction of Difference in the Early English
Caribbean*
by Jenny Shaw

*Natchez Country: Indians, Colonists, and the Landscapes of Race
in French Louisiana*
by George Edward Milne

Slavery, Childhood, and Abolition in Jamaica, 1788–1838
by Colleen A. Vasconcellos

*Privateers of the Americas: Spanish American Privateering from the United
States in the Early Republic*
by David Head

Charleston and the Emergence of Middle-Class Culture in the Revolutionary Era
by Jennifer L. Goloboy

*Anglo-Native Virginia: Trade, Conversion, and Indian Slavery in the Old
Dominion, 1646–1722*
by Kristalyn Marie Shefveland

Slavery on the Periphery: The Kansas-Missouri Border in the Antebellum and Civil War Eras
by Kristen Epps

In the Shadow of Dred Scott: *St. Louis Freedom Suits and the Legal Culture of Slavery in Antebellum America*
by Kelly M. Kennington

Brothers and Friends: Kinship in Early America
by Natalie R. Inman

CPSIA information can be obtained
at www.ICGtesting.com
Printed in the USA
LVOW11*0713020518

575670LV00006B/25/P